California

The Politics of Diversity

✳

California

The Politics of Diversity

SEVENTH EDITION

DAVID G. LAWRENCE
Professor Emeritus of Political Science
Westmont College

WADSWORTH
CENGAGE Learning™

Australia • Brazil • Japan • Korea • Mexico • Singapore • Spain • United Kingdom • United States

WADSWORTH
CENGAGE Learning

**California: The Politics of Diversity,
Seventh Edition**
David G. Lawrence

Publisher: Suzanne Jeans

Executive Editor: Carolyn Merrill

Acquiring Sponsoring Editor: Anita M. Devine

Associate Development Editor: Katherine Hayes

Assistant Editor: Laura Ross

Marketing Manager: Lydia LeStar

Marketing Coordinator: Lorreen Towle

Senior Marketing Communications Manager:
Heather L. Baxley

Design and Production Services:
PreMediaGlobal

Manufacturing Planner: Fola Orekoya

Rights Acquisition Specialist (Text, Image):
Jennifer MeyerDare

Cover Designer: Tony Saizon

Cover Image: Wojtek Buss/Photolibrary

Compositor: PreMediaGlobal

For product information and technology assistance, contact us at
Cengage Learning Customer & Sales Support, 1-800-354-9706

For permission to use material from this text or product,
submit all requests online at **www.cengage.com/permissions**.
Further permissions questions can be e-mailed to
permissionrequest@cengage.com.

Library of Congress Control Number: 2011936257

ISBN-13: 978-1-111-83353-4

ISBN-10: 1-111-83353-2

Wadsworth
20 Channel Center Street
Boston, MA, 02210
USA

Cengage Learning is a leading provider of customized learning solutions with office locations around the globe, including Singapore, the United Kingdom, Australia, Mexico, Brazil, and Japan. Locate your local office at **international.cengage.com/region**.

Cengage Learning products are represented in Canada by
Nelson Education, Ltd.

For your course and learning solutions, visit **www.cengage.com**.

Purchase any of our products at your local college store or at our preferred online store at **www.cengagebrain.com**.

Instructors: Please visit **login.cengage.com** and log in to access instructor-specific resources.

Printed in the United States of America
2 3 4 5 6 7 15 14 13

Brief Contents

PREFACE   xvii

1 Explaining California Politics   1

2 California's Political Development   20

3 Constitutionalism and Federalism: The Perimeters of California Politics   39

4 Direct Democracy in a Hyperpluralistic Age   58

5 How Californians Participate   80

6 Linking People and Policymakers: Media, Parties, and Interest Groups   100

7 Legislative Politics   122

8 Executive Politics   149

9 California's Judiciary   172

10 Community Politics   193

11 Budget Policy: The Cost of Diversity   219

12 Policies Stemming from Growth   242

13 Policies Stemming from Diversity   265

INDEX   285

Contents

PREFACE   xvii

1   Explaining California Politics   1

Introduction   2

How Diversity Explains California Politics   4

Land   4

Regions   4

Resources   5

People   7

Economy   10

How Political Theory Explains California Politics   12

Democratic Theory   12

Elite Theory   13

Pluralist Theory   13

Hyperpluralism   14

How Hyperpluralism Explains California Politics   14

The Constancy of Individualism   14

A Diversity of Interests and Cultures   15

Fading Majoritarianism   15

Structural Conflict   16

California: The Ironies of Diversity   17

Key Terms   18

Review Questions   18

Web Activities   *18*

Notes   *19*

2   California's Political Development   20

Introduction   21

The Idea of Political Culture   *21*

The Idea of Political Development   *22*

The Politics of Unification   22

Spanish "Rule"   *23*

Mexican "Control"   *23*

Statehood   *24*

The 1849 Constitution   *25*

The Politics of Modernization   26

The Gold Rush   *26*

The Big Four   *27*

Water   *28*

Other Modernizing Factors   *30*

The Politics of Welfare   31

The Progressive Movement   *31*

The Great Depression   *31*

Earl Warren   *32*

Edmund G. (Pat) Brown   *33*

The Politics of Abundance and Beyond   34

Key Terms   *36*

Review Questions   *37*

Web Activities   *37*

Notes   *37*

3   Constitutionalism and Federalism: The Perimeters of California Politics   39

Introduction: Rules and Boundaries   40

California's Constitution   41

What It Contains   *42*

What Makes It Distinctive   *44*

California and the Nation: The Boundaries of Federalism   45

Dual Federalism   *46*

Cooperative Federalism   *46*

Centralized Federalism   *46*

The New Federalism   47

Pragmatic Federalism   47

Federalism and California's Native Americans   48

California in Washington   49

California and the World: The Politics of Fences   52

Immigration   52

Trade   54

Conclusion   55

Key Terms   55

Review Questions   55

Web Activities   56

Notes   56

4   Direct Democracy in a Hyperpluralistic Age   58

The Impact of Progressivism   59

Progressivism: California Style   60

Selected Initiative Battles in California   61

Proposition 13: Give the Money Back   62

Propositions 187 and 209: Limits on Rights   64

Propositions 22 and 8: Limits on Same Sex Marriage   66

Propositions 215 and 19: Legalizing Marijuana   67

The Initiative Mess   69

Prospects for Initiative Reform   73

Progressive Cousins: Referendum and Recall   74

State Level Recalls   74

Local Level Recalls   76

Conclusion: The Legacy and the Paradox   76

Key Terms   77

Review Questions   77

Web Activities   78

Notes   78

5   How Californians Participate   80

Forms of Participation in a Democracy   81

Civic Engagement and Conventional Participation   81

The Exit Option   82

The Protest Option   82

The Role of Public Opinion   83

    What is Public Opinion?   83

    California's Major Pollsters   84

    How They Measure Public Opinion   84

Voters and Nonvoters in California   85

    Who Votes in California?   85

    Those Who Cannot Vote   86

    Those Who Will Not Vote   87

    Personal Factors   87

Elections and Campaigns in California   90

    California's Elections   90

    California's Campaign Professionals   91

    The Role of Money   92

    The Role of National Politics   93

California's Electoral Gaps   95

Conclusion: Divided by Diversity   97

    Key Terms   97

    Review Questions   98

    Web Activities   98

    Notes   98

6   Linking People and Policymakers: Media, Parties, and Interest Groups   100

Introduction   101

Mass Media   101

    Newspapers   102

    Television   103

    Radio   105

The Internet and Social Media   105

Political Parties   107

    Partisanship in California   107

    The Partisan Geography of California   108

    Political Parties: California Style   109

    How the Parties Are Organized   110

    Surrogate "Parties"   111

    Endorsement Politics   111

Interest Groups   112

    California Groups: Who Are They?   *114*

    How Interest Groups Organize   *115*

    What Interest Groups Do   *116*

Conclusion: Competing for Influence   118

    Key Terms   *119*

    Review Questions   *119*

    Web Activities   *120*

    Notes   *120*

7   Legislative Politics   122

Introduction: The Road to Professionalism
and Dysfunctionality   123

    California's Legislative History   *124*

What the Legislature Does   126

    Policymaking   *126*

    Representation   *126*

    Executive Oversight   *130*

    Civic Education   *130*

Getting There and Staying There   132

    Recruitment   *132*

    Why They Stay: Rewards of Office   *133*

    How They Stay: Reapportionment Politics   *134*

    The 2011 Reapportionment   *136*

Organizing to Legislate   136

    The Role of Leadership   *137*

    The Committee System   *139*

    The Staff   *139*

The Legislative Process   140

    Bill Introduction   *140*

    Committee Consideration   *140*

    Floor Action and Conference Committee   *141*

    The Governor's Role   *142*

The Third House   143

Conclusion   145

    Key Terms   *146*

    Review Questions   *146*

Web Activities   146

Notes   147

8   Executive Politics   149

Introduction   150

How Governors Lead   151

The Governor's Duties and Powers   155

Executive Powers   156

Budget Leadership   158

Legislative Powers   159

Judicial Powers   161

Other Powers   162

The Plural Executive: Competing for Power   162

Lieutenant Governor   163

Attorney General   163

Secretary of State   164

Superintendent of Public Instruction   164

Insurance Commissioner   165

Fiscal Officers   165

California's Bureaucracy and the Politics of Diversity   166

Functions of Bureaucracy   167

Power Sharing and Clout   167

Executive Branch Reform   168

Conclusion   169

Key Terms   169

Review Questions   169

Web Activities   170

Notes   170

9   California's Judiciary   172

Introduction   173

State Courts in Our Legal "System"   174

How California's Courts Are Organized   174

Trial Courts   175

Appellate Courts   176

Supreme Court   176

So You Want to be a Judge   176

   Entering the Profession   177

   The Right Experience   177

   Selection Mechanics   178

   Judicial Discipline   179

How Courts Make Decisions   181

   The Criminal Process   181

   The Civil Process   182

   Juries and Popular Justice   183

How Courts Make Policy   184

   Trial Court Policymaking   184

   Appellate Court Policymaking   184

Criminal Justice and Punishment   185

   Social Trends   185

   Sentencing Mandates   186

Conclusion   189

   Key Terms   190

   Review Questions   191

   Web Activities   191

   Notes   191

10 Community Politics   193

Introduction   194

   The Role of Community   196

   The Limits of Community Government   196

Counties   198

   The Shape of California Counties   198

   The Shape of County Government   200

   California's Troubled Counties   201

Cities   202

   How Communities Become Municipalities   204

   "Cities" Without "Government"   204

   How California Cities Are Run   205

   Cities and Counties: An Uneasy Relationship   209

Special Districts   210

   What Makes Them Special?   210

   The Stealth Governments of California   211

   Special District Politics and Problems   211

School Districts   212

Regional Governments   213

    Regional Coordination   214

    Regional Regulation   214

Conclusion: Diverse Communities, Diverse Governments   215

    Key Terms   216

    Review Questions   216

    Web Activities   217

    Notes   217

11 Budget Policy: The Cost of Diversity   219

Introduction: Budgeting as Public Policy   220

Where Budgeting Begins: The Economy   221

    Economic Diversity   221

    How California's Economy Affects Budgeting   221

    California's Local Economies   222

The Budget Process   222

    How California Budgeting Works   223

    Constraints on the Process   225

    Local Budget Processes   227

Types of Revenue   228

    Major State Revenues   229

    Local Revenue   234

Where the Money Goes   235

    State Expenditures   235

    Local Expenditures   237

The Need for Budget Reform   237

Conclusion: The Cost of Diversity   239

    Key Terms   239

    Review Questions   239

    Web Activities   240

    Notes   240

12 Policies Stemming from Growth   242

Introduction: Growth in California   243

    Why California Grew   244

    The Drumbeat of Growth   244

Structuring Local Growth   246

Slowing Growth in California   247

Water: Making Growth Possible   248

Storing Water   248

Moving Water   249

Water Policy Alternatives   252

Housing: For Many, the Impossible Dream   252

The California Dream   252

Housing Policy as "Filter Down"   253

The Housing Crisis and Beyond   253

Transportation: Stuck in Traffic   255

The Problem   255

California's Transportation Policies   257

Energy, Environment, and Climate Change   258

Energy   258

Environment and Climate Change   258

Policy Options   259

Conclusion: A New Growth Policy for California?   261

Key Terms   263

Review Questions   263

Web Activities   263

Notes   264

13 Policies Stemming from Diversity   265

Introduction: The Challenge of Diversity   266

Social Issues: Abortion and LGBT Rights   267

Abortion   268

LGBT Rights   269

Education: Coping with Growth and Diversity   270

Pressures on Education   270

Education Reform   272

Higher Education: An Uncertain Future   274

The Majoritarian Ideal   274

Rethinking the Plan   275

Higher Education for Undocumented Students   276

Social Programs   276

Welfare Policy   277

Health Policy   278

Conclusion   281
   Key Terms   282
   Review Questions   282
   Web Activities   282
   Notes   283

INDEX   285

Preface

The study of politics is the study of power: what it is, who has it, and how it is used. Political power, in particular, focuses on the ability in politics to control, change, or influence the behavior of others. Relative to California politics, political scientists examine the power of governors, legislators, judges, bureaucrats, political parties, interest groups, and ordinary citizens. They also observe the larger political environment in which these political actors work—the economy, demographic trends, and the structural features of the political system that both enable and constrain their work.

One major factor that drove the revisions in the seventh edition is the *power of change*. Change was seemingly everywhere one looked. In early 2011, Californians welcomed back to the governor's office Jerry Brown who had served as governor decades earlier. Upon his swearing in, a changed Brown confronted a changed state. The U.S. Census Bureau gradually released data from the 2010 census documenting various demographic changes taking place in the Golden State. Thanks to two propositions, California voters changed—rather revolutionized—how legislative and congressional districts would be drawn later in 2011. Changes in how state budgeting works enabled Democratic majorities in the state legislature to pass the 2011–2012 budget without a single Republican vote. Those and many other changes are reflected throughout this revision.

TEXT FEATURES

What has not changed in this edition is the fact that California politics remains affected by the diverse and hyperpluralistic nature of the state itself, particularly its people and the groups to which they belong. Political leadership is central to governing but leadership is affected by two other broad phenomena: the state's well-documented diversity and a variant of pluralism we call *hyperpluralism*. In all seven editions, we have tried to show two things: (1) how demographic, cultural, economic, geographic, and political diversity affect how politics actually works in California; and (2) how the exceedingly pluralistic nature of the state results in a highly competitive tug-of-war between ideologies, institutions, policymakers, political parties, interest groups, and voters. This tug-of-war makes effective, capable, long-range governing a constant challenge. In this political environment, policy successes do occur, but so do many instances of policy gridlock or only partial policy success.

As with many California political scientists, my teaching assignments included both California politics and American government. The seventh edition continues to apply important political science and American government concepts to the California experience. Devoting three chapters to public policy, it remains the most policy-focused general California government text on the market.

PEDAGOGICAL FEATURES

California continues to offer numerous pedagogical features that help students learn. Each chapter includes the following:

- A consistent perspective that makes sense to today's students
- An attractive and functional two-column design that aids in reading
- "In Brief" boxes and outlines that preview forthcoming content
- Chapter conclusions that revisit key points and tie them to book themes
- Boldfaced key terms that are referenced by page number
- Study questions that help students review and apply chapter content
- Extensive endnotes that provide opportunities for further reading and research
- Updated charts, tables, photos, quotes, boxes, and cartoons designed to amplify key points
- End-of-chapter Internet sources that encourage further exploration

REVISION HIGHLIGHTS

The seventh edition of *California: The Politics of Diversity* retains an organizational format familiar to many political scientists who teach American government courses. Its student-friendly writing style reflects my view that important ideas should be intelligible ones, especially in an undergraduate textbook. In terms of substance, the seventh edition involves cover-to-cover revisions that reflect the latest developments in California politics. They include the following:

- Analysis of the 2010 gubernatorial election including initiative results
- Initial coverage of Brown's "third" term as governor

- Incorporation of 2010 Census data throughout the text
- The 2011 reapportionment by the state's historic Citizens Redistricting Commission
- New sections on public opinion polling and the role of the Internet and social media
- The Bell, California salary scandal
- "Case in Point" vignettes—mini case studies that reinforce chapter ideas
- "California in Perspective" boxes—comparisons with other states and the nation as a whole
- Updates on California's chronic budget challenges, pension reform, the housing crisis, prison overcrowding, and California's version of the DREAM Act
- Reorganized chapters on voting, elections, parties, and interest groups

SUPPLEMENTS

As a Cengage Wadsworth text, *California* offers a number of attractive supplements that aid both professors and students; they consist of the following resources:

- An instructor's manual with test questions and other helpful instructional tips through Wadsworth's E-bank program. Please contact your Wadsworth representative for access.

ACKNOWLEDGMENTS

Textbook writing is a team effort. It involves many more people than a title page would suggest. I am indebted to several teams. The first is uniquely mine. From my own years in and around state and local politics, I must credit the many practitioners who have shared their political insights with me—former city council colleagues, internship supervisors, classroom speakers, journalists, and countless Sacramento Legislative Seminar panelists. Westmont College colleague Richard Burnweit has provided keen insights over the life of this book. As always, my wife and best friend, Carolyn, is my encourager and sounding board.

A second team consists of the good people at Cengage Wadsworth who provided helpful direction, assistance, and encouragement. They are publisher Suzanne Jeans, executive editor Carolyn Merrill, acquisitions editor Anita Devine, associate development editor Katherine Hayes, project manager PreMediaGlobal, permissions editor Roberta Broyer, marketing manager Lydia LeStar, marketing communications manager Heather Baxley, and photo researcher Mandy Groszko. Professor Dianne Long (California State Polytechnic University, San Luis Obispo) authored the instructor's manual and test bank.

A third team consists of the political scientists who reviewed all or some of *California* along the way. They include the following:

Theodore J. Anagnoson (California State University, Los Angeles), Jodi Balma (Fullerton College), Michele Colborn Harris (College of the Canyons), John H. Culver (California Polytechnic State University, San Luis Obispo), Jeff Cummins (California State University, Fresno), Robert L. Delorme (California State University, Long Beach), Lawrence L. Giventer (California State University, Stanislaus), Herbert E. Gooch (California Lutheran University), Jack Hames (Butte College), Drake C. Hawkins (Glendale Community College), Peter H. Howse (American River College), William W. Lammers (University of Southern California), Dianne Long (California Polytechnic State University, San Luis Obispo), Marilyn J. Loufek (Long Beach City College), Edward S. Malecki (California State University, Los Angeles), Donald J. Matthewson (California State University, Fullerton), Charles H. McCall (California State University, Bakersfield), John Mercurio (San Diego State University), Steve Monsma (Pepperdine University), Stanley W. Moore (Pepperdine University), Gerhard Peters (Citrus College), Eugene Price (California State University, Northridge), Donald Ranish (Antelope Valley College), John F. Roche III (Palomar College), Alvin D. Sokolow (University of California, Davis), Charles C. Turner (California State University, Chico), Richard S. Unruh (Fresno Pacific University), Linda O. Valenty (San Jose State University), JoAnn Victor (California State University, Long Beach), and Alan J. Wyner (University of California, Santa Barbara).

As helpful as these veteran colleagues were, I take full responsibility for the end product.

David Lawrence
Professor Emeritus of Political Science
Westmont College

1

✴

Explaining California Politics

Introduction

How Diversity Explains California Politics

    Land

    Regions

    Resources

    People

    Economy

How Political Theory Explains California Politics

    Democratic Theory

    Elite Theory

    Pluralist Theory

    Hyperpluralism

How Hyperpluralism Explains California Politics

    The Constancy of Individualism

    A Diversity of Interests and Cultures

    Fading Majoritarianism

    Structural Conflict

California: The Ironies of Diversity

    Key Terms

    Review Questions

    Web Activities

    Notes

IN BRIEF

In this introductory chapter, we survey the big picture of California politics. Many observers claim the Golden State is no longer the land of milk and honey, yet it continues to draw newcomers from the four corners of the earth. Why the differences in perception? The answer is in the diversity of California and how it is governed. This chapter will cover these two subjects.

The state's diversity has been its strength. The land varies from temperate coastal plains to rugged mountain ranges; from lush agricultural valleys to barren deserts. People divide California into several regions, but these divisions seem to be a matter of perception. Some divide the state into North and South; others see multiple and diverse regions. California is rich in resources, especially water and desirable climate. Moving the state's water supply around has increased the usability of the land. Throughout its history, waves of people have moved to and around California seeking a better life. These factors have resulted in a diverse economy—one of the world's largest.

How political scientists explain U.S. politics in general helps us understand California politics in particular. To answer the question "Who governs?" four theories have emerged. Democratic theory says the people do, usually through elected representatives. Elite theory claims that the upper classes exercise power and influence beyond their numbers. Pluralist theory contends that groups compete for power and policy advantage. Hyperpluralism, an emerging theory, contends that so many groups now compete and the political system is so complex that governing can become most difficult.

Although these theories seem incompatible, each helps to explain aspects of California politics. Evidence of hyperpluralism in California is growing. The outcome is a state of many paradoxes.

INTRODUCTION

Shortly before taking office in 2011, Governor-Elect Jerry Brown commented on the grim California economy and its toll on the state budget. "Because we are a divided state—North-South, Republican-Democrat, urban-rural—it becomes difficult to come to a consensus and a solution when they are as painful and difficult as they will be in the coming year."[1] His long years in politics and a prior stint as governor made him wise to the perennial challenge of matching the state's lofty policy goals with the economic and political realities that have described California throughout its history. In some ways, California could be likened to theme park roller coasters. People flock to both—enduring congestion in the process and experiencing the exhilaration of both ups and downs. In the Golden State, the highs include better jobs, economic opportunities, and living conditions than people could only have imagined back home, whether they are from Missouri or Mexico. People envision California as a place where these dreams can come true. The lows include periodic recessions, occasional droughts, smog, crime, crowded freeways, and unaffordable housing.

Some Californians endure the lows in order to appreciate the highs, but others find California, like the roller coaster, a bit too much. They flee the state for Washington, Oregon, Nevada, Colorado, and beyond. Or, they move within the state, seeking a calmer ride. As a whole, Californians' confidence in the future of the state can vary remarkably from year to year (see Figure 1.1).

Polling data confirm this roller coaster analogy. Pollster and analyst Mark Baldassare observed what he calls "the yin and yang" of California political life—"we might call it the New Economy meets the New Demography." That is, the economic optimism shared by many Californians at the turn of the new century was tempered by signs of trouble such as congestion, pollution, and increasing economic inequality; compounding the problem was a widely shared distrust of government. "Californians, by and large, did not believe that government had the ability to handle problems or that it even had their best interests at heart."[2] Within a few years, economic pessimism replaced optimism while many policy problems festered and political distrust grew. The confluence of these trends and

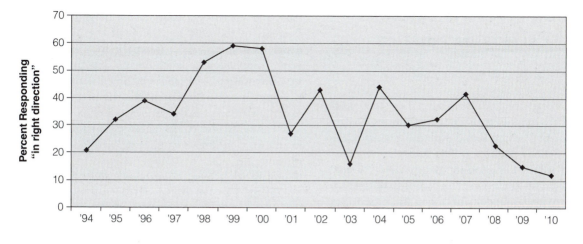

FIGURE 1.1 How Californians View California

When pollsters ask if California is going in the right or wrong direction, Californians' responses can vary significantly over the years.

Question: In your opinion, to what extent do these data affect perceptions of governmental institutions and policymakers?

NOTES: Results are based on representative statewide samples of about 1,000 California adults. The sampling error ranges from ±3.2 to 4.5 percentage points.
SOURCE: Successive surveys of *The Field Poll* (www.field.com/fieldpollonline/).

attitudes in part led to the 2003 recall of Governor Gray Davis and the election of optimistic political neophyte and action-movie hero Arnold Schwarzenegger. It also led to popular dissatisfaction with *his* performance by the time he left office. As Californians search for the good life, however they define it, they will need to adjust to the state's growing demographic diversity, regardless of election outcomes. A state senator summed it up succinctly: "We Californians have an opportunity, the necessity, the responsibility, to realize our great challenge ... the promise of a multicultural democracy in the global economy."[3]

As far as California is concerned, this search began centuries ago. In the 1500s, Spaniards desired to find and explore a mythical island of *California*. Writer Garci Ordoñez de Montalvo described this place as rich in "gold and precious stones"; its people were "robust of body, with strong and passionate hearts and great virtues." As for government, the queen "had ambitions

to execute nobler actions than had been performed by any other ruler."[4] Wealth and good intentions—what a combination! No wonder California has been called not only a state but also a state of mind.

Centuries later, California's official state motto captures that mythic search: "Eureka" (I Have Found It). The motto itself refers to the real gold many sought and some actually found. Symbolically, it refers to a host of images emanating from California: perpetually sunny days (advertised every year by Pasadena's Rose Parade); hope and opportunity; a chance to start over; plus gorgeous scenery and people to match (says Hollywood).

Chapter 1 introduces two approaches to understanding California politics. The first is the state's remarkable diversity. The second is a set of theories that political scientists use to explain aspects of American politics generally. These two broad approaches (diversity and theory) are revisited throughout the book.

HOW DIVERSITY EXPLAINS CALIFORNIA POLITICS

California always has been a compelling place. Few observers write about it without describing its physical diversity, and fewer still ignore its politics. To understand this huge state, one must understand how its public sector works. Political scientist David Easton defined **politics** as "the authoritative allocation of values for a society as a whole."[5] Politics occurs within the context of a **political system**. In our federal arrangement, there are 50 state systems and one national political system. These systems reflect ongoing patterns of human behavior involving control, influence, power, and authority. The process of making public policy, deciding "who gets what, when and how,"[6] exists within the context of a larger environment. The **political environment** is a set of social, cultural, economic, and physical attributes that inform and limit how politics is done. To begin this study of California politics, we must examine California's diverse environment—the land and regions of the state, and its resources, people, and economy.

Land

Diverse is truly the only word to describe the physical geography of California. The state's diversity is made possible in part by its sheer size. California's length covers the distance between New York City and Jacksonville, Florida. The nation's third-largest state in square miles (behind Alaska and Texas), California supports a rich variety of terrain.

Coastal communities enjoy moderate, semiarid Mediterranean weather in the South and wetter, cooler weather in the far North. Thick forests, including giant redwoods, occur in the North. In fact, 40 percent of the state is forested. The naturally barren South has been made less so over the years by farmers and gardeners alike. Numerous mountain ranges crisscross the state. The defining North/South range is the Sierra Nevada. Admired by naturalist John Muir, this magnificent mountain range is home to world-famous Yosemite National Park and giant sequoia trees. Farmers and urban residents to the west and south of the mountains depend on the Sierra's snowpack for year-round water supplies, the lifeblood of any arid state. Less-imposing coastal ranges help define the attractive but expensive environments around such places as Santa Barbara, Carmel, and Santa Cruz.

The transverse ranges, those mountains that lie in an east/west direction, once defined the limits of urbanization and, to some people's minds, the boundary between Northern and Southern California. The Los Angeles Basin (surrounded by the Sierra Madre, Tehachapi, Santa Ana, San Gabriel, and San Jacinto ranges) once kept its poor air quality to itself. But urban growth and automobile proliferation have spread smog over the mountains to communities on the other side (Palm Springs and Lancaster, e.g.) and locales as far away as the Grand Canyon in Arizona. The increasingly smoggy Central Valley supports some of the most productive agriculture in the world.

Below observable land lie two massive tectonic plates, the North American and the Pacific. The grinding of these plates results in long-term geologic features such as mountains and the short-term terror of potentially destructive earthquakes.

Regions

The configuration of the land influences how people settle on and use it—leading to regional differences. These differences are partly a matter of perception. Consider the idea of Northern and Southern California, the most familiar division of the state. People know Northern California for San Francisco (called simply "The City"), wineries, redwoods, heavy water-consuming crops such as rice, and mountain resorts such as Lake Tahoe. They identify Southern California with its warm days, wide beaches, automobile culture, show business, Latino roots, and, of course, smog. Some suggest that these two regions are actually two states divided by water. The North has it, the South wants it, and the North knows it. These North/South differences are deeply rooted. In 1859, less than a decade after statehood, the legislature voted to split the state in two, but the U.S. Congress disallowed it. Occasional efforts to divide California have surfaced ever since. The most recent efforts, in the 1990s, aimed to divide the state into either two or three states. These efforts seem motivated not only by classic regional differences but also by the mounting problems faced by a unified California—economic uncertainty, budget woes, population growth, and demographic diversity. In an advisory vote in 1992, voters in 31 counties considered a two-state proposal; it passed in 27 mostly northern counties. Although these efforts are doomed to failure, they do exemplify intense regional divisions in the state. Pundits have long since divided California from North to South into Logland, Fogland, and Smogland.

Perceptions aside, California is a state of many regions. Different observers have divided the state into anywhere from 4 to 14 distinct regions. Each is markedly different from the others based on geography, economy, populations, political behavior, and public attitudes.[7] Public opinion surveys and election analyzes of the four most populous regions—Los Angeles County, the San Francisco Bay area, the Central Valley, and the Orange County/Inland Empire region—document a number of differences (See Figure 1.2). In general, coastal Californians are more liberal and Democratic and those who live inland are more conservative and Republican. This plays out in legislative elections, initiative results, and views on public policy.[8] As a consequence, according to analyst and pollster Mark Baldassare, these regional differences make it difficult for Californians to unify and see themselves as members of one state. Indeed, "the major regions are drifting further apart at a time when there is a need to reach a statewide consensus on social, environmental, land use, and infrastructure issues."[9]

Resources

In addition to regional perceptions, a state's natural resources affect its politics. Ironically, California's most important resource is its most precious—water. One simply cannot underestimate what the availability and redistribution of water has meant for the Golden State. As writer Carey McWilliams once noted, "the history of Southern California is the record of its eternal quest for water, and more water, and still more water."[10] The entire state has been called a "hydraulic society," and it is easy to see why. Water has transformed parched land into the nation's salad bowl and fruit basket. Water has enabled imaginative people in a semiarid climate to control vast amounts of land or merely turn their yards into tropical and subtropical gardens. And most important, dams, canals, and aqueducts have channeled water from the North to the South, allowing millions of people to live where nature alone could support very few.

California's overall climate is itself a resource and has directly and indirectly caused the state's phenomenal growth. Americans have always been lured to California because of its weather. Years ago, winter exports of citrus and newspaper ads in the Midwest created a "Garden of Eden" image, which served as a magnet. Asked why he charged $200 an acre for seemingly worthless land, flamboyant speculator Lucky Baldwin retorted: "Hell! We're giving away the land. We're selling the climate."[11] Doctors would recommend California's milder climate to patients suffering from respiratory and arthritic ailments.

California's climate also has fostered elements of California's economy. Early movie producers found weather predictability helpful in shooting outdoor scenes. The films themselves became subtle advertisements for the Golden State. Farmers discovered that, given enough water, several harvests per year were possible. Developers and contractors found they could get away with cheaper, less-weather-resistant construction. Employers concerned with working conditions and living conditions for themselves found California an inviting destination. California's climate also fostered recreation-oriented "live for the weekend" lifestyles. Much leisure time can be spent outdoors—beach activities, snow skiing, fishing, water sports, camping, biking, hiking—the list is endless. Even at home, many Californians create their own micro-lifestyles, replete with expansive patios, pools, spas, barbecues, and gardens.

FIGURE 1.2 California's Regions

NOTE: The highlighted areas of California are the regions most used by the Public Policy Institute of California pollsters to document differing views of Californians based on geography.

SOURCE: Public Policy Institute of California.

Cartoon 1.1 The good life

Question: How do you define "the good life" in California in light of these periodic misfortunes?
SOURCE: Gary Brookins, *Richmond Times–Dispatch.*

All this has resulted in a subtle attitude found in the Golden State. Just as people thought they could change their destiny by moving to California in the first place, many believe they can engineer their destiny once they arrive. As Cartoon 1.1 implies, Californians seek what they call the "good life" despite hindrances of all sorts. They expect their state and local governments to deliver policies fostering and protecting a certain quality of life. They become disillusioned and angry when policymakers fail to meet those expectations. They give policymakers low marks in public opinion surveys, oust them from office if possible, or pass initiatives designed to sidestep policy processes.

People

California's resources have encouraged waves of human settlement. In short, diversity and growth characterize the demographics of California. As in the past, the state attracts immigrants from all over the world. Furthermore, they are settling throughout the state. Mexicans were never limited solely to

Los Angeles barrios, nor the Chinese to their Chinatowns. But the ethnic and geographic diversity of today's Californians is astounding. Iranians, Indians, Sri Lankans, Haitians, Koreans, Salvadoreans, Vietnamese, and others are moving to and throughout California in large numbers. By 2000, no racial group or ethnic group constituted a majority of Californians. In fact, a decade later, over 20 percent of the nation's non-white population lived in California. California's population currently is growing at a rate of nearly 1,000 per day. This trend can be seen in Figure 1.3.

Native Americans　California's first dwellers were widely-dispersed Native Americans living off the land in small communities. By 1823, there were about 400,000 tribal members living in California. As peaceful peoples, they were no match for the succession of more aggressive Spanish, Mexican, and Anglo-American settlers. Due primarily to disease imported from these settlers, they and their cultures were driven to near extinction. Today, Native Americans constitute less than one percent of its population and are discussed further in

Chapters 2 and 3. As a rule, they defy broad-brush generalizations. Some tribes remain poor while others have discovered newfound wealth and political influence by way of lucrative casino development and large-scale gaming.

Latinos By the time of Mexican independence from Spain in 1822, the remaining Native Americans plus a relative handful of Spaniards, Mexicans, and the offspring of mixed marriages between various groups populated the province of del norte. Like their predecessors, contemporary Mexicans and others from Latin America come to California seeking prosperity. Be they citizens, resident aliens, or undocumented workers, many Latinos work in the agricultural, manufacturing, and service sectors of the state's economy. Due to continuing in-migration and relatively high birthrates, they have become a sizeable cultural and socioeconomic force in the state. In 2010, Latinos constituted about a third of the entire state population. California's Department of Finance has projected that Hispanics (including Latinos) will become the largest ethnic group by 2016. Geographically, they are well-represented in most of California's regions and their political influence is on the rise. In one respect, Latinos have been known for low voter turnout, in part, because many of them are not yet citizens or are too young to vote. Yet a growing number of them have been elected to public office throughout the state. Population data and electoral returns suggest

that Latino political influence will grow in the future and that the rather diverse Latino community might not behave as a monolithic political force.[12]

Non-Hispanic Whites The Gold Rush of 1849 began what is known as the "American era." This provincial-sounding term refers to the successive waves of Euro-American citizens who moved to California from other parts of the United States. Within a year after gold was discovered at Sutter's Mill in 1848, roughly a third of the state's population was digging for gold in "them thar hills." Many with gold fever never intended to stay, but did. Others not only stayed but sent for their families to join them. Population figures tell the story. In 1840, Californians numbered about 116,000, including 110,000 to 112,000 Native Americans. Two decades later, they numbered 380,000, including only 30,000 Native Americans.

A second population rush followed completion of the Transcontinental Railroad in 1869. That last spike, joining the Central Pacific and Union Pacific railroads in Utah, linked California both physically and symbolically with the rest of the nation. For urban Americans, the lure of open space "out West" actually made possible a newly-emerging dream in the late 1800s—a single-family house on a single-family lot. But why California? For one thing, the Southern Pacific Railroad had received more than 10 million acres of Southern California land as a construction incentive.

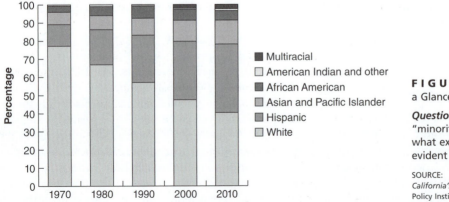

FIGURE 1.3 Californians at a Glance

Question: California is now a "minority majority" state. To what extent is this phenomenon evident where you live and work?

SOURCE: Hans Johnson, *Just the Facts: California's Population* (San Francisco: Public Policy Institute of California, May 2011).

Through shameless hucksterism and discounted train tickets, developers and the railroads lured many Midwesterners to the Golden State. Later, the mass production of automobiles allowed others to bypass trains altogether on their way to sunny California.

In the 1900s, additional waves of Americans moved westward to seek various employment opportunities. Beginning with Summerland near Santa Barbara in 1920, the discovery and drilling of oil led to new jobs and still more land speculation. The Depression-era jobless and Dust Bowl refugees (many were called Okies and Arkies for their home states of Oklahoma and Arkansas) came to California in search of any opportunity they could find.

John Steinbeck's *The Grapes of Wrath* fictionalized the real misery of these migrants and what they hoped for in California (see Box 1.1: California Voices). World War II brought numerous Americans to California for training and war production efforts. Soldiers and sailors who had never been west of the Mississippi River were stationed briefly in California on their way to the Pacific theater. Many of them vowed to return to California—for keeps—and they did. In 2010, white non-Hispanic Californians were about 40 percent of the overall population. These percentages have been declining and will continue to do so in the future.

African Americans   The war effort in California provided unprecedented employment opportunities for African Americans, many of whom migrated from the South. Their population in California grew 272 percent in the 1940s alone! In 2010, most of California's 2.3 million African Americans lived in the state's large metropolitan areas. As elsewhere, they have suffered racial discrimination and many lag behind other groups in education and income. They have held prominent positions in state politics including two Assembly speakerships (Willie Brown and Herb Wesson) as well as seats in Congress and the state legislature. According to the latest census, African Americans constitute only 6 percent of California's overall population. Because of modest birth rates and some migration out of California, black political clout appears to be lessening; the number of black officeholders has steadily declined since the mid-1980s.

Asian Americans   A succession of other minorities entered California over the years. Notable have been California's nearly 5 million Asian Americans (as of 2010), including those of Chinese, Japanese, Filipino, and Korean descent. Many Chinese were brought to the state during the Gold Rush or to work on railroad construction gangs. By 1870, nearly 150,000 of them were treated as virtual slaves by their employers. During economic downturns, they were considered as excess labor and had to retreat to their Chinatowns for protection and security.

Historically, Japanese Californians have also suffered oppression. Between 1900 and 1920 they increased from 10,000 to 72,000 and, to the dismay of whites, gained control of 11 percent of the state's farmland. Four years later, the U.S. Congress reacted by halting further Japanese

---

B o x 1.1   CALIFORNIA VOICES: Steinbeck on California

"I like to think how nice it's gonna be, maybe, in California. Never cold. An' fruit ever'place, an' people just bein' in the nicest places, little white houses in among the orange trees. I wonder—that is, if we all get jobs an' all work—maybe we can get one of them little white houses. An' the little fellas go out an' pick oranges right off the tree."

Question: To what extent are today's visions of California like or unlike those of Steinbeck's Depression-ravaged characters?

SOURCE: John Steinbeck, *The Grapes of Wrath* (New York: Viking Press, 1939), p. 124.

immigration. After Japan attacked Pearl Harbor in 1941, Californians of Japanese descent, including American citizens, were moved to relocation camps. Branded temporarily as "enemy aliens," Japanese Americans rose above this wholesale discrimination and economic dislocation to become successful both educationally and economically.

Filipino Californians, although sizeable in number, do not command the economic influence of either the Chinese or the Japanese in California. The Vietnam War resulted in an influx of Southeast Asians to California. Some have achieved material success in the Golden State, but others work at poverty wages in Southern California sweatshops.

Ethnic diversity in California also translates into language diversity. Census data indicate that over 42 percent of Californians speak a language other than English in the home; the national figure is less than 20 percent. In general, children speak English more fluently than the adults in these homes.

What do all this racial and ethnic data tell us? Whereas other parts of America have historically thought of diversity in biracial (black and white) terms, describing the people of California is much more complex, given the state's many racial and ethnic groups. Some observers ask: Will this multiethnic and multiracial mix we find in California lead to a divisive, Balkanized politics that emphasizes difference over unity? It depends.

Aside from policies related to race or ethnicity such as affirmative action, services to illegal immigrants, and bilingual education, polling data suggest that California's Asians, blacks, Latinos, and whites agree more often than not on a wide range of issues.[13] In the words of the nation's motto, there may well be more "unum" than "pluribus" on many issues. To the extent that diverse Californians view public life in similar terms, they embody what writer O. Henry once said of the state: "Californians are a race of people; not merely inhabitants of a state."[14] Furthermore, as you will see shortly, the "politics of diversity" in the Golden State is only in part a function of ethnic and racial diversity.

Economy

To the state's geographic and demographic diversity can be added economic diversity. To understand the politics of any state, knowing its economy is essential. Business and politics are closely intertwined. State and local policies can have an impact on economic growth, generally, particular economic sectors, and even individual businesses. The economy in turn provides the financial base for state and local policies. California's modern economy is large, postindustrial, diverse, driven by change, and affected by a tiered workforce.

1. *Size* By any measure, California's economy is huge. If it were a nation-state, its gross state (domestic) product (GDP)—in the range of $1.8 trillion—would make it the world's eighth largest economy (see Figure 1.4a). Compared to the other 49 states, California ranks first in a number of categories. While agriculture constitutes a small fraction of the state's economic output, it outproduces all other states. Despite recent job losses, it also ranks first in manufacturing. More Fortune 500 companies call California home than any other state.

2. *Post-Industrialism* California's economy is **postindustrial**, meaning it is characterized by a large and growing service sector, economic interdependence, rapid change, innovation, and advanced technology. As a general rule, traditional manufacturing has lagged behind services and trades in numbers of workers. This is especially true with "off-shoring," the transfer of manufacturing jobs overseas. Today's post-industrial service economy includes technology, education, research, finance, insurance, and real estate. It also includes both wholesale and retail sales of groceries, clothing, and a plethora of other consumer items. Taken together, the service sector includes both high-paying and low-paying jobs.[15]

3. *Change* California's economic history has been one of constant change. The Gold Rush encouraged a "rush" of workers. The

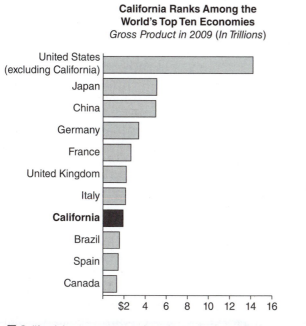

California Ranks Among the World's Top Ten Economies
Gross Product in 2009 (In Trillions)

- California's gross state product, the total value of final goods and services produced in state, was about $1.9 trillion in 2009, making it one of the world's largest economies.

- California accounts for 13 percent of the nation's output.

- The next largest state economy—Texas—is about 60 pecent the size of California's.

FIGURE 1.4a California: A Nation-Sized Economy

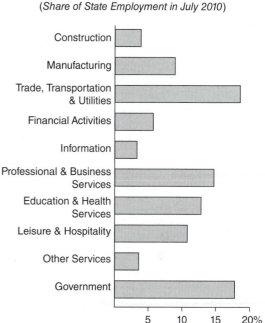

California's Employment Base is Diversified
(Share of State Employment in July 2010)

- California's distribution of jobs by sector is very similar to the nation's. Services, information, and government jobs are a slightly higher share of California's employment base, as compared to the rest of the country.

FIGURE 1.4b Where Californians work

SOURCE: Legislative Analyst's Office, *Cal Facts 2011: California's Economy* (Sacramento: Legislative Analyst's Office, January 2010). Accessed at http://lao.ca.gov/reports/2011/calfacts/calfacts_010511.pdf/.

expansion of railroads (including the invention of refrigerated rolling stock), plus government-financed water projects, secured agriculture as an economic mainstay. The discovery of oil fueled the state's emerging automobile-oriented transportation system. World War II spawned a military-industrial complex, which anchored the state's manufacturing sector. Finally, the technological revolution laid the groundwork for the service-based economy described earlier. Economic change today is international in scope. The health of foreign economies affects trade from California and many jobs have been outsourced or "off-shored" to

places like India. Asian nations have become major competitors in numerous industries, and Mexico's border towns have lured U.S.-and foreign-owned assembly factories called *maquiladoras*. California's workers are changing too. The state's labor force is older, more ethnically diverse, and more female than it once was.

4. *Diversity* California's economy is richly *diverse*. As Figure 1.4b portrays, California's employment base is highly-diversified, mirroring that of the nation. In many ways, this helps California weather difficulties faced by other states that lean on a relative handful of economic sectors for their economic health. This

diversity, however, did not shelter the state from the recent recession during which nearly 40 percent of the state's construction jobs were lost.

5. *A Multitiered Workforce* Lastly, California's workforce or labor pool consists of several tiers. The upper tiers consist of highly educated, well-paid employees in high technology, knowledge-intensive businesses, and organizations. Included are the fields of education, medicine, communications, law, finance, real estate, transportation, and government. The lower tiers consist of those working in low-paying, low-status service jobs found in retail outlets, the tourism industry, agriculture, and marginal manufacturing concerns. The top tiers have enjoyed rising income in recent decades; the lower tiers have actually experienced a precipitous drop in income, especially among male workers, leading to growing income disparities among the tiers. Immigrants constitute a growing share of California's workforce. While their incomes tend to be lower than native-born workers, Californians believe they are a benefit to the California labor market.[16]

HOW POLITICAL THEORY EXPLAINS CALIFORNIA POLITICS

As important as it is, a state's political environment alone (land, regions, resources, people, and economy) does not explain its politics. Politics deals with complex sets of human relationships involving influence and power. To understand the complexity of politics, theories help explain who governs and why. But not all political scientists can agree on a single theory. As a result, alternative theories have emerged, which we will briefly explore and apply to California politics.

Democratic Theory

According to traditional **democratic theory**, the answer to "Who governs?" is "All of us," in a sense. Two forms of democracy exist. *Participatory democracy* envisions rule by the many as described by the ancient philosopher Aristotle. *Representative democracy* suggests rule by the few on behalf of the many—the people. In a representative democracy, policymakers may negotiate and compromise with each other but are influenced and ultimately controlled by the electorate. Political scientist Robert Dahl thought an ideal democratic process must meet five criteria relative to "the people": equality in voting, effective citizen participation, enlightened understanding, final control over government's agenda, and inclusion (the application of rights and laws to everyone).[17] The American Founders thought that the states would play dominant roles in making representative democracy work.

Democratic theory partly explains California politics, especially its political ideals. The preamble to the state's constitution reads: "*We, the People* of the State of California, grateful to Almighty God for our freedom, in order to secure and perpetuate its blessings, do establish this Constitution" (emphasis added). It contains the state's own "Bill of Rights" and establishes various institutions of government that, on paper, are responsible to the electorate. Furthermore, voters have the power to adopt their own legislation (initiatives), approve or disapprove various laws passed by the state legislature (referenda), and remove elected officials between elections (recall). They can do all this on a statewide basis and in their respective communities.

Traditional democratic theory advances political ideals better than it explains political reality. A representative democracy assumes greater citizen interest than often is the case. In California, the politically disinterested and economically weak are clearly disadvantaged. The political equality presumed by democratic thought is largely missing. The result in California is the emergence of a two-tier polity. Some observers perceive a political dominance by an "affluent, politically active over class using its position to protect its privileges against the larger but weaker underclass."[18] They ask: Where is the "common good" between the haves and the have-nots? Democratic theory, then, needs to account for the relationship between government and wealth, the persistence of unequal subgroups in the polity, and what, if any, common ground exists between these unequal subgroups.

Elite Theory

Other theories also attempt to explain the origins and exercise of power. According to elite theorists, all societies naturally divide into two classes: the few who rule and the many who do not. Political power inevitably gravitates to the few out of necessity, what Robert Michels called an "iron law of oligarchy." As political scientist Harold Lasswell once put it, "Government is always government by the few, whether in the name of the few, the one, or the many."[19] Some elites consist of corporate owners and other wealthy persons who exercise political power directly or control those who do on their behalf.

As with democratic theory, elements of **elite and class politics** can be seen in California. Historically, one corporation, the Southern Pacific Railroad, wielded significant power. The "Big Four" (Leland Stanford, Collis Huntington, Charles Crocker, and Mark Hopkins) were successful businessmen. Controlling a virtual political machine, they shaped the state's early commerce, land development, and overall growth. Through his control of land and water, *Los Angeles Times* owner Harrison Gray Otis helped engineer Los Angeles' growth more profoundly than any city council could have. Elites are also evident in modern California. Some individuals continue to hold substantial power. For example, with little public notice, J. G. Boswell parlayed a Central Valley farm into a multinational agriculture-based empire through business savvy and political influence.[20] With that said, elites sometimes fail. One recent study documented the failure of Los Angeles elites in shaping both the city's image and citizen behavior.[21]

Furthermore, most elites today operate as groups. The state's media exercise considerable influence through major television stations and a small handful of newspaper chains. Among the most influential groups in Sacramento are large corporations or clusters of them, such as the California Manufacturers Association. The California legislature routinely provides tax incentives and other benefits to powerful economic interests and even single companies. Because they are frequently campaign contributors, when these groups speak, policymakers listen. Consider the 2010 election cycle. Compared to organized interest groups, individuals contributed only 19 percent of the $650 million spent on California candidates and ballot measures (followthemoney.org). Californians themselves sense the power of elites and distrust the results. According to a 2011 poll, 67 percent of respondents thought that the state government was "pretty much run by a few big interests looking out for themselves" instead of for the benefit of all Californians.[22]

As compelling as elite theory sounds, it, too, cannot fully explain California politics. The influence of the Big Four was ultimately broken in the Progressive era. Today, many California businesses of all sizes compete for power—reducing the influence of any one business. Some initiatives remain downright populist and still others that favor elite interests fail at the polls. For example, in November 2010, voters rejected business efforts to suspend the state's new global warming law and repealed certain business tax breaks granted by the legislature (Propositions 23 and 24). In short, because elites exist does not necessarily mean they win on, or even care about, all issues. California's elites tend to husband their resources for issues they regard as most important.

Pluralist Theory

Pluralist theory tries to correct aspects of both democratic and elite theory. Electoral majorities, a cornerstone of democratic theory, are something of a myth, given voter apathy. According to Dahl, "On matters of specific policy, the majority rarely rules."[23] Pluralists admit that groups are controlled by elites but observe many groups having access to, competing for, and sharing power. No single group dominates all the time. In many ways, American politics *is* group politics—a fluid process of competing interests winning or losing, rising or falling, as they seek to influence transitory issues. Interest group politics is readily observable at all levels of our political system. Pluralism's critics, though, argue that the push and pull of pluralist politics does not explain the inherent and systemic inequalities that persist in American life. Furthermore, interests must be organized; some perfectly legitimate interests, such as children or the homeless, rarely organize.

Pluralism is an attractive option for students of California politics. If you look up "Associations" in the Sacramento Yellow Pages (www.yellow.com/sacramento.html/), you will be amazed at the breadth of interest groups in the state's capital. Group-inspired lunch-hour rallies are a common sight on the Capitol steps. Proposition "wars" now feature dueling initiatives sponsored by opposing groups. Increasingly, ethnic groups are creating *multicultural pluralism* in California politics.

But not all politics in California can be labeled group politics. First, structural features of California's political system (its constitution and institutions) to some extent limit group power. Second, group competition alone does not explain the occasional rise of policy entrepreneurs—individuals who make a substantial difference, such as anti-tax crusader Howard Jarvis and, more recently, marijuana activist Richard Lee. Third, pluralism seems to suggest a satisfactory equilibrium among competing groups. But how does one explain policy indecision, delay, or paralysis—what is often called gridlock?

Hyperpluralism

Elements of truth in these three theories might suggest what Dahl calls an "American hybrid,"[24] but a nagging problem remains. All three presume that governing does, in fact, occur. Yet some observers claim that no one "rules" effectively anymore. State governments, California included, lurch from fiscal year to fiscal year. In a sense, recent budget crises serve to magnify the ongoing challenge of governing in the Golden State. In addition, initiatives sponsored by some organized interests, once passed, are challenged in court by other groups. Some political scientists call this state of affairs **hyperpluralism**. In this view, power is thinly scattered, not just widely or unevenly scattered as previous theories would suggest. The exercise of political power has become a highly competitive tug-of-war between institutions, policymakers, political parties, numerous interest groups, and voters.

Political scientists who hold this view are both describing a variant of pluralism and making a judgment about government's performance. They admit that the American system was intended to check power, not merely facilitate it. But they also believe checking power is different from preventing its exercise at all. Hyperpluralism seems increasingly helpful in explaining how aspects of American politics work. In explaining California politics, it is downright compelling. Let us consider it in more depth.

HOW HYPERPLURALISM EXPLAINS CALIFORNIA POLITICS

There is ample evidence of hyperpluralism in American politics, and in California politics in particular: individualism in political life, a growing diversity of group interests and cultures, the changing nature of majoritarian politics, and "built-in" or structural conflict. These **components of California hyperpluralism** are somewhat intertwined and dependent on each other.

The Constancy of Individualism

Individualism is a hallmark of American life, and it is nothing new. In the 1830s, French observer Alexis de Tocqueville correctly defined American individualism as "a calm and considered feeling which disposes each citizen to isolate himself from the mass of his fellows and withdraw into the circle of family and friends; with this little society formed to his taste, he gladly leaves the greater society to look after itself."[25] Recent scholars have observed the popularity of individualism among "middle Americans" and believe it exists at the expense of commitment to a larger community.[26] Individualism is a key tile in the mosaic of California politics. The proliferation of interest groups, the pursuit of leisure, gated communities, private security systems, solitary rush-hour commutes, and widespread gun ownership—a do-it-yourself law enforcement, of sorts—all suggest dependence on self rather than on society to fulfill both needs and wants. In a sense, even low voter turnout in California elections reflects individualism in a culture where political participation is considered optional and even unimportant. But individualism is not applied consistently. As writer Joan Didion reminds us, California's historic dependence on federal spending for water projects, highways, and defense contracts is "seemingly at odds with the [state's] emphasis on unfettered individualism that constitutes the local core belief."[27]

A Diversity of Interests and Cultures

One aspect of hyperpluralism is the range of interests that various groups bring to public life. The most fundamental interest is in civic life itself, what is called "civic engagement." Here the ethnic and racial diversity of California is not evident in voting or in other activities associated with public life—signing petitions, attending meetings, writing officials, making campaign contributions, attending rallies, and doing political party work. Research findings indicate that those Californians who are white, older, more affluent, homeowners, and more highly-educated evidence the highest levels of civic engagement. Relative to their numbers in the population, whites are overrepresented in virtually every political activity we associate with civic engagement.[28] Politically speaking, those Californians who have the greatest say are not those who arguably have the greatest needs.

Of those groups that do engage in community and public life, many represent relatively narrow viewpoints or advocate relatively narrow agendas. Some even define themselves and behave politically

in terms of one single issue—giving rise to what has been called *single-issue politics*. When public problems are viewed in such narrow terms, policy solutions seem obvious and clear cut, but only to the group espousing them. This leads such groups to hold their views with more determination and to communicate them with greater assertiveness. Some behave as grievance groups, out to correct negative treatment by the larger society. All this has increased group conflict in California and has decreased the potential for broader intergroup consensus. Absent a broader consensus, policymakers find that supporting certain groups has a price— the wrath of other groups.

Fading Majoritarianism

Another evidence of hyperpluralism is the changing nature of *majority rule*—a major principle of American politics. The nation's founders thought that, in a representative democracy, elected officials would seek the common good agreeable to a functioning majority. In California politics, a single public interest and a single majority seem to be endangered political species. In a sense, "minorities" already rule in the Golden State. On a statewide basis, a relatively small number of individuals and groups set legislative agendas and determine which issues make it to the ballot. A relatively small percentage of Californians who qualify to vote actually register to vote; an even smaller percentage turn out on Election Day; and only a *simple majority of those* determine election outcomes. In numerous California cities, there is no single ethnic majority. Ironically, while majority rule means less and less, some political ground rules in California require *supermajorities* to enact public policy. The state constitution requires a two-thirds majority of the legislature to raise taxes and a two-thirds popular vote to raise certain local taxes. Such numbers are often difficult to achieve.

Another aspect of fading majoritarianism is voter disinterest that leads to low voter turnout, at least in some elections. For example, of the more than 23 million eligible voters in California, only 17 million registered to vote for the 2010 June primary. Only 33 percent of those actually voted. Of course, fewer still voted for any particular candidate or ballot measure. Aside from high profile presidential races as we saw in 2008, election politics arguably can be viewed as a function of minority rule, not majoritarianism.

Structural Conflict

One reason California voters decide issues directly is that interest groups that sponsor initiatives want to bypass a cumbersome policy process in Sacramento. Many Californians, ready to assess blame for the results of that process, choose to replace their elected officials or limit their terms of service. Term limits have been increasingly adopted at the local level and have been applied to state legislators and constitutional officers thanks to Proposition 140 (1990).

Are elected politicians to blame? Only in part. California's political structure itself invites political conflict. First, the state's constitution in effect predestines a horizontal power struggle between the executive, legislative, and judicial branches. While praised as a necessary "checks and balances" feature of our form of government, it does foster political and policy conflict. Second, by dictating certain roles for local government, it guarantees a vertical power struggle between the "locals" (cities, counties, and special districts) and the state itself. Third, the initiative process allows voters to make policy and thereby circumvent and even contradict the very legislature they elect to make policy. According to journalist Peter Schrag, the result has been "an increasingly unmanageable and incomprehensible structure of state and local government that exacerbates the same public disaffection and alienation that brought it on."[29]

Theory	Evidence in California
Democratic theory	Initiative process
	Frequent elections
	Elected legislative bodies (state and local)
Elite theory	Big Four
	Major campaign contributors
	Policy entrepreneurs
	Policies benefitting the relative few
Pluralism	Proliferation of interest groups
	Group competition
	Dueling initiatives
	Multicultural pluralism
Hyperpluralism	Individualistic approaches to public life
	Power by nonmajorities
	Diversity of interests and cultures
	Supermajority vote requirements
	Structural conflict and policy gridlock

FIGURE 1.5 The Governing Theories in Brief

Did You Know ... ?

In response to the 2010 Census, 1.8 million Californians indicated that they were of two or more races.

Question: In the future, will racial categories be more difficult to keep distinct in California?

SOURCE: U.S. Census Bureau.

CALIFORNIA: THE IRONIES OF DIVERSITY

In this introductory chapter, we have surveyed California's rich **diversity**, the theories that help explain its politics, and the hyperpluralism that is increasingly evident. As California becomes more diverse and hyperpluralistic, several ironies have emerged. First, compared to other states, California has become both policy innovator and laggard. Over the years, it has "led the way" with such measures as Proposition 13 (which reduced property taxes) and "Three Strikes, You're Out" legislation (which imposed lengthy sentences for three-time felons), and the legalization of marijuana for medical use. Years ago, its investment in freeways was the envy of other states. In recent decades though, California's per capita spending on highways has declined considerably. In years past, other states imitated California's visionary 1961 master plan for higher education (which provided the structure for the state's community colleges and four-year universities). Yet recent spending on education at all levels has lagged the state's growth.

Second, the policy generosity of California's electorate and its government is cyclical, contested, and occasionally ambivalent. Consider budgeting. As diverse as California's economy is, the state's dependence on inherently volatile sources of revenue such as the income tax can significantly alter budget priorities. When tax revenues from stock options and capital gains fluctuate, mirroring the fluctuations in the stock market and technology sectors, California's state budget can experience both record surpluses and record deficits—all within a few years. These revenue gyrations force difficult and contested budget decisions. In terms of civil rights, policy generosity is tempered with ambivalence. For example, a growing number of Californians oppose discrimination against gays and lesbians but many of those still prefer not to sanction gay marriage itself.

Third, while policy paralysis often grips Sacramento, policy progress can be found closer to home. The state's 482 cities have developed entrepreneurial ways to raise needed revenue. Numerous counties have increased sales taxes to pay for transportation projects once thought to be the state's responsibility. Those Californians who can afford to (the upper tier) buy services their state or local government cannot afford or will not provide. Some have augmented meager public recreation programs with those of private groups like the YMCA. Some install their own security systems; others live in condominium or planned unit developments where neighborhood "quality of life" decisions are made by homeowner associations, not city councils. They transfer from troubled public schools to private ones or they resort to homeschooling. What does the bottom tier do? They rely on government programs despite the cuts, live by their wits, or simply do without.

The California portrayed in this chapter is of immense proportion. The challenges facing the most populous state in the Union are abundant to be sure, as they always have been. The capacity and potential for California governments to address these challenges is and always has been great. Its political system reflects a state "in which the best possibilities of the American experiment can be struggled for and sometimes achieved."[30] Political scientists search for theories to explain why California functions the way it does. While no single theory or approach will suffice, both the state's diversity and its hyperpluralistic political system seem useful in explaining California's current state of affairs.

As a subject of study, California politics is both fascinating and challenging. Due to term limits and demographic shifts, it is also ever changing. As you read this book, you will discover why.

KEY TERMS

political system (p. 4)

politics (p. 4)

political environment (p. 4)

postindustrial economy (p. 10)

a multi-tiered workforce (p. 12)

democratic theory (p. 12)

elite and class politics (p. 13)

pluralist theory (p. 13)

hyperpluralism (p. 14)

components of California hyperpluralism (pp. 14–16)

ironies of diversity (p. 17)

REVIEW QUESTIONS

1. Identify the ways in which diversity explains California politics.

2. Describe the various regions of California.

3. How have water and climate affected the state's growth?

4. What demographic groups have come to California and why?

5. Describe the five keys to understanding the state's economy. What makes it two-tiered in nature?

6. Illustrate each theory with California examples.

7. In what ways does hyperpluralism seem particularly apt in describing California politics?

8. Discuss and illustrate California's ironies of diversity.

WEB ACTIVITIES

California Home Page

www.ca.gov/

A good starting point, this site will take you in many different directions regarding life and politics in the Golden State.

California Department of Finance, Demographic Research Unit

www.dof.ca.gov/research/demographic

This "single official source of demographic data for state planning and budgeting" provides helpful information on population growth, change, and diversity in California.

U.S. Census Bureau

www.census.gov

You can find more census data on California by clicking Population Finder and Quick Facts.

NOTES

1. Quoted in Steven Harmon, "Jerry Brown, California Politicians Lay Out Grim Realities," *Contra Costa Times* (December 9, 2010).

2. Mark Baldassare, *A California State of Mind: The Conflicted Voter in a Changing World* (Berkeley: University of California Press, 2002), p. 1.

3. Quoted in Al Martinez, "Can We All Get Along?" *California Journal* 29 (Jan. 1998), p. 10.

4. Quoted in Andrew F. Rolle, *California: A History* (New York: Crowell, 1969), p. 34.

5. David Easton, *The Political System* (New York: Alfred A. Knopf), Chap. 5.

6. Harold D. Lasswell, *Politics: Who Gets What, When and How* (New York: McGraw-Hill, 1938).

7. Hans P. Johnson, "A State of Diversity in California Regions: Demographic Trends," *California Counts* (San Francisco: Public Policy Institute of California, May 2002).

8. Frederick Douzet and Kenneth P. Miller, "California's East-West Divide," in Frederick Douzet, Thad Kousser, and Kenneth P. Miller, *The New Political Geography of California* (Berkeley: Berkeley Public Policy Press, 2008).

9. Mark Baldassare, *PPIC Statewide Survey: Californians and Their Government* (San Francisco: Public Policy Institute of California, July 2001), p. 13.

10. Carey McWilliams, *Southern California: An Island on the Land* (Santa Barbara: Peregrine Smith, 1946, 1973), p. 183.

11. Quoted in Joseph S. O'Flaherty, *Those Powerful Years: The South Coast and Los Angeles, 1887—1917* (Hicksville, NY: Exposition Press, 1978), p. 23.

12. Baldassare, *A California State of Mind*, particularly Chap. 6: "The Latino Century Begins."

13. Zoltan Hajnal and Mark Baldassare, *Finding Common Ground: Racial and Ethnic Attitudes in California* (San Francisco: Public Policy Institute of California, 2001).

14. Quoted in Stephen Birmingham, *California Rich* (New York: Simon and Schuster, 1980), p. 13.

15. Neil Fligstein and Ofer Sharone, "Work in the Postindustrial Economy of California" *The State of Labor in California, 2002* (Berkeley: University of

California Institute for Labor and Employment, 2002).

16. Sara Bohn and Eric Schiff, *Just the Facts: Immigrants and the Labor Market* (San Francisco: Public Policy Institute of California, March 2011).

17. Robert A. Dahl, *Preface to Democratic Theory* (Chicago: University of Chicago Press, 1956), p. 124.

18. Dan Walters, *The New California: Facing the 21st Century*, 2nd ed. (Sacramento: California Journal Press, 1992), p. 20.

19. Harold Lasswell and Daniel Lerner, *The Comparative Study of Elites* (Stanford, CA: Stanford University Press, 1952), p. 7.

20. See Mark Arax and Rich Wartzman, *The King of California: J. G. Boswell and the Making of a Secret Empire* (Cambridge, MA: Public Affairs, 2003).

21. Ronald J. Schmidt, *This Is the City: Making Model Citizens in Los Angeles* (Minneapolis: University of Minnesota Press, 2005).

22. PPIC Statewide Survey, *Californians and Their Government* (San Francisco: Public Policy Institute of California, May 2011).

23. Dahl, p. 124.

24. Dahl, Chap. 5.

25. Alexis de Tocqueville, *Democracy in America, Vol. II* (J. P. Mayer and Max Lerner, eds.) (New York: Harper and Row, 1966), p. 477.

26. See Herbert J. Gans, *Middle American Individualism: The Future of Liberal Democracy* (New York: Free Press, 1988); Robert N. Bellah et al., *Habits of the Heart: Individualism and Commitment in American Life* (Berkeley: University of California Press, 1985).

27. Joan Didion, *Where I Was From* (New York: Alfred A. Knopf, 2003), p. 23.

28. Karthick Ramakrishnan and Mark Baldassare, *The Ties That Bind: Changing Demographics and Civic Engagement in California* (San Francisco: Public Policy Institute of California, 2004).

29. Peter Schrag, *Paradise Lost: California's Experience, America's Future* (New York: New Press, 1998), p. 12.

30. Kevin Starr, *California: A History* (New York: Modern Library, 2005), p. 344.

2

✵

California's Political Development

Introduction

The Idea of Political Culture

The Idea of Political Development

The Politics of Unification

Spanish "Rule"

Mexican "Control"

Statehood

The 1849 Constitution

The Politics of Modernization

The Gold Rush

The Big Four

Water

Other Modernizing Factors

The Politics of Welfare

The Progressive Movement

The Great Depression

Earl Warren

Edmund G. (Pat) Brown

The Politics of Abundance and Beyond

Key Terms

Review Questions

Web Activities

Notes

IN BRIEF

Chapter 2 focuses on the political culture and development of California. Understanding the variety of political subcultures found in California (traditionalistic, moralistic, and individualistic) helps to put in context the political and policy challenges facing the state today. California's political history is a progression of developmental stages: unification, industrialization, welfare, and abundance. Historic events and a succession of political and economic leaders have shaped each stage.

In the unification stage, Spanish and Mexican control gave way to what has been called an American era, which included statehood and the development of a constitution. The industrialization period featured the famous Gold Rush, the rise of the Southern Pacific Railroad, the development of water resources, the discovery of oil, and the impacts of World War II. The politics of welfare was noted for economic growth, progressive policies, and visionary leadership. During the politics of abundance period, growth and prosperity continue but some Californians question whether the state is beginning to choke on its success. At the end of the chapter, we consider whether the politics of abundance will continue indefinitely into the future and how the politics of diversity affects those perceptions.

INTRODUCTION

Why is California different from New York, besides its tendency to elect actors as governors? Both states have large, diverse populations, complex economies, megacities, huge state budgets, and geographic variety (seashore, mountains, farms, forests, etc.). Although Californians struggle to obtain water and New Yorkers do not, the similarities are there. Yet, Californians and New Yorkers know their states are different—and in profound ways. Political scientist Daniel Elazar calls these variations the "geology of political culture."[1] A primary difference stems from how they grew and changed as political and cultural identities. Chapter 2 surveys aspects of California's past that help explain its current political system. This process of growth and change is called "political development." Viewing California's history through the lens of political science is an essential prerequisite to understanding and contextualizing the state's politics today.

In 1949, the year of California's centennial, Carey McWilliams observed that the state, "the giant adolescent, has been outgrowing its governmental clothes, now, for a hundred years."[2] Today, he would likely underscore that point. This chapter helps us understand why that is the case.

The Idea of Political Culture

To understand the stages of political development found in California, we need to briefly examine the concept of political culture. **Political culture** is the product of historical events, migration and settlement patterns, and the presence of various social groups. It refers to *the shared beliefs, values, customs, and symbols of a society that affect how the society governs itself*. Political culture helps explain the policy choices made within political systems and why those choices vary between political systems.

Although in many respects the United States reflects one broad political culture, Elazar has identified three distinct political subcultures: traditional, moralistic, and individualistic.[3] Although the descriptions of each are largely impressionistic, they do help explain why some states are so different from each other. The **traditionalistic** political subculture is characterized by the dominance of a small, self-perpetuating, paternalistic ruling elite and a large, compliant nonelite. Its goal is to maintain the established social and economic order, rather than to provide wide access to the political system or initiate new policy. According to Elazar, this subculture had its historic roots in the preindustrial agrarian South.

The **moralistic** political subculture emphasizes a public-spirited citizenry dedicated to the common betterment of all its members. Widespread participation is both valued and expected. Dedicated, selfless, incorruptible public officials strive toward an assumed "general welfare." Politics is a high calling, not dirty work, and nonpartisanship is preferable to party politics. Government intervention in both the economy and society furthers the "public interest."

Elazar believes this subculture grew out of the religious values of Puritan New England.

The **individualistic** political subculture emphasizes the goals, aspirations, and initiative of private individuals or groups. Government exists to serve and facilitate these interests. Policymaking is transactional, a process of bargaining between self-interested individuals and groups. Public officials represent not only these people but also their own personal interests. The private citizen's attitude toward government is "Stay out of my way, let me do my thing, or at least help me do it." Elazar traces this subculture to the mercantile centers of the Eastern seaboard.

As more people immigrated to the United States and Americans already here migrated west, the features of these three subcultures moved and mingled as well. Historically, each of these three subcultures has played an important role in California's political development; elements of all three still exist. The *patron-client relationship* between California's Native Americans and the mission-era padres exemplified the traditionalistic subculture as does immigrant relations with the public sector today. Moralists moved into Southern California from the Midwest and brought with them pro-government values. They also came in such droves that government had little choice but to accommodate their need for housing, schools, and other services. Individualists came from the East Coast to Northern California. Today, the individualistic impulse can be seen in the attributes of many Californians who favor tax cuts while defending public services those taxes support or who oppose public services used by others. The blurring and stirring of these political subcultures help contribute to hyperpluralistic politics in California.

The Idea of Political Development

Political development refers to the growth and change that occurs within political systems. It includes 1) government's increasing capacity to manage its own affairs, respond to demands placed upon it, and do so in a stable manner; 2) an increase

in democratic values including the furthering of civil society, political participation, rule of law, and equality; and 3) an increase of economic specialization and complex social structures leading to group conflict and methods to resolve it.[4] Many political systems in the Western world have proceeded through distinct stages of political development—unification, modernization, welfare, and abundance.[5] These stages do not have neat beginnings and endings; they merge into each other.

Do states have their own stages of political development? To some extent. To be sure, the states together form a national political culture. Also, the nation's founding documents such as the U.S. Constitution have steered each state's political development in similar directions. Yet, the subsystems we call states entered the union at different times and are distinctly different in terms of the people they attracted, the economies they established, and the political practices they developed.

To view California's political history as its political development allows the student of California politics not only to understand the state's history but also to understand how the past informs the present. Larger than most nations, California has passed through all four stages of political development. To be sure, today's abundance does not affect all parts of the state and its people in equal measure. To analyze the present and anticipate the future, we must first make sense of the past—the goal of this chapter.

THE POLITICS OF UNIFICATION

During an early **unification** stage of political development, the primary function of government is making a society into a state. Government needs to establish its own central role, guard against early disunion, and develop a network of viable local economies. Early California from Native American times through the Gold Rush and statehood embodies this stage.

The West Coast has been a population magnet since prehistoric times. Archaeological evidence suggests that nomadic peoples from Asia once crossed a land bridge (now the Bering Strait) through Alaska and down the coast some 25,000 years ago. Native Californians were the eventual products of these early migration patterns. They were gatherers and coastal fishers. Spanish missionaries observed no pottery making, metallurgy, reading, or writing. In terms of language, there were at least 22 linguistic families and 135 regional dialects. No more than 1,000 spoke any single dialect. Native Californians were peaceable, nomadic, and needed little or no government. Because they lived "lightly on the land," they did not develop even a primitive technology. They resisted change, as well-meaning missionaries discovered, but were not resistant to the European diseases and violence that decimated their numbers.

The first nonnative visitors to California were European explorers who sailed California's coastal waters in the 1500s. They included Juan Rodriguez Cabrillo, Bartolome Ferrelo, and Sir Francis Drake. In 1579, Drake claimed the area north of modern-day San Francisco as Nova Albion (New England) 41 years *before* the Pilgrims touched shore at Plymouth.

Spanish "Rule"

Spain colonized Mexico in 1519 but did not extend its reach into Alta California until 1769. Governor Gaspar de Portola and Father Junipero Serra established a European settlement and Franciscan mission at San Diego. The missions (eventually numbering 21 and stretching from San Diego to Sonoma) were religious and evangelistic outposts intended to convert the Native Californians both to Christianity and to more "progressive" (European) lifestyles. As a colonial power, Spain promptly built military bases (*presidios*). Nearby civilian towns (*pueblos*) accommodated modest population growth. Local economies and primitive local, albeit colonial, governments grew up around these settlements. At the height of their influence, the Spanish numbered no more than 3,000 people

spread thinly along the California coast from San Diego to Sonoma. The relationship between the two groups was *patron-client* in nature: the ruled (Native Americans) supported or at least obeyed the rulers (military and church authorities) in exchange for relative security and safety. We should not exaggerate the governing influence of the missions: Only 20,000 out of 400,000 Native Californians worked and lived under mission authority.

Colonial governments are extractive in nature, but Spain found little to extract from Alta California. Distant, sparsely populated settlements needed no unification. To the responsible viceroy in Mexico City, California was "out of sight, out of mind." This inattention allowed economic competition between the missions and the presidios and pueblos to spill into open conflict. Spain's "rule" of Alta California lasted only 58 years, during which time British and French expeditions explored coastal lands. Russian traders sought valued animal furs and even established a settlement called Fort Rossiya (later called Fort Ross). Despite these incursions, Spain's long-term legacy to modern California includes continuing presence of her language, countless place names, and legal concepts such as communal water rights and community property.

Mexican "Control"

After years of Mexican frustration and Spanish inattention, Mexico obtained its independence from Spain in 1821. Ironically, the gold-hungry Spanish government abandoned Mexican California, unaware of the rich gold deposits to be discovered only a few decades later. California was now Mexico's colony—a distant and not too important province in Mexico's federal system. Concerned with solidifying its power base and unifying the rest of Mexico, the central government in Mexico City paid even less attention to California than had Spain. Feuds between the presidios and the missions and between the fledgling regions of California continued unabated during this Mexican era.

One act of unification during this time was to reduce the role of the church, which, in California, meant the vast mission enterprises developed under Spain. To do this, the Mexican government secularized the missions and distributed their massive land holdings to government loyalists.[6] Individuals could obtain 48,000-acre grants, and some influential families were able to accumulate *ranchos* as large as 250,000 acres. Many places familiar to Californians today derive their names from these ranchos. The myth of an idyllic, rural California persisted from the rancho period on. According to historian John W. Caughey, "With the rise of the ranchos, pastoral California reached its romantic zenith. Cattle roamed over a thousand hills. Horses became so numerous that they were hunted down to save pasturage for cattle."[7] The ranchos are long gone but some modern Californians continue the myth by developing "ranchettes" complete with horses, even in suburban communities. Less affluent residents move to inland areas in search of a more rural or possibly "pseudo-rural" lifestyle.

Another development during this period had nothing to do with Mexican policy. A gradual but steady trickle of rugged Euro-Americans found their way to California. These intrepid individuals included whalers, trappers, mountaineers, and adventurers. While some remained on the "wild side," others turned to farming and married into landholding Mexican families. Simply getting to California from the rest of the United States was a feat. After the adventurers proved it could be done (even the Donner party had survivors), more Americans arrived. By 1846, only 500 Americans were living in California, compared to 8,000—12,000 Mexicans. One such American was Lieutenant John C. Fremont, who favored westward expansion and had led several military expeditions into California. In 1846, a "Bear Flag Revolt" ensued between Mexican authorities, their supporters among the *Californio* population (native-born, Spanish-speaking Californians), and the American settlers, aided and abetted by Fremont and his associates. The symbol was a flag portraying a grizzly bear with the inscription, "California Republic." A version of it remains the state flag today. These motley bear flaggers seized Mexican horses, occupied Sonoma, and elected Fremont to head "The Republic of California." The effort was short-lived. Within a month, Naval Commodore John D. Sloat ordered his U.S. Pacific Squadron to sail into Monterey Bay, declaring "henceforth California will be a portion of the United States." Mexico's governance of California ended with its defeat by the United States in the Mexican American War of 1848.

What legacy did Mexico leave California after a mere 27 years of "control"? Mexico did not appear to exercise a unifying influence but, during its interim control, Mexico introduced several governing patterns that would become part of California's constitution, including a multitiered judicial system. Also, both Spain and Mexico left behind a traditionalistic political subculture. Vestiges of it remain today if one considers the relative powerlessness of California's newest immigrants. These many years later, the legacies of Spain and Mexico are not interchangeable. The most important difference in legacies is a matter of distance. Spain retreated to Spain—a continent and ocean away. Mexico retreated to the other side of a thin, porous border with California, as will be discussed further in Chapter 3.

Statehood

The unification stage of political development was completed with California's admission to the Union. To the Americans, California came to represent a logical stepping stone in meeting the nation's "manifest destiny." By the end of the war, Mexico "sold" not only California but also Nevada, Utah, and portions of Wyoming, Colorado, New Mexico, and Arizona, reducing its own land area by half. This $15 million bargain was known as the Mexican Cession. Ironically, U.S. President James Polk had offered $40 million for California alone in 1846, but Mexico refused to accept the offer. The *1848 Treaty of Guadalupe Hidalgo* concluded the war, ceded California to the United States, and granted U.S. citizenship and all its rights to the conquered peoples. Private property rights, important to

---

B o x 2.1   CALIFORNIA VOICES: Starr on the California Conquest

Historians have been wont to see the annexation of California by the United States as an act of conquest, a sideshow in the larger drama of Manifest Destiny and the Mexican War. Any close reading of Mexican California, however, suggests that even if the United States had never invaded Mexico or seized California by arms, California—as Richard Henry Dana, Jr. first put it—would in one way or another become American. At the very time that war broke out, Californios were negotiating

with the United States regarding the possibilities of a peaceful annexation. From this perspective, Josiah Royce, writing in 1886, considered the forcible conquest of California as the original sin of American California history. What was taken by force, Royce argued, would have been on the verge of being peaceably surrendered.

SOURCE: Kevin Starr, *California: A History* (New York: Modern Library, 2005), p. 65.

---

the wealthy *rancheros,* were maintained. California was now a U.S. territory under temporary military control (see Box 2.1).

The United States, despite its euphoric westward expansion and sense of mission, did not bring unification to California instantly. The state's fragmented governance structure was based on a now-collapsed Spanish system of *presidios.* Furthermore, the bits of gold found by James Marshall on the American River only nine days before the treaty was signed would bring anything but peace to America's newest possession. The news of gold in the Sierra foothills first reached other Californians who quite literally dropped what they were doing to stake their claims. These reports spread like wildfire across the nation. Colonel Richard Mason, the military governor of California, reported the discovery to President James Polk, sending along 230 ounces to prove his point: "I have no hesitation in saying there is more gold in the country drained by the Sacramento and San Joaquin Rivers than will pay the cost of the war with Mexico a hundred times over."[8] Polk mentioned the discovery of abundant gold in his December 1848 annual message: "Now that this fine province is part of our country, all of the States of the Union … are deeply interested in the speedy development of its wealth and resources."[9] Ostensibly, he was trying to sell the Congress on locating a branch mint in California. What

he sold was California itself. Professional advertisers could not have done a better job of it.

The 1849 Constitution

An important instrument in unifying a civil society is a *constitution.* This basic law provides general vision, establishes rights, creates political structures, and places limits on power and those who claim it. Theoretically, it is a contract between the government and the governed, and a covenant among society's members.

California's first constitution was the result of a constitutional convention held in the fall of 1849. The process was a curious mixture of elitism and pluralism. All 48 delegates were relatively young men. Thirteen had lived in California for less than one year. The nonnative Californians came from 13 other states and 5 other nations.[10] The goal of unification remained a challenge. Differences between Northern and Southern California promptly emerged. Closer to their Mexican roots, Southern Californians preferred territorial status, thinking that would give them the best of both cultures. Northern Californians generally favored statehood, sent a majority of the delegates, and eventually controlled the convention.

The convention produced a hybrid document that borrowed heavily from Mexico, Iowa, and New York (a number of delegates hailed from those states and Iowa's constitution was the shortest). **The 1849 Constitution** blended several theories of governing. The constitution began with a lofty, unifying preamble and a strong "bill of rights," reflecting democratic ideals. The idea of checks and balances (and the potential for structural gridlock) was found in a plural executive (a governor and several statewide officers) and a bicameral (two-house) legislature. Reflecting Mexican practice, it established a four-tier judicial system of elected judges. As elsewhere, suffrage (the right to vote) was limited to white males. Due to the *Californios,* the document was to be printed in both English and Spanish; so were all future official documents. The constitution won overwhelming voter approval in November 1849 and on September 9, 1850, Congress admitted California as the thirty-first state. California was to remain slave-free, a condition not applied to other ceded Mexican territories. At that moment, unification, to the extent California would ever experience it, was complete. The Mexican era ended; the North American era began.

In spite of its shortcomings (people demanded a new constitution only 30 years later), California's unifying document was considered a model worth imitating. Argentina's 1853 constitution was inspired by it. Argentinean Juan Bautista Alberti observed, "Without universities, without academies or law colleges, the newly organized people of California have drawn up a constitution full of foresight, of common sense and of opportunity."[11]

THE POLITICS OF MODERNIZATION

This sense of opportunity led to **the politics of modernization,** the next stage in the process of political development. This is a time when new political leaders emerge, a statewide economy is forged, and the political masses become fully incorporated—becoming the polity of the state. Government's purpose is to encourage economic modernization or industrialization. During this stage, California became a magnet of opportunity and a destination for those seeking jobs or simply a better way of life. Historic benchmarks during this stage were the Gold Rush, the rise of the Big Four, the industrialization of agriculture, and the consequences of World War II.

The Gold Rush

Discovery of gold created the mining frenzy we noted earlier. In retrospect, gold did not change California; the rush for it did. For a time, the population doubled every six months: from 9,000 in 1846 to 264,000 six years later. Seemingly overnight, a heavily Latino California become 80 percent Euro-American. The newcomers were primarily young, single men from every state in the Union and from as far away as Europe and China. A spirit of entrepreneurialism merged with hard labor and racism. Chinese immigrants were allowed to mine the gold but not own rights to it. Policing the mining towns was rough business. Committees of vigilance—*vigilantes*—often used violence to quell violence. While a few found the gold they sought, many more found unprecedented opportunities of other types. One luckless miner found he could make more money selling pants to other miners; his name was Levi Strauss.

Those who stayed created a new base for California's emerging economy. In effect, the Gold Rush jump-started the state's second stage of development by forming a nascent multiculturalism we experience today. It created numerous spillover effects (planned or unplanned consequences), such as heightened demand for goods and services. In turn, new demands for transportation improvements created still more opportunities for future entrepreneurs. The cultural change would be profound. According to writer J. H. Holliday: "In one astonishing year [1848-49] the place would be transformed from obscurity to world dominance ... from a society of neighbors and families to one of strangers and transients; from an ox-cart economy based on hides and tallow to a complex economy based on gold; from Catholic to Protestant, from Latin to Anglo-Saxon."[12] Lastly, it created a worker base consisting of individuals with steely nerve to take a risk, not just on gold, but on California itself.

Caughey thought the most important consequence was psychological: "the willingness to believe that the fabulous could be realized."[13] At least that was true for the new dominant majority, the Euro-Americans.

The Big Four

Four Sacramento merchants dared to believe that "the fabulous could be realized." Their actions furthered the economic growth of the state while making each of them very rich. As we noted, some Americans brought an individualistic political subculture to California; these men personified it. Their eventual political influence and abuse of it unleashed a political reform movement still felt today. Mark Hopkins, Charles Crocker, Collis Huntington, and Leland Stanford responded to the post-Gold Rush demand for improved transportation by forming the Central Pacific Railroad in 1861. Huntington was well connected in Washington, D.C. and served as the group's lobbyist. His efforts paid off. Congress designated this company responsible for the western portion of the ambitious transcontinental railroad and gave it both land and loans to begin construction. However, that was not enough. Stanford became governor and, in a move that would likely violate conflict of interest laws today, obtained additional loans and subsidies from the state legislature.

Because California developed or industrialized so rapidly in contrast to the rest of the West, the Big Four anticipated demand for plenty of transportation within the state. They acquired small railroad companies throughout California. One such acquisition was the **Southern Pacific Railroad** (SPR), the future namesake for the entire system. Eventually, they controlled 85 percent of the state's rails. This elite became a monopoly and behaved accordingly. By varying freight rates, they rewarded their friends and punished their enemies. This was not just laissez-faire capitalism at work. Local governments, desiring rail service and all its economic blessings, donated right-of-way property in addition to cash (euphemistically called "subsidies"). The land grab was substantial. For every mile of

track, SPR would receive up to 12,800 acres from the public domain. When San Bernardino refused its demands, the Southern Pacific retaliated by establishing nearby Colton as the site of a new depot. If shippers tried to move their goods along the coast by steamship, the Big Four would simply buy the steamship line and reset rates. As with other monopolies, Southern Pacific rates were higher than necessary, angering growing numbers of Californians. Frank Norris's 1901 novel, *The Octopus*, was a chilling and transparent description of how the Southern Pacific Railroad operated in the state (see Box 2.2).

Fearing that popular resentment might lead to state regulation, the Southern Pacific established a Political Bureau, a forerunner of the modern political action committee (PAC). Unlike today's PACs, which operate primarily in Sacramento, the Political Bureau was active at all levels of government. It controlled not only incumbent legislators but also party conventions and candidate nominations. In 1877, Stanford wrote Huntington, "The legislature elected I think is a good one and I apprehend less trouble [for example, rate control legislation] from it than from any preceding legislature for the last ten years—not a single unfriendly senator elected."[14] Others regarded that same legislature as the most corrupt in California's brief history.

As politically successful as the Big Four were, they could not cope with a national depression in the late 1800s that left many out of work. The unemployed blamed the railroads for importing poorly paid Chinese laborers who competed with whites for nonrailroad jobs. One such worker, the fiery Denis Kearney of San Francisco, helped found the radical Workingmen's Party. He was anti-Chinese and anti-Big Four. His incendiary rhetoric was prophetic given the reforms that would sweep the state in future decades: "The reign of bloated knaves is over. The people are about to take their own affairs into their own hands."[15]

Ironically, the same voters that elected a railroad-controlled state senate also authorized the calling of a constitutional convention—one noted for its anti-railroad temperament. Original state constitutions seem to need revision within several

---

B o x 2.2   CALIFORNIA VOICES: Norris on the Southern Pacific

The clerk brought forward a folder of yellow paper and handed it to Dyke. It was inscribed at the top "Tariff Schedule No. 8," and underneath these words, in brackets, was a smaller inscription, "Supercedes No. 7 of Aug. 1." For a moment Dyke was confused. Then swiftly the matter became clear in his mind. The Railroad had raised the freight on hops from two cents to five. All his calculations as to a profit on his little investment he had based on a freight rate of two cents a pound. He was under contract to deliver his crop. He could not draw back. The new rate ate up every cent of

his gains. He stood there ruined. "Good Lord," he murmured, "good Lord! What will you people do next? Look here. What's your basis of applying freight rates anyhow?" he suddenly vociferated with furious sarcasm. "What's your rule? What are you guided by?" S. Behrman emphasized each word of his reply with a tap of one forefinger on the counter before him. "All—the—traffic—will—bear."

SOURCE: Excerpted from Frank Norris, *The Octopus: A Story of California* (New York: Doubleday, Page and Co., 1904), p. 348–350.

---

decades and California was no exception. In California's case, the 1878–1879 convention coincided with economic troubles, anti-railroad fervor, and worker radicalism. The revised constitution literally banned the employment of the Chinese— "aliens who are or may become vagrants, paupers, mendicants, criminals, or invalids with contagious or infectious diseases."[16] Numerous anti-railroad regulations were imbedded into the constitution to prevent their easy removal. The delegates naively established a railroad commission, thinking such a regulatory body would be insulated from Big Four pressure. On the contrary, the commission proved no match for the power of the corporations and railroad interests. Furthermore, occasional regulatory victories were often voided by economically conservative courts. A popular political cartoon of the day entitled "The Curse of California" symbolized not only the power of the Big Four but also the elite theory of politics described in Chapter 1 (see Figure 2.1).

Changes in the larger political environment gradually lessened the influence of the Big Four and the massive company they left behind. Their political power was a house of cards based on a monopolistic rate structure and lack of competition. But in the 1880s, when a competing southern transcontinental railroad emerged (the Santa Fe), ensuing rate wars ruined their monopoly. As more towns obtained railroad service, local rivalries waned and company control was no longer

necessary. Further industrialization of California would depend less on parochial, intrastate concerns and more on national and international forces. As new transportation routes crisscrossed the state, political subcultures gradually merged. The railroads helped to both unify and industrialize the Golden State.

Water

A third factor in the modernization of California was water. This commodity affected both agriculture and urbanization in the state. A growing interstate network of railroad routes plus the advent of refrigerated rolling stock allowed the nation to enjoy an increasing variety of fruit and vegetables. The early padres, and later farmers, found that California's geography could accommodate at least some crops, anytime, anywhere in the state. This led not only to highly specialized farming but also a demand for adequate water. Specialty crops increased a farmer's return per acre, but only if there was a sufficient, continual supply of water. The state's endless cycles of wet and dry years produced a yo-yo economy from a grower's perspective.

The Great Drought during the 1860s spurred local irrigation efforts, especially in the great agricultural valleys of California. Instead of isolated farmsteads as found in the Midwest, California farmers settled in colonies. This allowed and, in fact, required

FIGURE 2.1 The "Curse of California"

Edward Keller's "The Curse of California" was published in *The Wasp* on August 19, 1882, and is regarded as the most influential political cartoon in California history. Keller employed the often-used octopus symbol to caricature the political and economic reach of the Big Four.

SOURCE: Courtesy of the Bancroft Library, University of California, Berkeley. *The Wasp*, 8/19/1882, Edward Keller.

them to cooperate on various water projects. These efforts included the diversion of water from the state's major river systems, rivers fed from a permanent snowpack in the Sierra Nevada.

The late 1800s and early 1900s witnessed numerous efforts to increase the volume and dependability of water. The Wright Irrigation Act of 1887 authorized the formation of local water irrigation districts, precursors to modern-day water districts. From that point on, the agricultural sector, in partnership with the state and federal governments, pursued the construction of dams, wells, canals, reservoirs, catchment basins, and aqueducts to move water ever farther from its source. In 1908, Los Angeles engineer William Mullholland and business leaders Harrison Gray Otis and his son-in-law Harry Chandler (successive publishers of the *Los Angeles Times*) spearheaded an effort to construct an aqueduct from the Owens River, east of the Sierras, to the San Fernando Valley. This project eventually sucked dry a previously productive agricultural valley.

The federal government played a major role in later water projects. In 1933, Congress appropriated start-up funds to initiate the Central Valley Project after a $170 million state construction bond went unsold. This effort to conserve, divert, and redistribute the Sacramento and San Joaquin Rivers turned family farms into agribusinesses. Three years later, the federally-financed Hoover Dam was completed, thereby creating Lake Mead. This massive effort to tame the mighty Colorado River garnered agricultural water for the Imperial Valley and still more water for Los Angeles. In addition, it produced huge amounts of electrical power, an additional prerequisite for urban growth in Southern California. Subsequent statewide water plans simply added to the patchwork of projects and confusing laws that constitute water policy in California. During this industrialization period, California would become one of the world's great "hydraulic societies," as Donald Worster put it.[17] Migrant workers during the Depression and later would provide the necessary labor required of industrialized agriculture. For more on water, see Chapter 12.

Other Modernizing Factors

The impact of the Gold Rush and visionary water planning were only two features of California's modernization. Several others deserve mention:

Oil Black gold was discovered in various parts of Southern California between 1900 and 1940, creating new economic opportunities. Unlike California's farmers and their crops, the oil companies faced tremendous obstacles shipping crude to distant out-of-state markets. They became vulnerable to overproduction and the vagaries of local demand within California. Producers of crude searched for various shipping methods, including oceangoing tankers and pipelines. Pipeline companies and oil producers became political adversaries. Eventually, the state regulated pipelines as common carriers (much like railroads); oil producers privately agreed to control production and set prices. They sought legislative help on occasion to maintain this balance.[18] By the 1990s, advanced refining facilities could supply both California and nearby markets. Oil helped to diversify California's mushrooming economy. Like yellow gold, early discoveries of black gold produced ripple effects—land speculation and further population growth. It became still another magnet drawing both job seekers and environmentalists concerned about oil-generated pollution. Finally, it gave major oil companies a significant and permanent stake in California politics.

World War II A second event that propelled California's industrialization was World War II. As noted in Chapter 1, the Great Depression drove people hoping for a better life to California. The nation's war effort, though, dwarfed Depression-era migration. Nearly 2 million people (including African Americans and whites from the South and Midwest) came to or through California to work in defense plants, neighboring communities, or military bases. A transportation network (thanks to the railroads) and plenty of water (thanks to the water visionaries) made wartime growth possible. California's location on the Pacific Rim during a war with Japan made wartime growth inevitable.

True, the military-industrial complex had a foothold in California long before World War II, with the establishment of the aircraft industry. But the war accelerated its growth and its impact on the urbanization of the state.[19] During the 1940s the state grew by 53 percent; more than one million people migrated to California just between July 1945 and July 1947. In addition to tremendous pressure on public services, these migrations furthered the blending of political subcultures in the state. The war itself fostered a pro-business climate. The thirst for defense contracts, **federal gold**, continued during the Cold War (1950s–1980s) and helped to forge an alliance between big business and big labor. Political moderates of both parties were elected to continue economic growth brought on by the war. By the 2000s, remnants of wartime California remained visible, including numerous World War II—era military bases that had never closed. Eventually, some bases would close and reduced defense spending would severely affect some defense-reliant California communities.

THE POLITICS OF WELFARE

Political development's third stage is the **politics of welfare**. In this stage, government's task is to shield the citizenry from hardship, manage a smooth-running economy, improve standards of living, and assist the less fortunate. It takes an industrial base to afford these activities. In California, several factors influenced this stage of development: the Progressive Movement, the Depression, and the leadership of two governors, Earl Warren and Edmund G. (Pat) Brown. Combined, they represented the state's moralistic political subculture on a grand scale.

The Progressive Movement

Although California's role as a modern welfare state came after World War II, the foundation for welfare politics was built earlier. California's version of the nationwide Progressive Movement,

led by Governor Hiram Johnson (1911–1917), eliminated the overbearing political influence of the SPR and stressed political individualism and nonpartisan-ship (see Chapter 4). Progressive reforms weakened political parties by requiring many officeholders to run as nonpartisans. The result was a nonpartisan public spirit to accomplish shared policy goals.

California experienced tremendous economic growth prior to the Depression as people poured into the state, lured by an increasingly diverse economy. Economic growth heightened people's economic expectations, soon to be dashed by the Depression. The Progressives in effect created a leadership vacuum by allowing voters to make decisions previously reserved for elected representatives. On a more subtle level, they increased the *expectation* of greater participation by the masses. This in turn fueled large scale demand for more services and greater benefits.

The Great Depression

The Depression itself accelerated demands for public assistance to those crushed by economic hardship. In 1934, novelist and socialist Upton Sinclair became the Democratic nominee for governor. His platform, End Poverty in California (EPIC), combined the goals of tax reform and public employment. Some voters, especially senior citizens, became Sinclair enthusiasts; big business labeled him a radical, a crackpot, and even a communist. Republican Frank Merriam won. Four years later, the same year *The Grapes of Wrath* was published, Democrat Culbert L. Olson won the governorship. Although he served only one term, he too developed ambitious policies to aid those untouched by progress in California.[20] What really helped California was the New Deal, which converted good intentions into actual assistance. The Works Progress Administration (WPA) funded projects from Shasta Dam and the Golden Gate Bridge to lesser-scale schools, libraries, and hospitals. Through what Kevin Starr calls the "therapy of public works," California seemingly built itself out of the Depression.[21] The experiences of this era suggested that Californians would support an array of policies to improve living conditions *if* they were proposed by competent, moderate, progressive leaders. Wartime California produced those leaders.

Earl Warren

World War II expedited the welfare era by pumping even more federal expenditures into the state's economy. Politically, it helped produce a coalition of business and labor dedicated to one common goal: a healthy economic future for California. Elected in 1942, Governor Earl Warren was just the leader this coalition needed. During the campaign, Warren, a progressive Republican, rejected incumbent Governor Olson's partisan pleas: "I am, as you know, a Republican. But, I shall make no appeal to blind partisanship, or follow any other divisive tactics."[22] Thanks to his popularity and a Progressive-era reform called cross-filing, he was nominated for reelection in 1946 by three parties—Republicans, Democrats, and Progressives. He won a third term in 1950, the only California governor ever to do so, and was a contender for the Republican presidential nomination in 1952. He resigned in 1953 when U.S. President Dwight D. Eisenhower appointed him Chief Justice of the U.S. Supreme Court.

Dorthea Lange/[LC-DIG-fsa-8b29516]/Library of Congress Prints and Photographs Division

Migrant mother
This 1936 photo of a migrant pea-picker and her children outside Nipomo, California, became a famous symbol of the Depression nationwide.

During Warren's tenure as governor, California made great strides in education and various social programs. In some respects, Warren continued a moralistic political subculture advanced by the Progressives. His social reforms included more generous old-age pensions, broadened unemployment insurance, improved medical care, and progressive labor legislation. Prison and mental-hospital reform were top priorities. He used his enormous popularity to push a progressive agenda through a Republican legislature. A massive freeway-building program was launched in 1947, financed through increased gasoline taxes. No wonder U.S. President Harry Truman once said of Warren, "He's a Democrat—and doesn't know it."[23] His one major legislative defeat was compulsory health insurance, an issue that would resurface some 40 years later.

Growing state services in the Warren years meant a growing bureaucracy. State employees swelled from 24,000 in 1943 to 56,000 a decade later. An expanding economy made this growth affordable and a 50 percent population increase made it necessary. Consistent with his "leadership, not politics" views, Warren hired experts rather than political cronies to run these growing state agencies. In the spirit of Progressivism, he appointed nonpartisan "committees of experts" to examine policy issues and propose policy recommendations. Historian Robert Glass Cleland credited the state's economy for all this policy vigor: "The war and postwar booms gave Warren only problems of prosperity to solve."[24] In fact, Warren was able to spend liberally *and* maintain a "rainy day" fund—a feat that seems quite unthinkable in contemporary California.

Lieutenant Governor Goodwin Knight succeeded Warren. Although more conservative than Warren, he adopted many of his predecessor's policies. California had become a relatively generous social welfare state, the populace supported that development, and politicians of both parties knew it. An implicit social contract was in place. California was to represent continual prosperity; government's job was to bolster and assure that prosperity. A political consensus was in place that would last for several decades.

Edmund G. (Pat) Brown

In 1958 Democratic votes finally caught up with Democratic registration trends and Pat Brown succeeded Knight as governor. Like Warren, Brown had been state attorney general and had avoided overly partisan election campaigns. He too avoided close ties with his own party. Under Brown's leadership, the state's Water Project was funded, providing the infrastructure to move vast amounts of water from the mountains to the growing Bay Area and Southern California cities. School and university enrollments mushroomed, as did requisite school construction, reflecting the state's continued growth.

Brown called for a master plan for higher education in 1959. This plan allocated different tasks to the University of California, the state colleges, and the junior colleges (as they were called then). Access to higher education by all Californians became part of the state's implicit social contract. Brown continued Warren's progressive welfare policies—an agenda he called **responsible liberalism**. In the area of civil rights, he pushed through the legislature various antidiscrimination measures and a Fair Employment Practices Commission to enforce them. Brown oversaw massive public construction projects including new college campuses, public schools, and a thousand miles of additional freeways. Brown was fortunate in that the freeways were largely funded by the *Federal Interstate Highway Act of 1956*. The state also became the regulator of air quality and the consumer's protector.[25] Responding to population and economic growth, public officials could not have imagined future growth that later Californians would no longer be willing to accommodate.

By 1966, unrestrained population growth, increased taxes, urban congestion, growing pollution, university campus unrest, farm worker strikes, and the 1965 Watts riot took their toll on Governor Brown. According to journalist and biographer Lou Cannon, "Many Californians who had previously voted Democratic blamed their grievances on government and no longer believed that they lived in the Golden State of their dreams and memories. California was a state "hungering for reform and a new sense of direction."[26]

Brown's successor was actor, liberal-turned-conservative, citizen politician Ronald Reagan. He spelled out his sense of direction in his January 1967 inaugural address: "The cost of California's government is too high. It adversely affects our business climate. We are going to squeeze and cut and trim until we reduce the cost of government."[27] Reagan soon learned that his "cut and trim" hyperbole was difficult if not impossible to implement. Most state spending was the product of legislative statutes or federal regulations, not gubernatorial wishes. Promising to cut government waste and "clean up the mess at Berkeley" (student protests were commonplace), Reagan did make substantial cuts in higher welfare, mental health, and higher education. But during his two terms as governor, the overall state budget doubled (from $5 billion to $10.2 billion). He even signed into law a major tax increase when a revenue shortfall necessitated it and the state's first-ever income tax withholding plan. This pragmatic conservatism also marked his years as American president (1981–1989).

THE POLITICS OF ABUNDANCE AND BEYOND

Ironically, responsible liberalism can produce negative reactions, even by those it helps. True, the standard of living had increased in California through both public and private spending. The state had moved into the **politics of abundance**. A growing economy provided the taxes to fund a social welfare state and a plethora of services Californians had come to expect. These policies were **majoritarian** in nature: The majority both paid for them and received their benefits. For instance, low-cost public higher education was available to every resident regardless of need. These policies not only were widely supported, they attracted still more people to the Golden State.

But when does growth become too much of a good thing? By the 1960s, many Californians were asking that question. Growth had funded their favorite programs but had also replaced orange groves with endless housing tracts and fueled freeway congestion, air pollution, and overcrowded parks and schools. Although many effects of growth are privately generated, Californians sensed that "politics as usual" was somehow to blame. Responsible liberalism apparently had become irresponsible. A succession of governors including Reagan would try to reverse the politics of growth, especially governmental growth, that had characterized the state's history. California entered an era of lowered expectations. Reagan's successor and Pat Brown's son, Jerry Brown (1975–1983 and 2011–), declared "small is beautiful" and claimed Californians were living in an **era of limits**, hardly the language his father would have used. Jerry Brown had rejected the bipartisan growth consensus of the Warren-Brown era. George Deukmejian succeeded Brown (1983–1991). As Reagan did, Deukmejian championed free enterprise; claimed government was the problem, not the solution; and rejected most tax and spending increases.

Political leaders in the 1970s and 1980s heeded Californians' pleas to preserve the "abundant state." If government was the problem, cut off its lifeblood— in a word, taxes. Elected officials imposed some of these tax limits in the annual budget process. Voters imposed others, such as Proposition 13 (which drastically cut property taxes). Buffeted by raging inflation and tax increases in the 1970s, they sincerely believed government revenue could be cut without reducing the services they enjoyed.

While governmental growth slowed down, the state's population growth did not. By the dawn of a new century, observers were conflicted over the future of Abundant California. Given the constant drumbeat of population growth (nearly 1,000 per day!), would there continue to be enough abundance to go around? This was a fundamental policy dilemma for Deukmejian's successor Pete Wilson (1991–1998) and subsequent governors, Gray Davis (1999–2003), Arnold Schwarzenegger (2003–2011), and (again) Jerry Brown (2011–). The 2001 electricity shortage due to, among other things, growing demand and inadequate supply reinforced this point. In 2006, Schwarzenegger proposed a massive building program in response to continuing growth pressures. In doing so, he hailed the leaders of yesteryear who "built the foundation of California's prosperity.... We must build a California eager to meet the challenges of the 21st century without reluctance or fear."[28] While he may have sounded like Pat Brown, the ensuing Great Recession derailed any such building plans. The recession clearly constrained any visionary impulses Jerry Brown may have had as he began his second stint as governor in 2011.

The California of Pat Brown and high expectations seems to be a thing of the past. The state's population is substantially larger and more diverse. California's current stage of political

Entering California

In 1975 cartoonist Dennis Renault captured the "era of limits" rhetoric of Governor Jerry Brown. To Californians used to the leadership of Governors Earl Warren and Pat Brown, the politics of later decades did seem to be characterized by lowered expectations.

Question: Does this cartoon speak to the California of today?

SOURCE: Dennis Renault, *Sacramento Bee.*

development—no matter what one calls it—has become a series of clashes, not only of competing political interests but also of diverse political and ethnic cultures. In short, hyperpluralism has replaced pluralism. All this in a new era of limits or at least perceived limits. Yet, even if California's growth rate slows, policymakers must accommodate still more Californians plus a backlog of past and current infrastructure demands. Yet, compared to decades past, a new political environment is now characterized by mistrust in public officials, revenue challenges, term-limited leadership, and a growing preference to bypass policymakers via the initiative process. According to Mark Baldassare and Ellen Hanak, these factors "make consensus building and planning for the future much more difficult than they were during the great building years of the mid-twentieth century. Those who believe that what California needs to meet future challenges is another great leader, a reincarnation of Governor Pat Brown, if you will, are not realistic about how the context of governance and planning has changed."[29]

When British ambassador James Bryce visited California in 1906, 2 million people inhabited the state. He asked, "What will happen when California is filled by 50 millions of people and its valuation is five times what it is now? There will be more people—as many as the country can support—and the real question will be not about making more wealth or having more people, but whether the people will then be happier or better than they have been hitherto or are at this moment."[30]

More than 36 million people later, his question remains compelling. The bipartisan pro-growth consensus that built California's social and physical infrastructure has collapsed and no alternative consensus has taken its place, despite Schwarzenegger's call for one. The reason appears to be a change in the political culture of the state. As noted in Chapter 1, the gap between the state's haves and have-nots is growing larger. The moralistic and individualistic political subcultures, which have historically lived side-by-side in California, seem at war with each other. Individualism may be winning. The state's upper tier, wanting to maintain the abundant state as they define it and remember it, readily participate in California's political system. Meanwhile, the lower tier, which participates to a lesser extent, in effect seems to be asking, "Where is the moralistic political subculture when *we* need it?" Caught in the middle, California's policymakers alternate between bold ideas and cautious actions.

What will political historians write of this period 50 years from now? What stage of political development will they be describing? Will a politics of abundance be replaced by a version of post-abundance, at least for some Californians, or will abundance and its successor live side by side in this diverse state? Or will contemporary Californians of all backgrounds unite behind the promise that California held for generations past and be willing to invest or reinvest in its future? As you read the balance of this book, consider these questions.

KEY TERMS

Political culture (p. 21)

traditional, moralistic, and individualistic subcultures (pp. 21–22)

Political development (p. 22)

politics of unification (p. 22)

Politics of modernization (p. 26)

The 1849 Constitutions (p. 26)

Southern Pacific Railroad (p. 27)

Black gold, federal gold (pp. 30–31)

Progressive Movement (p. 31)

responsible liberalism (p. 33)

politics of welfare and abundance (pp. 31, 34)

majoritarian policies (p. 34)

era of limits (p. 34)

REVIEW QUESTIONS

1. Describe Elazar's three political subcultures. How do they apply to California?

2. Describe political history as a process of political development. Define the four stages of political development used in this chapter.

3. Why are Spanish "rule" and Mexican "control" in quotes?

4. Describe the real impact of the Gold Rush?

5. Why were the Big Four so powerful and so resented?

6. How did California become a great "hydraulic society"?

7. What effects did World War II have on California's political development?

8. Describe the bipartisan growth consensus characterized by the governorships of Earl Warren and Pat Brown.

9. Describe the politics of abundance and why some Californians doubt its future.

10. What do you think will be the next stage of California's political development and why?

WEB ACTIVITIES

California Historical Society
(www.californiahistoricalsociety.org/)
The Golden State's official historical society provides historical data and numerous links to statewide and local resources. Included is another history time line.

Bancroft Library
(bancroft.berkeley.edu/collections/)

Short of a visit to UC Berkeley's Bancroft Library and its vast California collection, check out its digital collection on various California topics.

California State Library
(www.library.ca.gov/)
Click on the California History Section to determine what is available in the California History Room of the California State Library in Sacramento.

NOTES

1. Daniel Elazar, *American Federalism: A View from the States*, 3rd ed. (New York: Harper and Row, 1984), pp. 122–123.

2. Carey McWilliams, *California: The Great Exception* (Berkeley: University of California Press), p. 17.

3. Elazar, *American Federalism*, Chapter 4.

4. For further discussion of development, see Karen Orren and Stephen Skowronek, *The Search for American Political Development* (Cambridge, UK: Cambridge University Press, 2004).

5. A. F. K. Organski, *The Stages of Political Development* (New York: Alfred A. Knopf, 1965).

6. Secularization in this context meant converting the missions into parish churches (some remain so to this day), reducing the power of

the friars, and releasing mission land for nonmission uses.

7. John W. Caughey, *California: A Remarkable State's Life History* (Englewood Cliffs, N.J.: Prentice Hall, 1970), p. 114.

8. J. S. Holliday, *The World Rushed In: The California Gold Rush Experience* (New York: Simon and Schuster, 1981), p. 48.

9. James Polk, "Fourth Annual Message, December 5, 1848," in *Messages and Papers of the Presidents, Vol. V* (New York: Bureau of National Literature, 1897), p. 2487.

10. Paul Mason, "Constitutional History of California," *Constitution of the State of California (1879) and*

Related Documents (Sacramento: California State Senate, 1973), pp. 75–105.

11. Caughey, *California*, p. 215.

12. Holliday, *The World Rushed In*, p. 26.

13. Caughey, *California*, p. 191.

14. Ward McAfee, *California's Railroad Era: 1850–1911* (San Marino, CA: Golden West Books, 1973), p. 157.

15. Carl Brent Swisher, *Motivation and Political Technique in the California Constitutional Convention 1878–79* (New York: De Capo Press, 1969), p. 12.

16. Article XIX, "Chinese," 1879 Constitution.

17. Donald Worster, *Rivers of Empire* (New York: Pantheon Books, 1985).

18. Mansel G. Blackford, *The Politics of Business in California: 1890–1920* (Columbus, Ohio: Ohio State University Press, 1977). See Chapter 3: "The Oil Industry."

19. For an extensive analysis of the "metropolitan-military complex" in California, see Roger W. Lotchin, *Fortress California 1910–1961: From Warfare to Welfare* (New York: Oxford University Press, 1992).

20. See Robert E. Burke, *Olson's New Deal for California* (Berkeley: University of California Press, 1953).

21. Kevin Starr, *Endangered Dreams: The Great Depression in California* (New York: Oxford University Press, 1996), especially Part IV.

22. Quoted in David Lavender, *California: Land of New Beginnings* (New York: Harper and Row, 1972), p. 397.

23. Quoted in Hill, *Dancing Bear*, p. 100.

24. Robert Glass Cleland, *From Wilderness to Empire: A History of California* (New York: Alfred A. Knopf, 1959), p. 419.

25. For more on Brown's record see, Ethan Rarick, *California Rising: The Life and Times of Pat Brown* (Berkeley: University of California Press, 2006).

26. Lou Cannon, *Governor Reagan: His Rise to Power* (Cambridge, MA: Public Affairs, 2003), p. 9.

27. Quoted in James J. Rawls and Walton Bean, *California: An Interpretive History* (New York: McGraw Hill, 2003), pp. 458–459.

28. Governor Arnold Schwarzenegger's 2006 State of the State Address, January 5, 2006.

29. Mark Baldassare and Ellen Hanak, *Ca2025: It's Your Choice* (San Francisco: Public Policy Institute of California, 2006), p. 11.

30. Quoted in Dan Walters, *The New California: Facing the 21st Century*, 2nd ed. (Sacramento: California Journal Press, 1992), p. 7.

3

※

Constitutionalism and Federalism: The Perimeters of California Politics

Introduction: Rules and Boundaries

California's Constitution

What It Contains

What Makes It Distinctive

California and the Nation: The Boundaries of Federalism

Dual Federalism

Cooperative Federalism

Centralized Federalism

The New Federalism

Pragmatic Federalism

Federalism and California's Native Americans

California in Washington

California and the World: The Politics of Fences

Immigration

Trade

Conclusion

Key Terms

Review Questions

Web Activities

Notes

IN BRIEF

California is a nation unto itself. The most populous state in the Union, its economy dwarfs those of all other states and most nations. The state's political development is checkered with unique individuals, groups, and circumstances both historical and contemporary. Yet when California became the 31st state, it joined a preexisting nation, one with its own constitution and emerging political institutions and traditions. Ever since, California has affected and been affected by the nation as a whole. In recent years, it has been increasingly affected by its neighbors, especially Mexico.

In Chapter 3, we will focus on several perimeters or outer limits that affect California politics. First, we examine California's constitution as a rulebook to which policymakers, institutions, and voters must conform. California's constitutional development helps explain why its core document or rulebook is similar to or different from those of other states. It also helps to explain why some political fragmentation is essentially structural in nature. Second, we discuss California's role in affecting national affairs and public policy. In doing so, we examine the successive stages of federalism as they relate to California and how Californians attempt to exercise influence in Washington. The chapter concludes by surveying how California's borders create policy challenges not faced by most states.

INTRODUCTION: RULES AND BOUNDARIES

Western democracies place certain limits on governments. Some of these limitations may be rules that dictate how and under what circumstances power can be exercised, policy made, and by whom. State constitutions and local governing charters contain such rules. Other limitations take the form of boundaries that demarcate territorial jurisdiction. These are legal borders beyond which influence wanes and power means little. National and state borders, and city, county, and special district lines mark off the legal reach of most public policy efforts. From a state perspective, constitutions and federalism are the **perimeters of politics**—the outer limits that in effect contain the scope of political power.

Political scientists call the idea of limited government—government operating within certain rules—**constitutionalism**. American constitutionalism is derived from, among others, English political theorist John Locke (1632–1704). He believed that rights of the people and limits on those who govern them should be spelled out in a "social contract." Natural rights and rules governing the relationship between the people and government would occupy higher legal ground than ordinary laws (statutes passed by legislatures). In fact, the validity of those

laws would be measured against the constitution. Accordingly, changing a constitution should be more difficult than changing an ordinary law. Furthermore, any such change should be made by the people themselves.

Locke's views on governance (including the idea of separation of powers) deeply influenced the framers of the U.S. Constitution. They were largely successful in limiting the document to basic fundamental law and to only 8,700 words. It would be the "Supreme Law of the Land," superseding the Articles of Confederation. With revisions, the colonial constitutions became state constitutions in 1789. Despite their regard for Locke, the Framers rejected his idea of constitutional change by "the People." They believed in a republican form of government where only qualified voters would choose their representatives and only those representatives would make public policy. Ordinary citizens never voted on the original document and have never directly ratified its amendments.

America's constitutional history actually predates the U.S. Constitution. Those 13 original colonies possessed extensive governing charters reflecting their respective political cultures. Later states brought with them comparable experiences and traditions. Because the founding elites in each new state generally understood what limited government and civil liberties meant, and what basic institutions were necessary to govern, state constitutions were destined to look alike in many respects. Yet they were never intended to be clones of the federal document. For better or for worse, they would reflect not only those beliefs shared by American society as a whole but also the culture, traditions, and unique attributes of each state.

Over the years, some reformers have viewed state constitutions as jumbles of unnecessary trivia. They have sought to both strengthen governmental power and to eliminate what they consider unnecessary clutter. In their view, a state constitution should contain only basic, fundamental law and represent a governing consensus. A contrary view holds that constitutions are political documents—living, breathing expressions of policy conflict, not policy consensus. Constitutional language reflects not only compromise but also policy victories and defeats. The very rules of governing advantage some groups over others.

CALIFORNIA'S CONSTITUTION

California's current constitution is more than 54,000 words in length and has been amended more than 500 times, second only to Alabama.

Some of the document's most interesting provisions are certain amendments that will be discussed shortly. Yet the basic framework for California's government was established in the 1800s by two separate conventions producing two distinct constitutions.

The **Constitution of 1849** provided the basic structure of state government and a 16-section Declaration of Rights. Slavery was banned. Married women were granted separate property rights, the first such guarantee found in any state (see Figure 3.1). Certain policy directions were also set in this constitution. Provisions for public education were specified in some detail, and income from selected state lands was set aside for a future state university. Public debt of any magnitude was disallowed. This constitution lasted 30 years, longer than many observers thought it would. The voters repeatedly rejected legislative calls for a second constitutional convention, despite pleas that the state was "lawless, penniless and powerless."[1] Finally, a second one was held in 1878 amid population growth pressures (a 17-fold increase in only 30 years), farmer/railroad feuds, and the rise of the militant Workingman's Party. Many Californians thought constitutional reform would solve these problems.

The delegates to the 1878 convention generally represented three opposing interest groups: large financial interests (banks, corporations, and large

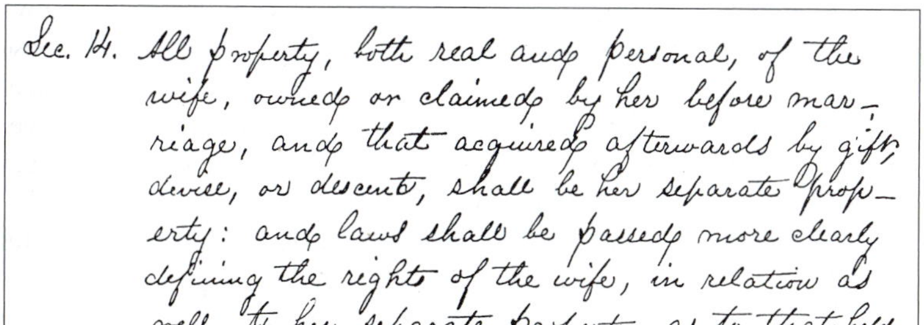

Sec. 14. All property, both real and personal, of the wife, owned or claimed by her before marriage, and that acquired afterwards by gift, devise, or descent, shall be her separate property: and laws shall be passed more clearly defining the rights of the wife, in relation as well to her separate property, as to that held in common with her husband. Laws shall also be passed providing for the registration of the wife's separate property

FIGURE 3.1 Women and the Constitution of 1849

At a time in American history when women were considered legally subservient to their husbands, California's first constitution suggested otherwise. Consider Section 14 of Article 11 (Miscellaneous Provisions) as it appeared in the original.

SOURCE: *The Original Constitution of the State of California, 1849: The Engrossed Copy with the Official Spanish Translation* (Sacramento: Telefact Foundation, 1965), p. 94.

landowners), farmers (opposed to the Southern Pacific Railroad and the tax system), and urban workers (alienated by both big business and the influx of Chinese). After 157 days of hard bargaining, they adopted the document on a 120–15 vote; on May 7, 1879, California voters ratified it.

The **Constitution of 1879** was three times longer than the old one and much more detailed. It was also viscerally anti-Chinese, containing provisions barring their immigration and employment. Meant to check the power and influence of the Southern Pacific Railroad, the new railroad commission was quickly captured by the SP itself, rendering it not only powerless but converting it into a new bureaucratic tool of the railroad. Contemporary analysts Joe Mathews and Mark Paul called the new document a civic disaster. "Much of the next half-century of political reform efforts in California would be devoted to undoing its worst provisions."[2]

Over the years, it California's constitution has grown still further just as the state has. Today, it is eight times as long as the U.S. Constitution. Over the years, many original provisions have survived intact. Others have been slightly revised. Entire new sections have been added, and other sections have been reorganized.

What It Contains

California's constitution illustrates features common to all state constitutions.

Duties of Government It reflects the particular obligations of state government overall and necessary institutions such as the governor, legislature, and judiciary. Because local governments are subdivisions of the state, the constitution must spell out their duties and powers. Therefore, extensive sections of California's constitution deal with cities, counties, special districts, and school districts.

Mistrust of Politicians California's constitution, like those of other states, has reflected historic mistrust of elected officials. This mistrust has been aimed at legislators as well as at governors. In the 1800s, the state legislature was considered so corrupt it was called

the Legislature of 1,000 Drinks and the Legislature of 1,000 Steals. As a result, its powers were sharply delineated. For instance, the 1879 document enumerated 33 instances in which the legislature was *prohibited* from passing laws. Governors have not been spared either. California's constitution requires the governor to share power with separately elected executive officers—the lieutenant governor, attorney general, secretary of state, treasurer, controller, insurance commissioner, and school superintendent plus numerous boards and commissions. In some respects, term limits for the legislature and statewide officers reveals a mistrust of both "career" politicians *and* the voters who continually reelect them.

Group Benefits Typical of other state constitutions, California's has conferred particular advantages or imposed various regulations on interest groups. Numerous provisions address corporations generally and a host of specific groups including financial institutions, the legal profession, the alcoholic beverage industry, churches, contractors, utility companies, the fishing industry, farmers, realtors, and transportation providers. One recent example is an Article 4, Section 19 provision guaranteeing gaming rights of California's Native American tribes. Although the constitution does not exactly mirror hyperpluralism as we use the term, any and all groups with requisite political power can use it to garner benefits for themselves or deny them to others.

Money California's constitution addresses taxation and finance in detail. Tax policies embedded in this document are used to benefit a plethora of interests: charitable groups, orchards and vineyards, historical preservation, nonprofit hospitals, the elderly, renters, homeowners, museums, and veterans. Unlike the federal government, state constitutions usually limit the amount of debt states and their subdivisions can incur. In California, the 1879 state limit of $300,000 remains, but Article 16 wording provides ample room for policymakers to borrow considerably more.

Clutter and Trivia Like other states, California's constitution is filled with clutter and trivia. This

I do solemnly swear (or affirm) that I will support and defend the Constitution of the United States and the Constitution of the State of California against all enemies, foreign and domestic; that I will bear true faith and allegiance to the Constitution of the United States and the Constitution of the State of California; that I take this obligation freely, without any mental reservation or purpose of evasion; and that I will well and faithfully discharge the duties upon which I am about to enter.

And I do further swear (or affirm) that I do not advocate, nor am I a member of any party or organization, political or otherwise, that advocates the overthrow of the Government of the United States or of the State of California by force or violence or other unlawful means....

F I G U R E 3.2   California's oath of office. Sometimes called a loyalty oath, this oath of office dates from 1952 and is found in Article XX of the California Constitution. Above is an excerpt.

Question: In recent years, several California teachers and professors have resisted signing this oath and some have been fired as a result. Is this oath an outdated Cold War relic or should it still apply given the nation's war on terror?

minutia must have seemed important at the time it was enacted. For instance, today's public school teachers can be grateful the state's constitution prevents their annual salaries from dipping below $2,400![3] In the early 1900s, the length of boxing matches and rounds was specified (12 rounds and three minutes, respectively). An 1849 ban on dueling remained in the constitution until 1970. A symbol of Cold War America is found in Article XX, Section 3. This 1952 provision requires virtually all public employees in the state to sign a loyalty oath (see Figure 3.2). Occasionally, the voters eliminate such provisions, but others remain simply because they are politically irrelevant. More important, some constitutional trivia remains because trivia is relative in a pluralistic society; what is undue clutter to one group might be economic survival to another. Even trivia represents hard-fought political conflict, winners and losers, and historical events in the life of a state. In a sense, it is pluralism at work.

Change   California, like other states, allows its basic document to change. Three methods are available. First is a **constitutional convention**. The legislature, by a two-thirds vote, may call for a constitutional convention. The last such convention was in 1878. California has not used this method as frequently or recently as other states. In

fact, voters have turned down such convention proposals on four occasions. In the 1960s, the legislature modified this method by appointing a "blue ribbon" constitutional revision commission to study the document and recommend changes for legislative approval and voter ratification. Overall, the revisions that survived voter approval resulted in a briefer, more streamlined document, at least by state constitution standards. In the mid-1990s, a 23-member Constitutional Revision Commission studied potential changes to the constitution. After two years of hearings and reports, it proposed a package of constitutional amendments to overhaul and streamline state and local government, but they died in the legislature. There have been renewed calls for a constitutional convention in recent years in the wake of the recent recession, continued hyperpartisanship, and what many consider governmental brokenness.

A second method is change by **legislative proposal**, a method common to all states. Individual members of the California Assembly and Senate propose legislative constitutional amendments and process them as bills. If two-thirds of their colleagues agree, measures are placed on the ballot for voter consideration. "Housekeeping" changes and more significant policy proposals have resulted from this method. For instance, in 2002 voters altered language in Article VI via Proposition 48, making it consistent with a prior court consolidation plan. A third method is the **initiative**, a product of the Progressive era. The initiative allows individuals and groups to bypass the legislature entirely by placing proposed statutes or constitutional amendments on the ballot. Proponents of an initiative constitutional amendment must gather valid signatures equal to 8 percent of the total votes cast for governor in the most recent gubernatorial election (807,615 during the period 2011–2015). To be enacted, initiative constitutional amendments require only a simple majority of votes cast. Eighteen states allow this method, but no state uses it more than California. Chapter 4 discusses the initiative process in depth.

What Makes It Distinctive

As we have seen, newer states leaned on the older constitutions for framework and language. Structurally, all state constitutions resemble the U.S. Constitution. Yet state constitutions invariably reflect their regional context, dominant political subcultures, historical experience, and subsequent political trends. At this point, we briefly spotlight several provisions in California's constitution that are quintessentially "Californian."

Power to the People As noted earlier, one significant result of California's Progressive movement, under Governor Hiram Johnson's leadership, was the addition of initiatives, referenda, and recall. None of these is provided for in the U.S. Constitution. The **initiative**, allowing voters to directly place constitutional amendments and statutory proposals on the ballot, was approved in 1911. The **referendum** allows voters to approve or reject statutes already passed by the legislature. In 2011–2015, initiative statutes and referenda required 504,760 valid signatures to be placed on a California ballot (five percent of the total votes cast for governor in the 2010 election). The **recall** allows the electorate to remove elective officials between elections. This provision applies to all elective officials at both the state and local levels,

including judges. Once thought impossible to accomplish at the statewide level (it takes the signatures of 20 percent of the votes cast in the last gubernatorial election), Governor Gray Davis was recalled in a 2003 special election.

The Right of Privacy Only eight state constitutions contain an explicit right of privacy, and California is one of them. Even though it is not specifically mentioned in the U.S. Constitution, the U.S. Supreme Court in *Roe v. Wade* (1973) established a right of privacy relative to reproductive choice.[4] California's original "Declaration of Rights" in 1849 did not include privacy. It read: "All men are by nature free and independent, and have certain inalienable rights, among which are those of enjoying and defending life and liberty; acquiring, possessing, and protecting property; and pursuing and obtaining safety and happiness."[5] In 1974, the year after *Roe v. Wade,* California voters replaced "men" with "people," and added "privacy" after "happiness." Although the emerging abortion controversy was not a key issue in its passage, this rewording has been used to support a prochoice policy in California.

Water Many states take water for granted, but not those in the West. California's history of drought, coupled with its agricultural potential, virtually required government's attention from the start. Over the years, much water policy has made its way into the constitution itself. A separate article is simply titled "Water" (Article X). Overall, these provisions encompass water development and regulation, water rates, riparian rights (rights of those who live next to a body of water); the water policy role of the state; protection of fish, wildlife, and scenic rivers; and needs of specific areas such as the Sacramento-San Joaquin Delta.

English Only The original 1849 Constitution was clear: "All laws, decrees, regulations, and provisions, which, from their nature, require publication, shall be published in English and Spanish."[6] The constitution itself was handwritten in both languages, reflecting California's two dominant cultures.

Possibly due to the influx of Euro-Americans during the Gold Rush, that bilingual requirement was eliminated in the *1879 Constitution*. Californians have struggled with this issue ever since. By the 1980s, California's bicultural identity was rapidly becoming bipolar (two cultures in conflict and poles apart). In some communities, the influx of immigrants from Asia and elsewhere suggested a multipolar state. Many white Californians were increasingly uncomfortable with the pluralism around them and the bilingual policies that resulted. In 1986, voters overwhelmingly approved Proposition 63, which declared English as the official language of the state. Its purpose was to "preserve, protect and strengthen the English language."[7] In 1998, they also rejected bilingual education in the public schools by approving Proposition 227. That said, "English Only" is not a universal policy. Multilingual ballots are commonplace and California's court interpreters are certified in at least 13 languages.

Proposition 13 In June 1978, California voters approved Proposition 13, a property-tax-cutting measure that fundamentally altered the relationship between the state and its local governments. The media widely portrayed its passage as the opening volley of a national tax revolt. Careful analysis suggests that the revolt was most successful in Western states with initiative provisions, like California.[8] It had a more subtle effect. It paved the way for former Governor Ronald Reagan's national antitax message two years later as he ran for the presidency. Although other states have adopted their own tax cuts in the intervening years, Proposition 13 captured the nation's attention like no other.

From a governing perspective, California's constitution has fostered fragmentation and gridlock in state politics and policymaking, key elements in hyperpluralism. The state's governors must share their power with other elected executives. Legislative prerogatives are curtailed or limited. Protections for powerful interest groups are sprinkled throughout the document. The initiative process allows well-funded interest groups and individuals, via the electorate, to share legislative power. California's constitutional clutter actually encourages litigation, as groups seek to clarify what a particular provision really means. This increases the policy role of the courts relative to the other branches.

California's constitution reflects all three political subcultures. Constitutional policies fostering education, water development, and other infrastructure investments, plus checks on corruption, connote a noble view of government characteristic of a moralistic political subculture. The individualistic political subculture (a more negative view of government) seems evident in efforts to curb political power and elevate individual rights. The traditionalistic political subculture (placing the powerful over the powerless) may be evident in a few scattered provisions such as public housing limits (Article 34) and English-only policies.

CALIFORNIA AND THE NATION: THE BOUNDARIES OF FEDERALISM

California's relationship to the national government, as with other states, has depended on both constitutional language and political practice. As times have changed, so has this relationship. The Tenth Amendment to the U.S. Constitution defines the general relationship that was supposed to exist between all the states and the national government: "The powers not delegated to the United States by the constitution, nor prohibited by it to the states, are reserved to the states respectively, or to the people."

The Founders never thought the national government would dominate the states in domestic policy. On the contrary, James Madison believed that, in most respects, the national government would be subservient to the states: "The State governments may be regarded as constituent and essential parts of the federal government; whilst the latter is nowise essential to the operation or organization of the former."[9] Alexander Hamilton considered citizens' loyalties to be primarily local. If national representatives were tempted to encroach on the states, "the people of the several States would control the indulgence of so extravagant an appetite."[10]

To modern-day Americans and Californians, these arguments seem both idealistic and unrealistic. The Founders simply could not have anticipated the profound changes that would take place in the federal system. In a sense, there has been no single federalism but rather multiple "federalisms" reflecting different historical eras, public demands, and alternative visions of who does what in our political system. Political scientists have grouped these federalisms into five historic periods.

Dual Federalism

This is the original pattern of which Madison and Hamilton wrote. From the founding to about 1913, the national government largely limited itself to activities specifically mentioned in the U.S. Constitution, such as national defense, foreign affairs, coining money, issuing tariffs, and maintaining a post office. The states were expected to make policy on domestic matters such as education, welfare, health, and law enforcement. Political scientists called this division of labor **dual federalism**; one compared it to a layer cake.[11] California achieved statehood during this dual federalism period. As a young state, it seemed preoccupied with its own political development. With few exceptions, such as aid for the transcontinental railroad, the federal presence in California politics was minimal and indirect.

Cooperative Federalism

As American society became more complex and the Industrial Revolution produced a national economy, the division of labor between the federal and state levels blurred. From 1913 to 1964, a **cooperative federalism** pattern emerged. A national income tax, two world wars, and the Great Depression combined to make both levels active policy partners concerned with health, welfare, transportation, education, crime, and other issues. Political scientists considered the marble cake with its intermingling of layers a better analogy to describe the relationship during those years. During this period, California benefited greatly from federal spending on water projects, New Deal programs, highway construction, and defense contracts.

Centralized Federalism

"He who pays the piper calls the tune," claims the old adage. As the federal government's capacity to tax and spend grew, it also became more than simply a cooperative partner in policymaking. The "feds" (as state and local officials call national-level policymakers) gradually established their own goals. U.S. President Lyndon Johnson's Great Society legislation in the 1960s epitomized the next stage, **centralized federalism**.

The rationale was simple: If policy problems are national in *scope*, they must be national in *nature*—requiring a centralized response. People assumed that states could not or would not provide policy leadership or needed funding. During this period, the Tenth Amendment lost so much of its meaning that political scientists were now describing federalism as a pineapple upside-down cake. Three methods used to centralize policymaking including preemptions, partial preemptions, and mandates. *Preemptions* are when federal policies supercede the authority of subnational governments (e.g. immigration). *Partial preemptions* occur when the federal government takes over a policy area but allows states to impose higher standards (e.g. some environmental regulations). *Mandates* are when the federal government imposes certain duties on subnational governments (e.g. housing undocumented prisoners). During this period, federal aid was commonplace. California followed the national pattern—relying on federal grants for everything from highways to health care but resenting the federal conditions ("strings") that accompanied the funding as well as the shift in control to "the feds." Increasingly, California officials had to lobby Washington, not just Sacramento, to get more funds and to avoid more strings.

The New Federalism

U.S. President Richard Nixon used the term **New Federalism** to describe his program that would share federal revenues with subnational governments with few conditions or strings attached. His General Revenue Sharing program delighted state and local officials in California and around the nation. The 1980s and the "Reagan revolution" continued this New Federalism in part. Building on his experience as California's governor, President Reagan sought to end centralized federalism and decrease the national government's overall role vis-à-vis state and local government. He blamed too many federal grant programs for "a maze of interlocking jurisdictions and levels of government [that] confronts the average citizen in trying to solve even the simplest of problems."[12] He hoped to return many responsibilities to the states and, short of that, to simply reduce spending on programs he disliked. After years of effort, Reagan even ended Nixon's revenue sharing program. Compared to previous decades, California and its local governments would be on their own, so to speak. As federal budget deficits ballooned in the 1980s, grant-cutting also became a deficit-control strategy, not just a way to implement Reagan's philosophy of federalism. Not wanting to fight a popular president, Congress often went along with these plans. During this period, federal controls never disappeared and sometimes grew. But overall, California policymakers learned to develop their own programs and revenue sources independent of federal policy.

Pragmatic Federalism

Today, the relationship between the federal government and subnational governments, including California, has been called **pragmatic federalism**—"a constantly evolving, problem solving attempt to work out solutions to major problems on an issue by issue basis."[13] By pragmatic, we simply mean that there is a certain level of political opportunism at work here. Pragmatic federalism expresses itself in two ways. First, the federal government (relative to the states) and states (relative to their local governments) use coercion in lieu of funding to achieve policy objectives. That is, public officials at each level do what they can to solve a particular problem while shifting the burdensome costs of doing so down the governmental chain. For example, Congress continues to preempt state and local authority over such issues as bankruptcy, environmental policy, transportation, water, and cable television regulation. It also requires states and local governments to implement federal policies without reimbursing the necessary costs, termed unfunded or underfunded mandates. For example, Congress routinely underfunds by half California's participation in the Medicaid program.

While complaining of federal coercion, California state officials often require local governments to provide various services (e.g. general assistance welfare), adopt various policies without providing requisite funding (e.g. recycling requirements), or preempt local action entirely (e.g. gun control). What do local governments do to respond to coercive state tactics? Located on the lowest rung of the intergovernmental ladder, local officials have little choice but to increase user fees and local development fees, privatize some services such as trash collection, or encourage "do it yourself" governments such as homeowners associations that maintain streets within their limited jurisdictions.

Second, due to federal government inaction on what states consider pressing issues, states have resorted to what some call "progressive federalism." Once a conservative argument intended to hamper governmental action in the days of dual federalism, political liberals have rediscovered "states rights" in order to address issues of health care, environmental regulation, medical marijuana, same-sex marriage, stem cell research, greater homeland security funding, immigration, and minimum wage increases. California's more progressive policymakers have sought to pass legislation in virtually all of these areas in response to what they consider policy gridlock, ideological opposition, or a lack of policy innovation in the nation's capital.[14]

B o x 3.1   Case in Point: No Child Left Behind and Race to the Top

Some federal policies supplement and sometimes supplant California's policies. For example, the federal No Child Left Behind Act of 2001 (NCLB)—the newest reauthorization of the decades-old Elementary and Secondary Education Act—requires annual and lengthy testing of all students, prompting one Bakersfield student to ask of a teacher "When are you going to teach us instead of just making us take tests?" Other requirements include "adequate yearly progress" by all states and state-issued "report cards" publicizing school-by-school data. It also subjects school systems to stiff sanctions if student progress is insufficient, a rule that tends to penalize California's racially mixed or low-income schools. These requirements have been particularly challenging to meet in California, even in schools where improvement is dramatic but not rapid enough for federal regulators. Education officials had to mesh NCLB with the state's own education reforms, including the high school exit exam. Budget cuts also made it difficult to meet the law's unrealistic growth targets and comply with its overly rigid accountability rules. U.S. President Barack Obama's own reform, Race to the Top (RTTT), was more incentive-based than NCLB but it too had its critics. They charged that RTTT perpetuated overreliance on test scores to accurately measure student achievement and embraced controversial reforms such as tying teacher evaluations to test results.

FEDERALISM AND CALIFORNIA'S NATIVE AMERICANS

Intergovernmental relations between the federal government, the State of California, and its many local governments leaves out an intriguing political entity—California's Native Americans. How do these semisovereign tribal governments fit into the federalism mix? As you read in Chapter 2, California's Native Americans were subjected to abuse, disease, violence, and death in pre-statehood California. Relegated to relatively remote, small-acreage reservations, their numbers and cultural influence dwindled. Their political influence was nonexistent. Until recently, they were among the state's poorest residents. Legally speaking, the federal government recognized American tribes as sovereign peoples, but this sovereignty has been compromised repeatedly. The federal government disregarded treaties and viewed the tribes as domestic dependent nations in need of federal guardianship. Native American achieved full American citizenship and voting rights in 1924. Today, Native American sovereignty is interpreted in various ways. For example, federal statutes and case law have established that states cannot tax or regulate the tribes. Off the reservations though, Native Americans are subject to state law like other citizens.

In the 1980s, these intergovernmental relationships began to change. A number of tribes nationally and in California had begun bingo concessions to augment their meager incomes. In 1987, the U.S. Supreme Court in *California v. Cabazon Band of Mission Indians* (480 U.S. 202) recognized the right of tribal governments to offer gaming on their own lands. One year later, Congress enacted the *Indian Gaming Regulatory Act*, a law specifying and restricting gaming practices. One requirement of the law was that tribal governments must enter gaming compacts with state governments to offer casino-style gambling. In 1999, Governor Davis signed such a compact with 61 of California's 109 tribes. Notable provisions addressed revenue-sharing with nongaming tribes, environmental protections, and labor matters. Proposition 1A ratified the compact's provisions in 2000 and locked them into the state constitution. Currently, 57 tribal governments operate casinos in California. Many are full service resorts offering dining opportunities and concert venues, much like Las Vegas. But remember, many tribes offer no gaming whatsoever. Their reservations may be too remote to support profitable casino operations. They receive some gaming proceeds nonetheless via a revenue sharing trust fund.

The popularity of Native American gaming has led to tremendous growth in the number, size, and scope of casinos in California, where they have a virtual monopoly on the activity. While the public has generally supported Native American self-sufficiency including gaming on tribal lands, casino expansion has spawned a number of political controversies. These controversies raise puzzling questions for policymakers and students of federalism. For example, because tribes need not pay traditional taxes, to what extent should they make "in lieu" payments to the State of California and the local jurisdictions where casinos are located? To what extent should tribes voluntarily abide by the same land use regulations required of their neighbors? Does Native American sovereignty extend to any nonreservation land a tribe might buy? These questions suggest that federalism as it relates to Native Americans in California is somewhat enigmatic. Whereas pragmatic federalism may characterize intergovernmental relations generally in America and the states, the presence, sovereignty, and power of California's gaming tribes suggest that a form of dual federalism actually may apply to tribal relations with California's state government. What we know for sure is that the newfound wealth of some California tribes has empowered them to exercise political influence, affect election outcomes, and utilize methods (lobbying, lawsuits, and protests) long available to other groups. It has also energized groups opposed to gaming in general and to the tribes' newfound political clout in particular.[15]

CALIFORNIA IN WASHINGTON

As with the other 49 states, California seeks to maximize its influence on federal policymaking, a process called intergovernmental lobbying. Compared to less diverse or smaller states, representing California in Washington is more challenging than size alone would suggest. In one notorious case, California's lack of clout once resulted in Congress awarding a federal earthquake research center to New York State rather than to earthquake-prone California.

In recent years, California has received in federal spending only 80 cents of every tax dollar it sends to Washington, making it a so-called donor state. Federal spending in the state includes everything from Social Security, Medicare, and Medicaid payments to military wages, college financial aid, and highway construction. This "balance of payments" problem is largely due to Californians' higher-than-average personal incomes (resulting in higher taxes paid), a significantly younger population (resulting in fewer Social Security payments), and a slippage in federal procurement spending.[16] Making matters worse are other federal inequities and priorities that disadvantage California. For example, homeland security reimbursements to California do not include related costs of the California Highway Patrol. Furthermore, state officials argue that federal funding does not recognize potential terrorist targets such as the state's ports, transportation facilities, and tourist attractions. Second, federal funding formulas may disadvantage California. For example, the higher cost of living in California is not factored into federal poverty calculations used to determine eligibility for several federal programs aimed at the poor. The state's housing rent for one year is often more than half of the federal poverty threshold. In San Francisco, it consumes all of it and then some.[17]

The reasons for California's relative lack of influence in Washington are numerous and complex. First, the rules of the federalism game have shifted in the last two decades. Earlier, lobbyists in Washington worked routinely with executive branch bureaucrats who controlled the distribution of grant monies. As both funding and federal programs were reduced in the 1980s, some grant decision making shifted from anonymous bureaucrats to members of Congress. As a result, California lobbyists found they had to influence the content of legislation, not just "touch base" with grant administrators. This trend put a diverse and conflict-prone state at the mercy of a more diverse and conflict-ridden Congress.

© David Marten

© David G. Lawrence

Morongo Casino Resort and Spa (Cazaban, California) and Chumash Indian Casino Resort (Santa Ynez, California)

Second, California may lack clout because of its distance both geographically and politically. Members of Congress may resent the state's sheer size and its role as a competitor for federal dollars. Washington veterans call this attitude the **ABC syndrome**—Anywhere But California.

Third, California's congressional delegation (two senators and 53 House members) is by far the nation's largest and most diverse. It faces both structural and ideological challenges. Structurally speaking, high-growth states such as California are outnumbered in the U.S. Senate, where each state,

---

Box 3.2   Case in Point: Dueling Views on Earmarks

In early 2010, the California city of Elk Grove requested a $250,000 federal grant for a teen resource center. The House member who represents Elk Grove, Republican Dan Lungren, was having none of it. In the light of mounting federal debt, he joined other Republicans in approving an unofficial one-year moratorium on earmarks as a way to reduce federal spending. "Look," he remarked, "as broke as the state of California is right now, the federal government is more broke." Democratic House members signed no such moratorium. Consequently, Democratic Representative Mike Thompson sought federal funding for a new building in Calistoga that would house an art facility and a teen center. And that was just one of 126 projects he was promoting through the earmarking process. As a group, the Democratic members of the delegation viewed earmarks as a way of "bring home the bacon" and respond to local concerns. It would be a dereliction of duty to do otherwise.

These two House members representing neighboring congressional districts were themselves miles apart in how best to represent their constituents. They also embodied why California's congressional delegation, the nation's largest, is less effective than size alone would suggest.

SOURCE: Rob Hotakainsen, "California's Congressional Delegation Divided Over Earmarks," McClatchy Newspapers (March 31, 2010). Accessed at www.mcclatchydc.com/2010/03/31/91363/californias-congressional-delegation.html/.

---

regardless of size, gets two senators and, accordingly, two votes. Ideologically speaking, the California delegation includes some of the most liberal and most conservative members in the entire House. Sharp ideological divisions exist not only between Republicans and Democrats but also within both parties. In addition, California's diverse political geography (north/south, coastal/inland, and urban/rural) creates diverse agendas within the delegation. While the challenge of uniting this diverse delegation has been likened to herding cats, cooperation is possible, as has been seen on such issues as disaster insurance, skilled worker visas, and criminal alien incarceration funding. In terms of earmarks, where individual members of Congress obtain project-specific appropriations for their states or districts, California numbers are unimpressive (See Box 3.2). According to the Citizens Against Government Waste, California ranked 40th in per capita earmarks for 2010. In dollar terms, this amounted to $17.19 per person. Hawaii ranked first at $251.78 per person.[18]

Given California's diversity of interests in Washington, several strategies have been employed to maximize the state's political effectiveness. First, growing numbers of the state's public and private interest groups now saturate the federal government with lobbying activity. Dozens of California counties, cities, special districts, and state agencies (including the legislature) are represented in Washington. All three public higher education systems (the community colleges, the California State University, and the University of California) employ registered lobbyists. Second, California's congressional delegation and California-based organizations have been most successful when they have framed their needs in broader terms and looked outside California for support. That is, they build coalitions. The broadest coalitions involve well-established associations such as the National Governors' Association, the Council of State Governments, or the National League of Cities. Narrower ones might involve regional allies (for e.g., the Western States Recycling Coalition). Because many issues come and go, California lobbyists must constantly build new coalitions to deal with new policy challenges. Third, California policymakers have discovered that it occasionally pays to downplay California's interests. State agencies have been known to quietly support or oppose a bill in Congress without actually acknowledging its impact on California. Private businesses from California, such as defense contractors and Silicon Valley technology firms, maintain the usual ties with home-district members but rarely coordinate their lobbying efforts.

CALIFORNIA AND THE WORLD: THE POLITICS OF FENCES

Just as federalism delineates the relationships between California and the national government, it is important to delineate the relationships between California and nation-states beyond its borders. According to former California Assembly Speaker Robert M. Hertzberg, "In no other era in the history of California have local interests been more directly tied to international concerns."[19] In fact, some analysts agree that California needs and deserves its own foreign policy.

International pressures on the Golden State are primarily twofold. First, California is by far the most popular destination for both legal and illegal immigrants. What made the state attractive to early immigrants makes it attractive today. Second, California's colossal economy—seventh or eighth largest in the world—is increasingly dependent on international trade. As the nation's largest exporter, the state relies on the ability to trade freely with Canada, Mexico, Europe, and its largest trading source—Asia. Much of California's "foreign policy" is related to immigration and trade. Here, the perimeters of California power are likened to literal and figurative fences. In general, policymakers have sought to heighten fences relative to immigration and lower them relative to trade.

Immigration

One gets the impression there are few fences between California and the world and immigration data bear this out. According to U.S. Citizenship and Immigration Services (USCIS), the foreign born now account for 27 percent of California residents, the highest proportion in the nation. The leading countries of origin have been Mexico, the Philippines, and China (see Table 3.1). While precise figures are illusive, experts believe that 10–12 million illegal or undocumented immigrants resided in the United States in 2009 and that roughly 2.6 million of those lived in California.

Given the numbers involved, immigration from Mexico, both legal and otherwise, receives the most attention by policymakers, the media, and ordinary citizens. Movement across California's border with Mexico is nothing new. Historically, the nation's approach toward Mexican workers, one shared in California, has been called the **flower petal policy**: "I need you, I need you not, I need you...."[20] That is, immigrants are welcome depending on whether the American workforce needs them. For instance, California welcomed Mexican immigrants after the Mexican Revolution of 1910 when Japanese and Chinese workers were unwelcome. During the Depression, people thought Mexicans were taking "American" jobs. But World War II resulted in another labor shortage, and Mexican labors were welcomed once again. Renewed deportation efforts occurred in the 1950s and early in the 1980s. Although the "I need you not" rhetoric has been common in recent years, in reality Mexican labor has been essential to numerous California industries including agriculture, garment, furniture, and electronics manufacturing, food processing, and tourism.

The attraction of *El Norte* to Mexicans is understandable. Mexico's minimum wage at the California border is roughly 57 pesos or $4.60 *per day*, compared to California's minimum wage of $8.00 per hour. This disparity has made the United States, and California in particular, economic magnets. Once they arrive and obtain jobs, frugal Mexican American workers often use excess income to support family members left behind. No wonder Mexico maintains ten consulates in California, more than any other nation.

Federal immigration policy in recent decades has focused on border enforcement. First, Congress passed the **Immigration Reform and Control Act of 1986 (IRCA)**. This law created an amnesty program leading to legal residency for more than three million foreigners, half of whom lived in California. About 75 percent of those were from Mexico. One purpose was to unite family members divided only by national boundaries. The children of these newly legalized aliens became fully eligible for any and all government services and benefits. California has received only a portion of the federal aid intended to cushion the fiscal impact of the IRCA.

Second, in 1994, the USCIS's predecessor, the Immigration and Naturalization Service (INS), launched "Operation Gatekeeper" to stem the tide of illegal immigrants pouring into California along the San Diego-Tijuana border—the busiest land-border crossing in the world. In 1996, Congress followed up with the **Illegal Immigration Reform and Immigrant Responsibility Act**. This law increased criminal penalties for immigration-related offenses and authorized the INS to hire more border patrol agents, construct new fencing, and employ new underground sensors and night-vision equipment. Furthermore, the law attempted to limit access to certain public benefits even by illegal immigrants, a provision later declared unconstitutional by the Supreme Court. In the years following the terrorist attacks of September 11, 2001, U.S. Border Patrol budgets and staffing increased dramatically.

Third, in 2005–2006, Congress debated further immigration reform including even tighter border security measures with Mexico, but House/Senate differences delayed final action. House legislation would criminalize the status of undocumented residents, initiate deportation proceedings for millions of them, and allow some to apply for immigration within proper channels used by legal immigrants. Senate legislation included many of those provisions but also included a temporary worker program for up to 200,000 workers who potentially could seek legal permanent residence, a measure favored by U.S. President George W. Bush. The only measure to pass Congress was the proposed construction of a 700-mile fence along portions of the 1,951-mile U.S.-Mexico border, much of it east of California.

Have the tightened borders of recent years stemmed the tide of illegal immigration? Apparently not. While the entry of undocumented immigrants has declined along the San Diego-Tijuana border, entry points have shifted eastward into more perilous desert terrain. To cope with these hostile conditions, some immigrants have paid thousands of dollars to border-wise *coyotes* or *polleros* to be smuggled into the United States and eventually to California. Deaths due to dehydration, exposure, and violence

have increased. Also, border crossings in urban areas are now so difficult, illegal immigrants already here hesitate to return to their countries of origin. In the past, many would repeatedly cross the border due to job availability, economic trends, and family emergencies. Keep in mind that many if not most immigrants to California, particularly from Mexico, have families in both places, resulting in many two-way border crossings. That said, it is so difficult to cross illegally, border enforcement ironically has kept many undocumented persons in California.[21] Furthermore, the prospect of better jobs and wages plus economic turmoil back home draws undocumented immigrants regardless of efforts to deter them.

Recent efforts in Congress and some states have emphasized the arrest and deportation of undocumented persons or even denying birth-right citizenship to their children born in the United States. Most of these efforts seem aimed at illegal immigration from Mexico. California policymakers have not been and likely will not be at the forefront of these efforts. In fact, the California Supreme Court in 2010 unanimously ruled that undocumented students may receive in-state tuition rates at California's public universities if they attended and graduated from a California high school.[22] This ruling affected an estimated 25,000 undocumented students. See Chapter 13 for further discussion of this topic.

What about immigration to California from Asia? While it has occurred throughout California's history and is considerable today as Table 3.1 suggests, current immigration from Asia seems much less controversial than immigration from Mexico and Latin America. The reasons may be several. First, nine in ten illegal immigrants come from Latin America. As a consequence, Asian and European illegal immigration do not receive the same level of scrutiny. Second, the United States and California border with Mexico is identifiable and presumably securable and even fenceable in the minds of many Americans and their policymakers. Routes to California from Asia are more difficult to identify, monitor, and enforce. Third, much immigration from Asia

TABLE 3.1   Leading Countries of Origin of Immigrants in California, 2009

Country	Number of immigrants in California
Mexico	4,308,000
Philippines	783,000
China	681,000
Vietnam	457,000
El Salvador	413,000
India	319,000
Korea	307,000
Guatemala	261,000
Iran	214,000
Canada	132,000
United Kingdom	125,000

SOURCE: U.S Census Bureau, *2009 American Community Survey* and *Just the Facts: Immigrants in California* (San Francisco: Public Policy Institute of California, April 2011) (Available at www.ppic.org).

lacks controversy because many immigrants bring high-level job skills needed in California's economy. Asians receive more employment preferences than do less-educated or -skilled immigrants from elsewhere.

Legal immigration presents its own challenges. In recent years, some of California's technology firms have outsourced certain tasks to nations with cheaper labor pools (such as India) or have replaced highly skilled and highly paid workers at home with lesser paid legal immigrants.

Trade

The impact of international trade on California is immense. In 2009, California exported $120 billion in goods to over 200 foreign markets. Such trade employs a million California workers. In contrast to immigration, the approach of California and the federal government to world trade has been to lower economic fences. In 1993, Congress passed the **North American Free Trade Act (NAFTA)** to encourage trade between Canada, the United States, and Mexico. Over time, it would eliminate tariffs

completely and remove many nontariff barriers to trade such as import licenses. By 2004, it had created the world's largest free trade zone with a combined gross domestic product of over $13 trillion. In 2000, Mexico surpassed Japan as the state's largest trading partner. NAFTA's specific impact may be good news or bad news depending on the industry and the locale. The San Diego area was a major beneficiary as foreign companies such as Sony and Samsung located there to take advantage of low-wage assembly-line labor south of the border. Four hundred miles north in Santa Cruz County, food processing plants closed, victims of soaring agricultural imports from Mexico and beyond.[23]

NAFTA has impacted immigration in some stunning ways. For example, the treaty allowed American corporations to dump government-subsidized corn on the Mexico market. The Mexican government compounded the problem by ending subsidies to their own subsistence farmers. Combined, these practices drove many small Mexican farms out of business which in turn forced now displaced agricultural workers to migrate north to work, including California.[24]

California's trade policy has been, at best, a work in progress. In the 1980s, it established the California World Trade Commission with offices in numerous foreign capitals. In 2003, these offices and the rest of the Technology, Trade, and Commerce Agency were closed down; critics claimed they were mismanaged and ineffective. In subsequent years, state officials discussed reestablishing a formal trade policy for the state, including the reopening of trade offices in China and elsewhere. Trade consultant Jock O'Connell discounts the need for official state representation: "The real California is superbly well represented in the form of 57,000 exporting companies.[25] In the meantime, California officials have collaborated with their international counterparts on a host of border-related issues including air pollution, poultry diseases, drug trafficking, and public health concerns. Yet, many observers agree that economic conditions and public policies in other nations, from Mexico to the outer reaches of the Pacific Rim, affect the politics of borders and fences more so than official efforts to improve bilateral relations.

CONCLUSION

California's position relative to the nation as a whole is most interesting. Its political development has resulted in constitutional provisions both similar and dissimilar to constitutions in other states. California's diversity is mirrored both in its constitution and in the variety of representatives it sends to Congress. Its sheer size makes it the focal point of media attention when voters dramatically alter their constitution. As a result, California can give birth to national political movements through such changes (e.g., Proposition 13 and the "taxpayers' revolt").

California's constitutional development reflects American political theory. The state constitution provides the basic elements of representative government—the cornerstone of American political thought. Political elites dominated California's two constitutional conventions and greatly influenced much of its language. Well-organized interests are amply provided for in the document. Yet the constitution allows for widespread group participation and has been partly responsible for the state's political pluralism. It also planted the seeds of hyperpluralism by dividing political responsibility, limiting some governmental powers, and, through the initiative process, compromising the notion of representative government.

California's size and diversity have affected its intergovernmental relationships. The state is both the automatic recipient of large amounts of federal spending and the source of resentment at the money being spent. But California's interests are so diffuse and its congressional delegation so diverse that the state rarely speaks with one voice, even when doing so would be in its own best interest. In its own midst, the growing power of California's gaming tribes has raised numerous questions of governance. Finally, California's relationships with the rest of the world present an ongoing challenge and reflect the politics of diversity. A solid black line on maps, California's border is in reality a porous screen door through which flow workers, families, jobs, and dollars. Efforts have been made to raise the fence in terms of immigration but at the same time lower the fence in terms of international trade.

KEY TERMS

perimeters of politics (p. 40)

constitutionalism (p. 40)

Constitution of 1849 and 1879 (pp. 41,42)

constitutional convention,

legislative proposal, initiative, referendum, and recall (pp. 43,44)

dual, cooperative, centralized, new federalism, and pragmatic federalism (pp. 46,47)

ABC syndrome (p. 50)

flower petal policy (p. 52)

Immigration Reform and Control Act of 1986 (IRCA) (p. 52)

Illegal Immigration Reform and

Immigrant Responsibility Act (p. 53)

North American Free Trade Act (NAFTA) (p. 54)

REVIEW QUESTIONS

1. Describe the concept of constitutionalism and illustrate from California's constitution.

2. Contrast the two California constitutions.

3. In what ways is California's constitution much like those of other states? In what ways is it different or unique?

4. California's constitution both planted the seeds of hyperpluralism and over time mirrored the political subcultures of the state. Illustrate this statement.

5. What developments were occurring in California during each stage of American federalism?

6. How has the reduced role of the federal government affected California? Given these conditions, how do Californians represent their interests in the nation's capital?

7. How is California politics affected by its proximity to Mexico and the Pacific Rim?

WEB ACTIVITIES

The California Constitution
(www.leginfo.ca.gov/const.html/)
The Legislative Counsel of California maintains this Web site, which contains a fully searchable copy of the state constitution. Contrast it to the U.S. Constitution.

The California Institute
(www.calinst.org/)
This nonprofit Washington, D.C.-based organization analyzes federal policy as it relates to California and advises the California delegation in Congress accordingly. The site helps you to assess the effect of a particular federal policy on California.

California Progress Report
(www.californiaprogressreport.com/)
This Web site illustrates progressive federalism by focusing on progressive state-initiated policies.

Progressive States Network (www.progressivestates.org) is its national counterpart.

Federation for American Immigration Reform
(www.fairus.org)
FAIR is an anti-immigration group that features some straightforward immigration data in California, both statewide and by county.

National Immigration Law Center
(www.nilc.org)
The National Immigration Law Center focuses on the rights of immigrants already in the United States and California.

NOTES

1. Hinten Helper, *The Land Of Gold* (1855), Quoted In Joe Mathews And Mark Paul, *California Crackup: How Reform Broke The Golden State And How We Can Fix It* (Berkeley: University of California Press, 2010), p. 21.

2. Ibid, p. 24.

3. See Article IX, Section 6, adopted November 4, 1952.

4. *Roe v. Wade,* 410 U.S. 113 (1973).

5. California Constitution, Article I, Section 1.

6. California Constitution, 1849, Article XI, Section 21.

7. Article III, Section 6, adopted November 4, 1986.

8. See Susan B. Hansen, *The Politics of Taxation* (New York: Praeger, 1983), p. 233.

9. "The Federalist No. 45," in Jacob E. Cooke, ed. *The Federalist* (Middletown, Conn.: Wesleyan University Press, 1961), p. 311.

10. Ibid., "The Federalist No. 17," pp. 106, 108.

11. Morton Grodzins, *The American System* (Chicago: Rand McNally, 1966), pp. 8–9.

12. U.S. President Ronald Reagan, "State of the Union Speech, January 26, 1982," *Public Papers of the Presidents, Vol. I* (Washington, D.C.: U.S. Government Printing Office, 1982), p. 75.

13. Parris N. Glendening and Mavis Mann Reeves, *Pragmatic Federalism: An Intergovernmental View of American Government*, 2nd ed. (Pacific Palisades, CA: Palisades Publishers, 1984), pp. 27–28.

14. For more background on this phenomenon, see Richard P. Nathan, "There Will Always Be a New Federalism," *Journal of Public Administration Research and Theory* 16 (October, 2006), pp. 499–510. See also www.californiaprogressreport.com/.

15. For two analyses of Indian gaming in California (both positive and negative), see UC Riverside's Center for California Native Americans (www.ccnn.ucr.edu) and Charlene Wear Simmons, *Gambling in the Golden State 1998 Forward* (Sacramento: California Research Bureau, 2006) (Available at www.library.ca.gov/crb).

16. For more on this imbalance in recent decades, see California Institute for Federal Policy Research, *California's Balance of Payments with the Federal Treasury FY 1981–2003* (February, 2005). (Available online at www.calinst.org/pubs/balance2003.htm.)

17. Deborah Reed, *Poverty in California: Moving Beyond the Federal Measure* (San Francisco: Public Policy Institute of California, 2006).

18. Citizens Against Government Waste, *2010 Pig Book* (Washington, D.C., 2011) (Available at www.cagw.org).

19. Robert M. Hertzberg, "Global California: Greater Legislative Participation in International Affairs," *Spectrum: The Journal of State Government* 76 (Fall, 2003), p. 22.

20. Daniel Levy and Gabriel Szekely, *Mexico: Paradoxes of Stability and Change* (Boulder, CO: Westview Press, 1987), p. 213.

21. Belinda I. Reyes, Hans P. Johnson, and Richard Van Swearingen, *Holding the Line? The Effect of the Recent Border Buildup on Unauthorized Immigration* (San Francisco: Public Policy Institute of California, 2002); and Hans P. Johnson, *At Issue: Illegal Immigration* (San Francisco: Public Policy Institute of California, 2006).

22. *Martinez v Regents of the University of California*, Ct. App.3 C054124 (2010).

23. Evelyn Iritani, "*NAFTA:* 10 Years Later," *Los Angeles Times*, January 19, 2004.

24. David Bacon, *Illegal People: How Globalization Creates Migration and Criminalizes Immigration* (Boston: Beacon Press, 2008); and Emilio Godoy, "Mexico: Experts Denounce Slant in Corn Subsidies," *Global Information Network* (September 16, 2010).

25. Quoted in Judy Lin, "California Lawmakers Refocus on Developing Foreign Trade," *Sacramento Bee*, June 19, 2006.

4

✴

Direct Democracy in a Hyperpluralistic Age

The Impact of Progressivism

Progressivism: California Style

Selected Initiative Battles in California

Proposition 13: Give the Money Back

Propositions 187 and 209: Limits on Rights

Propositions 22 and 8: Limits on Same Sex Marriage

Propositions 215 and 19: Legalizing Marijuana

The Initiative Mess

Prospects for Initiative Reform

Progressive Cousins: Referendum and Recall

State Level Recalls

Local Level Recalls

Conclusion: The Legacy and the Paradox

Key Terms

Review Questions

Web Activities

Notes

IN BRIEF

In a mature representative democracy, voters play a key role in governing. In a real sense, the "people" are sovereign, yet they do not behave in a political vacuum. Just as the public officials they elect are, the voters themselves are influenced by profound social, economic, and political forces they do not fully understand. Consider these questions: Why does the electorate vote so often in California? How can they throw out elected politicians without waiting for the next election? What empowers them to directly legislate on policy issues about which they know little or nothing? The average Californian is probably unable to give cogent answers to these questions. Yet that same person would heartily defend all those electoral powers as necessary in a democracy.

In Chapter 4, these questions are addressed first by unraveling the various layers of history that shroud the origins of the typical contemporary California voter. Beginning with political corruption and emerging urban problems during the "politics of modernization," we trace the rise of the Progressive movement in California; describe its continuing presence in modern politics; and examine the hyperpluralistic election system that has resulted. In the end, what emerges is something of a paradox in the Progressive legacy: The same reforms that gave voters ultimate power also have contributed to the policy and political gridlock we observe in California today.

THE IMPACT OF PROGRESSIVISM

It seems Californians are perennially voting, thinking about the next election, or recovering from the last one. They are inundated with more candidate and policy choices than most Americans could imagine. In some respects, Progressive reforms predestined this state of affairs. **Progressivism** was a turn-of-the-century political movement that sought to rid politics of corrupting influences, return power to "the people," and make government more businesslike. The movement both benefited and departed from a populist strain in American politics that distrusted political and economic elites. According to historian Richard Hofstadter, "Populism had been overwhelmingly rural and provincial. The ferment of the Progressive era was urban, middle-class and nationwide. Above all, Progressivism differed from Populism in the fact that the middle classes of the cities not only joined the trend toward protest but took over its leadership."[1]

The era from about 1900 to 1920 was one of social upheaval and intense political competition among social classes in the United States. The Progressive reformers were in the middle of this upheaval. Across the nation, these reformers were appalled by the political dark side of the Industrial Revolution. From coast to coast, new immigrant voters were routinely bribed by members of urban political machines. Unelected bosses of both parties easily controlled many city halls and statehouses. Rather than being above the dirt, political parties were rolling around in it.

Preoccupied by the demands of both machine bosses and corporate moguls, local and state legislators neglected the mounting problems faced by cities in the late 1800s and early 1900s: labor unrest, unemployment, poverty, and urban crowding. Political corruption was only part of the story. As urban problems mounted, the machine bosses were poorly equipped to manage the increasingly complex affairs of city hall. In what Hofstadter called a "status revolution," urban professionals, intellectuals, and muckraking journalists joined to expose the incapacity of the machines to govern effectively. The differences between these warring groups were profound. To the typical machine boss, politics was individualistic, the essence of good personal relations. To the Progressives, politics was a moral obligation to efficiently manage public resources for a larger public good.[2] They assumed there was one public and one public good achievable through consensus. Californians easily equate the Progressive era with the introduction of the initiative, referendum, and recall. Yet across the nation as well as in California, an entire set of other Progressive reforms was enacted to inhibit the influence of political machines. They included the following:

Direct primaries: The convention system of nominating candidates was easily controlled by bosses. Many states including California enacted a direct primary that bypassed party organizations. This enabled voters themselves to nominate candidates who would compete in general elections.

- *At-large elections:* At the local level, at-large elections, in which candidates run citywide rather than from a specific district or ward, were instituted to minimize machine control of individual votes and encourage citywide perspectives toward governing and policy issues. Today, the vast majority of local governments use at-large elections.

- *Nonpartisan elections:* Another reform removed party designations next to candidates' names on ballots. In California, this applied to all local and judicial offices requiring an election. Reformers thought that machine influence would lessen and that endorsements by "good government" groups would gain importance.

- *Merit systems and short ballots:* To further minimize the power of machines, the concept of a civil service was introduced. Government workers would be hired on the basis of merit—experience, training—not politics. Also, voters would directly elect fewer officials at the local level; in turn, these officials would hire civil servants to carry out the routines of government.

- *Professional management:* Related to the idea of merit, this reform created positions such as city manager, a professional administrator who would ideally be above and apart from politics. Today, most California cities have city managers or city administrators; counties and special districts have comparable positions.

PROGRESSIVISM: CALIFORNIA STYLE

California was a major center of Progressive-era activity. By the turn of the century, its politics exhibited many of the problems detested by the reformers. Analogous to the urban political machines elsewhere in the nation, California had its own statewide machine, the Southern Pacific Railroad. Its brazen and arrogant exercise of power became an easy target for the Progressives. Elsewhere in the United States, economic problems and social turbulence were blamed on new immigrants from Europe. In California, comparable problems were blamed on Chinese laborers and the railroad that originally employed them.

California Progressivism possessed five characteristics in common with the movement nationwide. First, it represented to some extent both the *individualistic and moralistic political subcultures* in California. On one hand, progressive reformers wanted to pursue their own agendas, unencumbered by big business monopolies or selfish labor union influence. They acted as if they were the heirs of the individualistic ideals of the liberal tradition. On the other hand, they possessed a moral sense. As historian George E. Mowry noted, the California Progressive "pictured himself as a complete individual wholly divorced from particular economic as well as class interests. Ready to do justice in the name of the common good, he was, in his own estimation, something akin to Plato's guardians, above and beyond the reach of corrupting material forces."[3] Historian Spencer Olin retitled an old hymn and called them "Onward Christian Capitalists."[4]

Second, Progressivism was *white and middle class.* According to Mowry, "the California progressive leader was a young man, often less than forty years old … probably had been born in the Middle West … carried a north European name … came of old American stock … was, in the jargon of his day, 'well fixed' … invariably a member of his town's chamber of commerce … until 1900, a conservative Republican."[5] Progressives were not just middle class; they were anti-upper class and anti-lower class. In 1908, the progressive *California Weekly* editorialized, "Nearly all the problems which vex society have their sources above or below the middle class man. From above come the problems of predatory wealth. From below come the problems of poverty and of pigheaded brutish criminality."[6]

Third, as with the rest of the nation, it was *urban* in nature. Although California Progressivism capitalized on agrarian unrest, its roots were in the state's emerging coastal cities. By 1910, 60 percent of California's population was urban; almost half lived in San Francisco, Los Angeles, and Alameda counties. In these places, the progressives waged war with organized labor, the Southern Pacific, and in San Francisco, a political machine controlled by Abe Ruef, a boss in the mold of New York City's legendary Boss Tweed.

Fourth, California Progressivism was *nonradical*. Its leaders were small business owners, lawyers, real estate operators, doctors, and journalists. As members of an upwardly mobile middle class, they were class conscious but not out to destroy those classes unlike their own. They sought to reduce the influence of one corporation, not to destroy the corporate idea. They rejected the socialist leanings of the labor unions, not labor itself. The Progressives sought to clean up government, not completely restructure it. Sensing even then a splintering of the state into diverse, hyperpluralistic groups, California's progressives, according to Mowry, "sought to blot out not only the rising clash of economic groups but the groups themselves, as conscious economic and political entities."[7]

Fifth, California's Progressives depended on entrepreneurial leadership—those dynamic individuals who could rally relatively unorganized interests against entrenched power structures. For instance, through the influence of wealthy physician John Randolph Haynes, Los Angeles was one of the first cities in the nation to adopt local versions of the initiative, referendum, and recall. Other cities in the state rapidly followed suit. Los Angeles was ripe for this reform. Collis Huntington of the Southern Pacific tried to control harbor facilities near Los Angeles and had made numerous enemies in the process.

Another leader was Hiram Johnson, a prosperous San Francisco attorney who had helped prosecute local political corruption. One target was San Francisco's Union Labor Party headed by "Boss" Ruef. He had masterminded the election of Mayor Eugene Schmitz and numerous San Francisco supervisors; he was eventually convicted of political graft. Another target was William F. Herrin, chief counsel of the Southern Pacific Railroad and head of its Political Bureau. Herrin had showered legislators with free railroad tickets and even bribed newspaper editors to receive positive coverage, a rare commodity for the SPR. A statewide reform group, the Lincoln-Roosevelt League, talked Johnson into running for governor in 1910. In a style reminiscent of Theodore Roosevelt, Johnson campaigned throughout the state by automobile (he boycotted trains for obvious reasons), promising at every stop to "kick the Southern Pacific Railroad out of politics."[8] Johnson and other Lincoln-Roosevelt candidates ran as progressive Republicans and won huge election victories that November.

At the height of their success, the Progressives in California energized state government and institutionalized all the reforms associated with the era. In some ways, modern reform-minded groups such as Common Cause, the League of Women Voters, the Public Interest Research Group (CALPIRG), and their online colleagues (CaliforniaProgressReport.org) have continued the Progressive tradition. They view their policy agendas as equally enlightened and have used the old reforms such as the initiative process to enact their goals. Twenty-three states eventually adopted the initiative, but no state uses it more prolifically than California.[9]

SELECTED INITIATIVE BATTLES IN CALIFORNIA

Progressive-era reforms are so familiar that modern Californians take them for granted. The reform that has become most familiar to voters is the initiative. In theory, the initiative would empower ordinary people to fight entrenched special interests. In reality, it quickly evolved into a weapon readily available to any group willing and able to use it. The individualist political subculture runs deep in California's political development, and it did not take long for individuals and groups to discover how valuable the initiative process could be. For example, in 1924—13 short years after its advent—Artie Samish, then employed by the Motor Carriers Association, used an initiative to stabilize taxes on bus companies (he later became an infamous lobbyist). By 1939, well-financed interest groups were initiating measures more often than ad hoc reform groups. This trend has continued to the present. Instead of using it as the safety valve it was intended to be, interest groups *and* politicians use it to bypass the legislature. A brief survey of several recent initiatives will demonstrate the evolving role the initiative has played in California's electoral politics. Each of these has followed the steps noted in Figure 4.1.

Proposition 13: Give the Money Back

The first of these initiatives, **Proposition 13**, is a classic measure rooted in California's real estate market. In the 1970s, California home prices skyrocketed and so did property taxes. Legislators and Jerry Brown, whose first stint as governor was from 1975 to 1983, could not agree on how to best provide tax relief. Homeowner frustration mounted. Los Angeles real estate developer and apartment owner Howard Jarvis proposed cutting property taxes by half and curbing their subsequent growth. He formed the populist-sounding United Organization of Taxpayers, which gathered a record 1.2 million signatures to qualify this historic tax reduction measure for the June 1978 ballot. Despite the dire predictions about its potential consequences, Proposition 13 passed with 64 percent of the vote. Nearly every electoral group measured by political scientists supported it. The consequences *were* dire. With property taxes cut by 57 percent, local services were slashed severely. Local governments, especially counties and school districts, appealed to Sacramento for help and became increasingly dependent on state funding to fill in

Courtesy of the California History Room, California State Library, Sacramento, CA

Hiram Johnson Campaigning
Progressive reformer Hiram Johnson speaks at a political rally.

revenue shortfalls. These "bailouts" became an annual feature of the state budget, and, in the process, local government lost a measure of its autonomy. The crowning blow to this autonomy was passage of the 1993–94 state budget, which not only eliminated the bailout but also transferred $2.6 billion in local property taxes to the state for education spending.

Another immediate consequence was the so-called "Proposition 13 effect." The measure limited property tax growth to only 2 percent per year, much less than real estate inflation at the time. Only when a property was sold would the tax jump dramatically (to 1 percent of the new price). Over time the property tax paid by two neighbors living in identical houses could vary substantially depending on when the homes were purchased.

How an Initiative Becomes a Law

According to California law, any policy idea considered the proper subject of legislation can become an initiative measure. Here are the steps that groups and individuals must complete for an idea to become a law via that process.

1. Write the text of the proposed law (the Legislative Counsel's Office provides assistance upon the request of 25 electors).

2. Request that the Attorney General provide a title and a brief summary of the chief purpose and points of the measure.

3. Upon completion of step 2, the Secretary of State prepares a calendar of filing deadlines. For example, proponents are allowed 150 days to circulate petitions and collect signatures (initiatives must qualify 131 days before the next statewide election).

4. Proponents circulate petitions and gather signatures, again within certain rules and detailed procedures. The petitions themselves must conform to certain format and other specifications.

5. Proponents file completed petitions with the appropriate county election offices; they in turn submit signature totals to the Secretary of State. If the list meets the minimum number of signatures required to qualify the measure, county officials use a random sampling technique to verify signature validity. If less than 95 percent of the sample is valid, the measure fails to qualify; if the submitted signatures are greater than 110 percent of the total number necessary, the measure automatically qualifies. If the random sample suggests that the number of valid signatures is between 95 and 110 percent, county elections officials must verify every signature—a so-called "full check." Results are submitted to the Secretary of State.

6. The Secretary of State deems an initiative qualified and notifies counties and proponents accordingly. The state legislature holds hearings on the measure but cannot alter it or prevent it from appearing on the ballot.

7. The initiative appears on the next statewide ballot and, if approved, becomes law immediately, unless the measure states otherwise. If the provisions of two initiative measures conflict, those of the measure receiving the most affirmative votes prevails. The legislature may amend or repeal an initiative statute but voters must agree to such changes (unless the measure provides otherwise).

FIGURE 4.1 How an Initiative Becomes a Law

SOURCE: Summarized from the California Secretary of State (www.ss.ca.gov/elections/initiative_guide/).

Due to more frequent turnover, the phenomenon affected residential more than commercial real estate. In 1992, the U.S. Supreme Court, in *Nordlinger v. Hahn*, upheld Proposition 13, including this desperate unequal treatment of property owners. Over the years, Proposition 13 made it exceedingly difficult to raise most taxes (a two-thirds vote of the people is usually required). It also encouraged local officials to levy myriad fees and approve land use projects that generated sales taxes not controlled by Proposition 13 (see Chapter 12). Lastly, it spawned a generation of political leaders loath to reform the measure or even question its wisdom, at least in public.

Propositions 187 and 209: Limits on Rights

The 1990s will be remembered as the decade when California voters decided to apply the initiative process to the topic of civil rights. **Proposition 187** was a 1994 attempt to curtail and penalize illegal immigration to California, and **Proposition 209** aimed to halt affirmative action in the state's public sector. Both measures illustrate some broader phenomena regarding direct democracy in the Golden State.

Proposition 187   Proposition 187, nicknamed the "Save Our State" initiative, was introduced by Republican State Senator Dick Mountjoy and a number of conservative, Republican-aligned organizations helped qualify it for the ballot and fund its campaign. Governor Pete Wilson embraced 187 and it quickly became a cornerstone issue in the fall gubernatorial election. Section 1 of the measure blamed illegal immigrants for "economic hardship"

and their "criminal conduct" for personal injury and damage.

The provisions of 187 sought to (1) exclude illegal immigrants from public schools and universities, nonemergency health care programs, and various public social services and benefits, (2) require state and local agencies to report suspected illegal immigrants to the state's attorney general and to the U.S. Immigration and Naturalization Service (INS), and (3) criminalize the printing and selling of false citizenship documents. As a practical matter, primary enforcement would be the responsibility of classroom teachers and school administrators, social workers, and police officers—not INS personnel. Although state and local governments stood to save an estimated $200 million in unused public services, they would have incurred millions of dollars in unreimbursed enforcement costs—in excess of $100 million in just the first year. In addition, some critics predicted that the state would likely loose up to $15 billion in federal funds due to conflicts with federal requirements. Critics also contended that 187 would run afoul of *Plyler* v. *Doe*, a 1982 U.S. Supreme Court case involving a Texas policy that withheld school funding from districts that educated the children of illegal aliens. The Court ruled that illegal aliens and their children, while not citizens, are persons and therefore protected by the equal protection clause of the Fourteenth Amendment.

The fall campaigns on both sides of 187 featured the usual vitriol we find so commonplace when California voters confront emotional, social issues. State Senator Art Torres referred to Proposition 187 as "the last gasp of white America in California." One controversial ad on behalf of Governor Wilson's reelection campaign featured film of illegal immigrants crossing Interstate 5 near the Mexico border with the narrator intoning "300,000 IMMIGRANT CHILD-REN IN PUBLIC SCHOOLS AND THEY KEEP COMING." Wilson won his reelection bid against Secretary of State Kathleen Brown with 55 percent of the vote and the proposition he so readily embraced passed with nearly 59 percent of the vote.

Immediately following the election, several lawsuits challenged the constitutionality of 187. Because it was to take effect immediately, several district court restraining orders halted its implementation pending judicial review. Initially, the state defended Proposition 187 and appealed district court rulings against it to the 9th Circuit Court of Appeals. But when Gray Davis became governor in 1998, he dropped the appeal. While Proposition 187 never became law, it catalyzed anti-immigration forces in California and, to many of the state's Latinos, linked the Republican Party with an anti-immigration agenda.[10]

Proposition 209 Two years after 187, Californians passed **Proposition 209**—the California Civil Rights Initiative. This measure amended Article I of the state constitution to read: "The state shall not discriminate against, or grant preferential treatment to, any individual or group on the basis of race, sex, color, ethnicity, or national origin in the operation of public employment, public education, or public contracting." In short, it banned affirmative action in California's public sector. The chief proponent of 209 was University of California (UC) Regent Ward Connerly who, in 1995, had successfully persuaded the UC Regents to repeal its own affirmative action-influenced admissions process.

Affirmative action's long history dates back to 1961. Then, U.S. President John F. Kennedy issued an executive order stating that government contractors needed to "take *affirmative action* to ensure that applicants are employed, and employees are treated during employment, without regard to race, creed, color, or national origin" (italics mine). U.S. President Lyndon Johnson expanded

the coverage of that order to include organizations receiving federal contracts and subcontracts; he also included sex on the list of attributes. His goal was equality not just as a policy goal but as a policy outcome. At the state level, such affirmative action programs included racial preferences in hiring, promotion, school admissions, scholarships, and financial aid. In time, some individuals complained that they were passed over in favor of less-qualified beneficiaries of affirmative action, what became known as reverse discrimination. For example, in the 1970s, the UC Davis Medical School reserved 16 spaces out of 100 for minority applicants. A white, male applicant, Allan Bakke, filed a lawsuit after UC Davis rejected him twice, even though his MCAT scores and grade point average exceeded those of the special admittees. In 1978, the U.S. Supreme Court ruled that, while the goals of affirmative action were laudable and universities needed diversity, inflexible quotas violated the equal protection clause of the Fourteenth Amendment. Affirmative action minus visible quotas continued at the University of California until 1995.

Proposition 209 sought to ban affirmative action entirely throughout the entire state. Proponents of 209 framed the measure as a way to ban reverse discrimination and uphold the colorblind ideals of the U.S. Constitution. "Vote for fairness … not favoritism!" urged the pro argument in the state voter guide. Opponents framed their arguments around the gains made by women and concluded their page in the voter guide by quoting retired general Colin Powell who declared that 209 "puts at risk every outreach program, sets back the gains made by women and puts the breaks of expanding opportunities for people in need."

In November of 1996, California voters passed 209 with 54 percent of the vote. Again, a series of lawsuits challenged the constitutionality of the measure. In 1997, a three-judge panel of the Ninth Circuit Court of Appeals ruled that 209 did not violate the U.S. Constitution and the U.S. Supreme Court refused to review the case. In 2000, the California Supreme Court upheld Proposition 209 by ruling that the City of San

---

B o x 4.1   A Once Sentence Policy

SECTION 1. This act may be cited as the "California Defense of Marriage Act."

SECTION 2. Section 308.5 is added to the Family Code, to read: *308.5. Only marriage between a man and a woman is valid or recognized in California.*

SOURCE: California Secretary of State.

Jose's minority and women-owned business preferences program violated its provisions.[11]

Propositions 22 and 8: Limits on Same Sex Marriage

The language in Box 4.1 was the actual text of **Proposition 22**, a controversial measure on the March 7, 2000, ballot. Those 14 words galvanized both supporters and opponents of gay rights and gay marriage in California. Although the proposition seemed simple enough, the issue it addressed was quite complex.

In an effort to seek societal recognition and fight discrimination, gay rights activists had demanded that gay marriages be given the same legal footing as heterosexual marriages. If they could achieve that in one state, presumably such marriages would need to be recognized in other states. The U.S. Constitution provides that "Full Faith and Credit shall be given in each State to the public acts, Records, and judicial Proceedings of every other State" (Article IV, Section 1). Concerned about that possibility, Congress passed and U.S. President Bill Clinton signed the *Defense of Marriage Act* in 1996. This law permitted states to not recognize gay marriages performed in other states. By early 2000, 30 states had passed similar laws.

The concerns of the gay community extended beyond the legal recognition of same-gender marriages. They feared that nonrecognition would result in the denial of various rights, including hospital visitations, inheritance, and dependent health insurance.

Prior to Proposition 22, California disallowed the marriage of same-sex couples but customarily recognized as legally valid all marriages occurring outside the state under Article IV. Proposition 22 proponents had become alarmed because Hawaii had come close to recognizing gay marriages and Vermont was on the verge of doing so (it legalized gay marriages in May 2000).

The impetus for Proposition 22 came from California State Senator William "Pete" Knight (R–Palmdale), who had unsuccessfully sought similar limits in the state legislature. For Knight, it was personal—his own son was gay and his gay brother had died of AIDS. Lining up to support the measure were various religious groups: the Mormon Church, the California Catholic Conference of Bishops, the state Republican Party, and the Hispanic Business Roundtable. Opposed were various gay-rights organizations: the American Civil Liberties Union, a number of labor unions, the California Democratic Party, and still other religious leaders. By the end of the campaign, Proposition 22's supporters outspent its opponents by a wide margin—$9.5 million versus $5 million. As usual, much of this money was spent on television advertising.

In the end, Proposition 22 passed with 61 percent of the vote. The only region to oppose it was the Bay Area; they rejected it by a 69–31 percent margin. The statewide margin of support for 22 was even higher than preelection polling would have predicted. Analysts speculated that large numbers of conservatives turned out because of a competitive Republican presidential primary campaign and effective get-out-the-vote efforts by groups such as the Traditional Values Coalition.

Gay-rights advocates were both disheartened and energized. Some thought they should seek to qualify their own pro-gay marriage initiative. Others thought that they should press their agenda in the state legislature. Most observers predicted that the struggle over gay marriage was hardly over. For one thing, Californians had become somewhat more accepting of gay rights in general. Polls suggested that fully 81 percent of Californians opposed discrimination based on sexual orientation and 54 percent thought that homophobia was morally wrong. In addition, it appeared that younger voters were more concerned about discrimination against gays than were older voters.[12] Gay rights activists became newly energized in early 2004 when, contrary to Proposition 22, San Francisco Mayor Gavin Newsome declared that same-sex unions marriages would sanctioned in his city. While his unilateral actions were immediately challenged in California courts, hundreds of gay couples wed in the months following his order.

In the aftermath of those well-publicized weddings, gay marriage opponents vowed to wage another initiative campaign—this time, placing the exact wording of Proposition 22 into the state constitution. They began circulating such a measure in late 2007. Why they believed they needed a constitutional amendment became clear when, in May 2008, the California Supreme Court rendered its own verdict on same-sex unions. In a 4-3 ruling, the Court declared that same-sex couples have the same fundamental "right to marry" as do heterosexual couples. The broadly worded decision appeared to invalidate any law that would discriminate on the basis of sexual orientation. By the time this decision was announced, **Proposition 8** indeed had qualified for the November 2008 ballot.

The fall campaign was vocal, emotional, and costly; campaign spending on both sides surpassed $73 million. The pro side (including a coalition of church groups) argued that the defeat of Proposition 8 would endanger the position of traditional marriage in society and would require schools to teach the acceptance of homosexuality. The con side (including gay rights, progressive-leaning, and still other religious groups) argued that same-sex unions are an important additional step on the road toward civil rights for all Americans. In the end, Proposition 8 passed by a 52.5 to 47.5 percent margin. But, as often occurs, the battle continued in the courts. After the California Supreme Court ruled that Proposition 8 was a valid amendment to the state constitution, opponents of the measure filed suit in federal court. In August 2010, a district court judge ruled that Proposition 8 violated the Due Process and Equal Protection Clauses of the Fourteenth Amendment. "Proposition 8 both unconstitutionally burdens the exercise of a fundamental right to marry and creates an irrational classification on the basis of sexual orientation."[13] The Ninth Circuit Court of Appeals stayed the ruling pending a federal appeal by Proposition 8 proponents. In 2011, the California Supreme Court reentered the fray by agreeing to consider whether Proposition 8's ballot sponsors could defend a state law when state officials refuse to do so.

Propositions 215 and 19: Legalizing Marijuana

A few weeks before California's 1996 general election, Senator Dianne Feinstein expressed concerns over **Proposition 215**, the Compassionate Use Act. This initiative statute proposed to legalize the possession and use of marijuana (cannabis sativa) for medical purposes, including serious illnesses and for relief of pain. Feinstein thought the measure was so badly worded that "you'll be able to drive a truckload of marijuana through the holes in it. While it seems simple, the devil is in the details, or in this particular bill, the lack of details." Unconvinced, voters passed it with nearly 56 percent of the vote. Six years later, Governor Davis signed SB 420, the Medical Marijuana Protection Act, which established an identification card system for medical marijuana patients. Presumably, this would enable such patients to avoid arrest by local police on the lookout for recreational users.[14]

Federal law continued to ban the use of marijuana for any purpose, medical or recreational, and two U.S. Supreme Court cases from California affirmed that position. In *U.S.* v. *Oakland Cannabis Buyer's Group* (2001), the Court agreed that federal Controlled Substances Act does not provide a medical exception because Congress at the time concluded that cannabis has no "currently accepted medical use." In 2005, the Court further ruled in *Gonzales* v. *Raich* that even if persons are cultivating, possessing, or distributing cannabis under state-approved medical marijuana programs, they remain in violation of federal law and subject to federal prosecution.[15] In 2009, U.S. Attorney General Eric Holder announced that the Justice Department would no longer enforce federal marijuana laws against medical users, cultivators, and dispensers in states that permitted medical use.

Proposition 215's goal of providing access to marijuana for medical uses has been highly successful to say the least. It has provided relieve for over 200,000 Californians and has encouraged the creation of cannabis cooperatives and dispensaries. While some physicians refused to prescribe it, others have done so for a wide variety of serious and not so serious disorders. In subsequent years, local officials have had to create their own laws and regulations in response to the roughly 1,000 dispensaries seeking to open around the state.

Given the cost of and frustration over the national war on drugs and public ambivalence about the harmfulness of marijuana, it was only a matter of time before an initiative would seek to decriminalize it altogether. It did so in November 2010 in the form of **Propostion 19**, which would have allowed anyone over 21 years of age to possess, cultivate, or transport marijuana for personal use. While local governments could regulate and tax the distribution of marijuana, the drug would still be illegal on school grounds. Marijuana-impared driving would be prosecutable just as drunk driving always has been. The pro legalization campaign emphasized the failure of the war on drugs, the influence of drug gangs and cartels, the potential to better regulate legalized marijuana, and the tax revenues that legalization would generate. (Cartoon 4.1 takes a poke at this idea). As they argued in the official voter information guide, "There is $14 billion in marijuana sales every year in California, but our debt-ridden state gets nothing from it." The con side argued that, unlike current law regulating alcohol consumption, Proposition 19 provided no standard as to what "driving under the influence" of marijuana really meant. If it passed, no California employer could meet federal drug-free workplace standards or qualify for federal grants. The major candidates for governor, attorney general, and U.S. Senate all opposed it as did Senator

Dan Carino/www.dancarino.com

Cartoon 4.1

Feinstein and outgoing Governor Arnold Schwarzenegger.

Despite opposition by the political establishment, the pro side raised by far the most campaign cash—$2.8 million versus $212,000 by those opposed to the measure. The fundraising advantage by the pro forces seemed to buy public initially. A September 2010 Field Poll found 19 in a slight lead by a 49 to 42 percent margin but it lost support in an October survey, where those numbers were reversed (42 percent in favor and 49 opposed). On election day, it lost by a 54 to 46 percent margin. Despite the result, the "Yes on 19" campaign was heartened by the large number of votes the measure did receive (more than Republican gubernatorial candidate Meg Whitman received), support among younger voters, and its relative strength in the Bay Area. They vowed to return in 2012 to "finish the job." Meanwhile, the medical marijuana industry continues to grow. One Oakland store, WeGrow, specializes in hydroponically grown marijuana and is called the "Walmart of Weed."

THE INITIATIVE MESS

The stories behind the preceding initiatives are typical of many others, and they point to some disturbing trends. Media titles give you a clue: "Initiatives: Too Much of a Good Thing," "Hiram's Folly?" "California Initiatives: Out of Control," "California: The State That Tied Its Own Hands," and "Is Direct Democracy Killing California?" Veteran journalist Peter Schrag believes today's initiative process has caused a "seismic shift in the state's political center of gravity."[16]

What has happened to this ultimate tool of the sovereign voter? To answer this question, one must think in terms of democratic theory and two faulty assumptions stemming from it. Before the initiative was instituted, there was *misplaced confidence in legislators as competent representatives*. In truth, legislators often dodge tough policy choices and favor the views of special interests over those of constituents,

especially when the two conflict. Consider this question: Are legislators primarily trustees using their own best judgment to represent the broad interests of their constituents or delegates following every constituent preference? The classic debate between trustee and delegate functions of legislators usually assumes constituents are voters back home, not the interest groups and lobbyists with whom contemporary legislators have much more contact.[17]

After the initiative process was established in California, there was *misplaced confidence in the voters as competent legislators*. Admittedly, political scientists do not always agree on this point. Years ago, Lester Milbrath did not expect the ordinary voter "to give a lot of attention to, and be active in resolving issues of public policy. Nor should we expect him to stand up and be counted on every issue that comes along."[18] Thomas Cronin takes a more generous view. He suggests that voters approach initiatives cautiously and vote against measures unless they see a direct personal or public benefit. "Voters who do vote on ballot measures do so more responsibly and intelligently than we have any right to expect." He further concluded that bad legislation is just as likely to come from the legislature as from the initiative process.[19] As you examine Table 4.1, a list of the November 2010 propositions, ask yourself how many voters would be as competent as legislators in making those decisions.

Many observers blame the state's initiative mess largely on the ease with which direct democracy can be used. A parade of reforms made this possible. In the 1960s, the same constitution revision commission that recommended professionalizing the state legislature also opened the initiative process to amateur policymakers—the voters—in some profound ways. First, it recommended ending the "indirect initiative," where the legislature could vote on the citizen initiative first. Second, it lowered the signature threshold for initiative statutes from 8 to 5 percent of the votes cast for governor in the most recent gubernatorial election. In doing so, an effort to discourage the proliferation voter-initiated constitutional amendments made signature gathering easier for all statutory initiatives. Following voter approval of these reforms, the legislature

TABLE 4.1   Propositions on the November 2010 Ballot in California

Proposition	Subject	% For	% Against
19	Legalizes marijuana under California but not federal law (initiative statute)	46.5	53.5
20	Empowers the Citizens Redistricting Commission to revise congressional districts (initiative constitutional amendment)	60.7	39.3
21	Establishes $18 vehicle license surcharge to fund state parks (initiative statute)	42.7	57.3
22	Prohibits state from borrowing or taking funds used for transportation, redevelopment, or local government (initiative constitutional amendment)	60.7	39.3
23	Suspends state's recently-enacted global warming law until economy improves (initiative statute)	38.4	61.6
24	Repeals legislation allowing businesses to lower their tax liability (initiative statute)	41.9	58.1
25	Lowers legislative voting requirement to pass a budget from 2/3 to simple majority; retains 2/3 vote to raise taxes (initiative constitutional amendment)	55.1	44.9
26	Requires certain state and local fees to be approved by 2/3 vote (initiative constitutional amendment)	52.5	47.5
27	Eliminates Citizens Redistricting Commission; transfers its duties to the legislature (initiative constitutional amendment and statute)	40.5	59.5

SOURCE: California Secretary of State (www.ss.ca.gov/elections).

liberalized the process further by permitting initiatives to appear on primary election ballots in addition to general election ballots. Consequently, initiatives could be passed with lower voter turnouts typical of primary elections. The legislature also ended the requirement that voters list their exact precinct number on petition forms (Can you name yours?). This saved signature campaigns the precious time it took to verify such data. Also, the California Supreme Court ruled in 1979 that shopping malls were not just private property but also the functional equivalent of town squares. To petition circulators, this decision was the functional equivalent of a welcome mat. In addition, initiative activist Ed Koupal discovered that petition circulators could amass huge numbers of signatures in shorter amounts of time by working in pairs outside stores; one with a clipboard would approach shoppers and other would gather actual signatures at a nearby table. Eighty an hour became commonplace.[20]

These changes in initiative rules and methods moved policymaking well beyond Sacramento and into every California community. Writer Carey McWilliams once called the state capital the "marketplace of California" where competing groups "bid for allotments of state power."[21] Now the initiative process itself has become California's new marketplace where multiple groups employ the initiative to achieve desired policy outcomes. As political scientist Elizabeth R. Gerber observed, citizen groups tend to use direct legislation to bring about policy change whereas economic and business groups tend to use it to block policy change.[22] Furthermore, the Progressive era assumption that initiatives would bypass political parties has proved to be untrue. In fact, California's political parties themselves encourage ballot measures to promote their own policy views, damage opposing parties, and rally voter turnout. Initiative backers also rely on political

---

B o x   4.2   CALIFORNIA VOICES: A Governor on Initiatives

Appearing outside a Burbank COSTCO store to support workers gathering signatures for a workers' compensation measure, Governor Schwarzenegger proclaimed: "I'm a hands on governor. I'm out here with a pen. I'm out here with a paper, saying, sign

here. I'm not one to sit around in Sacramento and do nothing."

SOURCE: Quoted in David M. Drucker and Dana Bartholomew, "Schwarzenegger Stumps for Workers' Comp Reform," *Los Angeles Daily News*, April 12, 2004.

---

parties and their supporters for endorsements and campaign contributions. In particular, Republicans have successfully used the initiative process to enact anti-tax and other conservative measures otherwise unachievable in a legislature controlled by Democrats.[23]

Widespread access to and use of the initiative process has had numerous consequences, some of which have been unintended:

1. *Big money can trump good ideas.* A significant feature of the initiative process today is the increased amount of money spent to affect the outcome. In fact, in recent election cycles, more money has been raised and spent on ballot measures than on state legislative races. For example, in the 2010 election cycle, California's state legislative campaigns raised over $67 million, while ballot measure committees raised over $204 million. In short, Californians spend far more on direct democracy than on representative democracy (www.followthemoney.org/). True, many ballot measures require large financial resources, but this does not mean that business groups invariably have the upper hand. Consumer, environmental, and public interest groups find considerable expenditures well spent if a favored regulation or bond issue is approved. To be sure, not all initiative campaigns require heavy spending, and heavy spending does not always ensure victory. For example, in 2010, proponents of Proposition 16, which would have required a two-thirds popular vote before local governments

could provide electricity service, spent over $46 million (and nearly all of that from PG&E Corporation, one of the largest private utilities in the state). Opponents spent only $136,000 but were victorious nonetheless. Also, some ballot measures never attain the visibility of higher profile measures and candidates. When voters have that little input, they often vote no.

2. *Unelected persons can rival the power of elected policymakers, including governors.* Some Californians have become **initiative entrepreneurs**, known for the measures they have supported or opposed: Howard Jarvis and Paul Gann (property tax cuts), Harvey Rosenfield (auto insurance reform), Mike Reynolds (three-strikes sentencing reform), Ward Connerly (affirmative action), Ron Unz (bilingual education), and Robert Klein (stem cell research). The process itself has spawned something of an initiative industrial complex. Although it takes only $200 to file an initiative with the Secretary of State, gathering a million or more signatures to qualify it for the ballot is no job for amateurs. Major firms such as Kimball Petition Management, Discovery Petition Management, and Arno Political Consulting hire independent subcontractors who in turn employ solicitors to collect signatures. What are they paid? According to Michael Arno, the going rate varies depending on the amount of time available to circulate a measure, the subject matter, time of year, and competition in California and other states. Recent per-signature rates have been $1.65–$2.35 for an initiative statute and $1.85–$3.00 for an

initiative constitutional amendment.[24] Using these firms, it is possible to garner more than 1 million signatures in barely a month. In fact, 90 percent of all initiatives require professional assistance.[25] Signature gathering specialists are joined by the standard assortment of campaign consultants, media buyers, and public relations firms. As John Balzar of the *Los Angeles Times* once observed, "California's biannual orgy of ballot initiatives is tops in the consulting world. … Here is a chance to get rich and do battle over the driving issues of the day—insurance, political reform, transportation—all without the distraction of a candidate."[26]

3. *Television becomes unduly important.* California's television stations do a remarkably poor job of covering the policy process in a representative democracy (see Chapter 6). Complicated, inside-the-capitol issues do not lend themselves to short, visually entertaining stories. Much legislative activity takes place behind closed doors and beyond the cameras. But direct democracy is different. Public opinion surveys suggest that television, in the form of news stories and especially paid political commercials, exerts more influence on initiative elections than any other information source but is the least useful in helping voters decide.[27] With well-funded ballot measures, television ads can saturate the airwaves months before voters receive their official voter information guides in the mail. Even if they were so inclined to do further homework—the 2010 general election official voter information guide ran 117 pages—prolific, often negative ads frame the issue in the minds of voters long before election day.

4. *Elected officials use it too.* Criticized as damaging representative government, the initiative has actually become another tool of representative government. Statewide officeholders—even governors—and legislators alike see it as a new route to public policy and electoral popularity. Policy gridlock in Sacramento has driven some policymakers to bypass their own process.

The initiative serves a variety of motives. Depending on the situation, it can be an opportunity for minority party members to go around majority party leaders; it can also be a policy vehicle for legislative mavericks or outsiders, a platform for higher office, or one more bargaining chip relative to pending legislation. As we discussed, Governor Wilson built at least part of his policy agenda around initiatives dealing with illegal immigration, three strikes, and affirmative action. Schwarzenegger did much the same on a host of issues (see California Voices). Upon assuming office for the second time, Governor Brown in 2011 called for a special election so that voters could approve his budget recommendations. Local officials rarely attempt statewide initiatives but in 2010 a coalition of them sponsored an initiative constitutional amendment that prohibited the state from borrowing or taking funds destined for transportation, redevelopment, or local government projects and services. It won with 61 percent of the vote.

5. *Successful initiatives expand government's workload.* To work at all, many measures require the legislature to fill in the missing details or enact implementing language. For instance, Proposition 20, the coastal protection initiative in 1972, required the appointment, staffing, and funding of a State Coastal Commission and several regional coastal commissions. The state coastal commission remains to this day. Proposition 71 (2004) created a stem cell research institute and Proposition 11 (2008) created a Citizens Redistricting Commission; both these groups required staffing and funding.

6. *Citizen initiatives enhance judicial power.* Students of American government know that courts interpret constitutions and review legislation accordingly. Because initiative statutes are voter-approved legislation, they present similar opportunities. Many are often poorly drafted, vaguely worded, or patently unconstitutional. A lawsuit is so likely that initiative drafters usually insert severability clauses; if the courts

find one section unconstitutional, the balance of the measure survives. In our dual judicial system, initiatives can be challenged in state or federal courts. Where the challenge is filed (court shopping) affects the outcome. California courts are more likely to uphold initiatives than are federal courts. As we noted earlier, the California Supreme Court upheld Proposition 8 that limited marriage only to heterosexual couples only one year after it ruled same sex unions constitutionally protected. The difference? According to the Court, with Proposition 8, the voters had spoken.[28] When courts at either level chose to review initiatives, they may invalidate entire measures or only those provisions they find to be unconstitutional. In recent years, the conservative majority of the U.S. Supreme Court has attempted to defer to the states where possible. It did so, for example, in 2003 when it upheld California's Three Strikes Law, enacted as Proposition 184. In *Ewing v. California*, the Court majority argued that "selecting sentencing rationales is generally a policy choice to be made by state legislatures, not federal courts."[29]

Clearly state and federal courts play important roles in the initiative process. Although they may infuriate initiative zealots, the courts can modify, rewrite, overturn, or uphold challenged initiatives. In effect, they repair faulty provisions or put the brakes on what they consider unconstitutional ones.

PROSPECTS FOR INITIATIVE REFORM

What we have called the initiative mess would be messier still if voters were less selective. The history of initiatives in California suggests that the vast majority of them never qualify for the ballot. Those that make it to the ballot face greater scrutiny than was the case with earlier signature campaigns. As Figure 4.2 indicates, during the decade of the 2000s, over half of all ballot measures failed. The failure rate during the decade's three special elections was substantially higher. Nonetheless, reformers are concerned about the growing reliance on initiatives by citizens and policymakers alike and the problems caused by the troublesome measures that do pass. What then are the odds of reforming the process? Not very good. In the mid-1990s, the California Constitution Revision Commission made three modest recommendations: (1) allow the legislature to rewrite an initiative before it is submitted to the voters; (2) limit initiative constitutional amendments to November elections when voter turnout is higher; and (3) permit the legislature, with the governor's approval, to amend statutory initiatives after they have been in effect for six years. The legislature has not acted on any of these recommendations.

Ordinary Californians appear to be ambivalent regarding the initiative process. Polls suggest they are relatively aware of its shortcomings as described in this chapter. They also admit that many

Number of ballot propositions	96
Number passed	47
Number failed	49
Success rate	49%
Failure rate	51%
Failure rate during special elections (2003, 2005, 2009)	94%

FIGURE 4.2 California Propositions in the 2000s

Question: Why are California voters particularly selective when voting on propositions during special elections?

SOURCE: California Secretary of State.

initiatives are confusingly worded, unnecessarily complicated, and often represent the concerns of special interests, not the state as a whole. Yet a majority of them believe that initiatives result in better decisions than those made by the legislature and the governor. Recent surveys suggest that a growing number of Californians are dissatisfied with how the initiative process is working.[30]

PROGRESSIVE COUSINS: REFERENDUM AND RECALL

In contrast to the initiative, two other Progressive-era reforms, referendum and recall, are much less used. For example, the referendum—sometimes called the veto referendum—gives voters the power to approve or reject legislative statutes. There are two kinds: **petition referenda** and **compulsory referenda**. The petition version is relatively rare but has been used recently. As with legislation, a referendum "yes" vote approves an already enacted law. For example, in 2003, the legislature approved and Governor Davis signed Senate Bill 2 that would have substantially expanded health insurance coverage for about one million California workers. Because the significant costs of this expansion would be borne by large and medium-sized employers, business groups and the California Chamber of Commerce succeeded in placing Proposition 72 on the November 2004 ballot. They succeeded; the measure failed by a slim 50.8 to 49.2 vote. In 2008, voters approved four referenda that attempted to nullify or "veto" four Indian gaming compacts approved by the legislature and Governor Schwarzenegger. These compacts allowed the four tribes in question to add 17,000 slot machines in exchange for paying the state a greater share of slot revenue. Propositions 94, 95, 96, and 97 all passed with over 55 percent of the vote.

The compulsory referendum, where voters must approve a legislative action for it to take effect, is more common. All constitutional amendments initiated by the legislature and all bond issues over $300,000 require voter approval. In recent years, bond issues have appeared on nearly every ballot as legislators seek additional revenue for schools, prisons, and transportation systems without raising taxes.

The mechanics of the referendum are simple enough. Compulsory referenda are placed on the ballot by the legislature. The petition referendum is another matter. Within three months of a law's passage, opponents may gather a requisite number of signatures to place the matter on the next regularly scheduled statewide ballot. Certain categories of legislation are exempt: calls for special elections, tax levies, urgency measures, and spending bills. To be successful, referendum advocates must gather 504,760 valid signatures within 90 days of a bill's enactment (the same number needed for initiative statutes during 2011–2015). But unlike referenda, initiative backers have 150 days to gather the necessary signatures. In short, the rules are stacked against petition referenda.

State Level Recalls

The **recall** allows voters to remove from office state or local elected officials before the end of their terms. California is one of 15 states allowing statewide recall; of 60 attempts, the 2003 recall of Governor Davis was the only successful one. In fact, it was only the second gubernatorial recall in American history (the first was North Dakota's Lynn Frazier in 1921). The hurdles to any statewide recall in California are substantial. To place a recall on the ballot, people must gather signatures equal to 12 percent of the votes cast in the previous election for that office (20 percent in the case of a state legislator). Signatures for a statewide recall must come from at least five counties (to prevent undue influence by megacounties such as Los Angeles).

The Recall of Gray Davis The historic recall of Governor Davis is instructive not only because it happened but also how it happened. Davis's troubles began in his first term (1999–2002) when the economic downturn of the early 2000s left voters feeling anxious, pessimistic, and angry. Furthermore, while blame for the 2001 energy crisis was widely shared (botched deregulation by a previous legislature and governor, speculative practices by Enron and other energy traders, and government inaction), Davis became the most visible culprit. While voters reelected Davis in 2002, they did so with a meager five percent margin against Republican businessman and political neophyte Bill Simon. Lost in the campaign rhetoric and prolific spending was an emerging budget crisis. His January 2003 budget was balanced (as all state budgets must be) with higher taxes, deep spending cuts, plus the usual accounting gimmicks but Californians were unprepared for such budget pain. Davis was rapidly becoming the center of the closest thing to "The Perfect Storm" one finds in politics.

In early 2003, antitax gadfly Ted Costa pushed the idea of recalling Davis for "gross mismanagement of California's finances" and other misdeeds. Secretary of State Kevin Shelley certified Costa's recall petition for circulation, giving him the constitutionally mandated 160 days to collect nearly 900,000 signatures. The drive sputtered for a time when funding ran short. U.S. Representative Darrell Issa, a wealthy car alarm magnate and former U.S. Senate candidate, came to the rescue—pouring roughly $1.7 million into the recall drive. Paid petition gatherers could now blanket the state. The signature drive was wildly successful with 2.1 million signatures in hand by the deadline.

Democratic Lieutenant Governor Cruz Bustamante had little choice but to set a fall election date. So, the question "Shall Gray Davis be recalled (removed) from the office of governor?" would be on an October 7, 2003, special election ballot. As was the custom in lower level recall elections, replacement candidates would appear on the same ballot. Comparatively low entry requirements—65 signatures and a $3,500 filing fee—encouraged 135 candidates to file, including a porn star, a porn publisher, and underemployed actor Gary Coleman. No wonder the British newspaper *The Guardian* called the recall "a circus fit for the fruit

and nut state." But media and public attention quickly narrowed to a handful of candidates and, by election day, the most viable candidates were Bustamante, Republican State Senator Tom McClintock, and movie star Schwarzenegger, who announced his candidacy on Jay Leno's *Tonight Show*. Early polling and media reporting presumed Davis would be recalled and attention quickly transferred to his potential replacements.

The entrance of candidate Schwarzenegger essentially altered the dynamics of this truncated 77-day campaign. The television media in particular covered his campaign to the virtual exclusion of other major candidates. Many aspects of the campaign were framed or reframed around him. Did *he* have the stuff to govern? Would *he* divide moderate and conservative Republicans? Would *he* debate his recall opponents? If so, would *he* measure up? Would *he* accept special interest campaign contributions? Would *he* discuss issues in more detail? The actual recall campaign was smothered in the process.

In the end, over 55 percent of voters chose to recall Davis and over 48 percent chose Schwarzenegger to replace him, an impressive plurality number given the field of other candidates. Support for the recall came from interior California and several coastal counties, including Orange and San Diego. They even constituted a substantial minority in vote-rich Los Angeles County. Recall opponents were concentrated in several northern coastal counties and in the San Francisco Bay Area. Although Schwarzenegger commanded the state's attention in his years as governor, do remember that the election itself was as much or more about recalling Davis as it was about electing Schwarzenegger. Given the confluence of events and the entry of a media-savvy celebrity candidate, the 2003 gubernatorial recall will likely remain a stunning if rare example of how a statewide recall election works.[31]

Other State Level Recalls Only a handful of other state level officials have been recalled in California, including a few legislators. In the mid-1990s, when the Assembly was evenly divided

---

B o x 4.3   Direct Democracy: How California Compares

Only seven states allow all three—direct initiative constitutional amendments, direct initiative statutes, and recall of elected officials. They are Arizona, California, Colorado, Montana, Nevada, North Dakota, and Oregon.

SOURCE: *Book of the States 2010* (Council of State Governments, 2010), 352, 350–372.

---

between Republicans and Democrats, Los Angeles area voters recalled Republican Paul Horcher for agreeing to support Democrat Willie Brown's continuance as speaker. Orange County voters ousted Doris Allen after she cut a deal with Brown in order to become something of a puppet speaker with Brown still brokering power. In one notable case, state senator David Roberti, who was about to be termed out of the legislature and was planning a bid for state treasurer, handily survived a 1994 recall election engineered by gun control opponents, but his $800,000 recall defense campaign drained resources from his state treasurer campaign; in the end, he lost that race. Roberti reflected that because a recall is a single subject special election, it is "designed for single-issue enthusiasts because they can maintain their enthusiasm and adrenaline ceaselessly."[32] In 2008, Republican State Senator Jeff Denham easily won a recall effort by Democrats angered over his budget votes.

Local Level Recalls

Recall is much more common at the local level (as is defeating incumbents at regular elections). A relatively small number of qualifying signatures make it quite feasible indeed. Such recall efforts are often characterized by bitter conflict. What angers local voters enough to recall an official? Most controversies involve unpopular policy decisions, personnel controversies, outrageous behavior, or other local issues. Consider these examples. Two Livingston city council members were recalled because they voted for a multiyear water rate increase. A Mission Viejo mayor was ousted after helping to increase council salaries by 100 percent

and supporting "lifetime" health care benefits for former council members. More than 70 percent of voters in the Big Flat-Oak Unified School District recalled an *entire* school board after they fired a popular high school math teacher. In 2011, the entire city council of Bell, California was recalled amidst a scandal involving exorbitant pay for themselves and several administrators. (See Chapter 10 for more on Bell).

CONCLUSION: THE LEGACY AND THE PARADOX

The legacy of the Progressive era cannot be overemphasized. In fact, it has fostered hyperpluralism. By kicking one group—the Southern Pacific Railroad—out of politics, Californians invited many other groups into politics. Numerous reforms at both the state and local levels were implemented in those early years. We take many of them for granted today, such as nonpartisan local elections and city managers. Some reforms, such as the referendum, have proved to be rather unworkable. Others, such as the local recall, have truly become the safety valve they were meant to be. The initiative gets the most attention and with good reason. Savvy individuals with enough money can qualify almost any pet policy or project for the ballot. But historically, most California initiatives have resulted from interest group activity and, more recently, major policymakers. Progressives defeated one powerful interest group and limited what they considered the negative influence of political parties, as Chapter 6 will attest. Inadvertently, they also strengthened the long-term role of California's interest groups for generations to come.

The process now appears to be a function of hyperpluralism in a technological age. As a result, some have called California a "hybrid democracy."[33] Interest groups participate via initiatives, not just statehouse bills. Truly revolutionary policy can result from this process, but so can policy paralysis. An initiative victory can be whittled away or substantially revised in its implementation. A stunning initiative victory or defeat can actually inhibit further discussion on the policy involved as with Proposition 13. The process has produced more choices and information about them than typical voters can handle. At the same time, it has produced media-centered campaigns that often insult voters' intelligence. Yet, for all its faults and abuses, contemporary Californians resist efforts to tamper with the system they have inherited. Voters may well realize that if they do not understand an issue, in spite of or due to an information blizzard on it, they can simply vote "No."

The initiative process is analogous to true-or-false tests. What voters face at the polls are highly technical issues with uncertain and far-reaching ramifications. Wise policy alternatives come in shades of gray, not black or white. Yet the voters are examined on these complex subjects with up or down decisions. No multiple-choice, fill-ins, or essay questions are allowed. The requirements of direct democracy are such that only the well educated and homework inclined can vote wisely. But a growing number of Californians do not fit that description. As we will see in Chapter 5, all Californians are affected by the state's policies, but a much smaller number actually participate in the system that produces those policies.

KEY TERMS

Progressivism
   (p. 59)
Progressive
   reforms
   (p. 59)

California
   progressivism
   (p. 60)
Propositions 13,
   187, 209, 22, 8,

215 and 19
   (pp. 62–69)
initiative
   entrepreneurs
   (p. 71)

petition and
   compulsory
   referenda (p. 74)
recalls (statewide
   and local)
   (pp. 74–76)

REVIEW QUESTIONS

1. What factors explain the rise of Progressivism nationwide? In California?

2. Who were the Progressives, and what did they achieve in California?

3. Describe and illustrate the initiative, petition referendum, compulsory referendum, and recall.

4. How do the initiative cases described here illustrate the pros and cons of the initiative process?

5. Describe the intended and unintended consequences of the initiative in California.

6. Is the process a mess as some believe?

7. Based on this chapter, are recalls a good idea? Why or why not?

8. What larger issues of California politics does direct democracy illustrate?

WEB ACTIVITIES

Initiative and Referendum Institute
(www.iandrinstitute.org)
As you will see from this site, California is not alone or unique in allowing voters to legislate.

California Secretary of State
(www.sos.ca.gov/)
Go to the elections area for progress reports on initiatives currently in circulation. If you want to circulate your own, complete how-to instructions are available.

National Institute on Money in State Politics
(www.followthemoney.org)
Click the national overview map, then California, for a plethora of campaign data including spending by and contributions to ballot measure committees.

Ballotpedia
(www.ballotpedia.org)
This community-contributed Web site, modeled after Wikipedia, contains volumes of information about initiatives, referenda, and recalls in California and elsewhere.

NOTES

1. Richard Hofstadter, *The Age of Reform: From Bryan to F.D.R.* (New York: Alfred A. Knopf New York, 1955), p. 131.

2. James Weinstein, *The Corporate Ideal in the Liberal State: 1900–1918* (Boston: Beacon Press, 1968), p. 3.

3. George E. Mowry, *The California Progressives* (Berkely, CA: University of California Press, 1951), p. 101.

4. Spencer C. Olin Jr., *California's Prodigal Sons: Hiram Johnson and the Progressives, 1911–1917* (University of California Press, 1968), Chap. 3.

5. Mowry, *The California Progressives*, pp. 87–88.

6. Ibid., 97.

7. Ibid, p. 102.

8. Quoted in Olin, *California's Prodigal Sons*, p. 26.

9. For a historical treatment of direct democracy in California, see John M. Allswang, *The Initiative and Referendum in California, 1898–1998* (Stanford: Stanford University Press, 2000).

10. For further analysis, see Andrew Wroe, *The Republican Party and Immigration: From Proposition 187 to George W. Bush* (New York: Palgrave Macmillan, 2008).

11. *Hi-Voltage Wire Works, Inc.* v. *City of San Jose* 24 Cal.4th 537 (2000).

12. Jennifer Warren, "Gays Gaining Acceptance, Poll Finds," *Los Angeles Times*, June 14, 2000.

13. *Perry* v *Schwarzenegger*, 704 F. Supp., 2d 921 (2010).

14. Scott Imler and Stephen Gutwillig, "Medical Marijuana in California: A History," *Los Angeles Times* (March 6, 2009).

15. *U.S.* v. *Oakland Cannabis Buyer's Cooperative*, 532 U.S. 483 (2001) and *Gonzales* v. *Raich*, 545 U.S. 1 (2005).

16. Peter Schrag, *Paradise Lost: California's Experience, America's Future* (New York: New Press, 1998), p. 189.

17. Political scientists regard legislators as *trustees* if they are primarily guided by personal conscience and as *delegates* if they are primarily guided by the wishes of the constituents who elect them.

18. Lester Milbrath, *Political Participation* (Chicago: Rand McNally, 1965), pp. 144–145.

19. Thomas E. Cronin, *Direct Democracy: The Politics of Initiative, Referendum and Recall* (Cambridge, MA: Harvard University Press, 1989), pp. 84–89, 210.

20. Joe Mathews and Mark Paul, *California Crackup: How Reform Broke the Golden State and How We Can Fix It* (Berkeley: University of California Press, 2010), pp. 30–34.

21. Carey McWilliams, *California: The Great Exception* (New York: Current Books, 1949), p. 213.

22. Elizabeth R. Gerber, *The Populist Paradox: Interest Group Influence and the Promise of Direct Legislation* (Princeton, NJ: Princeton University Press, 1999).

23. Daniel Smith and Caroline Tolbert, "The Initiative to Party: Partisanship and Ballot Initiatives in California," *Party Politics* 7 (2001), pp. 739–757.

24. Arno, Michael, Email communication, July 20, 2008.

25. John Marelius, "Petition Hawkers a Breed Apart," *San Diego Union*, April 16, 2005.

26. John Balzar, "Consultants: A Political Gold Rush in California," *Los Angeles Times*, June 12, 1989.

27. Mark Baldassare, *A California State of Mind: The Conflicted Voter in a Changing World* (Berkeley: University of California Press, 2002), pp. 212–219.

28. *Strauss* v. *Horton*, 46 Cal. 4th 364 (2009).

29. *Ewing* v. *California* 538 U.S. 11 (2003).

30. *PPIC Statewide Survey: Californians and Their Government* (San Francisco: Public Policy Institute of California, October, 2010)

31. For more on the Davis recall, see Larry N. Gerston and Terry Christensen, *Recall: California's Political Earthquake* (Armonk, New York: M.E. Sharpe, 2004) and David G. Lawrence, *The California Governor Recall Election* (Belmont, CA: Wadsworth, 2004).

32. Quoted in Laureen Lazarovici, "The Politics of Recall," *California Journal* 26 (July 1995), p. 21.

33. Mark Baldasarre and Cheryl Katz, *The Coming of Direct Democracy: California's Recall and Beyond* (Lanham, MD: Rowman and Littlefield, 2007).

5

✳

How Californians Participate

Forms of Participation in a Democracy

*Civic Engagement and
Conventional Participation*

The Exit Option

The Protest Option

The Role of Public Opinion

What is Public Opinion?

California's Major Pollsters

How They Measure Public Opinion

Voters and Nonvoters in California

Who Votes in California?

Those Who Cannot Vote

Those Who Will Not Vote

Personal Factors

Elections and Campaigns in California

California's Elections

*California's Campaign
Professionals*

The Role of Money

The Role of National Politics

California's Electoral Gaps

Conclusion: Divided by Diversity

Key Terms

Review Questions

Web Activities

Notes

IN BRIEF

Despite the image of a politically-involved citizenry, Californians' political behavior generally mirrors that of other Americans. Political scientists have categorized the political participation levels of Americans and Californians along a range from uninvolvement to voting and active campaigning. This chapter surveys the diversity of conventional forms of participation and two nonconventional ones—exiting the political system altogether and political protest. All of these forms are commonplace in California.

Short of formal political participation, Californians hold various opinions on politics and public policy—opinions that can sway policymakers. Pollsters survey and monitor those opinions using both scientific and unscientific methods. The traits of California voters are discussed, as are the reasons some Californians cannot vote and why qualified voters choose not to vote. Traditionally, Americans have identified with the major political parties, but they do so with greater diversity of motives than once thought. In California, these party identification patterns vary from region to region. Differences emerge between Northern and Southern California and between coastal and inland California. Emerging patterns of political behavior statewide suggest gaps among different groups of Californian voters and nonvoters—a sign of growing hyperpluralism in the state. Voters express themselves in numerous elections including presidential primary, state primary, general, and special elections. Aiding both voters and candidates are a plethora of campaign professionals and various state laws governing the conduct of those elections.

In that context, a steady parade of candidates and policy issues vie for the attention of Californians. Yet despite the political demands placed on them, Californians are much like other Americans in their political activity. Only a few are very involved, a larger number vote, and still others choose not to participate in any meaningful way. Specific groups of Californians differ from each other in their political behavior. Generalizing about voting behavior is a challenge. Voting is an individual, private act, and it is also a continuous activity. Electoral attitudes and behavior change and the motivations of voters and nonvoters are mixed. Also, voting is only one political behavior among many to measure and analyze. First, we consider the larger idea of political participation.

FORMS OF PARTICIPATION IN A DEMOCRACY

How ordinary citizens participate in a representative democracy has always intrigued political scientists. In recent years, they have identified and categorized the political activities of Americans. **Political participation** consists of individual or group activity intended to exercise influence in the political system. Methods used to exercise such influence are either conventional or nonconventional in nature, that is, inside or outside the norms considered acceptable by the larger society. We will explore briefly these channels of influence.

Civic Engagement and Conventional Participation

Political scientists have identified a wide range of civic activities engaged in by Americans. Voting is the most widely shared political activity with 71 percent reporting doing it regularly, followed by joining a political organization (48 percent), contacting political officials (34 percent), attending political meetings (29 percent), and making political contributions (24 percent).[1] Yet political participation is only one measure of community life. Many people participate in voluntary associations that political scientists call "civil societies." These include service organizations (Rotary, Lions, Soroptimists), youth clubs (Boys and Girls Clubs, Girls Inc.), and churches, mosques, or synagogues. Many parents are deeply involved in their children's schooling and sports activities. Yet there is growing evidence that many Americans are becoming less engaged with civic life. They may do charity work, but remain largely uninvolved in national, state, local, or neighborhood issues.[2]

These types of political and social behavior do not tell the whole story below the national level. In California, sizable differences in civic engagement and political participation are related to race,

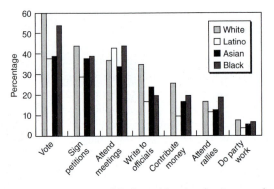

FIGURE 5.1 Political Participation by Race and Ethnicity

Question: What factors might explain the differences in the above graph?

ethnicity, language use, and in the case of immigrants, how long they have lived in California. Those Californians who are most active in civic life tend to be white, older, more affluent, more educated homeowners. As Figure 5.1 indicates, they not only vote more frequently than other groups, but they also participate in other political activities at higher levels, such as signing petitions, writing officials, and contributing money. Not surprisingly, the more intensive the activity, the less participation one finds among all groups. To some observers, these are troublesome findings. It appears that low-income and minority communities are less likely to be heard in the halls of government or in the prolific use of policymaking by way of initiatives.[3]

The Exit Option

Thus far, we have emphasized voting and other forms of civic participation. But what about those Californians who move from one community to another due to policy dissatisfaction? Those concerns may relate to traffic congestion, gang violence, school issues, or various quality of life issues. Arguably, this opting-out behavior also is a form of political participation, what we call the **exit option**.[4] For example, this form of participation applies to urban Californians who are fed up with crime, smog, and congestion. Given the chance,

some may move to interior California or points north or east—anywhere that is more affordable (equity refugees); or they pull their children out of ethnically diverse public schools and send them to less diverse, private ones (ethnic refugees). Some parents seek out charter schools, public schools that operate independent of local school boards and are designed to provide alternative educational experiences. Or they may homeschool their children—the ultimate educational exit option. In recent years, some California families have fled the state due to recession-induced job losses or housing foreclosures. Some California corporations have relocated or at least threatened leave, alleging that state policies are anti-business and corporate taxes are too high.

How people and businesses respond to political dissatisfaction depends on how invested they are in their communities. Those who are relatively satisfied with a local political system behave constructively—they speak up or express system loyalty in other ways, such as voting. Their level of investment in the community (home ownership, a job, or children in school) makes a difference. Low investors more easily opt for political neglect (such as not voting), exiting the system, or even protest or violence. Also, the availability of viable alternatives to the status quo determines what dissatisfied people do. For instance, for people to exit an unsatisfactory public school, feasible alternatives need to be either nearby (a neighboring jurisdiction) or affordable (alternative schools).

The Protest Option

Extreme levels of community dissatisfaction may result in the use of protest activities—the **protest option**. Sporadic political protest, both violent and nonviolent, has always been a part of America's political heritage. Historically, California has had its fair share. Most of the well-publicized incidents of protest and violence in California have been ethnic in nature. Consider the anti-Chinese demonstrations in San Francisco inspired by the Workingman's Party (1877); union strikes and the union-inspired bombing of the *Los Angeles Times* building (early 1900s); the "zoot suit" riots in

Los Angeles (1943); free speech and Vietnam War protests on university campuses (1960s); the Watts riot in Los Angeles following a controversial police arrest (1965); the 1992 Los Angeles riot following the acquittal of four Los Angeles police officers accused of beating motorist Rodney King; and a crowd of Oakland residents protesting the sentence of former mass transit officer who fatally shot and killed an unarmed citizen during an argument. Some protesters simply march through city streets to vent frustration as did immigrants protesting immigration reform or gay rights groups opposed to the passage of Proposition 8.

As forms of political behavior, political protest and violence are difficult to study. Developing a direct cause-and-effect relationship between arson or looting and some conscious political message can be rather speculative. To be sure, protest is a form of political behavior used by groups who lack more conventional resources. These groups, though, might not be able to articulate clearly or even accurately their motives. One study of the Watts riots in the 1960s found that rioters were not only expressing anti-white hostility but also anger over their own status in the larger society.[5] In many instances though, mob behavior lacks any civic purpose—it is simply mob behavior. Vandalism after a sporting event comes to mind. It is fair to say that the connection between protest and violence is tenuous, albeit related. *Not all protest is violent, and not all violence is protest.*

Immigration Protests
In 2006, roughly 500,000 Californians—citizens or not—take to the streets of Los Angeles to protest proposed immigration reforms considered by Congress.

THE ROLE OF PUBLIC OPINION

In a representative democracy, the opinions of the people matter—or at least they should. Strongly-held opinions lead to political action, and even weakly held opinions affect how people vote and relate to each other. As with the nation, the diverse opinions held by Californians contribute to the politics of diversity. On some issues, the state's political leaders have little or no direction from the public. On others, the views of the public are so conflicted; taking any position is bound to alienate some people. Holding an opinion may not qualify as political participation in an active sense. But it does provide the motivation for more active forms of participation such as voting, campaigning, demonstrating, joining a political party, and working through interest groups.

What is Public Opinion?

Public opinion consists of the collective beliefs, attitudes and values held by the citizenry. Relative to California, political scientists consider public opinion to be what Californians think about politics, public policy, and those aspects of life that affect politics and policy—"those opinions that governments find it prudent to heed."[6] At any given time, state and local officials believe they know what the public is thinking on a host of issues both large and small. Those officials may choose to ignore public opinion, follow it, or simply take it under advisement, but they do pay attention. In a representative democracy, they cannot afford not to. In California's hybrid democracy, where voters use the initiative process to make public policy, their opinions can take shape as policy decisions, not just policy perceptions.

California's Major Pollsters

Given California's size, polling organizations find it worthwhile to survey its citizens. Two of the state's major polling organizations are the Field Poll and the Public Policy Institute of California. The Field Poll is an independent political and public policy poll operated by the Field Research Corporation, a San Francisco-based national consumer marketing and public opinion research firm. Established in 1947 by Mervin Field to chart opinion trends in California, it is often quoted by national and state media organizations. The Public Policy Institute of California is an endowment-funded public policy think tank also headquartered in San Francisco. Its frequent statewide surveys provide policymakers, the media, and California residents with objective information on the opinions, perceptions, and policy preferences of the state's residents. Both of these polling organizations repeat similar questions over time having to do with the general mood of Californians. For example, "Is California moving in the right direction?" is a polling question repeated from year to year as we saw in Chapter 1. Whether the public mood is optimistic or pessimistic over the long term affects the ability of policymakers to make decisions requiring public support.

How They Measure Public Opinion

Finding out what Californians think is no easy task but polling is an attempt to do just that. There are two types of polls: straw polls and scientific polls. **Straw polls** are educated guesses as to what the public in general or a particular group of people is thinking. Various media organizations conduct such polls (person on the street interviews or Web site-based surveys) in order to gauge public support for or opposition to a particular policy. State political party conventions may conduct straw polls among the attendees to measure support for particular gubernatorial candidates or even presidential candidates. Some straw polls are done with focus groups. These relatively small gatherings of people may be questioned in order to construct a larger opinion survey or to obtain feedback on political commercials.

In contrast, **scientific polls** use a number of techniques to increase the likelihood that their results more nearly reflect the actual views of the larger population. *First*, scientific polls survey relatively large numbers of people. The larger polling organizations in California may sample 1,400-2,400 adults, substantially more than a straw poll would. *Second*, these polls do random sampling in order to give every potential respondent the same chance of being chosen. They may select key precincts, control for various ethnic groups, or randomly survey every tenth or hundredth household. In order to predict election outcomes, pollsters seek out those most likely to vote, not just those registered to vote. They may also employ computer-aided random-digit-dialing to include those with unlisted numbers or cell phones. *Third*, scientific polling also seeks to reduce or least admit to sampling error—the fact that a sample cannot accurately mirror the views of an entire population as if it had been polled. For example, one survey found that 51 percent of likely voters were willing to pay higher taxes to support higher education but that the margin of error for that group was 4.2 percent. This meant that the true result would be within 4.2 points of what would be the case if all likely voters were surveyed.[7] *Fourth*, pollsters try to ask the right questions. Wittingly or unwittingly, bias can creep into surveys so scientific surveys attempt to avoid wording that directs respondents to specific answers. Also, simple agree/disagree or approve/disapprove

	Approve strongly	Approve somewhat	Disapprove somewhat	Disapprove strongly
Total registered voters	37%	12	11	34
Democrats	22	11	13	49
Republicans	64	13	8	9
Non-partisans/others	32	14	12	37

F I G U R E 5.2 California's Views on Arizona's Illegal Immigration Law

SOURCE: Mark DiCamillo and Mervin Field, "California Voters Split Almost Evenly About Arizona's New Illegal Immigration Law," *The Field Poll, Release #2348* (San Francisco: Field Research Corporation, July 16, 2010), p. 3. (Accessed at www.field.com/fieldpollonline/).

answers rarely ascertain the intensity of opinion so pollsters often add "strongly agree" or "strongly disagree" to answer options. In Figure 5.2, notice how providing four answer options rather than two revealed how intensely partisan Californians viewed Arizona's 2010 immigration law.

The Field Poll questioned registered voters in California about Arizona's law giving police the right to question anyone who they think may be in the country illegally and ask them to produce documents to verify their legal status. Note the intensity differences between Democrats and Republicans.

VOTERS AND NONVOTERS IN CALIFORNIA

Of all the forms of political participation and expression, suffrage—the right to vote—is considered sacred. To better understand this central tenet of American democracy, political scientists examine voters (those who show up at the polls on Election Day or vote absentee), nonvoters (those who cannot or will not vote), and the electoral system in which voting takes place. The process before election day is analogous to a funnel that continually narrows the number of people until actual voters appear. Those who are eligible are considered to be the **voting age population** (VAP) or the electorate. For instance, in the 2010 gubernatorial election, California's voting age population numbered more than 23 million

people, and over 74 percent of those registered to vote. The next level down the funnel is number of officially registered voters for any particular election. The narrowest portion connotes **voter turnout**— those registered voters who actually vote in any particular election, whether in person or by mail. In the 2010 state general election, about 73 percent of those Californians registered to vote actually did so. This figure is less impressive if you consider the fact that only 52 percent of those eligible to vote actually did so.

Who Votes in California?

Political scientists want to know not only how many people vote but also who votes and what those voters are like. The Public Policy Institute of California surveys likely voters and infrequent voters on a regular basis. What characterizes the state's likely voters? Closely examine Figure 5.3, which provides data from a series of statewide polls. Some highlights include the following: Men and women are nearly equal in numbers. The largest age group is 55 and older. White voters constitute 6 percent of likely voters, a significantly larger percentage than their portion of the overall population. A majority of likely voters are college graduates. Democrats outnumber Republicans but self-described conservatives slightly outnumber liberals. Moderates or middle-of-the-roaders constitute 29 percent of California likely voters. About 42 percent of them have household incomes over

Gender			Ideology		
49 %	Male		31 %	Liberal	
51 %	Female		29 %	Middle of the road	
			40 %	Conservative	

Age			Own/Rent		
19 %	18–34		74 %	Own	
40 %	35–54		26 %	Rent	
41 %	55 and older				

Race/Ethnicity			Annual Family Income		
66 %	White		26 %	Under $40,000	
7 %	Black		32 %	$40,000 to under $80,000	
18 %	Latino		42 %	$80,000 or more	
6 %	Asian				
3 %	Others				

Education			Region		
17 %	No college		25 %	Los Angeles	
31 %	Some college		22 %	SF Bay Area	
52 %	College graduate		17 %	Central Valley	
			18 %	Orange/San Diego	
			9 %	Inland Empire	
			9 %	Other	

Party Registration		
44 %	Democrat	
18 %	Independent	
35 %	Republican	
3 %	Other	

FIGURE 5.3 California's Likely Voters: A Snapshot

These figures represent the combined results of eight PPIC Surveys conducted between September 2009 and July 2010. Over 17,000 people were questioned including likely voters, infrequent voters, and unregistered adults.

SOURCE: Public Policy Institute of California, *Just the Facts: California's Likely Voters* (San Francisco: Public Policy Institute of California, September 2010).

$80,000 and the vast majority are homeowners. An impressive 52 percent reside in Southern California, including Los Angeles County. We will discuss the contrast between likely voters and California's population shortly.

Those Who Cannot Vote

The health of representative democracy depends on voting. Yet California and other states have experienced rather high levels of nonparticipation, especially at the ballot box. Nonparticipation takes two forms: **structural nonvoting** (those disenfranchised by the rules) and **preferential nonvoting** (those disenfranchised by their own behavior and attitudes). We will explore both forms.

In our federal system, states administer all elections. "Universal suffrage" does not mean all people get to vote. In fact, states often establish barriers to voting, and California is no exception. As we noted, only 23.5 of 38 million Californians were legally eligible to vote in 2010. The other nearly 5 million included people in the following categories:

- Those under 18 years of age

- Noncitizens (documented and undocumented)

- Those who have moved to or within California within 15 days of an election

- Current prisoners and parolees (former prisoners regain their voting rights; those serving jail time for misdemeanor convictions may vote, by absentee ballot, of course!)

- The mentally incompetent (as determined by a court)

Surmounting these barriers is not enough. Individuals must formally register to vote by filing a brief registration form with the appropriate county office (usually a registrar of voters or the county clerk's office). During spurts of activity before big elections, these forms are available at shopping centers, in public buildings, and on street corners. Originally designed to inhibit voter fraud, registration requirements effectively inhibit many Californians from voting. Because one must reregister after every move, highly mobile groups (such as agricultural employees, some construction workers, and college students) find they are unregistered on Election Day. Recent surveys suggest that many unregistered Californians are relatively young Latino males and many of them are not U.S. citizens. Of those who are, many pay little or no attention to politics or political news.[8]

That said, registering to vote is getting somewhat easier. The 1993 National Voter Registration Act (called the motor voter law) required states to lower registration hurdles, for instance, by allowing people to register at motor vehicle or welfare offices. In fact, California DMV forms have voter registration forms attached to them. While millions of Californians have registered or reregistered under the law's provisions, some observers believe it has largely benefited those inclined to register anyway. In recent election cycles, Californians have been able to download user-friendly registration forms at the Secretary of State's Web site. In November 2002, voters rejected Proposition 52, a proposal to allow Californians to register on Election Day at their neighborhood polling places (as is done in several states and in Western Europe).

Those Who Will Not Vote

When political scientists, media pundits, and election officials bemoan low voter turnout, particularly in state and local elections, they refer to either eligible voters or registered voters who choose not to vote—**preferential nonvoters**. Why do otherwise qualified voters choose not to vote? The reasons can be divided into personal factors and structural factors.

Personal Factors

For many Californians, voting is a daunting task and not worth the trouble. In a 2005 study of infrequent voters and nonvoters, the major barriers to voting reflected both political alienation and personal factors. This is what they said:

1. Politics are controlled by special interests (66 percent of infrequent voters and 69 percent of nonvoters agreed).

2. "I don't feel that candidates really speak to me" (49 percent and 55 percent, respectively, agreed).

3. "It is hard to sift through all the information available to make good decisions on how to vote" (45 and 52 percent, respectively, agreed).

4. I am too busy with work and family" (43 and 46 percent, respectively, agreed).

5. "The issues are too confusing" (42 and 48 percent, respectively, agreed).[9]

Indeed, going to the polls on Election Day is only the temporary end of a long, information-laden campaign—replete with official voter pamphlets, constant television commercials, political "junk mail," door hangers, and precinct walkers. Many elections, especially those with multiple propositions, create information overload for average voters. For some, the cost of voting (including the homework involved) is not worth the trouble, especially if the benefit is not clear. Even those who turn out may not vote on every ballot item, a phenomenon called undervoting. For example, in 2008, nearly 1 million voters who voted for president declined to vote for Proposition 11, the landmark measure that radically altered how reapportionment works in California.

Another way Californians themselves make it easier to vote is to become absentee voters. The only expense is a first-class stamp. Growing numbers are doing so for every election by registering as "permanent mail ballot registrants." For the 2010 general election, nearly half of all voters did so by mail. As we shall see, this has affected how campaigns are waged.

The personal factor of age also affects voter turnout. Voter registration rates increase dramatically with age from 56 percent of 18–25-year-olds to 92 percent of those over 65. This is reflected in numbers of likely voters. Only 24 percent of adults aged 18–24 are considered likely voters; that percentage jumps to 78 percent of those over 65. While younger adults express little interest in politics compared to their older counterparts, basic demographics are at work here as well. Many younger Californians are also members of low propensity voter groups as well, such as Latinos.[10]

Structural Factors   The way the election system is structured also affects voting frequency. Primary elections, general elections, special elections, off-year elections, advisory elections—if it is Tuesday it must be Election Day, or so it seems. In 2008, Californians faced three statewide elections: the February presidential primary, the June state primary, and the November general election. Accordingly, many Californians pick and choose elections in which to vote. In general, they view higher-level elections to be more important than lower-level ones. Voter turnout drops successively from presidential to state to local elections. General elections witness higher turnouts than primary elections and presidential primaries are higher than primaries involving state offices (see Figure 5.4). With the presidential primary removed, the June 2008 state primary recorded the lowest turnout of registered voters ever—28.2 percent. Turnout in separate local elections normally hovers around 30 percent but can go lower. One study showed that where local government elections coincided with presidential elections, those elections experienced 36 percent more turnout than off-cycle, local-only elections.[11]

Other factors also affect voting numbers. Turnout drops in state legislative races where incumbents run unopposed. Special elections (to fill a legislative vacancy, for instance) attract minimal voter interest. When Californians have a chance to vote directly on well-publicized, easy-to-understand issues (initiatives and referenda), voter interest and motivation to turn out appears to increase. For example, the 2003 gubernatorial

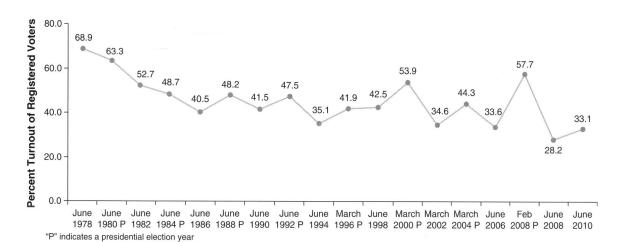

FIGURE 5.4 State Primary Turnout 1978–2010

SOURCE: California Secretary of State.

recall election combined voter anger (at incumbent Gray Davis), a celebrity replacement candidate (Arnold Schwarzenegger), and extraordinary media coverage, which resulted in a 61 percent voter turnout—on par with regularly scheduled gubernatorial general elections.

Political scientists also believe that voter turnout tends to increase where candidate races are reasonably competitive and either side has a chance to win. But voter turnout research in California's minority-majority congressional districts—where various minority groups constitute a majority of the voting population—alters somewhat this generalization. When Latinos or blacks are voting majorities, their respective turnouts increase significantly compared to their turnouts in Anglo-majority districts. Turnout among Latinos was particularly high in Latino-majority districts with Latino Congress members.[12]

Partisan Factors   Political scientists also know that voter turnout varies by political party. The conventional wisdom suggests that Republicans have somewhat higher turnouts than Democrats but that seems to depend on the election. In the 2008 presidential election, Democratic turnout generally mirrored their registration percentages. When these turnout gaps occur, the tend to benefit Republicans in

low-turnout elections. When party registrations are about even, major party candidates must appeal to California's independent voters who comprise a growing portion of the state's likely voters.

Regional Factors   All these general explanations apply to California as a whole but not to all parts of the state. Dramatic differences exist between the state's 58 counties. For the 2008 presidential election (when relatively high turnout would be expected), the highest turnout was in Marin County at 91 percent; the lowest was Merced County at 67 percent. Of those simply eligible to vote, Marin County again experienced the highest turnout at 78 percent; Kings County had the lowest at 46 percent. Why these inter-county differences? One explanation is that counties with high numbers of Latinos, immigrants, and other low-propensity voters tend to experience lower turnouts than those with lower concentrations of such groups.

What are the long-term trends in California? Even though presidential elections generate a great deal of voter interest and ultimately increased turnout, the long-term trend in state elections has been declining turnout. The 2008 contrast between a record low turnout in the June state primary and the near record high turnout in the November presidential election makes the point in stunning fashion.

Cartoon 5.1 The Election Was Yesterday

Question: How many California voters actually do the election homework portrayed in this cartoon? Eric G. Lewis.

ELECTIONS AND CAMPAIGNS IN CALIFORNIA

H. G. Wells once said "Democracy's ceremonial, its feast, its great function is the election." And so it is in California. Elections link average citizens to their government in profound ways. Public officials are to be held accountable periodically for what they do and say. Elections are important to policymakers, too, because they provide some measure of government legitimacy. In other words, voters grant officials they choose credibility and authority to act on their behalf. Policymakers occasionally misinterpret their election victories as mandates to do something in particular, especially if they win by wide margins. Aware of the complex factors that determine election outcomes, political scientists tend to discount the mandates so often claimed by election winners.

California's Elections

Californians are peppered with elections. Partisan elections for federal and state offices are scheduled in even-numbered years. State **primary elections** are where voters choose party nominees to run for Congress, the state legislature, and statewide offices. Primary ballots also include judicial candidates, some local offices, and ballot propositions (initiatives and referenda). In California, primaries occur on the Tuesday after the first Monday in June of even-numbered years. Thanks to Proposition 14 passed in June 2010, partisan candidates in 2012 on will run on a single ballot list and the two top vote getters regardless of party will face off in the general election. These **general elections** occur on the Tuesday after the first Monday in November. In some nonpartisan races where candidates did not receive the required simple majority of the vote to win in June (e.g. county supervisors), the general election serves as a run-off election between the top two candidates. Again, propositions may appear on general election ballots if they did not qualify in time for the June primary. Occasionally, the governor and legislature may call statewide **special elections** to consider certain propositions. The October 2003 recall of Governor Davis was a special election that also included two initiatives unrelated to the recall because they qualified for that statewide election. Local governments (cities, counties, special districts, and school districts) may schedule elections for June, November, or other times of their own choosing.

Presidential primaries where many delegates are chosen to attend national party nominating conventions occur every four even-numbered years and are a special case in California. After experimenting with early primaries in order to increase California's clout, (early March in 2000 and 2004; early February in 2008), the legislature in 2011 merged the 2012 presidential primary with the June 2012 state primary as a cost-saving measure.

Given the frequency of California elections, the prolific use of citizen initiatives, and the sheer size of the state, even willing, able, and qualified voters find the "great feast" difficult to manage. Election campaigns and the people who work in them link candidates and ballot measure activists to the voters whose support they seek.

California's Campaign Professionals

Campaigning for many offices in California is so challenging and arduous, candidates and ballot measure committees rely on political consultants to provide advice and actually run campaigns. California's first political consultants were Clem Whitaker and his wife, Leona Baxter, who established Whitaker and Baxter in the early 1930s. These two conservatives had close ties to the state's 700 newspaper publishers, and they helped defeat Upton Sinclair's bid for governor in 1934. One observer believes this particular campaign gave birth to the modern media-centered, professionally-managed campaign.[13] Contemporary California is home to all manner of campaign professionals—large and small, liberal and conservative, general and specialized. These people call California the "Golden State" for the campaign gold that can be mined there. For example, the firm of Winner and Mandabach Campaigns managed the four Indian gaming initiatives on the February 2008 ballot and, based on expenditures of roughly $74 million, likely earned over $11 million in fees.[14]

To run a candidate or proposition campaign in California requires a variety of consultants:

campaign managers, fundraisers, media experts, lawyers, accountants, and technology specialists. General campaign managers range from solo practitioners (found in smaller communities) to large firms located in Sacramento, San Francisco, or Los Angeles. They advise candidates on all aspects of campaigning, coordinate the use of specialists, and control the technology used in the campaign. Given the cost of campaigning in California, public relations firms adept at fund-raising are a must. They do direct mail or stage expensive dinners featuring "drawing card" celebrities, such as movie stars or recording artists.

Media specialists divide California into media markets, not electoral districts. Because politicians or would-be politicians do not think in those terms, media consultants are essential. They work with candidates and initiative campaigns to produce newspaper advertisements and broadcast commercials. All these media are tailored to specific markets and audiences. Because San Francisco voters are different from San Bernardino voters, appeals are customized based on geographic, demographic, and ideological differences. Candidates use television ads, not only to hype their own qualifications, but also to criticize opponents. Some are simple "comparison" ads; others are full-blown attack ads featuring ominous, insinuating voice-overs and unflattering photos. Today, upwards of half of California voters vote by mail, often weeks before Election Day. As a result, campaigns have been forced to spend earlier than was once the case; a last minute ad blitz might be too little, too late.[15]

Lawyers, accountants, and computer experts are also essential. California's campaign finance regulations, a direct consequence of the Watergate scandal in the 1970s, affect campaigns from the governor to sanitary district board member. State regulations require candidates to report campaign spending and to disclose personal income, which in turn requires legal analysis and careful bookkeeping, especially in the larger races. Increasingly, computer software allows campaigns of any size to manage the overall effort; maintain lists of voters, volunteers, and donors; generate correspondence; and compile reports required by California's Fair

Political Practices Commission. Webmasters are now essential to create and maintain campaign-based Web sites.

As we saw in Chapter 4, California's campaign professionals work to pass or defeat various initiatives. In these issue campaigns, consultants work closely with coalitions of like-minded interests (business, labor). This trend is understandable. In an era of term-limited state legislators, permanent interest groups believe elections are an increasingly important way to get their issues out before the public. From a consultant's point of view, issue campaigns are more lucrative; there are no spending limits on the "independent expenditure committees" that fund such efforts. Furthermore, issue campaigns are more impersonal; consultants avoid the headaches of candidate emotions and family pressures. As communications consultant Steve Hopcraft once observed, "Groups don't have a spouse."[16]

Polling specialists ask voters what they think about issues and candidates. Candidates may rely on instinct, letters to the editor, personal mail, or the statewide pollsters we described earlier. However, the most helpful polls are commissioned by particular campaigns. For example, benchmark polls taken before a campaign begins tell a candidate what issues are important, plus what the voters think of the candidate. Tracking polls, taken during the course of the campaign, reveal how the campaign is progressing and whether or not particular strategies are working. Focus groups test the reactions of a relative handful of voters to commercials and other political stimuli. All these techniques help pollsters measure the intensity of voter feelings and the impact of candidate messages.

Do election professionals make a difference in elections? Republican gubernatorial candidate Meg Whitman must have thought so. Her prolific media buys in 2010 were handled by at least 56 consulting firms. But other factors such as incumbency, political party strength, policy issues, candidate personality, and media coverage often water down the impact of big money. Win or lose, consultants appear to contribute to escalating campaign costs. In addition to retainer fees, consultants also often charge a percentage of whatever is spent so there

is little incentive to economize unless contributions fall short.

The Role of Money

Given the scope of election campaigns in California, raising the funds to compete electorally also raises concerns about the role of money itself. Former Assembly Speaker and State Treasurer Jesse Unruh once said, "Money is the mother's milk of politics." After assessing the modern role of money in election campaigns, he revised his adage: "Money has become clabber in the mouth of the body politic." Candidates and officeholders complain about escalating campaign costs but seem ready to raise and spend whatever it takes to win. Indeed, Governor Davis raised an average of $1 million a month during his first term in office, and Governor Schwarzenegger doubled that rate during his years in office. Candidates remind us that television ads and direct mail are costly and previous campaign debts need to be retired. But how much campaign fundraising is enough? No amount seems sufficient. Regardless of the amount raised, there are ways to spend or allocate every dime. Given the ready availability of campaign contributions and the prevalence of safe legislative seats, some candidates generate surplus funds to spend on behalf of other candidates or to bank for future campaigns.

Where do candidates obtain the funds necessary to run? *First*, wealthy candidates are allowed to spend unlimited amounts of their own money. But wealth does not ensure victory and can even be a hindrance. Meg Whitman's record personal expenditure of $141 million in a losing bid to become California's governor illustrates the problem. Assuming a massive campaign treasury is enough, such candidates think they can bypass or ignore the vast network of personal, party, and other relationships necessary to win modern campaigns. Second, candidates use direct mail, the Internet, or other means to attract small "grassroots" contributions. Although the amounts may be modest, these contributions signal broad-based support. Third, to bring in larger contributions, candidates seek contributions from the state's **political action committees** (PACs). The election arms of interest groups, PACs are the largest source of campaign funds for legislative and statewide races. Claiming that they simply want access, PACs commonly contribute to incumbents and to those legislators who control legislation of interest to them. In open seat elections, they may contribute to both sides, assuring some access regardless of who wins. Contributions often come by way of expensive Sacramento dinners, receptions, or other events such as golf outings or concerts; legislators routinely ask at least $1,000 per ticket. Many of these events coincide with the late-summer end of a legislative session when hundreds of bills of interest to these groups are scheduled for votes. Why Sacramento rather than the legislative districts where voters live? The capital is where full-time legislators spend much of their time and where lobbyists are situated. In fact these mutually convenient capital fundraisers are called "Third House events."

Contributions to candidate campaigns are strictly monitored in California. The **Political Reform Act of 1974** (Proposition 9) requires disclosure of campaign contributions and expenditures, regulates the organization of campaign committees, limits entertaining by lobbyists, and prohibits conflict of interest by local officials. The **Fair Political Practices Commission** (FPPC) was established to implement this law. Its staff monitors all nonfederal elections, issues advisory opinions, and conducts random audits. It also investigates charges of wrongdoing and fines candidates for missing filing deadlines, submitting inaccurate reports, sending deceptive mailers, and laundering contributions. For instance, in early 2008, State Senator Carole Migden (D, San Francisco) was fined a record $350,000 for 89 violations, many involving illegal use of surplus campaign funds. She lost a renomination bid the following June.

In 2000, voters amended the 1974 act by passing Proposition 34, which established contribution limits and voluntary expenditure ceilings for state candidates. At allowed the FPPC to adjust these limits and ceilings to reflect changes in the Consumer Price Index (CPI). The FPPC Web site lists current contribution limits for individuals and committees (www.fppc.ca.gov/). There are no limits on political parties. Their "soft money" spending is supposed to be used for party building and get-out-the-vote efforts. In fact, they are also used to attack opposing parties, candidates, and views. To get around Proposition 34 limits, individuals and interest groups now form "independent expenditure committees." These committees can raise and spend unlimited amounts of money on a particular candidate as long as they do not coordinate their efforts with that candidate's campaign. For example, in the summer of 2010, when Whitman was continuing her media spending spree, Jerry Brown benefitted from labor union committee-financed television ads. These expenditures allowed him to respond to Whitman's ads while conserving the relatively modest resources in his campaign budget for the fall campaign. What do loopholes like independent expenditure committees teach us? Like water, campaign money seems to flow around any reform obstacle in its path.

In short, meaningful election reform of any sort faces numerous obstacles. Incumbents are loath to create a level playing field and the courts think spending limits curtail free speech. Voters repeatedly reject using tax dollars for campaigning, as they did with Proposition 15 in June, 2010. Some reformers once recommended so-called Clean Money systems found in several other states. Under such systems, candidates raise small contributions, agree to limit overall spending, and obtain state funds to match those of privately financed opponents. But in 2011, the U.S. Supreme Court found those matching fund provisions violated free speech rights. In the meantime, California candidates compete in a system that favors large contributions or personal wealth.

The Role of National Politics

California is not an island and its elections do not exist in a vacuum. Increasingly, they play an important role in national politics. Four factors help explain this presence.

1. As was noted earlier, voter-approved initiatives often engender similar efforts in other states. Proposition 13 (1978) spawned similar tax-cutting efforts elsewhere. California's rejection of affirmative action in public programs (Proposition 209) encouraged such efforts in several other states. Ron Unz, the primary backer of a successful anti-bilingual education measure (Proposition 227), and Ward Connerly, sponsor of 209, traveled widely to advise policy activists in other states.

2. California is a significant source of campaign contributions sought by out-of-state candidates; so much so that political consultant Joe Cerrell characterized the state as a "big ATM in the sky."[17] During the 2008 presidential election, presidential candidates raised over $142 million from California donors, making it the top donor state (see Figure 6.2). Top recipients were Barack Obama with nearly $68 million; John McCain and Hillary Clinton trailed with $22–23 million each.

3. California candidates are compelling recipients of out-of-state campaign funds. National PACs join their in-state counterparts and numbers of individual donors join in to swell campaign coffers. Consider U.S. Senator Barbara Boxer. In the period 2005–2010, about 20 percent of reportable contributions (those over $200) came from out-of-state sources. One of those was EMILY's List, a campaign financing group that bundles checks from voters nationwide who support largely liberal and female candidates. Presidential candidates find California a compelling source of primary election campaign funds. Political scientist, Nelson Polsby, once called this "the Beverly Hills primary" with good reason.[18] While both major parties seek out campaign contributions in California, certain locales are favorites. Boxer's top locale for campaign contributions in 2010 was zip code 90210.

4. California's role in the selection of presidential nominees and in the election of presidents is anomalous. Because the state is the source of many convention delegates and by far the largest number of Electoral College votes—55 out of 270 needed to win—one might think candidates would need to devote considerable resources here. Think again, beginning with the primaries. Even though the California legislature frontloaded the primary election by placing it in early March (2000 and 2004) and early February (2008), many other states made similar moves, thereby diluting California's influence still again. In 2004, 20 states held their primaries or caucuses before California's March 2 primary, and California shared that date with nine other states. Democrat John Kerry became the presumed nominee before a single Californian voted. The 2008 primary, particularly the battle between Obama and Clinton, was much more competitive. Clinton won the primary but eventually lost the nomination to Obama. The major parties view winning differently in California. Republican rules give the plurality winner virtually all of the pledged delegates at stake. Hence, McCain won the presidential primary with only 42.3 percent of the Republican vote but won 93 percent of pledged delegates. Democratic Party rules allot pledged delegates largely in proportion to the popular vote percentages. So, despite the fact that Clinton won the popular vote with 51.5 percent of the Democratic vote, she garnered only 55 percent of pledged delegates.

Beyond calendar considerations and party rules, California is a daunting place to wage a presidential primary campaign. As *Los Angeles Times* reporter James Rainey put it, California is "too large to buttonhole many voters in person and with TV markets so expensive it can blow a campaign treasury to smithereens."[19] Even cash-rich campaigns find it profitable to spend media funds elsewhere. The California anomaly continues into the general election period. In recent presidential campaigns, public opinion polls, and election results have indicated consistent support in the Golden State for Democratic nominees since Bill Clinton in 1992. As a result, Republican candidates understandably spent their time and campaign resources where chances of winning were greater. As likely winners in California, Democratic candidates prefer to travel to and spend more money in those "battleground" states where such efforts could tip the balance. As one Obama strategist put it, "If we have to spend a dime in California, we're going to lose the election."[20]

Of course, the Electoral College determines who becomes president. In the last presidential election cycle, several groups sought to alter how California's 55 electoral votes would be allocated. Some Republicans sponsored a statewide initiative—The Presidential Election Reform Act—that would allocate California's electoral votes by the popular vote results in each congressional district (as is done in Maine and Nebraska). Such a change would give the Republican candidate a better chance of winning and, at minimum, would require Democratic presidential candidates to spend precious time and money in California. The effort to put the matter on the June 2008 ballot failed. Another group, the California-based National Popular Vote, proposed a novel reform wherein states would commit to allocate their electoral votes to the national popular vote winner. Obviously, it would take enough states totaling 270 electoral votes to concur in this reform to make it work. Some states passed such laws but Governor Schwarzenegger vetoed legislation that would have added California to the list.

CALIFORNIA'S ELECTORAL GAPS

The political participation patterns we have described must be viewed against a larger backdrop: recent demographic trends affecting both California and the nation. From a political behavior perspective, we see the emergence of two Californias—the state's richly diverse population on the one hand and the state's much less diverse electorate on the other. This two-California idea can be expressed in terms of a number of gaps.

Voter/Nonvoter Gap   The most profound gap is between *voters and nonvoters*. As California's population has grown, this gap has also grown because the segments of the population that are increasing the most are reflected in the electorate the least. This trend is occurring across the nation but, according to pollster Mark Baldassare, the trend "could be more problematic for California—a state that calls on its voters not only to elect representatives but to make so much policy through ballot initiatives."[21]

Consider the contrasting views of the two groups:

Typical Nonvoters	*Typical Likely Voters*
Want more active government	Want less active government
Favor more social spending	Favor less social spending
Support higher taxes	Oppose higher taxes
Oppose initiatives that limit government	Support initiatives that limit government

While it could be argued that nonvoters do not count because they do not participate, they do receive a variety of public services and pay taxes like voters; they do have a stake in the political system. Because many nonvoters are the most vulnerable Californians, this gap should be of concern to the state's voters.

Race/Ethnicity Gap   A second gap that reflects two different Californias is the *race/ethnicity gap*. This gap is expressed in Figure 5.5. Experts expect this gap to persist well into the future. While whites are projected to be only one-third of California's population in 2040, they are projected to still be a voting majority at that time.

The Age Gap   Embedded in the voter/nonvoter gap is the age gap. This refers to the fact that, compared to older voters, younger voters express less interest in politics, register to vote at lower rates, are less likely to vote, and are less likely to identify with the major parties. For example, in the 18–34 age group, only 19 percent are likely voters while 49 percent are not even registered to vote. In the over-55 group, 41 percent are likely voters and only 13 percent are not registered to vote. These likely voters are overwhelmingly white.[22]

The Partisan Gap   The 2010 midterm elections exposed a growing partisan divide in the United States. Various surveys of Californians also reveal growing gaps in the views of California Republicans and Democrats. More than Democrats, Republicans favor lower taxes and fewer public services. Over twice as many Democrats as Republicans favor a publicly financed universal health care system and believe that immigrants are a benefit to California. Sixty percent of Democrats favor the ability of same-sex couples to marry; only 23 percent of Republicans do. Fully 56 percent of Democrats favor the legalization of marijuana; only 30 percent of Republicans do. In recent years, Republicans have become even more conservative than in the past. Given this large and growing ideological divide between the major parties, it is understandable that hyperpartisanship would be reflected in the state legislature.[23]

The Gender Gap   A more subtle gap not reflected in this chapter's data is the *gender gap*—the margin of difference between the opinions and votes of men and women. In many elections, women side with the Democratic Party and their candidates in greater numbers than men do. For example, 58 percent of registered voters are women; only 42 percent of men are. In 1996, 55 percent of women voted for Bill Clinton while only 43 percent of men did—a 12-point difference. By 2004, the difference narrowed; 57 percent of women voted for Kerry while 53 percent of men did—a four-point difference. In the 2006 general election, men voted for Schwarzenegger in measurably greater numbers than women did. Understandably, female candidates do particularly well among women, as Obama discovered in California's 2008 primary. About 59 percent of women voters supported Hillary Clinton while only 34 percent supported Obama. This behavior is

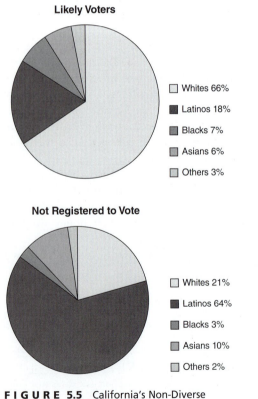

Likely Voters

- Whites 66%
- Latinos 18%
- Blacks 7%
- Asians 6%
- Others 3%

Not Registered to Vote

- Whites 21%
- Latinos 64%
- Blacks 3%
- Asians 10%
- Others 2%

FIGURE 5.5   California's Non-Diverse Electorate

SOURCE: Mark Baldassare, *At Issue: California's Exclusive Electorate* (San Francisco: Public Policy Institute of California, September 2010).

not universal. In 2010, more women voters preferred Brown than Whitman.

In years past, some observers expressed concern over these gaps, especially the dominance of affluent whites over the political process. For example, in the early 1990s, pollster Mervin Field proclaimed, "The agenda of the voting elites ... is obviously demonstrably different than those who do not vote. The more that non-voters become different than voters in color, in class, in attitudes toward life, we create and build threatening pressures which could easily explode and alter for the worse the future course of our precious democracy."[24] Such fears might subside over the long term. First, the portion of the electorate that is white is gradually declining. In a growing number of California cities, no ethnic or racial group constitutes a majority of the population. Second, while the proportion of white voters is declining, the educational and income levels of voters remain relatively high. As more ethnic and racial minorities assimilate and enter the middle class, they will to some extent vote as breadwinners and taxpayers, not just as Latinos, African Americans, or Asians. This will also influence party politics. Although Latinos often align themselves with the Democratic Party, only a third of them consider themselves to be liberal. For example, whereas 65 percent of likely Latino voters identify as Democrats, 33 percent consider themselves to be "middle of the road," and 35 percent as "somewhat" or "very" conservative.[25] Neither Democrats nor Republicans can afford to take for granted this growing group.

CONCLUSION: DIVIDED BY DIVERSITY

Once again, diversity helps explain how Californians participate in their political system. We see it in generalized forms of participation—varying degrees of civic engagement from attending meetings to exiting communities altogether or being involved in political protest. We see it in the wide spectrum of public opinions held by Californians on a host of political and policy issues. Various socioeconomic factors explain whether Californians can vote or indeed do vote. Campaign professionals must work with the state's plethora of elections and election rules in order to sort, sift, and attract California's electorate—or, more accurately, its diverse sub-electorates.

Whether the electoral gaps noted in this chapter are regional or based on race and ethnicity, age, partisanship, or gender, California's policymakers must cope with the biggest gap of all—the fundamental difference between California's overall population and the composition of its electorate. The importance of this gap for California politics cannot be emphasized enough. To the extent today's underrepresented groups choose to become part of the political process, profound changes could well occur in the future.

KEY TERMS

political participation (p. 81)

exit option (p. 82)

protest option (p. 82)

public opinion (p. 83)

straw polls and scientific polls (p. 84)

voting age population, voter turnout (p. 85)

structural and preferential nonvoting (p. 87)

election types: primary, general, special (p. 90)

political action committees (p. 93)

Political Reform Act of 1974 (p. 93)

Fair Political Practices Commission (FPPC) (p. 93)

electoral gaps; voter/ nonvoter, racial/ ethnic, gender, age, partisan (pp. 95–97)

REVIEW QUESTIONS

1. Survey the various forms of political participation identified by political scientists. Which forms most aptly describe your participation in the political system?

2. Why are the exit and protest options exercised by some Californians? Give some examples. Under what conditions might you consider these options?

3. How is public opinion expressed and measured in California?

4. Why do people not register to vote or, once registered, not turn out on Election Day?

5. Describe the various types of elections in California.

6. Why are campaign professionals so important in California's electoral process?

7. How do recent election results demonstrate trends in voter demographics, turnout, and behavior?

8. Describe the various electoral gaps in California. To what extent are they troublesome for the nation's largest and most diverse state?

WEB ACTIVITIES

The Field Poll
(www.field.com/fieldpollonline/)
Public Policy Institute of California
(www.ppic.org/)
These sites feature statewide polling data including the policy views, general attitudes, electoral preferences, and demographic attributes of California's electorate

California Voter Foundation
(www.calvoter.org/)
This site features numerous reports and election aids with the voter in mind.

California Secretary of State
(www.sos.ca.gov)
Click on "Elections" to locate registration forms, voter registration statistics, turnout data, and past election results.

Fair Political Practices Commission
(www.fppc.ca.gov/)
This site contains a wealth of information on campaign finance from a regulatory perspective.

NOTES

1. Sidney Verba, Kay Lehman Scholzman, and Henry E. Brady, *Voice and Equality: Civic Volunteerism in American Politics* (Cambridge, MA: Harvard University Press, 1995), p. 51.

2. Mark Baldassare, *California in the New Millennium: The Changing Social and Political Landscape* (Berkeley: University of California Press, 2000), pp. 34–36.

3. Katherine Ramarkrishnan and Mark Baldassare, *The Ties That Bind: Changing Demographics and Civic Engagement in California* (San Francisco: Public Policy Institute of California, 2004).

4. For an early analysis of the exit option and other responses to civic dissatisfaction, see William E. Lyons and David Lowry, "The Organization of Political Space and Citizen Responses to Dissatisfaction in Urban Communities: An Integrative Model," *The Journal of Politics* 49 (May 1986), pp. 321–346.

5. David O. Sears and John B. McConahay, *The Politics of Violence: The New Urban Blacks and the Watts Riot* (Boston: Houghton Mifflin, 1973), p. 199.

6. V. O. Key, *Public Opinion and Democracy* (New York: Alfred A. Knopf, 1961), p. 14.

7. *PPIC Statewide Survey: Californians and Their Government, January 2011* (San Francisco: Public Policy Institute of California, 2011).

8. Baldassare, *California in the New Millennium*, p. 31.

9. California Voter Foundation, *California Voter Participation Survey* (Davis, CA: California Voter Foundation, 2005). (Available at www.calvoter.org/).

10. Public Policy Institute of California, *Just the Facts: The Age Gap in California Politics* (San Francisco: Public Policy Institute of California, September 2007). (Accessed at www.ppic.org/).

11. Zoltan L. Hajnal, Paul G. Lewis, and Hugh Louch, *Municipal Elections in California: Turnout, Timing, and Competition* (San Francisco: Public Policy Institute of California, 2002).

12. Claudine Gay, *The Effect of Minority Districts and Minority Representation on Political Participation in California* (San Francisco: Public Policy Institute of California, 2001).

13. Greg Mitchell, *The Campaign of the Century: Upton Sinclair's Race for Governor of California and the Birth of Media Politics* (New York: Random House, 1992).

14. Expenditure data available at the Secretary of State Web site (www.sos.ca.gov).

15. Kate Folmer, "Absentee Voting Grows; Candidates Adapt," *San Jose Mercury News*, June 1, 2006.

16. Quoted in Noel Brinkerhoff, "Course Correction," *California Journal* 28 (December 1997), p. 44.

17. Quoted in Beth Fouhy, "Here Come the Democrats," *California Journal* 34 (March, 2003), p. 40.

18. Nelson W. Polsby and Aaron Wildavsky with David Hopkins, *Presidential Elections: Strategies and Structures of American Politics*, 12th ed. (Lanham, MD: Roman and Littlefield, 2007), p. 56.

19. James Rainey, "Delegate-Rich California Has to Share the Attention," *Los Angeles Times*, February 23, 2004.

20. Quoted in Cathleen Decker, "California's Moment in the Spotlight is Probably Over," *Los Angeles Times*, February 6, 2008.

21. Mark Baldassare, *At Issue: California's Exclusive Electorate* (San Francisco: Public Policy Institute of California, 2006).

22. See Public Policy Institute of California, *Just the Facts: California's Likely Voters* (San Francisco: Public Policy Institute of California, September 2010) and *The Age Gap in California Politics* (San Francisco: Public Policy Institute of California, September, 2007). (Accessed at www.ppic.org/)

23. Public Policy Institute of California, *Just the Facts: California's Partisan Divide* (San Francisco: Public Policy Institute of California, September, 2007) and PPIC, *California Voter and Party Profiles* (Public Policy Institute of California, September 2010). (Accessed at www.ppic.org/).

24. Quoted in Richard Zeiger, "Few Citizens Make Decisions for Everyone," *California Journal* 21 (November 1990), p. 519.

25. Public Policy Institute of California, *Just the Facts: Latino Likely Voters in California* (San Francisco: Public Policy Institute of California, September 2010).

6

✳

Linking People and Policymakers: Media, Parties, and Interest Groups

Introduction

Mass Media

Newspapers

Television

Radio

The Internet and Social Media

Political Parties

Partisanship in California

The Partisan Geography of California

Political Parties: California Style

How the Parties Are Organized

Surrogate "Parties"

Endorsement Politics

Interest Groups

California Groups: Who Are They?

How Interest Groups Organize

What Interest Groups Do

Conclusion: Competing for Influence

Key Terms

Review Questions

Web Activities

Notes

IN BRIEF

Chapter 6 examines various links between ordinary Californians and the policy institutions profiled in the next four chapters. In a representative democracy, these linkage efforts provide channels of access and influence for ordinary citizens; this input helps make the political system viable and legitimate to those citizens.

The mass media link Californians with policy processes primarily through newspapers and television. Newspapers provide substantial amounts of political news and guide public opinion by means of editorials and endorsements. Television has limits unique to the medium but reaches a huge audience in California. Increasingly, the Internet and social media are becoming factors in California politics. Thanks to the Progressives, political parties are weak in California, their powers limited either by law or practice. But thanks to the endurance of of two-party system, they remain important to many voters. Interest groups might well be *the* driving force in California politics. Groups represent every conceivable interest in the state and use a variety of resources to express their members' policy preferences to policymakers.

 INTRODUCTION

Chapter 5 examined the political behavior of Californians acting as individuals and groups. We analyzed how they participate in civil society and in politics, how they form opinions, and how they vote, or not vote. Subsequent chapters examine the formal governing institutions found in California's political system: the executive, legislative, and judicial branches of state government plus numerous local governments. Chapter 6 addresses those linkage activities and processes that connect individual Californians to those officials and institutions that make policy—what people think of as "the government." In a representative democracy, such linkage institutions provide channels through which citizens have input in the political system.[1] They help to inform ordinary citizens (the media), frame their political choices (political parties), and voice their policy preferences to the government (through interest groups). To be sure, direct democracy in California is its own channel of access and influence; it is so important to the state's politics both past and present, we treated it separately in Chapter 4. In Chapter 6, we will use linkages and channels of access and influence interchangeably.

In a representative democracy (where the people are sovereign, but delegate decision making to a relative few), these channels are essential. Power residing in "the people" is only latent (potential but unused) power until people have ways to express it. In California's evolving, complex, and pluralistic society, these channels are the only practical way ordinary citizens can speak or relate to those making policy on their behalf.

Scholars of American politics commonly focus on elections (discussed in Chapter 5), the media, political parties, and interest groups. At times these linkages work smoothly. Both the people and policymakers respectively get what they want and need. Indeed, democratic theory would suggest the two agendas agree much of the time. At other times, though, these linkage institutions might not serve their intended purpose, or they lose meaning to average citizens. When this happens, the ability to govern is affected. Some believe this is the condition of modern California politics. The media might not adequately inform the state's residents. Political parties and interest groups increasingly compete with one another, usually at the expense of the parties. Even during elections, the media and interest groups appear to exercise more power than parties. These developments affect the relationship between those who govern and those who are governed. Chapter 6 describes and evaluates each of these linkages and the role they play in connecting California's diverse citizenry and its government.

MASS MEDIA

A primary linkage or channel of influence in national and California state politics is the mass media. The **mass media** funnel information, opinion, and user-friendly analysis to large numbers of people without direct, face-to-face contact. They consist primarily of print media (newspapers and magazines), electronic media (radio and television), and new media (the Internet). Citizens and public officials alike depend on the media to send and receive messages. Their resulting power is enormous. When he was assembly speaker (one of the most powerful offices in the state), Willie Brown said, "The press has as much influence on public policy as I have."[2] To reinforce his point, consider that media organizations are the only businesses (yes, businesses) constitutionally protected as a check on the government.

In addition to mass media, various elite media (those catering to select groups) thrive in California. For decades, the now defunct *California Journal* covered state politics, personalities, and issues for an influential but small readership. Numerous print and Internet political newsletters (including *Capitol Weekly, California Progress Report, CalNews, Calbuzz,* and *California Watch*) provide timely inside news and gossip but their readership is small. Journalists specializing in California politics increasingly offer blogs alongside stories and columns.

So, on which of these news sources do Californians most rely? In one statewide survey, television was the most cited source of political news, followed by the Internet, newspapers, and radio. Newspaper readership is declining and the use of the Internet has dramatically increased (see Figure 6.1). Combined, these media warrant particular attention.

Newspapers

The rise of California's newspapers parallels the state's political development. Wealthy individuals and families managed the earliest newspapers. One example was James McClatchy of the *Sacramento Bee,* who in the late 1800s worked his way up to editor while gradually purchasing shares in the paper. His heirs gained control of the *Bee* and still own a portion of it. He fought for land reform (dividing huge landholdings that had survived statehood) and the transcontinental railroad; he also

When asked, "How do you get most of your information about politics?" Californians responded this way.

Media Type	1998/99	November 2010
Television	45	37
Internet	5	24
Newspapers	30	15
Radio	9	10

FIGURE 6.1 Political Information Sources in California

Question: What mix of media do you use to keep up with California politics?

SOURCE: Public Policy Institute of California, *Just the Facts: Californians' News and Information Sources* (derived from various PPIC Statewide Surveys) (San Francisco: Public Policy Institute of California, November, 2010).

fought against monopolies and environmentally destructive hydraulic mining. The McClatchy Company is now publicly traded and owns media properties across the nation.

The *Los Angeles Times* was decidedly more conservative than McClatchy's *Bee.* Harrison Gray Otis bought the *Los Angeles Times* shortly after a Southern California railroad project linked Los Angeles to points east. He preached probusiness, antiunion sermons in editorials while hyping the Los Angeles land boom in which he himself had invested. He cooperated with the Big Four, who shared his desire for economic growth, personal power, and enormous income. On the other hand, William Randolph Hearst's *San Francisco Examiner* was decidedly anti-railroad and friendly to Progressive reforms. During much of this period, newspapers from San Diego to San Francisco were owned by Republicans and espoused conservative values.

Today, California's newspapers have undergone substantial change since those early crusading years. Many have merged to create "one-newspaper" towns or have been acquired by out-of-town media chains, conglomerates, or wealthy individuals. For example, the Tribune Company now owns the *Los Angeles Times* (along with the *Chicago Tribune* and the Chicago Cubs) and billionaire investor Sam Zell now owns the Tribune Company. Nowadays, concerns over profitability and even survivability trump the traditional community and public service functions of newspapers. Once-thick weekday metropolitan dailes have thinned considerably as rounds of layoffs decimate newsroom staffs.

Large corporations may dominate the newspaper scene, but California is also home to many ethnic minority newspapers. For example, *La Opinion* is the largest Spanish language newspaper in the nation. In Los Angeles, only the *Los Angeles Times* has higher circulation. The media association New America Media lists roughly 800 California-based media outlets including print, radio, broadcast, and online versions serve groups including African Americans, Arabs, Armenians, Cambodians, Chinese, Hispanics, and Koreans. Many of these outlets operate below the radar of other Californians and the state's public officials. To the extent they reinforce subgroup identities, issues, and concerns, they may also reinforce the hyperpluralistic nature of California politics.

Despite readership declines, many Californians still depend on newspapers for state and local government news, but the quality and the quantity of the news they receive varies. The *Sacramento Bee* reports state politics heavily because its readers include not only elected officials but also thousands of state employees. Sacramento is, after all, a "company town." Only a small handful of large newspapers can afford to staff a Sacramento bureau; smaller newspapers have either combined forces or abandoned the capital entirely. Instead of traditional investigating reporting, they rely on wire services (Associated Press) and direct government sources (press releases).

Coverage of local politics is just as problematic. On the one hand, the large, metropolitan dailies (presumably read by California's urban majority) are too large to cover public affairs in the hundreds of communities that comprise their circulation areas.

On the other hand, smaller, more localized newspapers often lack the resources, regularity (many are published weekly), or desire to cover

political issues on a frequent basis, especially those that reach beyond their circulation base.

Are there any bright spots in this assessment of newspapers as channels of influence and access? Ironically, one bright spot might be technology. While it is portrayed as the major enemy of traditional print journalism, technology has actually made newspaper reading easier and more widely accessible. All major newspapers have Web versions and many of those are accessible at no charge to the reader. Furthermore, stories run throughout the day; one need not wait until tomorrow to see how the *Los Angeles Times* or the *San Francisco Chronicle* covers today's breaking story. Also, the Web site Rough & Tumble (www.rtumble.com) provides a daily compilation of California newspaper stories on state politics and public policy. While the long-term future of California's print newspapers may be bleak, for now, more of them are more accessible than ever before.

Television

The popularity of television has diminished the political influence of newspapers, especially among certain groups. As Figure 6.1 portrays, when asked where Californians get most of their news about the governor and the legislature, 37 percent of all respondents cited television; for Latino respondents, this figure jumped to 51 percent.[3] Given its pervasiveness in much of California's political life, television falls far short of its potential as a channel of access and influence. The reasons are several.

A Visual Medium Compared to other media, television focuses on the visual. To a news producer, a political story is not inherently interesting unless it is visually interesting. As one television producer admitted, his colleagues are interested in "slash, flash, and trash. They want the [story] to bleed, scream and yell."[4] In response, public officials deliberately employ symbols, stunts, or pseudo-events to make their messages visually interesting. Celebrity witnesses virtually guarantee media coverage of committee hearings that might otherwise go unnoticed. Celebrity-turned-governor Arnold Schwarzenegger staged made-for-media events to publicize his own policy agenda. In their defense, legislators claim they must resort to such measures to inform their constituents and shed light on the state's problems.

Media Bias   Many Americans claim the media are biased, that they treat the news in a partial, unfair manner. Some see an **ideological bias** where the media tend to favor Republicans or Democrats, conservatives or liberals. California journalists think this might be in the eye of the beholder. People want to see a story reported in a predetermined way and find fault if it is not. *Los Angeles Times* columnist George Skelton was asked about his partisan leanings to which he responded, "What am I? *I* don't know what I am." While many mainstream journalists consider themselves to be unbiased, over half of Californians who watch television news watch mostly cable television, where ideological bias is readily apparent (e.g. Fox News and MSNBC).

California reporters do examine what policymakers say and do and compare the differences. According to journalist Steve Scott, "We have a low threshold for hypocrisy." The media also seem attracted to inconsistency and the ironies that abound in politics. For example, during the 2010 gubernatorial campaign, billionaire Republican candidate Meg Whitman faced accusations that she retained a Latina housekeeper after finding out she had forged her immigration documents. Whitman's behavior seemed inconsistent for a candidate who had taken hard line anti-immigration positions during the primary race. The story ran for weeks and dogged the balance of her fall campaign.

Television in particular exhibits a **structural bias**. As a business, television structures news to minimize coverage of government and politics. It tends to focus less on politics and more on human-interest stories: entertainment, crime, sports, weather—anything but politics.

Reflecting on that dismal coverage, television columnist Howard Rosenberg suggested that the only way to attract media attention would be to "have the four leading candidates chase each other on a freeway."[5] Structural bias takes place in the context of fierce competition among stations for ratings and "market share." In addition, television's use of pictures—its primary product—can lead to false impressions. For instance, one study revealed that crime reports by Southern California stations followed a predictable narrative with two elements: crime is violent and perpetrators are nonwhite males.[6]

Sparse Coverage   When television does cover public affairs, the coverage tends to be sparse and shallow. News stories themselves tend to be brief—very brief—due to the inherent limitations of commercial television. The result is a lack of analysis—why events, political or otherwise, happen. For example, one study of California television news showed that violence dominated local news coverage. Furthermore, the emphasis was on the specifics of particular crimes, not on the underlying social conditions that contribute to violence.[7] Coverage of state politics has a similar quality to it, to the extent it is covered at all. Many stations neglect live coverage of the governor's State of the State speech but rather refer interested viewers to streaming video of the event on their own Web sites.

Another measure of television news coverage in California is how stations assign reporters. Sacramento-based news coverage had declined significantly from its zenith in the Reagan years—a phenomenon shared with other state capitals.[8] Local Sacramento stations still cover state politics and, on occasion, send footage to their network affiliates in Los Angeles and San Francisco. The Northern California News Satellite sells its state politics stories to client stations. Furthermore, the California Channel, the state's version of C-SPAN, provides live and archived cable broadcasts and Web casts of legislative floor sessions, committee hearings, news conferences, and other related programming.

Given its limitations, why does television news still hold promise as a linkage institution in California politics? In a word, size. The state has more than 90 local stations and more cable subscribers than any other state. Ninety-five percent of the state's households own television sets. More important, more than 85 percent of them live in only four media markets: greater Los Angeles, the San Francisco Bay Area, Sacramento, and San Diego. Access to those markets is a precious, costly commodity for public officials, election candidates, and interest groups. The sheer size of the Los Angeles television market (it reaches more than 50 percent of the state's voters) gives statewide candidates from Southern California built-in advantages over competitors from elsewhere in the state, especially if they have had prior media exposure.

In addition, television plays an important linkage role covering elections and crises. They do so through straight news reporting and through the airing of campaign commercials. Political advertising is prolific because it is the only realistic way candidates can reach voters. As a result, candidates often inundate newscast commercial time with messages unmediated by editors, reporters, and producers. The messages get through. Focus group research suggests that Californians are more likely to remember a candidate's television commercials than straight news about the candidate.[9] In covering crises, television has no peer; it has the capacity to provide nonstop news coverage of terrorist attacks, earthquakes, fires, and riots. Regular programming and much commercial time is suspended during such events. Crises in the nation's largest state often attract network attention.

Radio

As any reader will already know, most of California's radio stations are commercial enterprises featuring a variety of music formats. There are about 15 stations that use an all-news/talk format and about 30 public radio stations, some of which include some state and local news in their programming. One of the most public affairs—oriented of these is San Francisco's KQED. It

hosts daily reports and a weekly program called the *California Report* with extensive coverage of state issues, a program carried by other public radio stations across the state. Radio has something of a captive audience during commute times and much public affairs programming is scheduled for those rush hour times. Talk radio is tailored to those listeners and can be hard hitting and abrasive in tone. Listeners tend to self-select such programming and their views are largely reinforced, not challenged.

The power of minority-owned radio was powerfully illustrated during the anti-immigration protests of 2006. Spanish language radio personalities played a key role in organizing and inspiring those massive protest marches throughout California. Not only did they encourage those unprecedented turnouts, they helped set protest ground rules such as peaceful protests, no littering, and the use of American instead of Mexican flags.[10]

THE INTERNET AND SOCIAL MEDIA

Arguably, the growth of the Internet is revolutionizing U.S. and California politics. As we saw, Internet use in California doubled in less than a decade. In fact, it has overtaken television as a news source for younger adults, upper income residents, independents, and college graduates.[11] Media Web sites are ubiquitous, and both blogs and online political newsletters are within reach of most Californians.

While the Internet provides additional news options for California's news consumers, it is simply a must for the state's political elites including legislators, government workers, lobbyists, and the news media themselves. Online communication moves in two directions. According to one survey of these elites, receiving political information online (via Web sites, email, blogs, or podcasts) is on the rise, often at the expense of television usage.[12] In terms of disseminating information, the Internet is equally essential for those elites. Some ballot initiatives have relied heavily on the Internet to jumpstart the campaign process. Rare are candidates or issues without their own Web sites. Not only is the Internet an increasingly effective way to raise funds—Visa or MasterCard will do just fine—it communicates its own symbolic message.

How politically important is the Internet? The answer depends on the user. So far, the Internet seems to have attracted already well-informed Californians and political activists. But as a tool of persuasion, it tends to reinforce user views rather than convert undecided voters. According to Dan Schnur, "The Internet is a proactive medium. With television, you have to make a proactive decision to not watch the commercial. But with the Internet, you have to make an active decision to click, to participate. Base voters of each party are much more likely to do that than the undecided."[13] What about those Californians who are not yet wired, who for economic or other reasons do not communicate or consume information online? Will there eventually be a technological version of a second-class citizen? This worries some communications experts. According to Kassy Perry of the Perry Communications Group, "as more legislators, staff, and agency officials move online, many constituents who don't have access to the technology will find it harder to communicate with their elected and appointed officials."[14]

In terms of political access, will Californians ever be able to vote online? Technology seems to be inching, but only inching, in that direction. Voters can access voter registration materials via the Internet but security concerns and fears of election fraud have slowed down the prospect of online voting *per se*. Touch-screen voting devices are increasingly the norm at polling places but growing numbers of absentee voters must still fill out paper ballots as they have for years. That said, recent election cycles suggest that the Internet is becoming the driving force behind many campaign practices.

The most recent trend in the use of the Internet has been the rise of social media like Facebook and Twitter. In 2011, these networking sites were credited with aiding grassroots uprisings in the Middle East. Back home, a growing number of national figures have learned to communicate via Facebook and Twitter. But what, if any, is the impact of social media on California politics? While its influence is nascent, this we know:

- As of late 2010, there were more than 15 million voting-age Facebookers in California—a sizeable pool of potential voters and supporters of various causes.

- While official government Web sites have been slow to link with social media, California's interest groups and media routinely do so. Members and readers may refer news to their own friends and contacts.

- Both Facebook and Twitter now feature a "California Politics" Web site devoted to "blogs, news, and videos for California political junkies."

- Political parties are beginning to sense social media opportunities. In 2010, the state Democratic Party developed a Facebook application (friendsoutthevote.com/) that sifted through users' friends lists, matched them with party registration and voting data, and generated lists of Democrats who vote infrequently. The idea was to encourage the party's friends to nudge their non-voting friends to vote.

- YouTube allows Californians to "attend" interest group presentations, campaign events, and speeches. It also allows controversial actions by government employees captured on someone's cell phone to "go viral" feeding potential scandal.

- California's chief campaign regulator, the Fair Political Practices Commission (FPPC) has considered the possible regulation of the campaign uses of social media, as it regulates more traditional outreach efforts. According to FPPC Chair Dan Schnur, the decades old Political Reform Act needs some rewriting. "Our goal here is to meet the new challenges of 21st Century technology. There is no way the authors of the act could have anticipated that these types of communicating a campaign message would ever exist."[15]

POLITICAL PARTIES

In addition to the media, **political parties** also link citizens to their government. Parties are organized groups that (1) possess certain labels, (2) espouse policy preferences, (3) both nominate and work to elect candidates for public office, and (4) help frame government's postelection policy agenda. In American politics, they are found at all levels—federal, state, and local—though not in equal measure. Political parties come in three forms.[16] The *party in the electorate* refers to voters who hold partisan affiliations. The *party in government* refers to partisan elected officials and institutions, such as the legislature, which organize around party labels. These leaders (primarily governors and legislators) translate party positions into policy and personify the party in the minds of many voters. The *party organization* means the formal party apparatus: its structure, staff, budget, rules, and processes for achieving its goals. Here, we will discuss partisanship and its alternatives in California as well as how political parties are organized.

Partisanship in California

A **political party** is a relatively permanent coalition that exists to win public offices for its candidates, promote policy positions, and serve as a primary frame of reference for voters. **Party identification** is the extent to which citizens affiliate with, relate to, or support a specific political party. Identifiers believe support for a party makes their vote more meaningful. Unlike many multiparty systems elsewhere, the American two-party system presents relatively few choices. Voters respond to that lack by shading or qualifying their partisan loyalties. Common categories are: (1) strong Democrat, (2) weak Democrat, (3) independent-leaning Democrat, (4) independent, (5) independent-leaning Republican, (6) weak Republican, and (7) strong Republican. In general, the two major parties have been losing identification, a process called "dealignment," and independent voters have been increasing.

In California, both Republicans and Democrats have lost their share of registered voters. Since 1994, the percentage share of independents (those who check "Decline to State" on their registration forms) has grown from about 10 percent to over 20 percent in 2010. If these trends continue, independents could outnumber Democrats and Republicans by 2025—making California what some call an "unparty state." In the parlance of televised electoral maps (where red is Republican and blue is Democratic), California is gradually moving from blue to purple.[17]

What do we know about these independent voters? How independent are they? While there are "pure" independents, they tend to be more apolitical than leaners, tend to be less knowledgeable, and tend to vote less frequently. Of those who are more likely to vote, 38 percent lean Democratic and 30 percent lean Republican. Even the leaners can be unpredictable. More than Republicans and Democrats, independents think that California needs a viable third party though a majority do not support the Tea Party Movement. They may side with Democrats on environmental issues but with Republicans on tax issues.

California independents span the demographic spectrum. According to polls of likely voters (those who habitually vote), 21 percent of both whites and Latinos, 20 percent of blacks, and 30 percent of Asian Californians consider themselves to be independents. Still, recent election results have seen an alignment of most Latino voters with the Democratic Party. Some observers credit Latinos' recent voting behavior to Republican Party support for Proposition 187 (an anti-immigration measure) and Proposition 209 (an anti-affirmative action measure). These two measures in particular were voting motivators especially for newly naturalized Latinos.[18] Whether or not they officially register as Democrats, Latinos have been voting for Democratic candidates in impressive numbers. Their choices for president have been consistently Democratic. Bill Clinton won 63 percent of their votes in 1992; Al Gore, 75 percent in 2000; John Kerry, 68 percent in 2004; and Barack Obama, 94 percent in 2008. Whether Latino influence increases in the future depends on whether their citizenship and participation rates match their population growth.[19]

The Partisan Geography of California

Generalizations about party affiliation in California can be understood only in the context of the state's diverse geographical regions. Those regions have different voting habits and partisan loyalties. Pollsters often identify five distinct voting regions of California—Los Angeles County, the rest of Southern California, the San Francisco Bay Area, the rest of Northern California, and the Central Valley. Here we utilize presidential election data because turnouts are so much higher than in state elections.

A traditional divide has been between urban areas of Northern and Southern California.

Within Southern California, Los Angeles County remains a Democratic island amid a large and more conservative region. Inner-city African Americans remain loyally Democratic as do lower income Latinos and some urban whites. In 2008, Barack Obama garnered 67 percent of the vote there. The rest of Southern California is more white, middle class, and conservative than Los Angeles County. In 2008, Southern Californians outside of Los Angeles still favored Obama but by lesser margins—57 percent for Obama and 41 percent for John McCain.

Northern California, and especially the San Francisco Bay Area, is more liberal and Democratic than the rest of the state. In 2000, Bay Area voters preferred Gore over Bush by a 67 to 27 percent margin; eight years later, they preferred Obama over McCain by a 75 to 22 percent margin. This north/south divide remains important

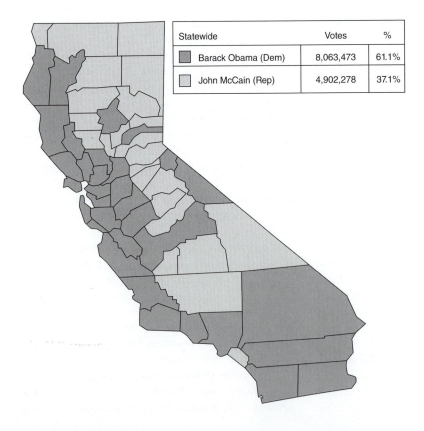

Statewide	Votes	%
Barack Obama (Dem)	8,063,473	61.1%
John McCain (Rep)	4,902,278	37.1%

FIGURE 6.2 California's Presidential Preferences, by County (2008)

SOURCE: California Secretary of State.

because nearly half of all likely voters in California are concentrated in Los Angeles County (25 percent) and the Bay Area (23 percent).

In recent years, analysts have noticed an east/west contrast between coastal and inland California. Note the contrasts portrayed in Figure 6.2. This map shows which 2008 presidential candidates won pluralities in each county. Most coastal Californians—and that means most Californians—preferred Obama over McCain. Reflecting a region-level realignment, voters in portions of the Central Valley and the mountain regions preferred McCain by varying margins. An East/West contrast is also evident in political ideologies. Various surveys suggest that Central Valley residents are more politically conservative and more Republican than other Californians. While there are pockets of Democratic strength in inland California, Frederick Douzet and Kenneth P. Miller observe that the state's "coastal region politically resembles New York state while the interior looks like Texas."[20]

Political Parties: California Style

Like the United States as a whole, California has a two-party system. Democrats and Republicans dominate at least partisan elections. But California's system is one of weak parties. To curb machine bosses such as San Francisco's Abe Ruef and corporate elites such as the Big Four, the Progressives established elements of a weak party system. *Direct primaries* allowed voters themselves to nominate candidates; *cross-filing* allowed the candidates themselves to run as Democrats, Republicans, or on occasion both; and *nonpartisan elections* blurred affiliations of judges and disallowed parties from endorsing or assisting local officeholders.

Many voters seem to prefer weak parties. Over the objections of party leaders in 1996, they approved an *Open Primary Law* (Proposition 198). It created a blanket primary that allowed voters to cross party lines and vote for any candidate, regardless of party label (that is, a registered Republican could vote for a Democratic candidate and vice

versa). This innovation enabled more than 1.7 million "decline-to-state" voters a chance to vote for partisan candidates. The blanket primary was employed for the 1998 June primary election and the March 7, 2000, presidential primary. But in late June 2000, the U.S. Supreme Court on a 7:2 vote overturned the law, claiming it forced parties to associate with those who do not necessarily support them, in violation of the First Amendment.[21] In reaction, a new election law established a "modified" closed primary that permits unaffiliated ("decline to state") voters to participate in a partisan primary if party rules permit it. The Democratic, Republican, and American Independent parties revised their rules accordingly. (In a notable exception, the Republicans disallowed independents from voting in their February 5, 2008, presidential primary.) As noted in Chapter 5, voters tweaked the system still further with Proposition 14 (2010). From 2011 forward, there would be a single ballot for primary elections for congressional and state elective offices. In this **top-two primary**, the two candidates for each office with the most votes, regardless of party, would advance to compete in the general election. In heavily Republican or Democratic districts, relatively, both nominees could be of the same party. Partisan primaries would still exist for presidential elections and party offices. Defenders of this reform believe more moderates will be elected because candidates have to appeal to a broader electorate. Critics believe the reform will increase campaign costs and decimate minor parties. Time will tell.

In California's weak party system, Democrats and Republicans control major offices in Sacramento. The rise of those independent voters we discussed earlier has not given rise to many office holders with an "I" next to their name. Based on how successful the parties were in electing governors and legislators, political scientists long regarded California as either "two-party competitive" or "modified one-party Democratic." During the 2000s, the label returned to two-party competitive.[22] After Progressive era reforms, Republicans dominated state politics from 1924 to 1957. Both parties were relatively competitive from 1958 to

1973, and Democrats dominated from 1974 to 1982. In recent years, Democrats have consolidated legislative control and, after two terms of Republican Schwarzenegger, regained the governor's office. They even gained legislative seats in 2010 when Republicans experienced numerous successes elsewhere in the nation. Today, one might be tempted to label California a "one-party" state but in a hybrid democracy, such "control" does not insure policy victories at every turn or even control over the policy agenda.

Minor or third parties widen voter choice at least for some voters. How does a third party qualify to be included on a California ballot? Two routes are possible: (1) signing up 103,000 registered voters (one percent of the total votes cast in the 2006 gubernatorial election), or (2) getting over one million registered voters to sign a petition seeking party qualification (ten percent of the total votes cast in the previous gubernatorial election). The first option is relatively easy; the second has never succeeded. To remain qualified, registration figures must remain above one-fifteenth of one percent of total state registration. The Natural Law Party failed this test and was disqualified in 2006. In addition to the Democrats and the Republicans, California's officially recognized third or minor parties include the American Independent Party, the Green Party, the Libertarian Party, and the Peace and Freedom Party. These minor parties represent the narrowest slice of the pie chart in Figure 6.3.

How the Parties Are Organized

Because the state elections code dictates how California parties are organized, party structures look very similar. California parties do not have precinct-level organizations common in "strong party" states. Therefore, the lowest level is the **county central committee**. Most voters elect these committee members in primary elections without really knowing who they are. These local committees do not "run" local party affairs, have few if any funds to disburse, and must compete for influence with elected officials and unofficial party clubs.

Political Party Registration Percentages

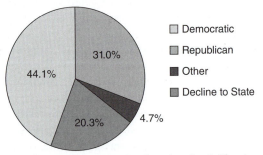

FIGURE 6.3 Party Registration in California, November 2010

Question: What rule changes could improve the success of minor parties in California? What do the major parties need to do to regain those registered voters who now call themselves "independents" or "decline to state."

SOURCE: California Secretary of State's Office (Accessed at www.sos.ca.gov/).

The **state central committee** is the key organizational unit for both Republicans and Democrats. Numbering in the hundreds, its membership is a hodgepodge of party leaders, elected officials, and appointees from the ranks of activist party members. Every two years, state central committee members meet to discuss policy issues, select party leaders, hear elected officials and major candidates speak, "network" with each other, and rally the party faithful. Historically, the Republicans have been more cohesive than the Democrats, who divide into multiple caucuses representing the disabled, women, labor, LGBT (lesbian/gay/bisexual/transgender), and seemingly every racial/ethnic group in the state. This devotion to group-specific interests has given the party a hyperpluralistic outlook. These party gatherings showcase, for better or worse, the current diversity that exists within both major parties. In the Democratic Party, liberals, moderates, and caucus groups fight among themselves. In the past, Republican Party conventions tended to pit fiscal conservatives against social issue conservatives and pragmatists against ideologues. Some intraparty differences also occur due to the state's geographic diversity. Many party activists from interior California have little in common with those from coastal and metropolitan areas apart from sharing party labels. As a general rule, party activists regardless of party tend to be more doctrinaire than the public at large. Many are ideologically brittle and lack the ability, willingness, and skill to compromise—traits that are expected of elected officials. During state party conventions, these activists may boo or shout down high profile candidates that are perceived as not being liberal or conservative enough to please "the base."

In addition to the state and county committee structures, the political parties in California send representatives to the national committees. Full time party chairpersons are selected to staff the state central committees. These positions often attract wealthy hyperactivists desiring to rub elbows with elected officials and party donors. Most are unknown to average voters; a notable exception was Jerry Brown who chaired the Democratic Party from 1988 to 1991, after his first stint as governor. As a rule, state party chairs are ineffective spokespersons for the party, but even their election at state party conventions can reveal ideological and issue splits within the party.

Surrogate "Parties"

If political parties are considered important linkage institutions in a representative democracy, what happens in states where parties are destined to be weak? In California, surrogate institutions have been created to replicate strong party functions. For example, a group of moderate Republicans in 1943 formed the California Republican Assembly. Because the group was unofficial, it was not regulated by state law and could endorse candidates. Their endorsement in a congressional race launched Richard Nixon's long political career. Today, this grassroots group claims to be the "conservative conscience" of the state Republican Party and usually endorses social issue conservatives. In 1953, Democrats organized the California Democratic Council (CDC). It helped the party's resurgence after 1958 and launched the career of former U.S. senator Alan Cranston. According to its Web site, it represents "the voice and activism of thousands of community Democrats."

Both these organizations organize into local clubs or chapters, hold grassroots conventions, and provide issue workshops for various party clubs around the state. These **surrogate parties** hold less meaning for the electorate today than once was the case. Nowadays, political action committees, candidate-centered campaigns, and media-driven elections conspire to limit party influence where it matters most: picking candidates and winning elections.

A recent twist on surrogate parties has been the rise of the **Tea Party movement** across the nation and in California. Spawned during the Great Recession, the Tea Party is conservative and even libertarian in thought, favoring smaller government, lower debt, and reduced taxes. They take their name from the Boston Tea Party, a protest by colonists opposed to British taxes on tea. The Tea Party is tied to California in a significant way, namely the Tea Party Express. This group was founded in 2009 to support the Tea Party movement nationally by way of a bus tour, rigorous fund raising, and other campaign activities. The Sacramento-based consulting firm, Russo Marsh and Rogers, formed the Express via its own political action committee— Our Country Deserves Better (OCDB). Sal Russo, a veteran political operative, is the PAC's chief strategies and former Republican assembly member Howard Kaloogian is its co-chair. Most of the funds raised by the PAC have paid for the services of the consulting firm that created it in the first place.

Endorsement Politics

Arguably the most important test of a strong political party organization is its ability to control the selection of nominees for public office. Short of hand-picking nominees, parties should be able to at least endorse them. In their quest for nonpartisanship, California's Progressives banned that practice in 1913. Through legislation and party practice, the ban was even strengthened to disallow parties from supporting or opposing preprimary candidates.

The surrogates endorse, but few listen. Occasionally, candidates unacceptable to their parties win primaries, as happened once when Democratic voters nominated a Ku Klux Klan member as a congressional candidate. In the 1980s, the U.S. Supreme Court intervened in California's party affairs by declaring the state ban on party endorsements unconstitutional. In a case involving San Francisco Democrats, the Court majority argued that such bans violated the parties' rights to spread their views and the voters' rights to inform themselves about candidates and issues.[23]

In 1996, a federal judge extended that reasoning and allowed party endorsements in judicial races and for other nonpartisan offices and in 2010, the Judicial Council of California lifted a ban on judicial candidates seeking those endorsements. Yet, California's major parties sometimes hesitate to make endorsements even in partisan elections. If they do endorse, they usually pick incumbents over primary challengers and office seekers who have paid their dues in party matters.

Whether parties endorse or not, another option is available, namely the use of **slate mailers**—large postcards listing "endorsed" candidates and propositions. Note the quotation marks. In many cases, distributors of these mailers are actually campaign-oriented businesses. While contributors are not disclosed, tiny asterisks reveal who paid to be included. These colorful mailers may sound official with titles like "Voter Information Guide." They may emphasize a particular theme (Official Law Enforcement Voter Guide) or tailor their messages to particular groups of voters. But, many are flatly misleading. For example, in 2010, the "Voting Guide for Republicans" recommended re-election of Democrat Bill Lockyer as state treasurer. It turns out he paid $60,000 to be listed in that mailer.[24] Some candidates feel pressured to pay for such "endorsements" or even blackmailed into doing so if the outfit threatens to "endorse" opposing candidates (see Figure 6.4).

While they appear to be unregulated and they largely are, slate mailer organizations must file with the California Secretary of State. In the 2009–2010 cycle, 90 of them were listed as active. As long as parties remain weak and propositions remain popular, slate mailers will likely remain a dubious, yet attractive, electoral tool.

INTEREST GROUPS

Interest groups are a significant force in national and state politics. It would be difficult to overemphasize their power and influence in California politics, both state and local. An **interest group** is a body of individuals who share similar goals and organize to influence public policy around those goals. Their development in U.S. politics was early and immediate. Founder James Madison considered the potential problem of "factions" in America (his term for both groups and political parties) but thought the new republic could control them. By the 1830s, Frenchman Alexis de Tocqueville observed, "In no country in the world has the principle of association been more successfully used or applied to a greater multitude of objects than in America."[25] By the 1950s, political scientists considered the activity of interest groups central to politics. Legislatures basically referee group struggles; victories come in the form of statutes—passed or defeated. The job of government in a pluralistic society is to manage conflict among groups.

State level interest group politics does not lend itself to easy generalization. The interest group environment varies from state to state. Because political parties are relatively weak in California, one would expect interest groups to be rather strong—and they are. But due to the size of the state and the scope of its government, interest group power is not concentrated among a few dominant interests. Depending on the issue, many groups not only actively participate but also actively compete on opposing sides of the same issue.

For ordinary citizens, interest groups provide still another important link to the political system. Multiple memberships are common. For instance, a local homebuilder is likely to be a member of a local builders group and the chamber of commerce plus several statewide groups, the Building Industry

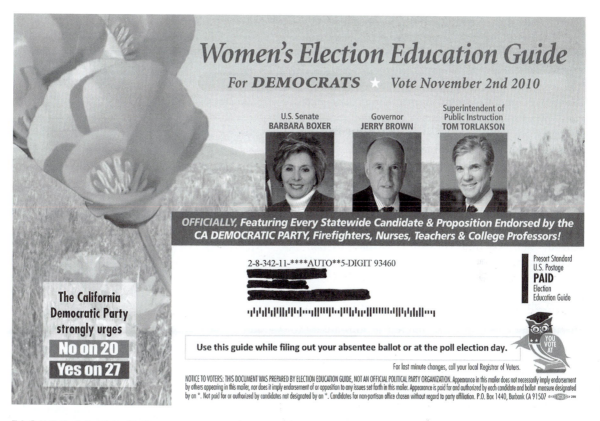

FIGURE 6.4 Slate Mailer

This particular slate mailer was sent to registered Democratic Party households in the Fall of 2010. Every proposition campaign position endorsed by the party paid to be included in this mailer. Note that the Party favored abolishing the Citizens Redistricting Commission (Proposition 27) and opposed adding congressional districts to the reapportionment duties of the commission (Proposition 20). Voters decided otherwise at the polls.

Association, and the Associated Contractors of California. These statewide groups provide the contractor with political access while furthering the broad interests of the building industry: environmental regulations, building code matters, land use controls, and growth policies. But builders are not just builders. They may also be members of churches, health insurance groups, automobile associations, and sporting groups. These interests are also organized at the state level to push their own public policy preferences.

Interest groups have an enormous impact on California politics and clearly contribute to its hyperpluralistic character. The Secretary of State's

official online lobbying directory runs more than 700 pages and is divided into individual registered lobbyists, lobbying firms, and lobbyist employers (www.sos.ca.gov/prd/Lobbying-Directory.pdf). Other groups, including local chapters of statewide groups, operate below the state level to sway county governments, cities, special districts, and school districts. For example, local chambers of commerce often have government relations offices that monitor and influence local government decision-making from a pro-business perspective.

The development and growth of interest groups paralleled the political development of the Golden State. By winning the war against the

Southern Pacific Railroad, the Progressives in effect invited other interest groups to participate in California politics. Furthermore, the development of the state's political system coincided with the industrial revolution, the rise of corporate California, and the development of a complex economy. Private sector interest groups multiplied as a result. As the scope of government enlarged, so did the number of government employees. They formed their own interest groups (such as the American Federation of State, County, and Municipal Employees, AFL-CIO). By century's end, an increasingly active state government, spurred by new policy demands and a shrinking federal role, required constant vigilance by an ever-growing corps of interest groups.

California Groups: Who Are They?

In contemporary California, interest groups are as diverse as the state itself. Together, they resemble the interest group system in the nation's capital. This hyperpluralistic maze of groups can be divided into five categories based on primary interest or motivation.

1. *Economic Groups.* These groups are primarily motivated by money—income, profits, better salaries, or the economic health of a company or trade. In their view, business regulations, tax policies, labor/management issues, access to markets, occupational safety, and environmental rules can mean financial gain or loss. They range from individual companies to trade associations to employee groups. Some of the biggest, measured in lobbyist spending, include the Association of California Insurance Companies, the Western State Petroleum Association, the California Cogeneration Council, the California Manufacturers Association, ARCO, and Chevron.

2. *Professional Groups.* Professionally motivated groups both provide member services and represent group interests in the policy process. They possess economic interests, to be sure, but are also concerned about the regulation of their particular professions. It is common for the state to both regulate entry into certain professions and oversee their conduct. Notable California examples include the California Teachers Association, the California Medical Association the California Bar Association, and the California Trial Lawyers Association.

3. *Public Agency Groups.* These groups represent various units of government at the state and local level. Representative are the following: the League of California Cities, the California State Association of Counties, the California Association of Councils of Government, the California Special Districts Association, the Association of California Water Agencies, and the California District Attorneys Association. At least 85 separate cities hire their own lobbyists. As sovereign governments, California's gaming tribes lobby individually and collectively via the California Nations Indian Gaming Association. The state even lobbies itself; executive branch agencies routinely defend their own interests at legislative hearings.

4. *Cross-Cutting Groups.* These groups do not fit neatly into other categories even though they share some overlapping interests. Cross-cutting groups attract members from other groups due to social, ethnic, ideological, religious, or emotional ties. Illustrative are California Church Impact, the California Association to Abolish Slavery and Trafficking, the Sierra Club, and the Drug Policy Alliance Network. Scholars and policymakers alike call some of these groups "public interest" groups or PIGs because their policy goals are not solely economic or professional in nature. Such groups regard themselves as public interest groups because *they* believe their causes serve a larger public interest or an underrepresented group.

5. *Miscellaneous.* This catch-all category simply means that some California groups defy reasonable classification. Where do you place the Americans for Smokers Rights, the California Coin Dealers, the California Equine Council,

---

---

or California Trout, Inc.? Some groups are ad hoc or single issue in nature: They temporarily organize around a "hot" issue or legislative bill or an initiative. When the issue dies, so do they. Still other groups defy simple classification because they spend only minimal or sporadic amounts of time on public policy matters.

6. *Local Groups.* We should not ignore the many interest groups at the local level in California. Of course, some are local chapters of statewide groups such as the Sierra Club, the Chamber of Commerce, and local teachers union affiliates. They provide "on the ground" support for statewide policy positions and are available to lobby legislators during frequent district visits. Others are purely local, focusing on issues of local or regional interest. For example, the San Francisco Bay Area interest groups focusing on mass transit issues have included the Bay Area Transportation and Land Use Coalition, People on the Bus, Access BART Coalition, Say NO to BART!, Rescue Muni, Train Riders Association of California, and Marin Advocates for Transit.

As is the case in national politics, the power of California interest groups ebbs and flows depending on economic trends, and whether their interests match the interests of those in power. For example, the California Chamber of Commerce had extraordinary access to Governor Schwarzenegger because they endorsed him and shared his pro-business agenda. The power of labor unions largely depends on the health of the sectors they represent. The clout of unions representing traditional blue-collar trades has fallen as manufacturing jobs have declined in numbers or moved out of state. Today, the power of public sector unions (school teachers, various state employees, law enforcement officers, and health care workers) reflects the growth of those sectors and their claim on public budgets. No wonder public sector unions now contribute more to political candidates and ballot measures than do traditional trade unions.[26]

People often confuse interest groups with lobbyists. **Lobbyists** those individuals who represent interest groups in the policy process. In California, they prefer to be called "legislative advocates." All in all, there are more than 1,100 groups or individuals who actually lobby the state government (and are duly registered as lobbyists with the Secretary of State). There are so many of them, they have their own group—the Institute of Governmental Advocates (www.californiaiga.org).

How Interest Groups Organize

Interest groups in California have found there is no best method of organizing to function as linkage institutions. The following patterns are common.

In-House Lobbyists Because policymaking greatly affects their interests, some businesses find that hiring their own in-house lobbyists is the most effective route to adequate representation. For instance, ARCO, Chevron, Allstate Insurance Company, Ford Motor Company, and United Airlines represent themselves in the political process. Some public sector agencies, such as the City and County of Los Angeles, also have offices in Sacramento. For good measure, many of these interests hire contract lobbying firms to augment their own employees.

Associations Many individual entities join together around common goals. If you type in "associations" at the Sacramento Yellow Pages Web site, the scope of these groups becomes readily apparent. One can almost fill in the blank: The California Association of Nurserymen, Nonprofits, HMOs, Winegrape Growers, or Suburban School Districts. These are only a handful of the myriad associations found in the capital. Such groups link members to the policy process through numerous meetings, legislative briefings, and newsletters. The larger ones command substantial resources for lobbying and campaign activity. Because policy priorities are established only at periodic meetings, some associations find it difficult to respond quickly to changing policy developments. Relatively small associations find it economical to contract out even their own management functions.

Contract Lobbyists   Known as "hired guns" in the lobbying world, contract lobbying firms represent multiple clients often in the same general subject area such as education, health, or insurance. Examples of large firms include KP Public Affairs, California Advocates, A-K Associates, Advocation Inc., and California Strategies and Advocacy. KP is regarded as one of the largest, employing 17 lobbyists and serving more than 70 clients ranging from Hertz and Google to the Barona Band of Mission Indians. Some contract lobbyists are former legislators, legislative staff members, and administration officials who apply their knowledge of the process and the policymakers involved. State law requires a cooling off or waiting period before former legislators can lobby their former colleagues.

"Brown Bag" Advocates   These modestly funded groups may be associations or individuals. Their lack of financial resources sets them apart from the lobbying firms and associations. Large campaign contributions and lavish receptions—tools of the trade for large groups and big firms—are out of the question for groups such as the interfaith group JERICO: A Voice for Justice. Instead, these groups rely on networks of intense believers. For instance, the Children's Defense Fund champions the needs of poor children and relies on a combination of grassroots activism, a telephone network, and "white

hat" issues to provide what clout they have. The availability of email and social networking helps groups like these mobilize their members over particular issues.

What Interest Groups Do

When interest groups come to mind, the image is of lobbying—testifying at committee hearings or entertaining legislators. But interest group representation is more complex than that. Several tactics are employed to link group members to the political system.

Public Relations   Interest groups want the general public to know that their respective goals are similar. For instance, subtle and not-so-subtle television commercials equate an oil company with a venerated public television series or as protector of the state's wildlife. Numerous companies have "adopted" public school classrooms to further their image in the community and throughout the state. Many interests now rely on Sacramento-based public relations firms to help craft and sell their messages to the media and other attentive publics. For example, Perry Communications Group offers its clients expertise in these areas: public affairs, issues management, media relations, event planning, advocacy and coalition building, multicultural communication, social marketing, and (even) reputation management.[27]

Electioneering   Once regarded as risky business, interest groups now work both to elect their friends and to defeat their enemies and they do so both directly and indirectly. The development of political action committees has allowed all manner of groups to contribute directly to legislative campaigns through essentially paper organizations registered with the FPPC. Some cannot afford to contribute much (the brown baggers) or legally cannot (government groups, such as the League of California Cities). To hedge their bets, some PACs contribute to both sides, especially in open-seat elections where no incumbent is running. As noted earlier, PACs feel obligated to attend pricey

Sacramento testimonial dinners and "legislative briefings." The money pours in continually whether or not it is an election year. As a result, incumbents often amass huge campaign war chests even before they announce their reelection plans. In recent years, the largest campaign contributors have been a revolving door of casino interests, energy companies, utilities, candidate committees, and both public sector and trade unions (see Table 6.1).

If interest groups wish fund a campaign unencumbered by contribution limits or onerous reporting, they can make indirect contributions through "independent expenditure committees." Because candidates do not control the raising or spending of those funds, these efforts are outside the authority of the FPPC. Anyone or any group can give any amount. According to the National Institute on Money in State Politics, "independent expenditures

TABLE 6.1 Top-10 Contributors to California Campaigns, 2010, by Sector

Top Sectors	Total $ (in millions)
Candidate Self-Finance	$182.4
Electric Utilities	$49.9
Public Sector Unions	$38.8
General Trade Unions	$23.6
Insurance	$23.4
Candidate Committees	$18.6
Party Committees	$15.8
Oil & Gas	$13.4
TV and Movie Production/Distribution	$12.2
Pro-Environmental Policy	$11.8

NOTE: The presence and order of groups on these lists vary depending on the nature of elections that particular year and the presence of certain ballot measures. As noted earlier, Meg Whitman's personal infusion of $141 million into her gubernatorial campaign accounts for the sudden rise of the first category.

SOURCE: National Institute on Money in State Politics (Accessed at www.followthemoney.org) Check this site for updated figures.

are the single largest loophole contributors use to circumvent state limits on direct campaign contributions."[28] Many observers believe that this presumed divorce between contributions and candidates is an artificial one at best. Office holders are invariably aware of those interests that helped elect them and will be mindful of them when making policy decisions.

Influencing Propositions As noted earlier, interest groups can sponsor, support, or oppose various statewide ballot measures. Of course, this is a form of electioneering but it avoids the normal legislative process in most respects. Some of these efforts combine altruism with traditional self-interest. For instance, the California Building Industry Association worked closely with the legislature to craft a massive $9.2 billion school facilities bond measure—Proposition 1A. It passed in November 1998 with more than 62 percent of the vote. What was in it for the home-builders? Lesser-known provisions in "1A" included limits on school fees charged to developers and other pro-developer provisions. The builders in turn pumped $2.5 million into the winning campaign.[29] Money and clout do not always persuade voters. In the 2010 primary election, the utility giant PG&E contributed nearly all of the $46 million spent in support of Proposition 16. This measure would have required a two-thirds popular vote for public jurisdictions to enter the energy business, such as generating and selling electricity. It lost to a campaign that raised only $136,000.

Political consultants aid interest groups in this process and sometimes even initiate initiatives. Some have been known to "test market" issues to see whether direct mail would be a profitable tactic. If so, these consultants shop around for interest groups to back them. To fellow consultant Joe Cerrell, these people propose initiatives "so they can make money. It's become a straight business."[30]

Lobbying Lobbying is what interest groups do to influence policymakers. It includes monitoring legislation, drafting bills for legislators to introduce, testifying at public hearings, and contacting individual members and/or their staffs. Lobbyists also pay attention to the executive branch, where agencies issue rules and otherwise implement legislation. Their most important asset is credible, albeit one-sided, information on how a legislative bill or an agency decision will affect their group. According to Patrick McCallum, a Sacramento lobbyist who specializes in higher education, "Much of what we do to be effective lobbyists requires being very analytical. Having a technical understanding of why the regulation was created in the first place, why it's there, and its potential impact on your client. Taking a formulaic regulation or statute and 'tweaking' it, using this technical knowledge to legally recreate the regulation in a way that's advantageous to the client, protecting and supporting the client's best interests."[31] Term limits have presented interest groups and lobbyists with newfound challenges. Influence based on long-time friendships with veteran legislators disappears as veterans leave. Lobbyists must continually start over with new members, who in turn leave within a few years. Because lobbyists are often called the Third House of the legislature, we discuss them further in Chapter 7.

Influencing Appointments   California's executive branch not only presents lobbying opportunities, it offers interest groups a place at the table via appointments to several hundred boards and commissions. Some boards regulate or oversee particular professions or businesses (such as the California Architects Board and the California Board of Accountancy) so it behooves professional associations to make sure the "right" members are appointed. To an interest group, the right appointment may be someone with professional expertise and a sympathetic ear. To a governor, it may be an old friend, a longtime supporter, or a termed-out legislative ally. The governor nominates most board and commission members, subject to confirmation by the State Senate. With a few exceptions like the California Coastal Commission, most boards and commissions operate well outside public view or media coverage unless they render a controversial decision or the governor attempts a controversial appointment.

Litigation   Interest groups often find the courts making policy through interpreting the state constitution, legislative statutes, and administrative rulings. Therefore, in many situations, the most effective method of participation by an interest group is to litigate. Increasingly, this is the case over budget matters. For instance, during the Fall of 2010, the California School Boards Association sued Governor Schwarzenegger because he vetoed a bill requiring county mental health offices to serve special needs students and the requisite funded needed. The veto essentially shifted the responsibility for mental health to financially strapped school districts. Months later, Governor Brown faced a bevy of lawsuits by redevelopment agencies, advocates for the disabled, and others challenging various cuts in his 2011 budget. In some cases, California is merely a convenient venue to file high profile suits. For example, a Sacramento mother, aided by the Center for Science in the Public Interest, filed a class action lawsuit against McDonalds, claiming that the chain used toys to lure children into consuming nutritionally unhealthy Happy Meals.

If interest groups do not qualify as litigants, they can file *amicus curiae* (friend of the court) briefs to explain their position in court cases. These legal arguments provide information or advocate a particular result. This is done at every level of California's legal system. For example, the recent initiatives seeking to ban same sex marriage and the ensuing court cases stemming from those initiatives fostered dozens of amicus briefs on every side of the issue.

CONCLUSION: COMPETING FOR INFLUENCE

California's linkage institutions indeed connect Californians with their policymakers. They essentially compete with each other based on different priorities. *The media compete for consumers.* The media are daily conduits of political and governmental news, if readers, listeners, and viewers bother to pay attention. During election campaigns, California's television stations link candidates and issue campaigns to voters through paid political advertising. The importance of the Internet and social media is just beginning to be felt as they link Californians to the public square.

Political parties compete for voter attention— unsuccessfully it seems. They face competition from the media, public officials who owe them little, and the variety of constraints—legal and otherwise—placed on parties in California. Parties are augmented by "surrogate" parties, for-profit "endorsers," and campaign professionals working for both candidates and causes.

The most formidable competitors to California's political parties are a plethora of interest groups.

Interest groups compete for policymaker attention; at this they have been highly successful. Theodore Lowi once called this "interest group liberalism," where "the most important difference between liberals and conservatives, Republicans and Democrats, is to be found in the interest groups they identify with."[32] These groups seemingly represent every agenda, population segment, economic interest, social value, or walk of life in the state. In California, where voters commonly make policy via citizen initiatives, interest groups compete for their attention as well. Increasingly, the size, scope, complexity and diversity of the Golden State is mirrored in and represented by these groups. In a sense, California politics today is a hyperpluralistic mix of interest groups clamoring for access, influence, and power.

KEY TERMS

mass and elite media
(pp. 101, 102)

ideological and
structural bias
(p. 104)

political parties and
minor or third
parties (pp. 107, 110)

party identification
(p. 107)

top-two primary (p. 109)

county and state central
committees (p. 110)

surrogate parties (p. 111)

Tea Party movement
(p. 111)

slate mailers (p. 112)

interest groups (p. 112)

lobbyists and lobbying
(pp. 115, 117–118)

REVIEW QUESTIONS

1. Illustrate the concept of linkage with each in institution in California politics?

2. How did newspapers evolve in California?

3. What are television's shortcomings as a linkage institution in California politics?

4. How might the Internet and social media affect California politics in the foreseeable future?

5. How are the major parties organized in California, and why are they so weak?

6. In what ways do surrogates and slate mailers augment political parties?

7. Trace the rise of interest groups in California and describe the means they use to exercise political influence.

8. To what extent do interest groups mirror the diversity of the state and contribute to hyperpluralism?

WEB ACTIVITIES

Political Parties

(www.cadem.org)
California Democratic Party

(www.cagop.org)
California Republican Party

These are the chief party Web sites in California's version of our two-party system. They include party descriptions, news, events, and platforms.

Rough & Tumble

(www.rtumble.com/)
Updated daily, this site links you to California newspaper articles and columns dealing with state and local government and politics.

Secretary of State

(www.sos.ca.gov)
Extensive data on political party qualifications as well as interest group spending on elections and lobbying

National Institute on Money in State Politics

(www.followthemoney.org)
Locate California to access election data including interest group contributions to candidates, ballot measures, and party committees

NOTES

1. Linkage was first coined by V. O. Key, *Public Opinion and American Democracy* (New York: Knopf, 1961), Chap. 16 and developed further by Kay Lawson in *Political Parties and Linkage: A Comparative Perspective* (New Haven: Yale University Press, 1980).

2. "Mr. Speaker: A California Journal Interview," *California Journal* 17 (January 1986), p. 13.

3. Public Policy Institute of California, *Just the Facts: Californians' News and Information Sources* (San Francisco: Public Policy Institute of California, November 2010).

4. Steve Scott, "Tube Dreams," *California Journal* 30 (May 1999), p. 29.

5. Quoted in Lou Cannon, "Bleeders Sweeping Leaders Off California TV," *Washington Post,* May 23, 1998, p. A6.

6. Franklin D. Gilliam Jr. and Shanto Iyengar, "Prime Suspects: The Influence of Local Television News on the Viewing Public," *American Journal of Political Science* 44 (July 2000), pp. 560–573.

7. Lori Dorfman et al., "Youth and Violence on Local Television News in California," *American Journal of Public Health* 87 (August 1997), pp. 1131–1137.

8. Jennifer Dorroh, "Statehouse Exodus," *American Journalism Review* (April/May, 2010). (Accessed at www.ajr.org).

9. Mark Baldassare, *California in the New Millennium: The Changing Social and Political Landscape* (Berkeley: University of California Press, 2000), pp. 40–42.

10. Teresa Watanabe and Hector Becerra, "How DJs Put 500,000 Marchers in Motion," *Los Angeles Times,* March 28, 2006.

11. Public Policy Institute of California, *Just the Facts: Californians' News and Information Sources* (San Francisco: Public Policy Institute of California, November 2010).

12. "California's Political Elite Relying on Internet More, TV Less," *Government Technology* (February 17, 2006). (Accessed at www.govtech.net/magazine/).

13. Quoted in Sandy Harrison, "Online Campaigning Comes of Age," *California Journal* 35 (May, 2004), p. 29.

14. Quoted in Ibid.

15. Brian Leubitz, "FPPC Wants to Regulate Social Media," *Calitics* (August 2, 2010) (Accessed at www.calitics.com).

16. Frank J. Sorauf and Paul Allen Back, *Party Politics in America,* 6th ed. (Boston: Scott Foresman/Little Brown, 1988), p. 10.

17. Mark Baldassare, "Purple Vote is Growing," *Riverside Press-Enterprise* (April 9, 2006).

18. Adrian D. Pantoja, Ricardo Ramirez, and Gary M. Segura, "Citizens by Choice, Voters by Necessity: Patterns in Political Mobilization by Naturalized Latinos," *Political Research Quarterly* 54 (December 2001), pp. 729–750.

19. Jack Citron and Benjamin Highton, "When the Sleeping Giant is Awake," *California Journal* 33 (December 2002), pp. 42–46.

20. Frederick Douzet and Kenneth P. Miller, "California's East-West Divide" in Frederick Douzet, Thad Kousser, and Kenneth P. Miller, eds. *The New Political Geography of California* (Berkeley: Berkeley Public Policy Press, 2008), p. 36.

21. *California Democratic Party, et al.* v. *Jones, Bill, CA Secretary of State* 99–0401 (2000).

22. See Thomas M. Holbrock and Ray Lajara, "Parties and Elections," in Virginia Gray and Russell L. Hanson, eds., *Politics in the American States: A Comparative Analysis,* 9th ed. (Washington, D.C.: CQ Press, 2007).

23. *Eu* v. *San Francisco County Democratic Central Committee, 489 U.S. 214 (1989).*

24. Dan Walters, "Slate Mail is Just Junk, But Costly," *Sacramento Bee* (October 24, 2010).

25. Alexis de Tocqueville, *Democracy in America* (New York: Alfred A. Knopf, 1945), p. 191.

26. John Howard, "What's Good for Business Is Good for California," *California Journal* 35 (December, 2004), pp. 46–50; and John Howard, "California Labor's Big Shift" *California Journal* 35 (November, 2004), pp. 7–13.

27. Perry Communications (www.perrycom.com/ services).

28. Quoted in Fair Political Practices Commission, *Independent Expenditures: The Giant Gorilla in Campaign Finance* (Sacramento: FPPC, 2008).

29. Cynthia H. Craft and Kathleen Les, "School Bonds," *California Journal* 29 (November 1998), pp. 28–35.

30. Quoted in Peter Schrag, *Paradise Lost: California's Experience, America's Future* (New York: New Press, 1998), p. 211.

31. Kathy Mulcahy, "Q & A With Higher Education Lobbying Expert," LobbyingFirms.com (September 14, 2010).

32. Theodore Lowi, *The End of Liberalism: The Second Republic of the United States*, 2nd ed. (New York: Norton, 1979), p. 51.

7

✴

Legislative Politics

Introduction: The Road to Professionalism and Dysfunctionality
California's Legislative History

What the Legislature Does
Policymaking
Representation
Executive Oversight
Civic Education

Getting There and Staying There
Recruitment
Why They Stay: Rewards of Office
How They Stay: Reapportionment Politics
The 2011 Reapportionment

Organizing to Legislate
The Role of Leadership

The Committee System
The Staff

The Legislative Process
Bill Introduction
Committee Consideration
Floor Action and Conference Committee
The Governor's Role

The Third House

Conclusion
Key Terms
Review Questions
Web Activities
Notes

IN BRIEF

California's legislature illustrates many of the challenges facing California politics. Increasingly, the legislature also represents the diversity of the Golden State. Once dominated by rural interests and the Southern Pacific Railroad, its powers were tightly drawn by the Progressives in the early 1900s. After decades of stagnation, the legislature became more professional in the 1960s and, through reapportionment, more reflective of the state's urban growth. Since the 1970s, the legislature has gradually become more partisan and increasingly deadlocked—reflecting the state's growing diversity of interests. Furthermore, the aftermath of Proposition 140, which established term limits in 1990, has raised serious questions about the long-term policy role of a once-envied institution.

The California legislature performs a variety of functions: policymaking, representation, executive oversight, and civic education. Most legislators attain office through a combination of personal initiative and sponsorship by legislative and party leaders. Until Proposition 140, the legislature offered attractive political careers to its members; it still offers opportunities for advancement from one house to another, to statewide offices and Congress, and to influential lobbying positions.

In doing its business, the legislature relies heavily on a handful of leaders, including the Assembly Speaker and the Senate President pro tem. A combination of committees and leadership posts provide structure for the legislative process, one that seems simple on paper but which actually boils with internal politics. Lobbyists provide essential information to members and committees while representing a diversity of interests in California.

Nowadays, the California legislature faces a variety of challenges: a growing number of conflicting interests, social change, economic turmoil, and a restive public dissatisfied with the legislature's performance.

INTRODUCTION: THE ROAD TO PROFESSIONALISM AND DYSFUNCTIONALITY

Question: Which state pays its legislators more than any other state but forces them to leave office as soon as they gain valuable experience?

Answer: California.

Indeed, the California state legislature is an anomaly. It makes statutory policy for the largest state in the Union, incubates political leaders, and is an enviable place to act on behalf of the public interest. It was once regarded as the most professional of all state legislatures and, in many ways, it still is. But today's challenges are sobering. Member tenure is term-limited, campaigns are exorbitantly expensive, and the policy stakes are higher than ever. The legislature is an easy target of criticism. In fact, no matter who occupies the governor's office, the legislature usually fares far worse in job approval surveys. Believers in representative democracy placed great confidence in legislatures.

While admitting the executive would share lawmaking power, political philosopher John Locke viewed legislative power as supreme. American colonial legislatures viewed themselves as mini-parliaments. The Framers assumed Congress would be first among the three federal branches. In the early 1800s, state legislatures were modeled after the Congress and were considered superior to Congress as policymaking bodies. After all, states had larger policy responsibilities. But by the late 1800s, state legislatures had fallen into disrepute. British observer James Bryce summed up a prevailing attitude: "If [the legislature] meets, it will pass bad laws. Let us therefore prevent it from meeting."[1] By the 1980s, state legislatures had become much more professionalized institutions capable of making effective public policy. Larger staffs, higher salaries, and longer sessions marked this "institutionalization." But by the early 1990s, these trends had backfired. The public began to lose confidence in their legislatures as policymaking bodies. Today, state legislatures are undergoing a process of "deinstitutionalization." That is, they are affected more now than ever before by outside forces beyond the control of legislative bodies—public opinion, the media, voter-imposed term limits, and interest groups.[2]

California conforms to this trend. Angry Californians passed Proposition 140 in November 1990. As noted in Chapter 4, this initiative limited assembly members to three two-year terms and senators to two four-year terms. The measure also sought to eliminate the legislature's retirement system and severely cut its operating budget. Although the California Supreme Court overturned the retirement system ban for all members, it upheld the balance of 140.[3] The introduction of term limits has shaken the California legislature to its very core, affecting virtually every aspect of the institution. References to it appear throughout this chapter.

California's Legislative History

Criticism of the California legislature is as old as statehood. In fact, the institution has always reflected the state's different political eras. Its history includes the early years, the Progressive era, stagnation amid change, reform, the golden years, and life after Proposition 140.

The Early Years   In the mid-1800s, the state legislature was an amateur body dominated by farmers and beholden to the Southern Pacific Railroad (SPR). People considered the members of the legislature to be dishonest drunks—the legislature of "1,000 steals" or "1,000 drinks." In 1849, it consisted of 16 senators and 36 assemblymen. By the second constitutional convention in 1878, it had grown to its current size, 40 senators serving four-year terms and 80 assembly members serving two-year terms. The combination of frequent elections, part-time politicians, and domination by the SPR's Political Bureau led to a corrupt "political machine" atmosphere and fueled the rise of the Progressives.

The Progressive Era   Under the righteous indignation of the Progressives, Hiram Johnson assumed the governorship in 1911. That same year, voters approved constitutional amendments limiting what the legislature could do, plus how and when it could do it. They even specified the number of days the legislature could meet. More importantly, they approved the initiative, a reform that would eventually compete with the legislature for policy-making power. Yet the voters did not support every antilegislature proposal. Between 1913 and 1925, they rejected six referenda to create a unicameral (one-house) legislature—an idea some Californians still favor. During this period, the legislature lost an important political role in appointing U.S. senators due to the passage of the Seventeenth Amendment to the U.S. Constitution in 1913. It required direct election of senators.

Stagnation Amid Change   From the 1920s to the 1960s, California experienced tremendous growth and change. Urban and suburban populations surged as did the economy. The Depression and World War II brought federal programs and dollars to California. The legislature did not fully reflect these changes; in fact, it resisted them. Like the Congress, representation in the lower house (the Assembly) was based on population; in the upper house (the State Senate), it was based on area. No county could have more than one senator (the so-called **Federal plan**). The result was skewed representation. In fact, as late as the 1960s, San Diego, Los Angeles, and Alameda counties claimed half the state's population but sent to Sacramento only one senator each. As a result, rural interests predominated and policymaking was fractionalized more by region than by partisanship.[4] Meanwhile, interest groups grew in number as the state's economy became more complex. In the process, individual lobbyists such as the colorful Artie Samish gained enormous influence and power.

Reform   In the 1960s, two events led to substantial legislative reforms. First, a legislatively appointed Constitution Revision Commission recommended a series of constitutional amendments allowing the legislature to govern most of its affairs (such as setting salaries and determining calendars). In 1966, voters approved Proposition 1A by a 3 to 1 margin. Spearheading this effort was Assembly Speaker Jesse

Unruh, who became something of a nationwide guru for legislative professionalization. Under his leadership, the legislature aggressively pursued a policy agenda apart from the governor's. To this day, an unoccupied desk remains on the Assembly floor to memorialize Unruh's legacy. Second, federal courts ruled against California's "Federal plan" in 1965. Both houses in a state legislature would have to be reapportioned on the basis of "one person, one vote."[5] The post-reapportionment election of 1966 produced immediate change. Compared to the old guard, many new legislators were younger, better educated, possessed more professional backgrounds, and represented more minorities. They also seemed more partisan in their dealings with each other.

The Golden Years The 1960s and 1970s ushered in still more reforms such as the two-year session adopted in 1972. This allowed bills to remain alive longer, avoided time-consuming reintroductions, and gave bills greater chance of passage. A robust economy allowed the legislature to spend generously on both public policy and on itself. Staffs and salaries grew steadily. Among the 50 states, the California legislature was rated number one by the Citizens' Conference on State Legislatures in 1973.[6] All was not well, though. Proposition 9 (1974) addressed what the public considered an all-too-cozy relationship between legislators and lobbyists. It limited campaign finances and lobbying practices and disallowed campaign work by state-paid legislative staff. Those elected after Proposition 13 passed in 1978 seemed more rigidly conservative than their veteran colleagues. The breakup of the postwar bipartisan consensus (favoring active government and greater spending) appeared complete.

Inching Toward 140 Voter approval of term limits in 1990 was the culmination of several developments. First, divided government (Republicans controlling the governor's office; Democrats, the legislature) became routine and led to well-publicized policy gridlock. Second, the initiative process increasingly supplanted the legislature as the driving policy force in California. Third, while some voters were gradually "dealigning"

from their respective parties (considering themselves to be independents), legislators were becoming *more* partisan in their dealings with each other. Fourth, the media began to spotlight how campaign funds were raised and spent. Then Assembly Speaker Willie Brown doled out excess campaign funds of his own to loyal colleagues.[7] Brown engendered both grudging respect and fear on the part of colleagues. Some observers believe that the primary motivation for 140 was to remove Brown from office. While the African American speaker was a source of enmity, other members added to the public's growing frustration with the legislature. They readily sought out service on so-called **juice committees** because industries most interested in those committees would contribute to the committee members' political campaigns.[8] The whole business looked tawdry to ordinary voters. After several well-publicized bribery scandals, the public's general regard for the legislature plummeted.

Today's Dysfunctionality By the late 1990s, California had experienced 100 percent turnover in its legislature and the revolving door continues. Proposition 140 has profoundly affected the legislature in one area after another. Compared to the past, post-140 legislators are younger, and fewer are former staff members. Latinos, women, and those with local government backgrounds have increased in number. Member turnover has meant higher staff turnover and less experience—some say competence—all around. In addition, power has shifted in various ways. The Senate has gained influence as veteran, but termed-out, assembly members and staffers join the Senate. Relative to the less-experienced legislature, the governor has gained more power. Lobbyists are as knowledgeable as ever but must now work harder to get legislators' attention both in Sacramento and in the members' districts.[9] Term limits are not the only culprit. There is a greater ideological divide between Republicans and Democrats than in the past. Couple this hyperpartisanship with a two-thirds vote requirement to raise taxes and the results include budget gridlock and overall inefficiency.[10]

WHAT THE LEGISLATURE DOES

Amid all this change, the California legislature still remains at the core of politics in the Golden State. As with all legislatures, its functions are varied. We discuss four broad and overlapping ones: policymaking, representation, executive oversight, and civic education.

Policymaking

The first function of a legislature is policymaking. California's legislature addresses a stunning variety of policy issues each year. Among the more than 700 laws that took effect on January 1, 2011, were bills that did the following:

- Regulated the trans fats bakeries could use in fried pastries

- Allowed local governments to ban mobile billboards

- Repealed a 60-year old law requiring the state to seek a "cure" for homosexuality

- Eased the transfer from community colleges to California State University

- Made an infraction the sale of electronic cigarettes to minors

In California, there are three types of legislation: bills, constitutional amendments, and resolutions. **Bills** are proposed statutes (laws at the state level) and can be introduced only by legislators. Even the governor's budget (itself a bill) must have a legislator's name on it.[11] **Constitutional amendments** originating in the legislature require a two-thirds vote of the members and a concurrence of a majority of voters at a subsequent election. **Resolutions** are merely statements representing the collective opinion of one house or both on miscellaneous subjects. They may commend individual Californians, praise a champion sports team, or express a popular opinion on some fleeting issue (see Box 7.1). The most important bill and most important set of policies the legislature adopts each year is the state budget.

Representation

A second legislative function, *representation,* sounds simple enough. In a representative democracy, legislators ideally reflect or act on the wishes of those who elect them. In reality, representation is complex and operates on a variety of levels. This is especially true in a diverse and hyperpluralistic state like California.

Geographic Representation   The first level of representation is geographic. Forty senators and 80 assembly members represent the particular interests of their home districts. Given the state's diversity, from densely urban districts near the coast to sparsely populated districts in the interior, a multitude of geographic perspectives translate into a multitude of policy perspectives and priorities. Sometimes these differences are manifest in *local bills* that affect only one district. For instance, one such bill reorganized ferry service on San Francisco Bay. Legislators may also form coalitions with like-minded members based on common geographic interests, as coastal lawmakers do on offshore oil drilling or Bay Area members do on transportation issues.

Social and Cultural Representation   At another level, legislators often represent the characteristics of constituents back home. Overall, legislators usually approximate their districts in terms of race, religion, or ethnicity. In recent years, there has been a surge of Latino and female legislators. In fact, in 2009 California ranked second among the 50 states in the percentage of Latino legislators at 23 percent; New Mexico easily ranked first with 44 percent. In 2011, California's legislature ranked 16th in the percentage of female legislators (26.7 percent).[12] While legislators arguably seek out the good of California as a whole, they also desire to "represent" their racial, ethnic, or other affinity group. For example, several caucuses (Latino, Black Caucus, Asian, and LGBT—Lesbian, Gay, Bisexual, and Transgendered) are organized around this motivation. California's female legislators are sensitive to family and

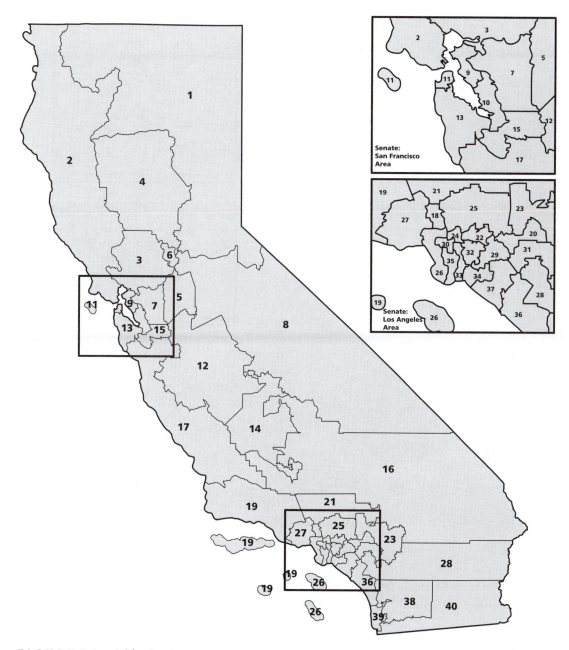

FIGURE 7.1a   California's Senate Districts

SOURCE: California Citizens Redistricting Commission.

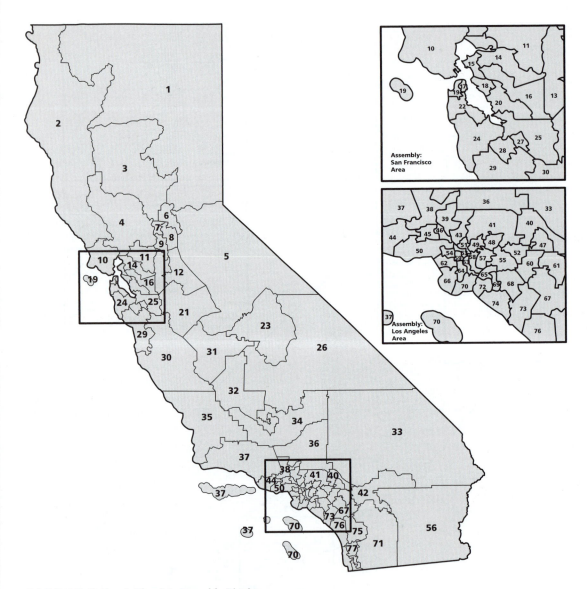

FIGURE 7.1b California's Assembly Districts

SOURCE: California Citizens Redistricting Commission.

health issues and consider themselves uniquely qualified to deal with them.[13] Their bipartisan caucus also seeks to increase the participation and representation of women in state government. Sometimes, social representation is highly personal. Four legislators once formed a "family caucus" to support and defend state programs for the mentally disabled; their reason quite simply was that each has a family member in need of such programs. Note Table 7.1, profiles the 2011–2012 legislature in term of partisan and group identities.

Box 7.1   Case in Point: How Many Bills Are Too Many?

By the February 18, 2011 deadline to submit bills for consideration, California legislators had submitted 2,323 of them—an average of about 19 per member. That is actually less than the 40-bill cap per member set in the early 1990s. Granted many of the new bills were merely resolutions such as declaring "Spay Day" or creating a "Parks Make Life Better" Month. Others were somewhat more substantive: banning caffeinated beer, altering the definition of extra virgin olive oil, and providing tax incentives to build commercial space vehicles in the Mojave Desert.

In light of a looming $25 billion budget deficit, Governor Jerry Brown asked the legislature to control

the volume of bills it considers. "I think there are definitely too many laws, just as there are too many regulations." His admonition will likely be as successful as those of his predecessors. What seems like policy trivia to average Californians can heighten a legislator's name recognition, raise needed campaign cash, or appease a favored interest group. And then there is the matter of time. As Republican consultant Rob Stutzman put it, "These legislators show up, they're not here for very long and they want to do everything they ever thought of."

SOURCE: Adapted from Michael J. Mishak, "State Lawmakers Are Being Urged to Scale Back the Number of Laws They Propose," *Los Angeles Times*, March 6, 2011.

Specific Representation   Individual constituents sometimes need specific representation, that is, individual attention. Constituent service, called "casework," is the vehicle through which this function takes place. For instance, many constituents seek help dealing with assorted state bureaucracies such as the Department of Motor Vehicles. Casework often involves little more than researching pending bills or listening to callers vent their

frustrations over the telephone. District office staffers, including college and university interns, do the bulk of this work.

Functional Representation   Functional representation refers to the specific policy interests and preferences that legislators bring to Sacramento. Former teachers, farmers, or city officials might logically gravitate to education,

TABLE 7.1   The Legislature at a Glance, 2011–12

	Senate (40)		Assembly (80)
Democrats	25		52
Republicans	15		28
Women	12		22
Latinas	(1)		(2)
Latinos	7		13
African Americans	2		6
Asian Americans	3		7
LGBT*	2		5
Former Assembly Members	37	Former Senate Members	4

*Lesbian, Gay, Bisexual, Transgendered

SOURCE: Data from legislators' Web sites; compiled by Richard Burnweit.

agriculture, or local government committees. Other members might wish to represent key industries in their districts, such as computer technology. As Table 7.2 portrays, the legislature's policy committees are organized around a rich diversity of functional interests. Although constituents may not routinely think in these functional terms, interest groups do. Each committee is monitored by a familiar assortment of interest groups (such as the Aging and Long Term Care Committee by senior groups).

Perceptual Representation Legislators themselves perceive their representational roles in different ways. British philosopher and member of Parliament Edmund Burke once distinguished between trustee roles and delegate roles. **Trustees** rely primarily on their own best judgment when voting on legislation rather than the wishes (fleeting wishes, thought Burke) of their constituents who elected them. **Delegates** lean primarily on those constituent wishes and deliberately seek them out. Modern political scientists have added the politico role. **Politicos** combine the two roles depending on how controversial specific issues are locally.[14] For instance, even though he harbored personal reservations about several "Three Strikes" bills, which imposed long sentences on repeat criminal offenders, then State Senator Leroy Greene concluded he would nonetheless support them. "I'm going to vote for these turkeys because my constituents want me to." These perceptions are not static. One study of the California Assembly suggested that, over time, legislators change their role perceptions. Why? It could be that legislators vote inconsistently or do not think about whether they are trustees, delegates, or politicos.[15]

Executive Oversight

A third function of California's legislature is **executive branch oversight**. The state constitution mandates some of these oversight activities. For instance, the Senate must confirm various gubernatorial appointments to commissions (such as Fish and Game, Public Utilities, and the University of California Regents). Both the Senate and Assembly confirm gubernatorial appointments to fill vacancies in constitutional offices. Like Congress, the legislature can remove statewide officeholders and judges through a rarely used impeachment process. The Joint Legislative Audit Committee works with the Bureau of State Audits to assess the financial and operational activities of various state agencies and programs. Such investigations may uncover various spending abuses by state employees. To maintain its own independence and objectivity, the Bureau of State Audits is itself overseen by another independent group, the Little Hoover Commission (formally called the Milton Marks Commission on California State Government Organization and Economy).

A routinely used oversight tool is the "power of the purse." This term actually refers to several processes. In the **authorization process**, the legislature gives authority for an agency program to exist. In the **appropriation process**, the legislature creates spending authority, thereby allowing the agency to implement the program. Through the annual budget, authorization, and appropriations processes, the legislature can evaluate agency performance and set its own spending priorities. In doing this work, legislative committees hear from executive branch officials as much as from private sector lobbyists.

Civic Education

The final function involves the *civic education* of constituents. Legislators are expected to educate people about the legislative process and California politics generally. In Sacramento, they meet with district constituents, students, professional lobbyists, and many interest group members who visit the Capitol. Legislators explain their version of how the process works and why favored legislation is so difficult to pass or afford. On occasion, they (or their staffs) write newspaper opinion pieces. Back in the districts, legislators speak to service clubs and community gatherings,

TABLE 7.2   California's Standing Legislative Committees

Assembly (30)	Senate (22)
Accountability and Administrative Review	
Aging and Long-Term Care	Agriculture
Agriculture	Appropriations
Appropriations	Banking, Finance, and Insurance
Arts, Entertainment, Sports, Tourism, and Internet Media	Budget and Fiscal Review
Banking and Finance	Business, Professions, and Economic Development
Budget	Education
Business, Professions and Consumer Protection	Elections and Constitutional Amendments
Education	
Elections and Redistricting	Energy, Utilities, and Communications
Environmental Safety and Toxic Materials	Environmental Quality
	Governance and Finance
Government Organization	Governmental Organization
Health	
Higher Education	Health
Housing and Community Development	
	Human Services
	Insurance
Human Services	Judiciary
Insurance	Labor and Industrial Relations
Jobs, Economic Development, and the Economy	
Judiciary	Natural Resources and Water
	Public Employment and Retirement
Labor and Employment	
Local Government	Public Safety
Natural Resources	
Public Employees, Retirement and Social Security	Rules
Public Safety	Transportation and Housing
Revenue and Taxation	Veterans Affairs
Rules	
Transportation	
Utilities and Commerce	
Veterans Affairs	
Water, Parks and Wildlife	

SOURCE: California State Assembly and Senate.

issue press releases, hold "office hours," and confer with local chapters of statewide groups. Each activity provides an opportunity for them to explain the process and their views on policy. In many ways, the members' Web sites serve the same function.

These four legislative functions commingle constantly. A constituent complaint about the Department of Motor Vehicles might lead to a member inquiry about how the department operates. Urban and rural legislators sit side-by-side on committees, learning to appreciate the geographic diversity they bring to their work. Historically underrepresented groups in the legislature, such as African Americans and Latinos, form their own bicameral caucuses to make social representation more visible and deliberate in the eyes of colleagues. Those more theoretical roles also intermingle. Legislators who think they are "trustees" relative to their districts often behave like "delegates," not of their constituents but of interest groups with whom they more routinely work.

GETTING THERE
AND STAYING THERE

Why people seek *any* public office is an interesting question to political scientists. Joining a legislature often means giving up one's privacy, normal family life, career continuity, and, for some people, substantial income. What motivates California candidates is especially fascinating. Because being a legislator is a full-time job (and then some, legislators would argue), a member must maintain two residences, even if one is a small Sacramento apartment. Family dislocation (Where do you put the kids in school? What about a working spouse?) and frequent travel to the district creates stresses most Californians can only imagine. What about resuming a career after a term-limited legislative stint? Is that even possible? Yet the price is worth it to many members, who attempt to convert their beliefs into public policy.

Recruitment

The initial decision to run for the legislature is determined by both personal desire and requests by others. Three patterns of candidate recruitment have emerged in California.

Self Starters   Some individuals run for the legislature because they desire to implement policy preferences or begin political careers. They talk themselves into it. Some come from local offices such as school boards, city councils, and county boards of supervisors. They figure they can do as good a job as the legislators they meet coping with state policies and legislative mandates. Other aspiring legislators become interested in the impact of state policy on their own professions. Farmers, doctors, and members of "brokerage" occupations (law, real estate, and insurance) often fit this category. Some gain valuable policy and political experience as staff members in Sacramento or in district offices. Others spend large sums of their own wealth to run for office, claiming independence from special interests.

Sponsorship   Some legislative candidates are sponsored by or recruited to run by others. In California, sponsorship comes not so much from local party officials but from legislative leaders in Sacramento. In recent years, the Assembly speaker, Senate president pro tem, and partisan caucus staffs have provided both encouragement and campaign funding to promising candidates. This is possible because legislative leaders can raise substantial surplus funds well beyond what they need for their own reelection efforts. What do these legislative leaders look for in potential candidates? They generally seek candidates who will be good legislators *and* who will support them in future leadership battles. The ability to win always helps! In contested primaries, these Sacramento benefactors usually wait for a primary winner to emerge and then provide support for a fall general election campaign.

Combination Pattern   In recent years, many legislative races have featured a combination of self-starting and sponsorship. Given the entrepreneurial nature of California politics and the historically weak local political parties, many candidates need self-starter qualities, such as a burning ambition to run and win. Yet these people alone cannot marshal the resources needed to win. Remember, compared to many states, California's legislature is relatively small: 40 senators and 80 assembly members who represent more than 38 million people. That translates into huge districts—roughly 950,000 people per Senate district and 475,000 people per Assembly district. No other state legislature has near these per-district populations (See Table 7.3). Face-to-face voter contact in some districts necessarily gives way to political advertising. Media costs, the largest chunk of any modern campaign budget, are expensive in California. Unless a candidate is wealthy, outside help is essential. Once they are nominated, legislative candidates may be showered with resources including endorsements, party assistance, funding from legislative leaders, PAC contributions, and soft money expenditures.

The Power of Incumbency Once elected, incumbents enjoy tremendous advantages when running for reelection. They attract the vast majority of PAC contributions, can "draft" staffers as campaign aides, command media attention, and benefit from districtwide name recognition. In partisan primary elections, the vast majority of incumbents run unopposed by a member of their own parties. Interestingly, in the case of presumably competitive open seat primaries—where incumbents are vacating office voluntarily or due to term limits—one candidate per office per party is

commonplace. This suggests considerable candidate sorting even before candidates file nomination papers.

Why They Stay: Rewards of Office

Given the frustrations of the legislative life in California (hyperpartisanship, gridlock, short tenures guaranteed by term limits, incessant travel, and family pressures), one might wonder why legislators want to stay and hate to leave. What drives them to remain? For instance, why do they run for Senate when their Assembly terms expire? The reasons are several.

Policy Achievement Given the problems and challenges facing California, finding solutions and crafting statewide policy is a primary goal for many legislators. These members have genuine public service goals, and they operate in Sacramento and back home with those goals in mind. Serving on just the right committees and moving into leadership positions on those committees are paramount to policy achievers. Post-term limit members bring a sense of policy urgency, knowing they have only a few years to enact their preferences into law.

Material Benefits Many state legislatures provide poor salaries and working conditions. Not in California where an independent citizens compensation commission sets members' annual salaries. In 2011, a legislator's salary was $95,291, the nation's highest. Legislative leaders such as the Assembly speaker and the Senate president pro tem earn

TABLE 7.3   **California in Perspective: State Legislative District Populations (2009, in 1000s)**

	State Senate	State Assembly/House
California	931	466
U.S. Average (50 states)	157	57
Vermont	21	4

NOTE: Vermont's lower house had only 4,172 persons per district because it is a small state and its lower house has 150 members, almost twice the membership of California's Assembly.

SOURCE: *Book of the States, 2010* (Washington, DC: Council of State Governments, 2010); 2010 Census.

somewhat more. On top of that, out-of-town legislators receive a tax-free $142 stipend for unvouchered living expenses each day their house is "in session," a figure which can upwards of $30,000 in largely tax-free compensation annually.[16] As a result, brief "check-in" sessions are commonplace, even when there is little business to conduct. Additional benefits include an automobile, cell phone, health insurance, trips to the district, and funds to hire staff and rent office space. Critics call these expenditures unwarranted "perks," but others consider them the normal cost of running the nation's largest state.

Psychic Satisfaction   If legislators do not bring big egos to Sacramento, they acquire them there. They have many staff members to help with policy, research, personal, party, and leadership responsibilities. Members experience other psychic rewards; lobbyists, constituents, and virtually everyone they meet pay deference to them, its own form of celebrity. As a former Senate leader put it, "When you're in Sacramento, the entire city is dedicated to making you feel important and special."[17]

Careerism, Then and Now   Careerism and political ambition are related. According to political scientists, political ambitions may be discrete (short-term service with return to private life), static (making a long-run career out of a particular office), or progressive (using an office as a stepping stone to still higher office).[18] Until Proposition 140, the California legislature had become known as a hothouse for political careers. The power of incumbency and relatively safe districts assured some job security. By state legislative standards, the pay and perks were good and needed to be, because the work was increasingly full-time. Considered a dead end in many other states, legislative service in California allowed rapid advancement and rewarded political ambition and policy entrepreneurship. California lawmakers viewed and used their positions as springboards to higher office.

Proposition 140 has had an impact on careerism in two ways. For some, it effectively aborts a long-term career as an elected official. For others, it alters the stepping-stone process. In what has been called the term limits shuffle, legislators constantly cast about for other offices—federal, state, and even local—to extend their public careers. Some land appointments to head executive branch agencies or sit on relatively obscure but well-paid boards and commissions.

The election of Arnold Schwarzenegger as governor threatened to alter legislative ambitions still further. First, in 2004 he suggested that the California legislature return to its pre-1960s part-time status, accusing it of not having enough to do and producing "strange" bills when it did act. While his proposal may have been a playful poke at legislative Democrats, it stirred up latent wishes on the part of some to further deprofessionalize the legislature. Second, he threatened to abolish many of the boards and commissions that had become well-paid career parachutes for at least some termed-out legislators. Third, he backed efforts to transfer the task of reapportioning legislative districts from the legislature itself to either a panel of judges or an independent citizens commission.

How They Stay: Reapportionment Politics

To understand reapportionment, you must understand the motives of legislators. Willingness to stay in office is not the same as staying; ask any incumbent who loses a reelection bid. But incumbents generally know what it takes to get elected time and time again. More than challengers, they can afford the campaign techniques described in Chapter 5. Also, they fully understand that campaigning is territorial: The boundaries of a legislative district can spell victory or defeat. How are these boundaries drawn? After each decade, the U.S. Census Bureau counts the population and gathers other demographic data. Historically, **reapportionment** involved the legislature redrawing district lines for the U.S. House of Representatives, the State Assembly, and the State Senate to reflect population growth and movement within the state. As with other bills, the governor would need to sign any reapportionment plan. The California Constitution requires that any plan consider, to the extent possible, the "geographic integrity" of existing city and county boundaries.

In reality, the legislature rarely followed that constitutional guideline because population shifts and communities of interest are not the only factors in redrawing district boundaries. Reapportioning districts for partisan or other advantage is called **gerrymandering**. There are three types: (1) **Partisan gerrymandering** means either "splintering" a district (dividing either Republicans or Democrats among several districts to dilute their strength) or "packing" a district (say, concentrating Democrats into one district to enhance election chances for Republicans in other districts). (2) **Incumbent gerrymandering**, a long-standing one in California, protects incumbents regardless of party. Often called "sweetheart" gerrymandering, this type is sometimes found under divided government conditions. That incumbents protect each other should hardly be surprising. (3) **Racial gerrymandering** has historically been used in the United States to dilute the strength of racial minorities. In recent years, it has been used, often in the South, to concentrate minority voting strength—often ensuring victory for minority candidates. Although this goal may be laudable, the U.S. Supreme Court has rejected the most obvious racial gerrymanders as a violation of the Fourteenth Amendment's equal protection clause.

When California legislators faced the task of redistricting, previous reapportionment efforts colored their efforts. Consider the 1980s, when a Democratic legislature redrew legislative district lines to the advantage of its own party members. Republicans countered with three initiatives challenging the new plans, but the voters rejected them. Eventually, the state Supreme Court upheld the original plan, ruling that the state constitution allows only one plan per decade. Bitter Republicans vowed to prevail after the next census.

By the early 1990s, partisanship was only one factor among many in the redistricting equation. Growth and ethnic diversity were other factors.

The 1980s saw tremendous population growth, especially in interior California. This was bound to threaten incumbents as district maps would have to be redrawn substantially. In addition, a growing number of minorities in California wanted not only a voice in the reapportionment process but also new districts that would reflect their interests. Furthermore, the *Voting Rights Act of 1965* (as amended in 1982 and interpreted by the courts) required state legislatures to *create* racial and ethnic majority voting districts if at all feasible. Political scientist Bruce Cain called this form of racial gerrymandering the "affirmative action gerrymander."[19]

In 1991, after a prolonged redistricting stalemate between Republican Governor Pete Wilson and legislative Democrats, the state Supreme Court appointed a panel of "masters" (retired judges) to redraw the districts presumably from scratch, taking into account those legal mandates. The resulting 1992 reapportionment plan dealt a stunning blow to many incumbents—forcing some into retirement, others into campaigns against colleagues, and still others into premature stepping-stone races. Following Proposition 140, that reapportionment was truly a bitter pill for California's legislature.

The 2001 reapportionment was an altogether different experience. With little or no debate, the State Senate approved the new maps on two votes: 38 to 2 and 40 to 0. The Assembly approved the maps on a bipartisan 58 to 10 vote. What happened to the rancor of earlier battles? First, sizeable voting majorities in the Assembly and Senate (50 to 30 and 26 to 14, respectively) gave Democrats a substantial advantage in redrawing the maps; Republicans were at their mercy. Just retaining current Republican districts would be something of a victory for them. Second, although California's ethnic minorities had been growing in the 1990s, eking out still more "minority-majority" districts was unlikely. In the end, the 2001 reapportionment process was a classic incumbent protection effort. As a result, it locked in (to the extent redistricting can) Democratic majorities and prior gains made by the state's minorities. It also locked into place, but did not further reduce, the minority status of California's Republican lawmakers.

The 2011 Reapportionment

The 2001 reapportionment angered both reform groups and voters. One group, the politically moderate Democratic Leadership Council branded the state one of the "Dirty Dozen" states that, through gerrymandering, rigged elections and suppressed voter turnout. Only a handful of legislative seats changed parties during the 2000s, plausibly reducing voter turnout because election outcomes were foregone conclusions.[20] Other analysts traced the ideological extremes in the California legislature (more conservative Republicans and more liberal Democrats than in the past) and the policy gridlock that ensued to safe districts gerrymandered by incumbents.[21]

While angry voters rejected a Schwarzenegger – backed measure to transfer redistricting power from the legislature to a panel of retired judges, they did approve a ground-breaking reform in 2008. **Proposition 11** was an initiative constitutional amendment and statute granting remapping authority over legislative districts and the five-member Board of Equalization (BOA) to a 14-member independent Citizen Redistricting Commission. In 2010, an initial group of 30,000 interested individuals was winnowed down to 4,500 applicants and eventually 14 commissioners by a complex and laborious selection process. In November 2010, voters added to the commission's purview California's 53 congressional districts that had been exempted under Proposition 11. The transfer was complete. The voters had removed all redistricting authority from the state legislature for the first time in the California's history. The new commission began its work in earnest in 2011 by hiring staff, digesting newly released 2010 Census data, holding hearings across the state, and drafting new maps to meet an August 15 deadline.

What would be different this time? Seemingly everything. The commission itself was made up of five Democrats, five Republicans, and four others but none were seasoned politicos or even related to them. In addition to meeting various federal requirements (one person, one vote), district boundaries had to 1) maintain the geographic integrity of cities, counties, neighborhoods, and "communities of interest," 2) be geographically compact, and 3) nest two Assembly districts into one Senate district and ten Senate districts within one BOA district. Furthermore, the commission could *not* favor particular incumbents, political candidates, or political parties. Muddying these unchartered waters were the initial census results. The Latino population had grown substantially in the 2000s as had inland California. It was likely that coastal districts might be larger in size but fewer in number. The final maps approved by the Commission in August 2011 made many state legislative and congressional districts more competitive and viewed incumbents neutrally.[22] Fearing a dilution of their voting strength, both the Republican Party and some Latino groups vowed to fight the new maps. In the meantime, affected candidates scrambled to conform their 2012 ambitions to the new maps.

ORGANIZING TO LEGISLATE

No matter who redraws legislative districts, making laws is still the legislature's primary task. Thousands of bills may be introduced during each two-year session of the California legislature. When the great jurist Oliver Wendell Holmes observed that "every opinion tends to become a law," one might have thought he was commenting on California's legislature. On paper, the process of making a law seems straightforward enough. In reality, it is complex and fraught with intrigue and, on occasion, chaos.

The California Constitution requires a bicameral legislature, consisting of a lower house (an 80-member Assembly) and an upper house (a 40-member Senate). Assembly members serve two-year terms; senators, four-year terms. Under Proposition 140, assembly members are limited to three terms; senators to two. Although both houses behave similarly in many respects, there are differences. The state Senate is more prestigious due to its smaller size and longer terms. Senators tend to be more politically experienced; many gained that experience in the Assembly. Senators can seek still higher office in the middle of their terms without losing their seats—a "free ride." Compared to the Speaker-dominated

Assembly, senators are more independent. Each finds publicity easier to attain. As a body, the Senate can more easily challenge a governor by not confirming gubernatorial appointments that require Senate confirmation. Also, the Senate seems quieter and more deliberative than the rough-and-tumble Assembly.

How does the legislature itself organize to do its work? The process in both houses leans heavily on leadership, a committee system, and professional staffs.

The Role of Leadership

Groups large and small need leaders to manage what they do. Legislatures are no different. In his study of state legislative politics, Alan Rosenthal listed six different leadership tasks: organizing for work, processing legislation, negotiating agreements, dispensing benefits, handling the press, and maintaining the institution.[23] California's legislative leaders perform each of these tasks. The key positions are discussed below.

Assembly Speaker   One of the most fascinating offices in California politics is the **Assembly Speaker**, the pinnacle of what used to be called a "self-inflicted dictatorship." Once elected by the entire Assembly, the majority **party caucus** has chosen recent speakers. A party's caucus is its total membership in the chamber when gathered to do business. Speakers sometimes must court minority party votes when majority control of the Assembly is marginal. Speakers balance power and policy—perpetuating their own power while using it to achieve policy goals. In part, this is done by controlling committees: determining the number and titles of committees, assigning all members to committees (with the exception of the Rules Committee), controlling the selection of other leadership positions within the Speaker's party, managing floor action, enforcing Assembly customs, and assigning office space and some staff. When asked why he had assigned a newly elected critic of his a smelly, windowless broom closet of an office, then-speaker Willie Brown replied, "I didn't have anything smaller." No wonder he nicknamed himself the "ayatollah of the legislature."

Jesse Unruh was the first assembly speaker to buttress the role of the office. Under his leadership in the 1960s, the Assembly became a powerful policymaking force in state government. Brown occupied the post from 1980 to 1996. He was the first African American to hold the post and served longer than any predecessor. His lengthy tenure provided leadership, stability, and operational predictability. His policy expertise, ability to craft legislative deals, and fundraising prowess kept his post secure.

What have term limits done to this once mighty office? The results are mixed. On the one hand, term limits allowed more assembly members to seek the speakership and that resulted in a number of firsts. Cruz Bustemante became the first Latino speaker and other Latinos followed including Los Angeles Mayor Antonio Villaraigosa, Fabian Nunez, and John Perez who was chosen speaker in January 2010. Perez has substantial background in organized labor and is openly gay. His immediate predecessor was Karen Bass who became the first African American woman in the nation to head a legislative body. On the other hand, term limits have posed a fundamental problem for Assembly speakers. The majority party must choose between relatively inexperienced colleagues who can gain experience and provide continuity in the Speaker role (Perez had only one year of Assembly experience when he was tapped), or veterans who must leave the post within a few years of accepting it. In short, they become power-limited lame ducks the moment they assume the speakership.

Other Assembly Posts   Several other leadership posts round out the legislative elite in the assembly. The *speaker pro tempore* is a member of the Speaker's party and exercises the powers of the Speaker in the latter's absence. Although this individual is technically chosen by the entire Assembly, the Speaker's choice gets the nod. The speaker pro tem usually presides during floor sessions, allowing the Speaker to mingle with other members. The *assembly majority* and *minority leaders* are selected from their respective party caucuses. They represent caucus interests on the Assembly floor; the latter communicates minority wishes to the Speaker. Several whips monitor legislation and secure floor votes from caucus members. The Assembly Rules Committee exercises institutional leadership by selecting many legislative staff members, studying legislative rules, and referring bills to committees. Its nine members include four members each from the Democratic and Republican caucuses; the Speaker appoints the chair.

Senate President pro tempore In the U.S. Senate, the vice president can preside and vote in case of a tie, but rarely performs either function. In the California Senate, the lieutenant governor has comparable powers but also rarely uses them. Day-to-day leadership is in the hands of the **president pro tempore** (pro tem for short). Although the entire senate votes to fill this post, the majority party invariably chooses one of its own. David Roberti (D, Van Nuys) occupied the post from 1980 to 1994, roughly paralleling Speaker Brown's tenure. In 1994, he was succeeded by Bill Lockyer (D, Hayward). When Lockyer resigned to

run for attorney general in 1998, the Democrats picked John Burton (D, San Francisco). This colorful, longtime political operator brought passion, emotion, intensity, and integrity to the job. In 2004, the termed-out Burton was succeeded by Don Perata (D, Oakland), a former school teacher, known for his prowess at deal making and fundraising. In late 2008, he was succeeded by Darrell Steinberg (D, Sacramento). The *California Political Almanac* called Steinberg a "tour de force as a legislator—highly intelligent, ethical to a fault, and a creature of such hard work that he sometimes exasperates colleagues and staff."[24] On paper, this post appears to be less powerful than the Assembly speakership. But, because of longer terms and individual tenures, the senate president pro tem post rivals the Assembly speakership in many respects. Much of the pro tem's power stems from chairing a five-member *Rules Committee*. The other four members consist of two senators from each party caucus. Its powers are comparable to both the Assembly Speaker and the Assembly Rules Committee.

AP Photo/Rich Pedroncelli

Photo of Senate President Pro Tem Darrell Steinberg (left) and Assembly Speaker John Perez

The Committee System

To carry out their policymaking responsibilities, modern legislatures must organize into committees—much as Congress does. The committee process recognizes that screening legislation takes specialization and division of labor. California's legislature is divided into numerous committees. Combined, they form a *committee system*: the web of relationships among a number of committees required to enact policy.

Several kinds of committees constitute the committee system in California's legislature. The job of permanent **standing committees** is to process legislation. In other words, they formulate public policy (see Table 7.2 for a complete list of these committees). Members seek assignment to certain policy committees because of former occupations, current policy interests, or the possibility of receiving campaign contributions. Some women legislators have preferred to serve on committees dealing with human services issues such as children and welfare.[25] We already noted a preference for committees that control legislation of interest to potential campaign contributors—so-called juice committees. Examples include the Assembly Government Organization Committee and the Senate Insurance Committee. Apart from election considerations, policy committees give members opportunities to develop policy expertise and address the great and not-so-great issues facing the Golden State.

Several other committees deserve mention. **Fiscal committees** handle bills that require the spending of money. Both houses have appropriations and budget committees devoted to this task. Members seeking power, prestige, or institutional importance covet these assignments. **Conference committees** are convened if the two houses produce different versions of the same bill; their job is to iron out the differences and send unified bills back to both houses for final passage. **Select committees** study various issues facing California with long-term solutions in mind. Both houses have dozens of them. They cover topics ranging from e-commerce, the Colorado River, and wine to California-Mexico relations, school safety, and

mobile homes. Various **joint committees** include members from both houses. They consider matters of common concern such as fisheries, the arts, and homeland security.

Why all these seemingly extra committees? They can give needed visibility to emerging issues such as border conflicts and school safety. But they also create added chairmanships, opportunities to hire additional staff, and pools of potential campaign contributors. Not only are there more committees than in the past, many standing committees—the workhorses of the legislature—are larger than ever. For example, of its 80 members, fully 27 are on the Assembly Budget Committee. Scheduling conflicts are commonplace and quorums are illusive as members juggle their time. According to Jim Knox, executive director of California Common Cause, "The idea of members listening to actual testimony at these hearings has become sort of quaint." As a result, committees are less deliberative than in the past.[26]

The Staff

One mark of a professional legislature is a professional staff. Before the California legislature became full-time in the 1960s, a few staff offices met its needs for information and analysis: the Legislative Counsel of California (created in 1913 to help draft bills), the California State Auditor (established in 1955 to provide fiscal oversight of state agencies), and the Legislative Analyst's Office (created in 1941 to give nonpartisan advice on fiscal and policy issues). The Analyst's annual *Analysis of the Budget Bill* can run to nearly 1,600 pages. Over the years, it has developed a national reputation for expertise, solid analysis, and nonpartisanship.[27] In some ways, these offices have been islands of objectivity in a sea of subjective, partisan wrangling. That is, they serve the legislature as an institution and not the agendas of individual members.

As committees grew in number, so did committee staffs. In Sacramento, professional committee staffers are called "consultants." Given the many policy hats members must wear, the expertise these consultants provide is essential to the committee system. They may earn as much as or more than their elected bosses. In addition to the consultants, each house maintains separate staff to analyze pending bills and to do long-range research. Leadership staffs assist the house officers for both parties. Party staffs assist the respective party caucuses. In addition to secretaries and clerks, both houses employ undergraduate-and graduate-level interns to perform a variety of tasks. Some interns land full-time jobs as a result. More than a few have eventually become legislators.

Proposition 140 affected the legislative staff system in direct and indirect ways. Historically known for their expertise and relative objectivity, many legislative staffers have become more partisan in recent years. According to some critics, advocacy has overshadowed analysis, and political operatives have eclipsed policy experts. Initially, term limits cut staff budgets; years later they seem to have created a staff-level brain drain, as many move on to lobbying positions. Capitol insiders think this flux in staff has hobbled the legislature, but others think staff expansion itself has exacerbated the legislature's problems. To some, armies of staff and reams of paper have replaced policy vision and political fortitude.

THE LEGISLATIVE PROCESS

In truth, passing most legislation requires neither vision nor political courage. Constituents back home could hardly care less about many bills; most are minor changes to existing law, business regulations, and policies that affect the relative few. But all bills, large or small, even the budget bill, must survive the same process. As Figure 7.2 shows, the flow of legislation is quite simple—on paper. Internal deadlines impose additional structure on the process. For example, the last day to introduce a bill is in late February. The last day for bills to be passed out of a house or origin is in late May. August 31 is the last day for each house to pass bills. Fiscal committees impose and must meet additional deadlines. Beyond the deadlines and behind the scenes, informal processes work to

speed up, slow down, pass, or defeat bills. When people quote German Chancellor Otto Von Bismarck—"Laws are like sausages, it is better not to seem them being made"—they likely are referring to these informal processes.

Bill Introduction

An idea for a law can come from any number of sources, such as staff, lobbyists, executive agencies, constituents, and the member's experience. For example, one legislator introduced a bill requiring a vote of the people before local libraries could privatize their operations after discovering that such efforts result in higher costs and reduced service. The Legislative Counsel's office takes that idea and drafts the necessary legal language. The legislator who formally submits a bill is its author and is expected to shepherd it through the process; coauthors or cosponsors lend their names as supporters but do little else. Members must introduce bills by late February, but what if they are not ready by then? They can introduce "spot bills" containing nonsubstantive language that will be eventually replaced with substantive changes the author really wants. This is not to suggest that legislators initiate all bill ideas. Some observers estimate that a third of all bills are actually "sponsored" by interest groups, a fact that is not readily apparent in the formal legislative process.[28]

Committee Consideration

In both houses, the respective Rules Committees assign bills to committees for hearings. The fate of a bill may hinge on which committee hears it. All spending bills must be heard by each house's appropriations committee. During a typical hearing, the committee hears testimony on the bill from its author, government agencies, and/or interest groups. Managing enough committee votes for a "do-pass" recommendation can be tricky business. A majority of all committee members is required whether or not they are in attendance when a vote is taken. Given multiple committee memberships, hectic schedules, and the sheer number of

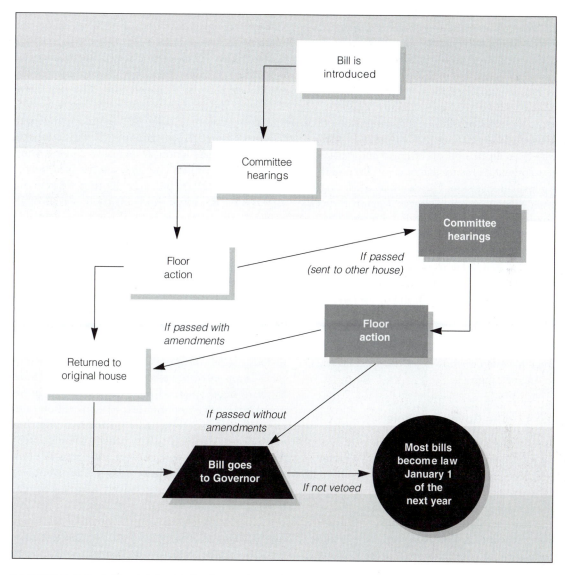

FIGURE 7.2 California's Legislative Process in Brief

SOURCE: Legislative Council of California.

bills, simply getting supporters to be there at the right time is a challenge. Ways to kill a bill include assigning it to more than one committee or calling for a committee vote when supporters are absent. Given the plethora of bills each session, some committees are awash in bills, preventing careful analysis of each one during the hearing process.

Floor Action and Conference Committee

On each house floor, garnering enough votes is equally challenging. Majorities of 41 in the Assembly and 21 in the Senate are required to pass legislation, even if there is only a bare quorum at the time.

A two-thirds vote is necessary on the annual budget and for emergency bills (those taking immediate effect). Yet during floor debate, amendments to the bill may be offered and voted on by a simple majority *of those present.* Because it is so easy (numerically speaking) to amend a bill compared to passing it, floor amendments can be used to substantially modify a bill even to the point of killing it. The ultimate modification is called GANDA or "gut and amend." Here, the entire contents of a bill are stripped and replaced with new content, a practice that often occurs near the end of a legislative session. For example, a bill originally dealing with how schools classify English learners was completely rewritten to ban the proposed DNA testing of UC Berkeley freshmen. While gut and amend appears to violate the legislature's own rules (amendments must be germane to the original bill) the rules are ignored as needed. Amendments aside, the generic process that began in the house of origin repeats it self in the second house. A conference committee resolves inter-house differences. If its members cannot agree with the conference report, the bill dies. Conferees have been known to rewrite bills well beyond original language.

The Governor's Role

If a bill passes both houses, the governor may sign it (making it law), do nothing (making it law without a signature), or veto it. As in Congress, a vetoed bill then requires an extraordinary two-thirds vote of both the Assembly and the Senate for it to become law. The mere threat of a veto can halt a bill's progress or alter its content. Understandably, this is more commonplace when the governor and the legislature are of different parties or when personal relations between the governor and affected legislators are strained.

If Figure 7.2 does not reveal the nuances of legislation, it also does not communicate the rhythm or pace of the legislature. The beginning of a term moves rather slowly. By the end of a legislative session (usually late summer), the pace becomes frenetic. At that point, the textbook process becomes fiction as legislators "hijack" and rewrite scores of bills and bypass what were once-essential committee hearings. During the closing days and weeks, some legislators try to slip through local bills (benefiting individual constituents or single groups). Numerous interest group sponsored bills are considered during the day while fundraisers targeting those same interests are scheduled at night. Upward of 1,500 bills may be considered during those final weeks.

As you reflect on the legislative process in California, remember that the job of the legislature is to both pass and *not pass* legislation. Bills fail for various reasons. Of course, a bill might lack widespread support or be unacceptable to the governor. Schwarzenegger vetoed more than 300 bills in his first year as governor. But less obvious reasons also exist. Some members may introduce bills but expend little effort on their behalf. Merely introducing bills (along with the requisite press releases) may placate some groups or constituents. Members may cast "yes" votes on relatively harmless legislation to appease legislative colleagues; this has been the nature of logrolling throughout legislative history. If a bill dies, especially a bad one, a legislator can breathe easier while blaming committees,

---

B o x 7.2   A State Senator's Lament

Amid new efforts to cap the number of bills the California State Legislature considers each year, some legislators voiced deeper concerns about how the legislature goes about making policy. State Senator Mark Wyland (R-Carlsbad) would prohibit any bill introductions during the first year of a two-year legislative session. "We don't address the fundamental problems facing the state of California and we don't do it because we are in a bill factory, There's not a single major issue that we analyze in depth."

SOURCE: Karen de Sa, "A Push to Rein In the Leverage Lobbyists Have Over California Lawmakers," *The Mercury News* (July 21, 2010; updated November 1, 2010).

the leadership, "special interests," a media blitz, the governor, or whomever for its defeat.

THE THIRD HOUSE

In many ways, the legislative process requires lobbying by interest groups. In a representative democracy, interest groups would have to be invented if they did not already exist. Chapter 6 outlined the role of interest groups as linkage institutions in California politics. They organize in different ways to express their policy preferences and serve their members. The professionals they employ to affect the policy process are called *lobbyists*. Sacramento's lobbyists influence the legislative process in six distinct ways.

1. *Making campaign contributions.* Contributing to campaigns is not lobbying *per se*. But because so many fundraisers occur in Sacramento, lobbyists are expected to attend. Legislators and lobbyists alike agree that this practice is more used to "buy" access rather than votes on specific bills. Because contributions are made on a year-round basis, lobbyists sometimes make them—and

legislators sometimes solicit them—at the same time bills of interest to those lobbyists are being considered. This perceived "pay to play" atmosphere is particularly evident near the end of legislative sessions when fundraising events multiply much like the bills awaiting action. The practice is unseemly even to some legislators. According to former Assembly member Nicole Parra, "It's happening while bills are moving and despite the fact that we're all professionals and you never talk about legislation, it's just too close—not illegal, just too close for comfort."[29] Some interest groups such as local governments are barred from making campaign contributions (they would be using tax revenues to do so) so they must rely all the more on lobbyists and former local officials who are now legislative allies.

2. *Simply being there.* If a physical presence in Sacramento was optional, many groups would locate elsewhere. But because timing is so important in the legislative process, lobbyists need to be on hand to monitor or "watchdog" bills as they proceed through the legislative labyrinth. Being there also includes making

---

B o x 7.3   Case in Point: A Newbie Enters the Fray

In recent years, it appeared that Mark Zuckerberg and his colleagues at Facebook were simply growing their wildly popular social networking Web site, and growing rich in the process. That is, until the Palo Alto-based company learned of "The Social Networking Privacy Act," a California State Senate bill introduced by Senate Senator Ellen Corbett in February 2010. The act would have required businesses like Facebook to refrain from displaying personal information like home addresses and phone numbers of users under 18 years of age. Doing otherwise would result in civil penalties. The motivation was to protect minors from sexual predators and others who might misuse such information. Examples of such abuse were increasing alongside the growth of Facebook itself.

Company executives must have become worried when SB 1361 passed the State Senate on a 25-4 vote in April 2010 and headed to the Assembly for consideration. Within weeks, Facebook had hired Gonzalez

Public Affairs to represent its interests in Sacramento and its particular interest in the assembly version of SB 1361. According to Senator Corbett, "By the time it got to the Assembly, the opposition lobbying had begun." While her staff sought input from Facebook, "it appears they just worked in the background to kill the bill." And kill it they did. According to Secretary of State filings, this lobbying victory was a bargain in the lobbying world, costing Facebook less than $7,000.

Critics claim that Facebook should have worked more closely with TechNet, a lobbying coalition that includes Google and Microsoft, rather than become the "public face" of opposition to user privacy. According to one, the effort "places a giant bulls-eye on the company by elected officials as the poster boy for privacy regulation."

SOURCE: John Letzing, "Facebook Makes Foray into California Lobbying," *MarketWatch*, October 27, 2010.

friends and establishing numerous contacts with legislators and their staffs. Capitol hallways, elevators, the sixth-floor eatery, and members' offices all serve as contact opportunities. Lobbyists may be in hot pursuit most any time. A veteran lobbyist once noted that, during lengthy committee hearings members "have to go to the bathroom sometime!"

3. *Knowing the process.* Simply being there is not enough. An intimate knowledge of the process and of the personality quirks of members and their staff is essential. Any legislature is a par-liamentary labyrinth characterized by a host of written and unwritten rules. The written rules involve the intricacies of the legislative process discussed earlier. Unwritten rules might encompass everything from how members address each other to what they wear. This is why so many successful lobbyists have been former members or staffers.

4. *Providing information.* The most important role a lobbyist can play is giving legislators, commit-tees, and staff accurate, detailed information on a bill, especially its impact on their clients. Lobbyists should be and often are masters of the subject encompassed by a bill. Appealing to common sense and logic works especially well on minor bills where other pressures might be absent. On controversial matters, "winning on the merits" is less fruitful. A related technique is the use of a silver bullet—a piece of inform-ation that, if made public, would prove too damaging for a bill to survive. If there is opposition to a particular bill, groups often propose amendments to make a bill more acceptable or even harmless. Observers believe term limits has increased the informational power of lobbyists and interest groups, the new repositories of institutional memory.

5. *Coalition building.* Many interest groups believe there is strength in numbers. Accordingly, they develop coalitions with each other to help craft policy or defeat policies injurious to their interests. Given the umbrella structure and generalized interests of the California Chamber of Commerce, the Chamber hosts 24 such coalitions addressing topics like Latin American trade and free trade. Holding large coalitions in place is not easy. Several environmentally-oriented members left the AB32 Implementation Group after learning that other members including some of the state's largest polluters, were working to water down the state's landmark global warming law.[30]

6. *Grassroots lobbying.* An increasingly common lobbying technique is the use of **grassroots pressure**. Because legislators of necessity pay attention to constituents back home, grassroots efforts help mobilize them and connect them with their representatives on specific policy issues—even single bills. Modern technology and the presence of term limits makes "farming the membership" both feasible and effective. According to public relations executive Katherine MacDonald, "Grass-roots efforts work more now because new legislators tend to be more grass-roots based and less Sacramento based."[31] As a result, they respond to organized phone call, letter, fax, and email campaigns. A variant of grassroots lobbying is **crowd lobbying**. Here, interest group members gather in Sacramento for briefings and to play "lobbyist for a day," as they roam statehouse hallways. The more organized wear business attire, sport nametags, meet legislators and staff, and may even testify at a hearing. Others, sometimes busloads of them, rally on the Capitol steps to voice their views. That said, not all constituents are equal or equally significant to legislators. Successful lobbyists know how to cultivate those constituents closest to legislators or how to help their clients become significant constituents worth listening to.[32]

In short, the lobbyists, or the third house, represent one point of a legislative triangle. The other two points are legislative committees (both members and staffs) and executive branch agencies (their legislative liaison offices). These triangles or issue networks exist on every subject of permanent interest in state government. They best portray the three-way communication and influence pattern that characterizes the legislative process.

Public school teachers march in Sacramento to protest proposed education spending cuts.

CONCLUSION

California's legislature is the most professionalized in the nation. Its well-paid members work full time and can rely on ample resources to make informed public policy.[33] But this body has faced daunting challenges in recent years. Term limits have diluted legislative competency, erased institutional memory, and transferred policy influence and expertise to the third house and the executive branch. In many ways, the initiative process has provided a viable alternative to the California legislature and the very notion of representative government for interest groups, individuals, and even public officials themselves. Reapportionment practices have lessened electoral competition, hardened partisan views, and reduced bipartisan approaches to policymaking in general and the state budget in particular. Future challenges might well include the state's growing diversity. Although legislatures are intended to represent the people of a state, representation in modern California is no easy matter. As noted, California is becoming increasingly diverse in every sense of the word—culturally, ethnically, socially, and economically. Pluralism is giving way to hyperpluralism. The legislature is increasingly a place where conflicts between diverse groups unfold. Historically, the legislature has best represented the social, economic, and political upper tiers of California—those who can afford to organize. Occasionally, it represents the problems faced by the relatively poor or powerless. In political theory, it is an institution designed potentially to represent pluralistic interests, but, in reality, it most effectively represents the state's business and economic elites. For instance, despite recent budget shortfalls, business interests received additional tax breaks from Republican *and* Democratic legislators, ostensibly to create new jobs. Other groups will need to amass political power to match their growing numbers if they are to have comparable clout in the state capital.

Due to Proposition 140, reapportionment, and the newfound electoral clout of women and Latinos, a more diverse group now serves in California's legislature. Many of these new members bring fresh ideas and zeal to "get things done" within their limited terms of office. Others bring inexperience to a complex legislative process. Will they exhibit the professionalism that once marked California's legislature or be able to surmount the dysfunctionality that many believe is the norm today? Time will tell.

KEY TERMS

Federal plan (p. 124)

juice committees (p. 125)

bills, constitutional amendments, resolutions (p. 126)

trustees, delegates, politicos (p. 130)

executive branch oversight (p. 130)

authorization and appropriation process (p. 130)

reapportionment and gerrymandering (pp. 134, 135)

partisan, incumbent, and racial gerrymandering (p. 135)

Proposition 11 (p. 136)

party caucus (p. 137)

Assembly Speaker and Senate President Pro Tem (pp. 137, 138)

standing, fiscal, conference, select, and joint committees (p. 139)

grassroots pressure and crowd lobbying (p. 144)

REVIEW QUESTIONS

1. Briefly survey California's legislative history.
2. Describe the functions legislatures perform.
3. In what ways do legislators perceive their own roles?
4. How are legislative candidates recruited? Why and how do they manage to stay?
5. Describe the power of the Assembly Speaker and other leadership posts.
6. Explain how the committee system represents both a diverse state and ambitions of legislators.
7. If you were to redraw the legislation flow chart to reflect informal processes and rules, what would it look like?
8. As a lobbyist, how would you most effectively deal with today's legislature?

WEB ACTIVITIES

California Assembly and Senate
(www.assembly.ca.gov/ and www.senate.ca.gov/)
These sites provide current schedules, district finders, member directories, links to legislation, various caucuses, and other California government Web sites.

Legislative Analyst's Office
(www.lao.ca.gov/)

Here you have access to the same policy expertise available to the legislature.

Legislative Counsel of California
(www.leginfo.ca.gov/)
This is an excellent gateway site leading you to bill information, state laws, legislative information, and related publications.

NOTES

1. James Bryce, *The American Commonwealth, Vol. 1,* 2nd ed. (New York: Macmillan, 1891), p. 536.

2. For more analysis, see Alan Rosenthal, *The Decline of Representative Democracy: Process, Participation, and Power in State Legislatures* (Washington, D.C.: CQ Press, 1998).

3. The U.S. Supreme Court ruled term limits for members of Congress (that had also been imposed by Proposition 140) unconstitutional in *U.S. Term Limits v. Thornton,* 514 U.S. 779 (1995).

4. For more on this period, see William Buchanan, *Legislative Partisanship: The Deviant Case of California* (Berkeley: University of California Press, 1963).

5. *Reynolds v. Sims* 377 U.S. 533 (1964).

6. The 50 legislatures were judged on how functional, accountable, informed, independent, and representative they were. See Citizen's Conference on State Legislatures, *The Sometime Governments: A Critical Study of the 50 American Legislatures,* 2nd ed. (Kansas City, MO: CCSL, 1973).

7. See Richard A. Clucas, *The Speaker's Electoral Connection: Willie Brown and the California Assembly* (Berkeley: University of California Press, 1995).

8. See A. G. Block and Stephanie Carniello, "Putting on the Squeeze," *California Journal* 18 (April 1987), pp. 178–180; and Delia M. Rios, "Squeezing the Juice from Committee Assignments," *California Journal* 12 (March 1981), pp. 109–110.

9. This parallels the national experience with legislative term limits. See Thad Kousser, *Term Limits and the Dismantling of State Legislative Professionalism* (Cambridge: Cambridge University Press, 2004).

10. For a broad ranging essay on the state of California's legislature, see Chap. 6 "The Legislature" in A.G. Block and Gerald C. Lubenow, eds. *California Political Almanac 2007–2008* (Washington, D.C.: CQ Press, 2007).

11. This "author system" is described in William K. Muir Jr., *Legislature: California's School for Politics* (Chicago: University of Chicago Press, 1982), Chap. 3.

12. National Conference of State Legislatures, *Women in State Legislatures* 2011 (Washington, DC: National Conference of State Legislatures, 2011) (Accessed at www.ncsl.org/).

13. For extensive research on this topic, see Sue Thomas, *How Women Legislate* (New York: Oxford University Press, 1994); relative to California, see the "Women in Politics" issue of the *California Journal* 32 (December 2001).

14. A classic study of legislative roles can be found in John C. Wahlke et al., *The Legislative System: Exploration in Legislative behavior* (New York: Wiley, 1962).

15. Kent C. Price, "Instability in Representational Role Orientation in a State Legislature: A Research Note," *Western Political Quarterly* 38 (March 1985), pp. 162–171.

16. In 2009, the California Citizens Compensation Commission cut base legislative salaries from $116,291 to $95,291 in the wake of a severe recession. Later, they cut the per diem from $173 to $142.

17. Quoted in Eric Bradley and Michael Rothfeld, "Duvall Incident Spotlights Politicians' Perks in Capital," *Los Angeles Times* (September, 11, 2009).

18. Joseph A. Schlesinger developed this classic division in *Ambition and Politics: Political Careers in the United States* (Chicago: Rand McNally, 1966), p. 10.

19. Bruce E. Cain, *The Reapportionment Puzzle* (Berkeley: University of California Press, 1984), pp. 166–168.

20. Mark Dunkelman, *Gerrymandering the Vote: How a Dirty Dozen States Suppress as Many as 9 Million Votes* (Washington, D.C.: Democratic Leadership Council, June, 2008). (Accessed at www.dlc.org/).

21. Eric McGhee, *Legislative Reform* (San Francisco: Public Policy Institute of California, 2007).

22. *Just the Facts: California's 2011 Redistricting: The Commission's Final Plans* (San Francisco: Public Policy Institute of California, August 2011).

23. Rosenthal, *The Decline of Representative Democracy,* pp. 162–177.

24. A.G. Block and Gerald C. Lubenow, eds. *California Political Almanac 2007–2008* (Washington, D.C.: CQ Press, 2007), p. 199.

25. Although gender differences are not dramatic, men and women do have different policy priorities including committee preferences, according to a multi-state study that included the California legislature. See Sue Thomas and Susan Welch, "The Impact of Gender on Activities and Priorities of State Legislators," *Western Political Quarterly* 44 (June 1991), pp. 445–456.

26. See Anthony York, "Capitol Whispers," *Political Pulse* (January 30, 2004).

27. Elizabeth Hill, "California Legislative Analyst's Office: An Isle of Independence," *Spectrum: The Journal of State Government* 76 (Fall, 2003), pp. 26–29.

28. Karen de Sa, "A Push to Rein In the Leverage Lobbyists Have Over California Lawmakers," *The Mercury News*, July 21, 2010.

29. Quoted in Shane Goldmacher, "While Budget Waits, California Legislators Collect Campaign Contributions," *Sacramento Bee,* August 12, 2008.

30. Ali Winston, "Green Firms Balk at Coalition's Lobbying Effort," *San Francisco Chronicle*, January 18, 2010 (Accessed at www.sfgate.com).

31. Quoted in Laureen Lazarovici, "The Rise of the Wind-Makers," *California Journal* 26 (June 1995), p. 18.

32. For more on legislative strategies of interest groups, see Jay Michaels and Dan Walters, *The Third House: Lobbyists, Money, and Power in Sacramento* (Berkeley: Berkeley Public Policy Press, 2002).

33. Peverill Squire and Gary Moncrief, *State Legislatures Today: Politics Under the Domes* (Boston: Longman, 2010), p. 79.

8

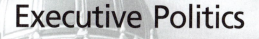

Executive Politics

Introduction

How Governors Lead

The Governor's Duties and Powers

Executive Powers

Budget Leadership

Legislative Powers

Judicial Powers

Other Powers

The Plural Executive: Competing for Power

Lieutenant Governor

Attorney General

Secretary of State

Superintendent of Public Instruction

Insurance Commissioner

Fiscal Officers

California's Bureaucracy and the Politics of Diversity

Functions of Bureaucracy

Power Sharing and Clout

Executive Branch Reform

Conclusion

Key Terms

Review Questions

Web Activities

Notes

IN BRIEF

Administering California's state government is the responsibility of the executive branch; administering that branch and providing overall political leadership for the entire state falls to the governor. In Chapter 8, we survey the office of governor, other executive officers, plus a sizable bureaucracy—all of whom compete for power and leadership in the Golden State.

California's post-statehood governors have run the gamut in personality, governing styles, and political skills. Most have been forgotten by history, but others have provided uncommon leadership and made a mark on the state through policy entrepreneurship. Governors exercise a variety of duties and powers, including executive powers, budget leadership opportunities, legislative and judicial power, plus roles such as the state's commander in chief and chief of state. They share power and leadership authority with several other separately elected leaders, the most powerful of whom is the attorney general.

In addition to those top posts, California's bureaucracy numbers over 300,000. They exercise functions common to all bureaucracies, and in doing so diffuse executive leadership and administration still further. Yet, they deliver state services and personify state government to many Californians. California's executive branch both mirrors and attempts to govern a diverse state. In the process, it is limited by political and organizational fragmentation that resists efforts to reform it.

INTRODUCTION

California voters did a remarkable thing in November of 2010. They elected a governor with actual gubernatorial experience. Edmund G. Brown, Jr., known to all as "Jerry," handily trounced former eBay executive Meg Whitman to regain the governorship after a 27-year absence. He was almost 73 years old when he took office in January 2011, making him the state's oldest governor, and the nation's oldest for that matter. At 37, he was one of the state's youngest governors when first elected to the office in 1974. In those early years, Brown proved to be a fiscal conservative, more so than Governor Ronald Reagan according to some observers. A result was one of the largest budget surpluses in state history. Brown developed a reputation as a cheapskate, foregoing a new governor's mansion and the customary chauffeured limousine. On social issues, he was much more liberal, appointing anti-death penalty judges and diversifying the executive branch with women and minorities. He sponsored many environmental initiatives and tried to slow down what he saw as rampant spending on freeways and other public works projects. He was fond of saying "There is no free lunch." "This is an era of limits and we all had better get used to it." "Small is beautiful."[1]

Decades later, when he campaigned for governor in 2010, he harked back to his previous record

as governor. More than Whitman, he was better prepared to tackle the state's looming budget deficits. Knowing how Sacramento really worked, he was better prepared to negotiate with the legislature. In television ads, he told voters that, at his age, he had nothing to fear making the hard choices necessary to move California forward. In a nod to the political realities of 2010 and to blunt any criticism of his as "tax and spend liberal," he vowed to seek voter approval for any tax extensions or increases.

After taking office in 2011, Brown discovered that his era of limits now included how far his prior experience could carry him in today's Sacramento. In the Sacramento of his day, legislators of opposing parties socialized after hours and worked toward compromise in order to pass budgets and approve legislation. Veteran legislators admired his father, Governor Edmund G. "Pat" Brown, and powerful legislative leaders like Assembly Speaker Willie Brown were able to control their caucuses and discipline their members. Policymaking was a matter of cutting deals "inside the building," as insiders called the Capitol. Brown himself was more distant and less social than his father. But, knowing how "old" Sacramento worked, the new Governor Brown met with hesitant Republicans, attended their social events, and even appeared before committee hearings. He was far more amenable to political schmoozing than in the old days.

In the short term at least, his efforts to win enough minority Republicans to pass a budget or even to put a tax extension on the ballot were not enough. And many political analysts knew why. While Brown was older, wiser, and more experienced than he was when he was first governor, Sacramento—indeed the state—had changed. According to Republican strategist Tony Quinn, "Brown has treated this [budget crisis] as an inside ballgame. That's his central problem." Democratic strategist Steve Maviglio elaborated on that point: "The political dynamics now are nothing like when he was first governor." Factors such as term limits, safe legislative districts, and the two-thirds legislative majority needed to raise taxes has resulted in a minority party "not interested in halfway anymore."[2]

Brown's initial reintroduction to Sacramento and the governor's office suggests that gubernatorial leadership depends on a fluid mix of many factors—actual job performance, electoral moods, the health of the economy, legislative friends and enemies, formal powers, structural constraints, partisanship, and one's own personality.

Executive branch politics is both fascinating to watch and complicated to study. State governors perform many of the same tasks American presidents do, but governors usually are out of the national spotlight—usually. The 1992 budget stalemate between Governor Pete Wilson and the legislature occupied the national media for weeks, as did Gray Davis's recall and Arnold Schwarzenegger's election. Brown's election over Whitman in 2010 was national news not only because of Brown's long absence but also because she broke all personal spending records in her quest. The formal powers of governors, like those of presidents, are not exhaustive. Both must compete for influence in a system full of checks and balances. Political scientist James MacGregor Burns once described presidential power as "essentially the power to dicker and transact."[3] This is all the more true of American governors. Let's examine the political and administrative setting in which California governors operate.

HOW GOVERNORS LEAD

The governor operates in a complex pattern of executive leadership. On the one hand, California's governor is at the apex of the political system—more powerful than any other individual. On the other, the entire executive branch exemplifies the themes of this book. It regulates and/or provides benefits to virtually every group or issue in the state, in effect mirroring the diversity that is California. As such, the executive branch (appointed officials, career civil servants, and other workers) represents the state's population. But given how the executive branch is organized and structured, it also exhibits its own form of hyperpluralism: diluted and shared power, politically independent offices and agencies, and many avenues for interest group influence. Legislators debate policy, help constituents, and collectively pass legislation. Although voters often consider their own legislators political leaders, the legislature's primary role is more to provide representation than to provide leadership. Even the legislative leaders discussed in Chapter 7 provide institutional leadership, not statewide political leadership. This function necessarily resides in the governorship. But the state's diversity and fragmented political system present numerous roadblocks to leadership.

Experience with colonial governors on the East Coast taught the original colonies a lesson: To prevent autocratic governors, constitutionally weaken their offices. As newer states copied older state constitutions, they also limited gubernatorial power. California did so, too, even though it had experienced relatively weak colonial governors under Spain and Mexico.

Table 8.1 lists all California governors from establishment of statehood to the present. Three observations are in order. *First,* few early governors are memorable to contemporary Californians. Strong executive leadership was neither valued nor experienced in those years. The most familiar nineteenth-century governor, Leland Stanford, is better known for his membership in the Big Four and for the university he

AP Photo/Rich Pedroncelli

Governor Jerry Brown speaks on the state budget in 2011

T A B L E 8.1   The Governors of California

Governor	Party	Years	Terms
Peter H. Burnett	D	1849–1851	<1
John McDougaf	D	1851–1852	<1
John Bigler	D	1852–1856	1
J. Neely Johnson	A[†]	1856–1858	<1
John B. Weller	D	1858–1860	<1
Milton S. Latham	D	1860	<1
John G. Downey*	D	1860–1862	<1
Leland Stanford	R	1862–1863	<1
Frederick F. Low	R	1863–1867	1
Henry H. Haight	D	1867–1871	1
Newton Booth	R	1871–1875	1
Romualdo Pacheco, Jr.*	R	1875	<1
William Irwin	D	1875–1880	>1
George C. Perkins	R	1880–1883	<1

Governor	Party	Years	Terms
George Stoneman	D	1883–1887	1
Washington Barlett	D	1887	<1
Robert H. Waterman*	R	1887–1891	1
Henry H. Markham	R	1891–1895	1
James H. Budd	D	1895–1899	1
Henry T. Gage	R	1899–1903	1
George C. Pardee	R	1903–1907	1
James N. Gillett	R	1907–1911	1
Hiram W. Johnson	R	1911–1917	>1
William D. Stephens*	R	1917–1923	>1
Friend W. Richardson	R	1923–1927	1
C. C. Young	R	1927–1931	1
James Rolph, Jr.	R	1931–1934	<1
Frank F. Merriam*	R	1934–1939	>1
Culbert L. Olson	D	1939–1943	1
Earl Warren	R	1943–1953	>2
Goodwin J. Knight*	R	1953–1959	<1
Edmund G. "Pat" Brown	D	1959–1967	2
Ronald Reagan	R	1967–1975	2
Edmund G. "Jerry" Brown	D	1975–1983	2
George Deukmejian	R	1983–1991	2
Pete Wilson	R	1991–1999	2
Gray Davis	D	1999–2003	>1
Arnold Schwarzenegger	R	2003–2011	2
Edmund G. "Jerry" Brown	D	2011–	

[†]American Party

[*]Lieutenant governor succeeded to governorship

Question: To what extent and on what basis will recent governors be memorable a century from now?

founded. *Second,* throughout most of its history, the California governorship has been a rapidly revolving door. Service of less than one term was common among early governors. In 1860, Milton Latham served all of five days! He quit to replace a U.S. senator shot in a duel. Hiram Johnson was the first governor to serve more than four years. He took office in 1911, was reelected in 1914, and resigned to serve in the U.S. Senate in 1917.

Third, as the table shows, lengthy service as governor is a recent phenomenon. Keep in mind that Proposition 140 established term limits—two four-year terms for governors and other statewide executives even though that limit had become an informal custom. Earl Warren served more than two terms and governors from Pat Brown to Wilson each served two four-year terms. The 2003 recall prevented Davis from serving a second term to which he had been elected. Presumably, eight years gives a governor ample time to form an agenda, exercise leadership, and implement priorities. Ironically, the records of recent governors suggest that lengthy tenure alone does not necessarily guarantee effective leadership.

The governor's annual salary of \$173,987 is among the nation's highest and would seemingly reflect the office's leadership role.[4] In reality, several California public employees, including public health administrators, top public university administrators, and many local government managers, earn more.

Like other elected executives, California governors do not exercise power in a political vacuum. Borrowing heavily from research on the American presidency, Robert Crew identified five variables that affect gubernatorial leadership.[5] We will apply them to gubernatorial politics in California. They include the governor's personality, political skill, political resources, the overall political environment or context, and strategic considerations:

1. *Personality.* Highly personal factors such as motivation, behavior, and character affect how governors lead. California governors have possessed diverse personality traits. For instance, Hiram Johnson was tenacious and persuasive; Warren, competent and well liked; Pat Brown, confident and active; Reagan, gregarious and surprisingly flexible. During his first stint as governor, Jerry Brown was aloof and philosophical; George Deukmejian was persistent and stubborn; Wilson was tough yet pragmatic. Davis was called a "Lone Ranger," a governor short on people skills. Disavowing "politics as usual," Schwarzenegger brought to the office star power, a desire for action, and a willingness to challenge legislative opponents. He also did little to ingratiate legislators and cultivate their support. Naturally, the personalities of governors affect how they approach the job, relate to staff and legislators, and communicate with the public.

2. *Political Skill.* California governors need extraordinary political skill to push their priorities through the legislature and the state's bureaucracy. These skills involve working successfully with legislative leaders, political party operatives, the media, and interest groups. For instance, Warren sponsored nonpartisan "town halls"— inviting thousands of concerned citizens to Sacramento during a legislative session. Reagan mastered the art of sounding ultra conservative (to please his followers) while acting with moderation (in recognition of political reality). Schwarzenegger alternated between media-driven public confrontation and private negotiation (often in his cigar-smoking tent just outside his Capitol office). Unlike his earlier experience, Jerry Brown began his first year as governor in 2011 wooing legislative allies and opponents in order to address the state's budget crisis.

3. *Political Resources.* Such resources come from inside or outside the governor's office. Internal resources include the amount of time, information, expertise, and energy a governor has. External resources include party support in the legislature, public approval, electoral margins, and professional reputation. Johnson could attribute his success to a legislature controlled by fellow Progressives. Republican Wilson possessed the experience and largely moderate political views that historically have been valued by Californians. Davis enjoyed Democratic majorities in the legislature, allowing him to obtain several education reforms. Public opinion itself is a political resource. Schwarzenegger's political strength ebbed and flowed largely in concert with his job approval ratings as published by several polling organizations. Brown began his second tenure as governor with positive approval ratings (41 percent positive, 21 percent negative, and 31 percent had no opinion). In contrast, only 16 percent of voters approved of the job the legislature was doing.[6]

4. *Political Context.* The term **political context** refers to factors in the external environment that affect a governor's performance. California's economy is one such factor. Recent economic troubles are nothing new. Depression-era governors were hurt by national economic turmoil. Post-World War II governors (Warren, Goodwin Knight, and Brown) took advantage of a growing economy and the taxes it generated. More recent governors have endured recessions, sagging revenues, and huge budget deficits. A second external factor is the state's political environment. This includes the electorate's partisan and ideological leanings. It also includes the political era during which a governor serves. Each era witnesses its own governing coalitions, expressions of political culture, and an overall political mood expressed by the public. Public confidence in the future of the state as measured in public opinion polls (see Chapter 1) provides an upbeat political context in which governors can maneuver. The other side of that coin—when the public's mood sours and public confidence in the future fades—imparts a decidedly downbeat context in which to govern.

5. *Strategic Considerations.* Given the factors mentioned, each governor must craft a strategy to achieve desired goals. This involves a game plan to deal with the legislature and methods to gain interest group and popular support. Previous strategies in California have involved large-scale, ambitious programs such as water projects and the master plan for higher education. Wilson took office espousing "preventative government": programs to reduce the dependence of California's children on government. Schwarzenegger faced skeptical legislators and continuing budget deficits that narrowed to some extent his policy options. In 2011, Brown advocated a "tough love" approach—giving the voters a choice between cutting taxes and severely reducing government services.

Timing is an important strategic consideration for governors. Relatively few windows of opportunity exist—times when governors can pursue a policy agenda with some hope of success. These windows are determined by routine political cycles, such as the election calendar and the annual budget process. As with presidents, California governors normally experience brief "honeymoons" of popularity and support early in their administrations. Astute governors take advantage of this phenomenon. For instance, Schwarzenegger administratively cancelled a controversial car tax increase within minutes of taking office, fulfilling a campaign promise by doing so. Windows of opportunity often close during election years, especially if tax increases are contemplated. Every other year, the entire Assembly is up for election, as is one half of the Senate. During recessions, when revenues cease to grow or even shrink, those windows might never fully open. Because so many policy issues depend on adequate funding, revenue levels themselves open and close windows of opportunity.

THE GOVERNOR'S DUTIES AND POWERS

Whether resources are in their favor or not, California governors possess a wide range of duties and powers. In terms of public expectations, their responsibilities to lead the state outstrip their actual formal powers. The range of powers that are discussed below are both formal and informal. They stem from both the constitution and political necessity. They are both visible and invisible to the general public. Some powers the governor must share with the legislature or other executive branch agencies. Others are relatively unchecked by competing forces. Compared to the personal and institutional powers of all 50 governors (including shared executive power, tenure potential, party control, and the powers of appointment, budget, and veto), California's governor ranks somewhere in the middle. But remember, that is an average. On a scale of 1 to 5 (where 1 represents gubernatorial weakness and 5 strength), California's governors have been assigned a "1" in terms of shared executive power and a "5" in terms of their veto power.[7]

Executive Powers

The governor is first and foremost the chief executive officer of the state. According to the California Constitution, the "supreme executive power" of the state is vested in the governor. "The Governor shall see that the law is faithfully executed."[8] Although this is much easier said than done, the governor possesses several powers to achieve this goal.

Organizing a Personal Staff   The governor's **inner circle** consists of a chief of staff and a variety of assistants called "secretaries," assigned to legislative matters, administration, the press, appointments and scheduling, and legal affairs. Top personal staff members often are veteran associates of the governor. *Their* staffers are often young, energetic, recent college graduates with workaholic schedules. The administrations of Reagan and Deukmejian were known for rather hierarchical staff relations (resembling a strict organization chart), whereas Brown had a relatively loose "spokes of the wheel" arrangement. In this latter style, numerous individuals had relatively free access to the governor. Given Schwarzenegger's lack of public sector experience, his initial appointments included former Wilson aides and staffers from several business-oriented interest groups; later he even hired as chief of staff Susan P. Kennedy, a onetime Democratic party official and Davis appointee. Many observers noted that the greatest personal asset Jerry Brown brought to the governorship in 2011 was his closest confidant and wife, Ann Gust Brown.

Making Appointments   Although 99 percent of executive branch employees belong to a civil service system, the governor appoints several thousand individuals to various administrative, board, and commission posts. Many are "at pleasure" appointees who serve as long as the governor wishes them to. They include the governor's personal staff and high-level administrators. Some governors, including Schwarzenegger, borrow selected appointees from various departments to augment their own office staffs. Most appointees are "term" appointees, including board and commission members, who serve a fixed number of years. During a governor's term, still others will need to be appointed to fill vacancies and judicial retirements. What motivates these appointments in addition to administrative needs? First, governors can diversify their administrations. For instance, in a departure from previous practice, Brown named numerous ethnic minorities and women when he was first governor. Second, they can reward their friends and political allies. Schwarzenegger appointed a number of personal friends and political associates to various regulatory boards. Watchdog groups complained of cronyism, charging that many of his appointments favored the industries the boards were established to oversee on behalf of the public.[9]

Managing the Executive Branch   California governors have their own versions of presidential cabinets. Notice Figure 8.1, an organization chart of the state's executive branch. Wary of the huge number of appointees reporting directly to him, Governor Pat Brown reorganized a plethora of departments into several **superagencies**. Subsequent governors have reorganized a bit, but the super agency structure remains. These agencies include (1) Business, Transportation, and Housing; (2) Environmental Protection; (3) Health and Human Services Agency; (4) Resources; (5) State and Consumer Services; and (6) Youth and Adult Corrections. All these people are part of the governor's *cabinet,* but they are less powerful than their "super" titles would suggest. For instance, within Business, Transportation, and Housing are CalTrans, Housing and Community Development, Commerce, and the Highway Patrol. Each operates like a semi-autonomous fiefdom, well outside the governor's routine attention span. These agency secretaries, joined by the education secretary and several other departments (Food and Agriculture, Finance, Labor and Workforce Development, and Veterans Affairs), make up the governor's

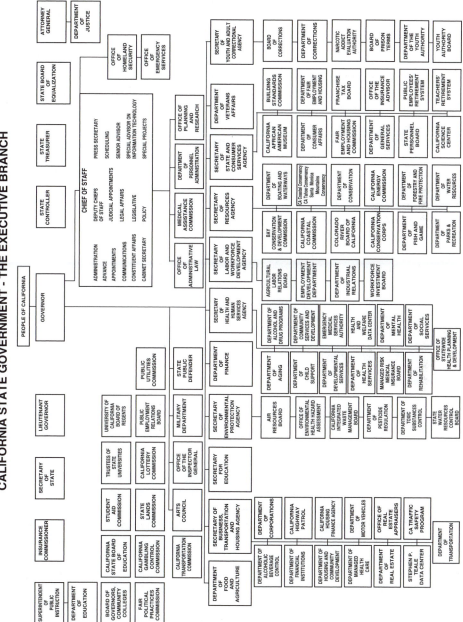

FIGURE 8.1 Executive Branch Organization Chart

Question: Which parts of the executive branch do you think cost the most? Compare your answer with budget data in Chapter 11.

13-member cabinet. These various agency heads vary in importance. The director of finance is a crucial appointee, given the governor's budget responsibilities. As a group, the governor's cabinet is less a policy body than a collection of executive branch appointees.

Issuing Orders The "executive power" of California's governor also includes the ability to take action independent of the legislature. A primary vehicle to do this is the **executive order**. Such orders usually involve a series of "whereas" statements detailing the reasons for the order followed by this language: "NOW, THEREFORE I, EDMUND G. BROWN, JR., Governor of the State of California, by virtue of the power and authority invested in me by the Constitution and the laws of the State of California, do hereby issue this order to become effective immediately." Following that are the substantive actions the governor wishes to take. One of Brown's first items of business in 2011 was to issue an executive order mandating a 50 percent cut in cell phone and smart phone use by government agencies.

Budget Leadership

Although the constitutional language "supreme executive power" sounds impressive, what requires the governor's constant attention is the state's budget (discussed further in Chapter 11). The California Constitution requires the governor to submit a budget to the legislature within the first ten days of each calendar year. A tremendous amount of preparation goes into the submission of that "budget bill." The state budget is the premier policy statement for California and governors want their priorities reflected in it. The process is twofold. The **internal budget process** (within the executive branch) begins the previous July when the governor, through the Department of Finance (DOF), submits a "budget letter/price letter" to all executive agencies and departments. The budget letter relays the governor's policy priorities, whereas the price letter contains fiscal assumptions (such as the rate of inflation) used to determine budget

baselines. During the rest of the year, departments and the DOF haggle over which figures will emerge in the governor's January budget.[10]

The **external budget process** pits the governor against the legislature. This part of the process is the most visible to the public and clearly the messiest from the governor's standpoint. At this stage, the governor shares budget power primarily with the Assembly Budget Committee, the Senate Budget and Fiscal Review Committee, and the Legislative Analyst's Office. Each has a staff that examines and often second-guesses the governor's figures. When stalemates occur (they often do when revenues and expenditures do not easily match), a parallel group—the "Big Five"—usually emerges to further haggle over the budget bill. The governor and two caucus leaders each from the Assembly and Senate form this group.

The constitution also requires that the legislature enact the budget bill by June 15 and for the governor to sign it by June 30, the last day of each fiscal year. It once mandated an extraordinary two-thirds legislative vote on the budget, but the voters reduced that threshold to a simple majority in 2011. It still takes a two-thirds vote to raise taxes and many fees—an important component of any budget process. Not surprisingly, budget stalemates occur among the Big Five.

July 1 might pass without a budget as pundits declare the largest state in the Union "broke." On one occasion, creditors and employees have been paid in registered warrants (called "IOUs") until a new budget is enacted. Less publicized conflicts occur regularly. When revenues are down, budget makers argue over where to cut spending; when revenues are up, they argue over new spending ideas versus new tax cuts.

Once a budget is passed, additional spending requests plus new revenue projections require further adjustments during the fiscal year. Although the governor's budget power seems to dissipate during legislative debate on the budget bill, the governor's power over an approved budget is substantial. The most formidable tool the governor has at this point is the **item veto**. This refers to the governor's ability to reduce or reject any item in an appropriations (spending) bill. Including

California, 42 governors have this power. Notice Figure 8.2, a portion of a veto message attached to a 2011 budget bill. Here, Brown deleted a modest amount from the Commission on the Status of Women and explained his rationale for doing so. Item vetoes can add up. Deukmejian, known in Sacramento as "Governor No," vetoed about 1,700 expenditure items totaling nearly $7 billion during his two terms.

A final word on the governor's budget powers is in order. Many parts of the overall budget are difficult to control. They include separate spending decisions made by voters through initiatives (Proposition 98's funding requirements for education), particular revenues dedicated to certain uses (gas taxes for highway expenditures), or automatic spending increases called COLAs (cost of living adjustments). All these "un-controllables," as political scientists call them, amount to a significant majority of the entire state budget. They substantially limit the ability of the governor to control spending and, therefore, policy.

Legislative Powers

California governors must deal constantly with the legislature and not just on the annual budget. They must exercise legislative leadership to achieve a host of other policy goals. California's most successful governors, legislatively speaking, were admired and respected by many legislators, used bipartisanship, and enjoyed high public approval ratings. But many California governors experienced significant political conflict because they brought profoundly different perspectives to their leadership role.

- *Party Differences:* The most telling source of conflict occurs when the governor is of one major political party and the legislature is controlled by another major party. In recent decades, Republican governors and Democratic legislative majorities have clashed on taxes, welfare spending, and many other issues. In contrast, Davis and legislative Democrats had to temper efforts to impose an activist agenda the public might not support. In light of persistent budget problems, Schwarzenegger initially appeased both Republicans and Democrats—the former by opposing tax increases and the latter by postponing many deep program cuts. Subsequently, he became more aggressive and combative in pushing a variety of budget and political reforms. Unified party control does not necessarily connote smooth interbranch relations. For instance, fellow

---

"I object to the following appropriations contained in Senate Bill 87." With this simple declarative sentence, Governor Jerry Brown "blue penciled" thirty different spending items in the state's new 2011–2012 budget. In this instance, he unilaterally reduces spending for the Commission on the Status of Women:

Item 8820-001-0001—For support of Commission on the Status of Women. I reduce this item from $465,000 to $265,000 by reducing:

(1) 10-Administration, Legislation, Research and Information from $467,000 to $267,000.

I am reducing this item by $200,000 to help bring ongoing expenditures in line with existing resources. Given our constrained state resources, this reduction reflects the need for government to focus on its core functions. While the statutory goals of the Commission are worthy, I continue to believe there are other formal and informal venues for policy development and advocacy that do not require General Fund expenditures.

Notice that many of these vetoes are not all that dramatic. Brown's actions cut only $24 million from an $86 billion budget. In most cases, item vetoes shave modest amounts off legislative appropriations as a way to control spending in a tight budget environment, reinforce the governor's own spending priorities, or make some other point to the legislature as a whole or one or more members who pushed the item.

SOURCE: California Governor's Office (www.gov.ca.gov).

FIGURE 8.2 Item Veto Message

Democrats in the legislature overrode a number of Brown's vetoes in the late 1970s and, decades later, only reluctantly agreed to his proposed budget cuts.

- *Constituency Differences:* At times, differences in perspective between a governor and the legislature can be traced to constituency differences. Legislators represent individual, more homogeneous districts whereas the governor represents the entire state population, as diverse as it is. The needs of the whole state might not square with the constituent views of a particular Assembly or Senate district. For instance, a governor must balance the water needs of the entire state, not just those of farmers or city dwellers, as individual legislators might. Some parts of the state might hunger for economic development and growth; others might actively oppose it.

- *Interest Differences:* Legislators are particularly responsive to the views of individual interest groups, as noted in Chapter 7. Governors try to represent the larger "general interest" of the state and, in doing so, seem more willing to step on interest group toes in the process. For example, Schwarzenegger alienated some business and Republican allies by defending the state's global warming law. Brown received a great deal of electoral support (campaign contributions and votes) from public employee unions but was forced to advocate policies to which they were opposed.

- *Responsibility Differences:* When California legislators want to diffuse blame, they can easily point their fingers to committee chairpersons, legislative leaders, or insensitive fellow legislators from elsewhere in the state. Governors cannot spread the blame for failure nearly as far. If they try, their own leadership ability is questioned. Furthermore, the public tends to lay singular responsibility on the governor. California's polling organizations measure the *governor's* popularity, not each legislator's.

Governors employ several resources in dealing with the California legislature: an overall legislative program, the general veto, calling special sessions, and personal relations. They work in the following ways.

- *Legislative Program:* Each January, the governor presents a "State of the State" speech, much like the president's "State of the Union" speech. This is an opportunity to fashion a coherent set of policy priorities by which legislation might be evaluated. California governors never command media attention comparable to that received by presidents, though. Many television stations rarely carry more than excerpts of the State of the State speech. In response, governors often stage symbol-laden media events as when Schwarzenegger staged the refueling of a hydrogen-powered Hummer, symbolizing his commitment to alternative, clean energy.

- *General Veto:* As noted earlier, the item veto allows the governor power to "blue pencil" a particular expenditure contained in an appropriations bill. A **general veto**, like the president's veto power, allows the governor to reject an entire nonspending or authorization bill. Figure 8.3 features Brown's general veto of SB 69 and AB 98, the bills that constitute the Democratic majority's budget for 2011-2012. He points out flaws in both the budget and the budget process.

- *Special Sessions:* In the past, when the legislature was not in session, governors would call **special sessions** to deal with pressing matters. Modern legislative sessions are virtually year round, so fewer special sessions are needed. But governors still call them now and then. In December of 1989, Governor Deukmejian called one in response to the Loma Prieta earthquake in the San Francisco Bay Area. In mid-2006, Schwarzenegger called a special session of the legislature to address prison overcrowding and related reforms.

■ *Personal Relations:* One of the governor's most potent but underrated legislative tools is good

> June 16, 2011
>
> To the Members of the California State Legislature:
>
> I am returning Senate Bill 69 and Assembly Bill 98 without my signature.
>
> In January, I presented a balanced budget solution with a mix of deep spending cuts and temporary tax extensions subject to voter approval. My plan would put these extended revenues in a lockbox, ensuring that they are only used to protect education and public safety. It would also address California's long term fiscal crisis by substantially paying down the $35 billion wall of debt built up over the last decade.
>
> Yet Republicans in the Legislature blocked the right of the people to vote on this honest, balanced budget.
>
> Meanwhile, Democrats in the Legislature made valiant efforts to address California's budget crisis by enacting $11 billion in painful cuts and other solutions. I commend them for their tremendous efforts to balance the budget in the absence of Republican cooperation.
>
> Unfortunately, the budget I have received is not a balanced solution. It continues big deficits for years to come and adds billions of dollars of new debt. It also contains legally questionable maneuvers, costly borrowing and unrealistic savings. Finally, it is not financeable and therefore will not allow us to meet our obligations as they occur.
>
> We can – and must – do better. A balanced budget is critical to our economic recovery. I am, once again, calling on Republicans to allow the people of California to vote on tax extensions for a balanced budget and significant reforms. They should also join Democrats in supporting job creation and ending tax breaks for out-of-state companies. If they continue to obstruct a vote, we will be forced to pursue deeper and more destructive cuts to schools and public safety – a tragedy for which Republicans will bear full responsibility.
>
> Sincerely,
>
> Edmund G. Brown, Jr.

F I G U R E 8.3 A General Veto Message

SOURCE: California Governor's Office (www.gov.ca.gov).

interpersonal relationships. For example, Reagan cultivated the press corps. Warren and Pat Brown were known for their warm relations with legislators, but Jerry Brown and Deukmejian were more distant and cool. Even members of his own party detested bachelor Brown's spartan lifestyle and unconventional tactics in the 1970s. Initially, Schwarzenegger capitalized on his larger-than-life persona by giving legislative leaders coveted personal attention, but later preferred "going public" to cultivating personal relationships with legislators. Returning to the governor's office, now married Jerry Brown was happy to host social events for both Republican and Democratic lawmakers, noting "That's a very important part of how the Legislature works."[11]

Judicial Powers

Gubernatorial power also involves the judiciary or can be essentially judicial in nature. For instance, the governor's appointment power extends to the judicial branch, as explained in Chapter 9. When a vacancy occurs on the California Supreme Court or the Courts of Appeal, the governor makes the appointment. Governors even appoint superior court judges when vacancies occur between elections. These appointments can add up. By the end of Governor Deukmejian's two terms, he had appointed nearly two-thirds of all state judges.

Like American presidents and appointments to the U.S. Supreme Court, governors can leave their imprints on state supreme courts. Deukmejian's appointments were moderate conservatives with pro-business credentials. Brown's appointments in the 1970s and early 1980s reflected his desire to create opportunities for minorities and to shake up the legal system. His selections included several firsts: Chief Justice Rose Bird (the first woman), Cruz Reynoso (the first Latino), and Wiley Manuel (the first African American). Once appointed, appellate justices must face the voters.

Bird, Reynoso, and another justice, Joseph Grodin, were ousted in 1986, in part because they opposed the death penalty.

The governor's purely judicial powers involve **clemency** (or acts of mercy). First, the governor may *pardon* an individual convicted of a crime. This means releasing someone from the consequences of a criminal conviction. Second, the governor may *commute* or reduce a sentence. For example, in late 2005, Schwarzenegger refused to grant clemency (reducing his death sentence to life without parole) to Crips gang cofounder and convicted murderer Stanley "Tookie" Williams, who, without admitting guilt, had become an antigang advocate while in prison. Williams was executed shortly thereafter. Third, the governor may issue a *reprieve* (the postponement of a sentence). Fourth, the governor may reverse parole decisions by the Board of Prison Terms, a power only three states grant their governors. For example, Schwarzenegger reversed a board decision to parole a dentist convicted of killing three patients through fatal doses of a general anesthetic. Fifth, the governor may *extradite* a fugitive to another state from which the fugitive has fled. Governor Brown once refused South Dakota's request in the 1970s to extradite Dennis Banks, a militant Native American, fearing he would not receive a fair trial.

A related task is more legal and political than judicial in nature. Along with the attorney general, the governor largely determines which court cases the state pursues at the appellate level. These cases involve appeals in which the state is a party or other cases on which the state wishes to take a stand. These top executives are not obligated to defend every state decision or policy, especially if they come from citizen initiatives. For instance, both Governor Schwarzenegger and then Attorney General Jerry Brown refused to defend in court Proposition 8, the anti-gay marriage law.

Other Powers

During times of crisis and public disorder, the governor's role as *commander in chief* of the California National Guard (the state militia) comes into play. The scenario usually involves a local riot or disturbance, the inability of local police to restore order, a mayoral request for National Guard assistance, and the deployment of guardsmen to restore order. In 1965, Pat Brown deployed 1,000 guardsmen during the Watts Riot. In 1992, Wilson sent 7,000 guardsmen to riot-torn Los Angeles, and in 1994, he sent a smaller number to Northridge to help with earthquake relief efforts. In 2006, Schwarzenegger bowed to federal pressure and reluctantly sent 1,000 guardsmen to the California/Mexico border to augment federal border enforcement efforts.

Last, governors are *chiefs of state*. As such, they greet foreign dignitaries, address interest group conventions, accompany presidents who are traveling in California, cut ribbons on public works projects, and process a huge volume of mail. School children write governors, assuming they exercise far more power than we have discussed. Consider this one: "Dear Governor Reagan: I wrote you once before about having to go to school on my birthday—and nothing happened. My next birthday is a month away and I am wondering what your plans are. Let me hear from you soon. Jeff."[12]

THE PLURAL EXECUTIVE: COMPETING FOR POWER

As considerable as the governor's powers are, they are circumscribed in some profound ways. A significant limitation is called the **plural executive**—an array of executive officials with cabinet-sounding titles who are separately elected and politically independent of the governor. Cabinet members in Washington serve at the pleasure of the president and can be removed at any time. California governors (plus many other governors) can only wish they had that power. Many comparable state office holders are elected directly by the people. This reflects a historic mistrust of gubernatorial power. Although competition for power understandably ensues, a plural executive does not necessarily hinder a governor's leadership role. The duties of some of these elected officials are largely administrative in nature; independent political power is neither feasible nor possible or consequential. That said, these executives may come from political parties other than the governor's and may publicly oppose the governor's agenda. Their own gubernatorial ambitions may color their relationship with the incumbent governor.

Lieutenant Governor

The least-threatening office of the group is lieutenant governor. California governor Friend W. Richardson (1923–1927) never held the post but sized it up succinctly: "to preside over the senate and each morning to inquire solicitously after the governor's health." In 1998, former Assembly Speaker Cruz Bustamante won this office, the first Latino elected to statewide office since 1878. During 2003, he opposed the recall of Davis but also waged a losing campaign to replace him. He was followed by former Insurance Commissioner John Garamendi and, in 2011, former San Francisco mayor Gavin Newsom. The lieutenant governor's annual salary is $130,490.

Because lieutenant governors rarely preside over the California State Senate and modern governors tend to be quite healthy, what do lieutenant governors do? First, they sit on various boards, including the Regents of the University of California, the Trustees of the State University System, the State Lands Commission, and the Commission for Economic Development. Politically ambitious lieutenant governors eke whatever publicity they can from these memberships and maximize (or exaggerate) their related policy accomplishments. Second, the lieutenant governor becomes acting governor the minute the governor leaves the state, an obvious holdover from days of slower travel and communication. This is problematic when the two are not elected as a team, that is, they can be of opposing parties. For instance, when Democratic Governor Jerry Brown traveled the nation running for president, Republican Lieutenant Governor Mike Curb

hastened to appoint a judge before Brown could return. There is an irony then when California governors are mentioned as possible presidential candidates. Incumbent governors can ill afford the absenteeism required to wage a national campaign.

Politically speaking, the lieutenant governor is in a "Twilight Zone" of sorts. The responsibilities assigned to the office rarely embrace the great issues facing California. The media all but ignore the office, giving its occupants few opportunities to communicate with the voters who elect them. Accordingly, the office is a slippery stepping stone at best. In California's history, only six lieutenant governors have become governors. Reformers would like to either abolish this post—six states seem to manage without it—or at least require the governor and the lieutenant governor to run on the same party ticket (a requirement in 23 other states). Yet, polls show that most Californians favor the status quo.

Attorney General

In contrast to the lieutenant governor, the state attorney general is quite powerful. Former Attorney General Robert Kenny (1943–1946) once quipped: "A smart A.G. could practically take over the state from a dumb governor—if he had a mind to." In fact, the attorney general is the second most powerful position in California's executive branch. This office oversees the state's Department of Justice, which employs 5,000 people, including 1,000 attorneys. Historically, the "A.G." has truly been a stepping stone to higher office. Attorneys General Earl Warren, Pat Brown, George Deukmejian and, most recently, Jerry Brown each became governor. Although some have come from legislative backgrounds (Dan Lungren was a congressman and Bill Lockyer state senator), others have been prominent, politically active district attorneys (Warren, Evelle Younger, John Van de Kamp, and Kamala Harris). Harris, a two-term San Francisco District Attorney succeeded Brown when he was elected governor in 2010. She is the first woman, the first

African American, and the first South Asian in California to hold that office. The position pays $151,127 per year.

In criminal matters, the department conducts investigations, argues all appeals above the trial court level, and nominally oversees local district attorneys and county sheriffs. On rare occasions, the department even prosecutes local crimes if a district attorney refuses to as it did with the "Hillside Strangler" case in 1981. In civil matters, the attorney general and his army of department lawyers advise other state agencies and represent them in court either as prosecutor or defense counsel. The office also prepares titles and summaries for all ballot measures. Even this otherwise routine task can be controversial as Brown discovered in 2008. When Proposition 8 was submitted to his office, he altered the draft summary to read that the measure seeks to "eliminate the right of same-sex couples to marry." The measure's supporters thought that the wording was too argumentative and biased.

Secretary of State

In terms of discretionary power, the secretary of state stands in stark contrast to the attorney general. Whereas the nation's secretary of state is essentially a minister of foreign affairs, California's Secretary of State is essentially a clerk of records and elections. As archivist, this official maintains all current and historical records. This $130,490-per-year post also possesses many election-related duties (preparing and distributing statewide voter pamphlets, processing candidate papers, certifying initiative petitions, publishing election results, and tracking campaign donations and expenditures). Also, the secretary of state decides early on which candidates warrant a place on California's presidential primary ballot.

Historically, the position of secretary of state was so routine and devoid of controversy, it was held by a father/son team (Frank C. and Frank M. Jordan) for nearly all of the period between 1911 and 1970. Although Jerry Brown once occupied the office (1970-1974), most secretaries of state rarely move up the political ladder and most generate little controversy or fanfare. In one notable exception, Kevin Shelley gave the office unwelcome publicity when he was accused of fiscal irregularities and verbally abusing his staff. More recently, former state senator Debra Bowen won election to the post in 2006 and was reelected in 2010. She has taken a particular interest in the integrity and verifiability of new balloting technologies such as touch screen voting machines.

Superintendent of Public Instruction

One of the most plural, indeed fragmented, arrangements in California's executive branch is the Superintendent of Public Instruction. Several features of this $151,127-per-year office set it apart from other statewide elective offices. First, unlike other members of the plural executive, the position is officially nonpartisan, reflecting the notion that education and "politics" should not mix. Second, the superintendent does not "superintend" in the dictionary sense. Rather the office shares responsibility for the 1,200-employee Department of Education with an 11-member Board of Education appointed by the governor. Furthermore, even though 80 percent of school funding flows through this department, the actual task of education takes place locally in over a thousand school districts. In recent years, an increasingly visible partner has been the federal Department of Education as it implements the 2001 No Child Left Behind Act and, more recently, the "Race to the Top" funding program. This governance structure has been a perfect formula for policy fragmentation and diffusion of educational responsibility.

Consequently, in hyperpluralistic fashion, governors, superintendents, the state board, legislators, local educators, and interest groups continually battle over education policy and funding (see Chapter 13). State Senator Jack O'Connell, a legislative veteran in the area of public education, won election to the post in 2002 and 2006. Many of his educational priorities and reforms were overtaken by recession-driven spending cuts and federal programs that compromised state goals. Succeeding him in 2011 was former teacher and Democratic state legislator Tom Torlakson.

Insurance Commissioner

In 1988, California voters "pluralized" still further the executive branch by approving Proposition 103. They authorized auto insurance rate reductions and joined eight other states that have an elected insurance commissioner. Prior to "103," the governor had appointed the commissioner. This is the only office in California's plural executive to have been created by the initiative process. The commissioner heads the state's Department of Insurance, which regulates the insurance industry in California, and is paid $139,189 annually. The insurance commissioner enforces the state's insurance code, approves industry mergers, pursues industry fraud, levies fines for insurance wrongdoing, and controls insurance rates. Arguably, this office would play a major role in implementing heath care reform.

The goal of protecting insurance consumers is more problematic than one might think. Republican Commissioner Chuck Quakenbush resigned in disgrace in 2002 after diverting and misspending insurance funds intended for Northridge earthquake victims. A deeper problem stems from the elective nature of the post itself. For years, consumer groups viewed the Department of Insurance as little more than a cheerleader for the politically powerful insurance industry. Making the post elective rather than appointive may have worsened the problem as candidates seek campaign contributions from the very industry they are seeking to regulate. Wealthy occupants of the office like Steve Poizner (2005–2011) can fund their own campaigns but why should wealth be an unwritten qualification for this post? In 2010, former Democratic Assembly Member Dave Jones was elected commissioner, after taking little if any insurance industry funding.

Fiscal Officers

While all members of California's plural executive are elected and therefore require campaign funds, the job descriptions of some of them center around money: collecting it, investing it, and disbursing it to pay the state's bills. These offices are the controller, treasurer, and Board of Equalization.

- *Controller* As the chief fiscal officer of the state, the controller pays all bills, monitors all state accounts, audits various state and local programs, and earns $139,189 per year. In addition to managing dispersements of over $100 billion annually, this official sits on nearly 80 boards, committees, and commissions, including the Franchise Tax Board (which collects the state's income tax) and the Board of Equalization (which collects other taxes). Controllers who have sought to run for governor have experienced victory and defeat. Davis, who served from 1986 through 1994, used his membership on the State Lands Commission to publicly oppose oil drilling and toxic waste dumping, a popular stance among California's environmentalists and his party's base. eBay executive Steve Westly was elected in 2002 but relinquished the office in 2006 to run unsuccessfully for the Democratic nomination for governor. Former Board of Equalization member John Chiang was elected in 2006 and reelected in 2010. In the wake of a pay scandal in the city of Bell, he released the salaries of many local government employees.

- *Treasurer* If the controller writes the state's checks, the treasurer handles the money while it is in the checking account. Because there is a lag between when revenue is received and when it is spent, the treasurer invests it in the interim. Obviously the goal is to obtain the highest possible interest rates for money on deposit. Another important responsibility is to sell state bonds (a form of borrowing discussed in Chapter 11). Because this revenue funds major construction (such as water projects, school construction, and affordable housing) and must be paid back with interest to large financial institutions, the treasurer tries to obtain the lowest possible rates. The treasurer oversees the investment of nearly $100 billion in state and local moneys and sits on pension boards that invest the retirement assets of millions of public employees and school teachers. Because the treasurer decides who gets to resell revenue bonds to investors, investment firms have been known to contribute to treasurers' election campaigns, a questionable practice given their economic stake in the office. Although Jesse Unruh enhanced the powers and clout of this office during his long tenure (1974–1986), it also remains a rather slippery stepping stone to higher office. A series of politically ambitious individuals including Kathleen Brown (Pat Brown's daughter and Jerry Brown's sister), Matt Fong, and former Democratic Party chair and businessman Philip Angelides have attempted to run for higher office from this precarious perch. Termed-out Attorney General Bill Lockyer became treasurer in 2006 and was reelected in 2010. The salary for this office is $139,189.

■ *Board of Equalization* The last fiscal office in California's plural executive is the Board of Equalization, which consists of four elected individuals plus the state controller, who serves ex officio (without vote). Districts, representing more than 9 million people each, elect the four. These four, who earn $130,490 per year, are largely invisible to average Californians, even when campaigning. The Board administers and collects nearly $50 billion in sales taxes, excise taxes, and fees each year. This organizational relic was placed in the 1879 constitution to assess Southern Pacific Railroad's property, a needed reform at the time. To this day, the board sets the market value for public utilities and railroads and, as a quasi-judicial body, hears franchise and income tax appeals. Progressive reformers would be aghast to know that board members often collect substantial campaign contributions from groups with which the board does business. Although critics call this board—the only elected one in the nation—outmoded, efforts to fold it into the Franchise Tax Board have failed.

CALIFORNIA'S BUREAUCRACY AND THE POLITICS OF DIVERSITY

Any large, diverse state with a complex economy and a comprehensive state government will possess a substantial bureaucracy. California boasts one of the nation's largest. Virtually every aspect of life in California is touched in some way by the state's executive branch and the people that work in it. Roughly 350,000 full time employees work for a host of departments, agencies, boards, and commissions. Is this number high or even too high? It depends on one's perspective. If you consider the ratio of state employees to the state's overall population—a more realistic measure of bureaucratic size—that number has declined over time. In fact, the number of state employees per 1,000 Californians was consistently higher in the 1970s than it has been in recent years.

Several hiring systems govern state employees. Over 130,000 are governed by the tenure and hiring practices of the University of California and State University systems. Most of the rest operate under **civil service**—the idea that permanent employees should be hired and evaluated on the basis of merit, not politics. This means competence and expertise rather than political connections and clout. California's civil service system, like those of other states, was modeled after the federal *Pendleton Act of 1883* and Progressive-era opposition to patronage. Created in 1934, the State Personnel Board administers the overall civil service system, hears appeals from aggrieved employees or job applicants, and led in implementing the state's affirmative action program before Proposition 209 abolished it. The Department of Personnel Administration handles all issues subject to collective bargaining including salaries, benefits, job classifications, and training. In 2011, Governor Brown proposed merging these two agencies into a single California Department of Human Resources, a move estimated to save nearly $6 million annually.

Functions of Bureaucracy

Even the briefest survey of California's bureaucracy demonstrates the magnitude of government and the diversity of its work. A majority of all state employees works for the two university systems or in the area of public safety (prisons, highway patrol, the Department of Justice, and the courts). The fastest growing group has been correctional employees; their numbers have doubled over the last two decades, reflecting a growing prison population.[13]

The primary purpose of California's bureaucracy is implementation—carrying out policies and laws approved by the legislature and even the voters (through initiatives). Most of the myriad day-to-day activities of bureaucracies are required to implement policy. The following sampling of various state agencies illustrates some of these activities. The Highway Patrol *patrols* state highways and *monitors* school bus transportation. The Department of Alcoholic Beverage Control *licenses and regulates* the manufacture, sale, purchases, possession, and transportation of alcoholic beverages. The State Banking Department *protects* Californians against financial loss at state-chartered banks. The Integrated Waste Management Board *promotes* recycling and composting. The California Department of Transportation *builds, maintains, and rehabilitates* the state's roads and bridges. The Department of Fair Employment and Housing *enforces* the state's civil rights laws that ban various forms of discrimination. The Department of Health Services *manages* numerous health programs. The Air Resources Board *establishes* clean air standards and *researches* anti-smog approaches.

To the extent that the various layers of government in California contribute to hyperpluralism, the same can be said about California's bureaucracy. Excepting higher education, virtually all state agencies, departments, offices, and boards coordinate their activities with similar local government efforts, or they may actually direct those efforts. Consider just K—12 education. The State Board of Education selects textbooks for grade levels K—8, develops curricular frameworks, approves local waivers from state regulations, and oversees the credentialing of teachers. The Commission on Teacher Credentialing certifies teacher preparation programs in the state's colleges and universities. The Department of Education communicates education policy to school districts, approves instructional materials, and provides curriculum leadership. Local school districts receive and account for state funds, deliver education per state standards, administer state-designed tests, cope with enrollment growth, and innovate wherever they can.

All these functions have produced mountains of paperwork in the Golden State. No matter where one turns, there are regulations to follow, forms to fill out, and fine print to read. The title of a 1995 Little Hoover Commission report on California's bureaucracy summed it up—*Too Many Agencies, Too Many Rules.*[14] Critics would claim little has changed since then. But they would do well to remember this: Given the state's size, complexity, and diversity, California's bureaucracy is bound to be large, complex, and diverse. Furthermore, as the editors of the *California Almanac* put it, "Wrapped in red tape they may be, but bureaucrats are the technicians that keep the machinery of state government humming."[15]

Power Sharing and Clout

California's bureaucracy also shares power with the federal government. Most federal aid destined for the state and even local governments passes through state agencies. Structurally, you can think of these relationships as a fiscal version of a picket fence. For example, the portion of federal gas taxes returned to the state funnel through the Department of Transportation (Caltrans) to various state or local transportation improvements (see Figure 8.4). Certain state agencies rely on counties to channel the delivery of state services such as foster care, welfare, and public health.

The clout of California's public employees comes not only from what they do but also from their ability to organize. Borrowing labor practices from the private sector, most state employees are organized into more than 20 different bargaining

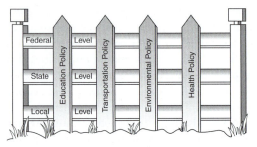

FIGURE 8.4 Picket Fence Relationships in California

Executive branch and administrative relationships between all three levels of our political system (including grants and rulemaking) resemble a picket fence. For instance, a federal education program involves vertical communication between officials in the federal Department of Education, the California Department of Education, and local school systems.

SOURCE: From Lawrence. *America: The Politics of Diversity*, 1E. © 1999 Wadsworth, a part of Cengage Learning, Inc. Reproduced by permission. www.cengage.com/permissions.

units, represented by 12 unions. The largest is the California State Employees' Association, representing over 140,000 active and retired civil servants. There are also specific unions representing specific professions in state government. The largest is the Service Employees International Union that represents nearly 100,000 state workers from nurses to bus drivers. Over 30,000 prison guards belong to the California Correctional Peace Officers Association (CCPOA). As their Web site declares, this group represents "the men and women who walk the toughest beat in the state."[16] As union members, state employees deal with many personnel-related issues such as collective bargaining rights, and sexual harassment, plus the administration of pension plans. In 1992, they heavily supported the passage of Proposition 162, which gave public employee pension boards greater power to manage their own affairs. In the past, the legislature occasionally "borrowed" (some say "raided") assets from the pension plans to help balance state budgets. The two largest boards are CalPERS (the Public Employees Retirement System) and STRS (the State Teachers Retirement System).

As in other states, California's public employees have been subject to a great deal of scrutiny in the wake of the recent recession. Critics have decried what they regard as overly generous public sector salaries, fringe benefits, and retirement packages. Accordingly, there have been frequent calls to reform, reduce, or eliminate public pensions as has been done in much of the private sector. Even a state agency recommended reduced pensions for current workers. Other observers point out that state workers and retirees account for rather modest portions of the state's budget. More than 70 percent of all state spending is "local assistance"—going to schools, local government, health care providers, and poor families.

Executive Branch Reform

When Schwarzenegger campaigned for governor, he vowed to "blow up the boxes," that is, reorganize the workings of state government. It made for colorful, Terminator-like election rhetoric but one had to wonder at the time how much he knew of those boxes that constituted the executive branch. If not then, he would later learn that 339 separate boards and commissions shared power with executive branch agencies and departments. One such board, the Unemployment Insurance Appeals Board paid each member over $128,000 per year for work easily managed by civil service workers and administrative law judges. Most board members were in fact term-out legislators. As governor, he would witness the legislature create still more of these groups such as the Ocean Protection Council and the Commission on Latino/Latina Affairs. Calling the state government a "mastodon frozen in time," Schwarzenegger appointed a 275-person team—the California Performance Review—to study the executive branch and make recommendations for reform. Their 2,700-page, six-inch-thick report contained more than 1,000 recommendations including the elimination of more than 12,000 jobs, the abolition of 118 boards and commissions, and the streamlining of still other agencies where policy redundancy was routine.[17]

Reform proponents praised the report, the billions of dollars in anticipated savings, and the promise of greater accountability. Critics claimed that the cost savings were exaggerated and that many of the proposals centralized too much power in the governor's office. In response to the findings, the governor pledged to use the report to create a "21st century government for the future of California." "We cannot just chip away at the edges of our state's problems. Sometimes a surgeon has to cut in order to save the patient."[18] The governor later lost interest in that ambitious reform agenda and larger budget woes preempted it in his second term. By the time he left office, he had even appointed some former staffers to boards he once would have eliminated. Facing continued budget deficits, successor Brown submitted a 2011–2012 budget premised on eliminating 37 boards and commissions, including that insurance appeals board.

CONCLUSION

The themes of hyperpluralism and diversity emerge from a review of California's executive branch. Executive leadership in California is a diffused phenomenon. Power is shared between the governor, other statewide elected officials, plus a huge bureaucracy. California governors, as elsewhere, can employ several resources to enhance their leadership potential. Historians regard Hiram Johnson, Earl Warren, Pat Brown, and Ronald Reagan as gubernatorial giants. They clearly made the most of the power they had. But they governed in a simpler time over a smaller and less diverse California. Today's governors wield substantial formal powers, but even these are shared by the legislature, a plural executive system, and at times, the voters themselves. The office's most singular duties are constitutionally mandated, such as submitting a budget, exercising veto power, and performing various judicial roles.

The vastness of California's bureaucracy in some respects mirrors the diversity of the state itself. As Figure 8.1 suggests, virtually every economic sector and demographic group is represented in and/or regulated by the executive branch. The state's bureaucrats can wield a great deal of power but commonly share it with the judiciary or legislature. Reformers increasingly believe that the gridlock between the executive branch and the other branches is the source of California's governing problems. But given the enduring idea of checks and balances in American politics, others believe gridlock is a price worth paying to avoid unchecked executive and bureaucratic power.

KEY TERMS

political context (p. 155)

inner circle (p. 156)

superagencies (p. 156)

executive order (p. 158)

internal and external budget processes (p. 158)

item and general veto (pp. 158, 160)

special session (p. 160)

clemency (p. 162)

plural executive (p. 162)

civil service (p. 166)

REVIEW QUESTIONS

1. Apply Crew's gubernatorial leadership variables to Governor Jerry Brown and other recent California governors. What did Brown discover about leadership since his first two terms as governor?

2. Of the governor's duties and powers, which do you think are the most and least important?

3. What advice would you give California governors on how to maximize their budget powers?

4. In what ways does California's plural executive increase political fragmentation and encourage hyperpluralism?

5. If you wanted to use a statewide elective office as a stepping stone to the governorship, which would you seek, not seek, and why?

6. In what ways can California's bureaucracy exercise power independent of the governor? Is the bureaucracy itself a function of hyperpluralism?

WEB ACTIVITIES

Governor's Office
(http://gov.ca.gov/)
This site features biographical information, speeches, press releases, executive orders, video blogs, and volumes of other information related to the current governor.

State Agencies
(www.ca.gov/CaSearch/Agencies.aspx)
This directory leads you to a stunningly long list of agencies, departments, divisions, boards,

commissions, and other state entities with links to each one. The scope and diversity of California's executive branch is readily apparent.

Capitol Weekly
(www://capitolweekly.net)
This newspaper includes many articles and features of interest to all Californians and public sector workers in particular, including job postings, salary data, and policy decisions affecting those workers.

NOTES

1. For more information on this era, see John C. Bollens and G. Robert Williams, *Jerry Brown in a Plain Brown Wrapper* (Palisades, NY: Palisades Publishers, 1978).

2. Quoted in Carla Marinucci, "Jerry Brown Faces New Political Game at Capitol," *San Francisco Chronicle*, March 27, 2011.

3. James MacGregor Burns, *Leadership* (New York: Harper and Row, 1978), p. 388.

4. All the salary figures in this chapter represent reductions made in 2010 by the California Citizens Compensation Commission; legislative salaries were reduced at this time as well.

5. See Robert E. Crew Jr., "Understanding Gubernatorial Behavior: A Framework for Analysis," in Thad Beyle, ed. *Governors and Hard Times* (Washington, D.C.: Congressional Quarterly Press, 1992), pp. 15–27.

6. Mark DiCamillo and Mervin Field, "Voters Approve of Governor Brown's Job Performance by a Two to One Margin. Legislature Continues to be Seen in a Very Negative Light," *The Field Poll, Release#2371* (San Francisco: Field Research Corporation, March 22, 2011). (Accessed at www. field. com/fieldpollonline/).

7. Political scientist Thad Beyle has ranked the powers of all 50 governors using numerous variables. For links to his calculations, go to www.unc.edu/~beyle/.

8. California State Constitution, Article V, Section 1.

9. Peter Nicholas, "Governor's State Board Choices Raise Charges of Cronyism," *Los Angeles Times*, April 2, 2007.

10. For more on the budget process, see John Decker, *California in the Balance: Why Budgets Matter* (Berkeley: Institute of Governmental Studies, 2009)

and Richard Krolak, *California's Budget Dance: Issues and Process,* 2nd ed. (Sacramento: California Journal Press, 1994).

11. Jack Chang, "Jerry Brown's Wife is Vital Campaign Partner," *Sacramento Bee,* September 22, 2010; last modified November 28, 2010.

12. Quoted in Helene Von Damm, *Sincerely, Ronald Reagan* (Ottawa, Illinois: Green Hill, 1976), pp. 162–163.

13. California Budget Project, *Professors and Prison Guards: An Overview of California's Workforce* (Sacramento: California Budget Project, April, 2010).

14. This report and other reform oriented reports on California's executive branch can be found at www.lhc.ca.gov/.

15. A.G. Block and Gerald C. Lubenow, eds. *California Political Almanac 2007–2008* (Washington, D.C.: CQ Press, 2007), p. 75.

16. Little Hoover Commission, *Public Pensions for Retirement Security* (Sacramento: Little Hoover Commission, February, 2011).

17. California Performance Review. (Accessed at http://cpr.ca.gov/report/).

18. Quoted in Peter Nicholas, "Schwarzenegger Vows to 'Make Every Use' of Overhaul Plan," *Los Angeles Times,* August 4, 2004.

9

✴

California's Judiciary

Introduction

State Courts in Our Legal "System"

How California's Courts Are Organized

Trial Courts

Appellate Courts

Supreme Court

So You Want to be a Judge

Entering the Profession

The Right Experience

Selection Mechanics

Judicial Discipline

How Courts Make Decisions

The Criminal Process

The Civil Process

Juries and Popular Justice

How Courts Make Policy

Trial Court Policymaking

Appellate Court Policymaking

Criminal Justice and Punishment

Social Trends

Sentencing Mandates

Conclusion

Key Terms

Review Questions

Web Activities

Notes

IN BRIEF

California's judiciary shares power with the legislative and executive branches. As in other states, it is divided into two levels: trial courts and appellate courts. Lower courts handle major disputes and offenses and hold preliminary hearings on more serious matters. Trial courts decide matters of fact; appellate courts matters of law. All cases are either criminal (wrongs against society) or civil (disputes among individuals and/or organizations).

Lawyers who want to be judges must become politically involved. Although all judges in California must eventually face the voters, most assume the bench through gubernatorial appointment. In a representative democracy, judges need to be both independent and politically accountable—a difficult balance to achieve. Judges are also accountable to professional standards policed by the California Commission on Judicial Performance.

Judges make case-specific decisions in addition to public policy. At the trial court level, cases follow a predictable chronology, including various pretrial activities designed to avoid trial, the trial itself, and the sentence or judgment. Appellate justices have the most leeway in making public policy, as recent state supreme courts demonstrate. The judiciary's most visible policy role involves criminal justice, especially cases involving the death penalty.

Although the legal profession does not reflect California's growing ethnicity, judicial policymaking in California is influenced by both the state's diversity and its population growth. While carrying out its own policy role, California courts also share power with the legislative and executive branches.

INTRODUCTION

Fact: A parent in Granada Hills, California, sues a Little League executive after he is told to stop smoking during a game. The parent claims emotional distress.

Fact: Losing a citizen initiative campaign, an interest group sues the state to prevent its implementation.

Fact: Death row inmate, Richard Ramirez, spends more than 20 years filing appeals to his 1989 death sentence.

These examples illustrate some broad trends occurring in California and the nation. First, we are a litigious society. Americans increasingly view all manner of problems and even public policies in legal terms. Lawyers and laypersons alike assume that for every wrong there must be a legal remedy, usually determined in a court of law. Second, there has been an explosion in the number of lawyers in U.S. society. Of all U.S. lawyers, about one in seven practices in California. In 2011, there were more than 170,000 active attorneys in California; thousands more join the state bar each year.[1] More lawyers likely mean more lawsuits. Third, the crush of civil and criminal cases has bogged down California's busiest court systems. At any one time in Los Angeles County

there are more than one million small claims and civil cases in process; resolving many of them can take years.

Despite all the litigation, Californians' knowledge of the legal system is rather spotty. In a State Bar Association survey, 53 percent of the respondents could not identify the nation's Bill of Rights; 48 percent did not know that defendants are presumed innocent until proven guilty; and 68 percent were unaware that they had only limited liability if someone used their name to make an unauthorized purchase. Yet 90 percent knew it took a .08 or higher blood alcohol level to be convicted of adult drunk driving; 95 percent realized that both parents could be liable for child support; and 95 percent knew that husbands could be prosecuted for spousal rape.[2]

Given the role of law in California's political system, what courts, judges, and juries do affects all Californians. The judiciary has always shared power with the legislative and executive branches. Conflict among them is increasingly common. At times it seems judges have the final say; at other times, they seem only to contribute to the policy gridlock occurring in the nation's most populous and diverse state. This chapter examines California's legal system and its policymaking role, how it is organized, and what its participants do.

STATE COURTS IN OUR
LEGAL "SYSTEM"

I use the term "legal system" advisedly. The federal *Judiciary Act of 1789* actually created a dual system of courts, national and state. The federal courts deal with matters arising from the U.S. Constitution, civil cases involving regulatory activity, plus a relatively small number of criminal offenses. Fifty separate state systems address matters arising from state constitutions, civil matters, and most criminal offenses. State courts handle the vast majority of all court activity in the nation.

California is only one of those 50 systems, but it is not simply a copy of the others. Each state's judiciary reflects to some extent its political culture and history. The independent spirit that characterized California's history was bound to be reflected in its legal system; in fact, its Supreme Court has developed a national reputation for independence from the federal judiciary. Unlike many Southern states that used a "states rights" philosophy to impede federal civil rights efforts, California's courts have viewed independence in progressive terms. The state's "independent-state-grounds" doctrine assumed that when state and federal constitutional provisions are similar, California could interpret those provisions more expansively or liberally. This view, pioneered by the late State Supreme Court Justice Stanley Mosk, expanded individual rights beyond those granted by the U.S. Supreme Court—a doctrine called "independent-state grounds."[3] In several celebrated cases, the California Supreme Court struck down the death penalty before its federal counterpart did, rejected the state's method of financing public education (a decision the U.S. Supreme Court has refused to make), and invalidated a citizen initiative that would have banned fair housing laws.[4] This exemplifies **judicial federalism**: the ability and willingness of different court systems to produce potentially diverse, fragmented, and contradictory policy.

California's independent-minded judiciary does not operate in a vacuum. Some people prefer to resolve their legal disputes at the federal level. California has four federal district courts located throughout the state. It is possible for state and federal courts to hear the same kinds of cases (civil rights and liberties), a phenomenon called "concurrent jurisdiction." As a result, Californians can "shop" for the level—federal or state—most likely to give them the desired result. Challenges to voter-approved initiatives are often filed in federal court. Examples include Propositions 187 (immigration), 209 (affirmative action), and 8 (same sex marriage).

If decisions by the federal district courts in California are appealed, they go to the U.S. Court of Appeals for the Ninth Circuit. This court is famous for its own judicial independence. In fact, the U.S. Supreme Court has rebuked this circuit court for frustrating California's efforts to execute death row inmates. More than most federal appellate courts, the Ninth Circuit handles cases involving diverse populations and sweeping social changes. The judges themselves admit that California provides them with a variety of cutting-edge issues because of the state's size, diversity, and independence from federal policies. Occasionally, the U.S. Supreme Court itself overturns California law and policy. For example, in 2011, it ruled in *Brown v. Plata* that overcrowding in California state prisons amounted to cruel and unusual punishment, in violation of the Eighth Amendment of the U.S. Constitution. To add teeth to their decision, they ordered the state to drastically reduce its prison population.[5]

HOW CALIFORNIA'S COURTS
ARE ORGANIZED

California's judicial system is the largest in the world, consisting of more than 2,000 judicial officers divided into three tiers of courts. These layers divide the judiciary's caseload within the system

California Supreme Court
1 chief justice, 6 associate justices
- Hears oral arguments in San Francisco, Los Angeles, and Sacramento
- Has discretionary authority to review decisions of the Courts of Appeal and direct responsibility for automatic appeals after death penalty judgments

Courts of Appeal
105 justices
- 6 districts, 18 divisions, and 9 court locations
- Review the majority of appealable orders or judgments from the superior courts

Superior Courts
1,499 judges, 437 commissioners and referees
- 58 courts, one in each county, with from 1 to 55 branches
- Provide a forum for resolution of criminal and civil cases under state and local laws, which define crimes, specify punishments, and define civil duties and liabilities

FIGURE 9.1 California Court System

Question: Should death penalty cases go directly to the Supreme Court or work their way through the courts of appeal like other cases?

SOURCE: Judicial Council of California.

while allowing ample opportunity for litigants to appeal unfavorable decisions (see Figure 9.1). Let's briefly look at each layer, beginning where most cases start—at the bottom.

Trial Courts

On the lowest rung of the judicial ladder are the state's trial courts. Called **superior courts** in California, they are triers of fact; they determine who is right or wrong in civil disputes and who is innocent or guilty in criminal cases. Until recently, there were both municipal courts and superior courts. The municipal courts handled minor criminal offenses (punishable by fines or jail time), infractions (fineable violations of state statutes or local ordinances), and civil claims of $25,000 or less. In 1998, the passage of Proposition 220 allowed municipal and superior court functions to merge into the superior courts.

All state trial courts are now organized in this manner. In recent years, there have been roughly 1,600 authorized judges and 400 commissioners and referees with authority to act as judges. In addition to all felony and civil disputes, the superior courts serve as family, juvenile, and probate courts. Depending on the county's size, superior court judges either hear a wide variety of cases or specialize in a particular area of the law: juvenile, family, probate, or criminal. They are paid about $172,000 per year, plus benefits. Cases may be decided by juries or only judges (bench trials). California's **Three-Strikes Law** (which imposes a minimum 25-years-to-life sentence for defendants with two or more prior felony convictions) has significantly increased the workload for some trial courts. Facing a possible third strike conviction, many defendants opt for jury trials rather than plead guilty. The law itself requires copious record keeping by local court personnel. Supporting the judges are professional court administrators who manage court personnel, budgets, and workloads. Because more than 30 percent of criminal arrests in California are illicit-drug-related, many counties have established "drug treatment courts" that combine the standard judicial process with community drug treatment services.

The volume of trial court cases in California is staggering. Superior courts handle over nine million filings annually, most of those criminal in nature.

In addition to court consolidation, California's judiciary has experienced other recent improvements. The *1997 Trial Court Funding Act* transferred financial responsibility for the trial courts to the state. The purpose of this law was to stabilize and make more equitable judicial services across the state. Then Chief Justice Ronald M. George called it "without a doubt one of the most important reforms in the California justice system in the 20th century."[6] California has also increased court interpreter services, and with good reason. On any given day, more than 100 languages might require translation in the state's courts.

Appellate Courts

District Courts of Appeal hear appeals from superior courts and quasi-judicial state agencies. They are geographically divided into six districts. Unlike superior courts, they normally decide questions of law, not fact. For instance, instead of deciding guilt or innocence in a car theft case, California's 105 appellate justices typically sit on three-member panels to determine if legal procedures were applied properly in that case. (Was the suspect informed of his or her rights? Did the judge instruct the jury properly?) If legal errors did occur, they can order a new trial. Although appeals are common, appellate courts dismiss most of them. At that level, there are no "trials" as such, no witnesses or juries. The justices read trial court transcripts and occasionally hear oral arguments by opposing attorneys. They spend hours in private legal research, not in the courtroom. When they hear cases, they usually sit as panels of three. Because the California Supreme Court also declines to hear most cases appealed to it, appellate court decisions are often final. Appeals rarely involve life-or-death, earthshaking issues. As one California appellate justice put it: "If 90 percent of this stuff were in the United States Post Office, it would be classified as junk mail."[7] The Courts of Appeal process about 24,000 filings annually and dispose of about 11,000 matters through written opinions. Less than ten percent of those are deemed significant enough to warrant publication.[8] Appellate justices earn about $209,000 annually; presiding justices earn somewhat more.

Supreme Court

The **California Supreme Court** is at the pinnacle of the system. Its purpose is to raise important constitutional issues and to maintain legal uniformity throughout the state. When it speaks, other courts listen—not only in California but also in other states and throughout the federal judiciary. Due to heavy volume, this court must be selective in what it chooses to hear and what it chooses to say. The Supreme Court averages about 9,000 filings annually but issues only 110–120 written opinions. Its seven justices spend most of their time in legal research and opinion writing. They hear oral arguments for only one week of every month they are in session. The court consists of a chief justice and six associate justices. The associate justices earn about $215,000; the chief justice earns about $234,000.

If the Supreme Court is so selective, what kinds of cases is it willing to hear? First, much of its work is civil in nature, reflecting the legal problems of California businesses. Second, all death penalty cases are "automatic appeals"; they bypass the appellate courts and must be heard directly by the Supreme Court. In its 2008-2009 term, the Court considered 24 new death penalty appeals and disposed of 50 such cases. Most of these cases are over a decade old by the time they reach the court and when they do, they consume huge amounts of the Court's time and resources. The records in these cases can approach 10,000 pages in length and numerous motions require the court's attention even before formal hearings occur. Some appeals languish because lawyers are unwilling to represent such clients. Third, as noted in Chapter 4, the widespread use of initiatives fosters litigation and, ultimately, interpretation by the California Supreme Court. Recent examples include gay marriage, medical marijuana, and stem cell research.

SO YOU WANT TO BE A JUDGE

A law school official once said that A-students become law professors, B-students become judges, and C-students become rich! A judgeship is a noble goal regardless of grade point average. Judges earn much less than senior corporate law partners, but the pay is reasonable; plus, a judgeship offers a level of prestige no law firm can match. Several steps are required to become a judge. Given the number of judicial officers and active attorneys in

Supreme Court of California

Chief Justice Tani Cantil-Sakauye was sworn into office on January 3, 2011.
She is only the second woman and the first Asian-Filipina American to serve as California's chief justice. For a full biography, go to www.courts.ca.gov/2664.htm/.

SOURCE: California Supreme Court.

California (2,000 and 170,000, respectively), only a small percentage will ever achieve this elusive goal.

Entering the Profession

To become a judge, one must first become a lawyer, but this was not always the case. In the past, nonlawyers could serve as justices of the peace. Today, virtually all California judges are law school graduates. To practice law, the state constitution requires all practicing lawyers to join the State Bar Association of California, a quasi-official group that oversees the admission and discipline of the state's attorneys. Applicants to the state bar must pass a three-day state bar exam, considered one of the nation's toughest. It is common for nearly half of exam takers to fail, sometimes repeatedly. That

badge of honor is shared by governors Jerry Brown and Pete Wilson, former California Supreme Court Justice William P. Clark, Los Angeles Mayor Antonio Villaraigosa, and countless lesser knowns. The best overall preparation for the exam is law school. California boasts 18 American Bar Association-accredited and 16 state-accredited law schools, plus assorted unaccredited schools and correspondence law courses.

Who employs California's lawyers? About three-fourths are in private practice. The rest work in government, private industry, education, or other contexts. The demographic makeup of both the California bar and bench does not mirror California as a whole. While they are gradually becoming more diverse, both the bar and the courts remain largely male and white. One of the most significant demographic changes is the influx of women in the legal profession. While nearly 30 percent of the state bar and bench are women, that number will likely grow if law school admission trends continue. Racial and ethnic minorities have more progress to make. They constitute only 17 percent of the state bar and only 19 percent of the state bench.[9]

A major challenge facing the legal profession in California is equal access to legal representation. As we have seen repeatedly, two Californias are evident—in this case, those who can afford legal representation and those who cannot. While public defenders represent indigent defendants in criminal cases, civil cases are more problematic. There are relatively few legal aid lawyers compared to other private attorneys in California. The State Bar of California is addressing this by encouraging more attorneys to volunteer a portion of their time for the public good ("pro bono" work).

The Right Experience

Few California lawyers are situated to become judges. To be considered judgeship material, lawyers find they need a network of personal, legal, and political relationships. When asked what it took to become a California Supreme Court justice, former

Justice Mathew Tobriner recommended going to high school with someone who planned to become governor.[10] After law school, most lawyers settle into private practice or work for government. They become involved in a local bar association and may dabble in partisan politics. Attending political fundraisers helps, and contributing to a governor's campaign helps a great deal. Many judges appointed by recent governors have contributed to their campaigns. One's legal specialty also affects one's chances of becoming a judge. Young lawyers grinding out billable hours for high-powered law firms may find little time, energy, or incentive for politics. Of those who practice criminal law, aspiring judicial candidates are likely to be district attorneys, not defense attorneys.

Selection Mechanics

The formal steps to becoming a judge vary, depending on the court level. All levels in California employ a version of the **Missouri Plan**, which combines both elections and appointments. This hybrid method is based on two assumptions: (1) fellow lawyers can best assess the attributes of judicial candidates, and (2) in a representative democracy, ultimate accountability to the voters is important, even for judges.

Trial Courts   At the local, trial court level, voters elect judges for six-year terms in officially nonpartisan elections (once again, thanks to the Progressives). Reelection is virtually guaranteed. What lawyer wants to run against a judge, lose, and then face that judge in court? Many judges resign or retire from the bench between elections, in which case the governor appoints a replacement to fill out a term based on recommendations from the local bar and political allies. Judges themselves can fill some vacancies by appointing commissioners, lawyers who act as judges on a temporary basis. These lawyers gain invaluable experience they can tout if a permanent judgeship opportunity arises.

Although some political scientists refer to judges as "politicians who wear robes," local judicial elections have been staid affairs. Judges raise modest campaign support from fellow lawyers and the business community, but rarely wage the kind of combative election campaigns voters see in other branches of government. There is little or no precinct walking, television advertising, or direct mail flyers. Maybe a few yard signs or newspaper ads. But times are changing. Due to their own campaign inexperience, judges increasingly employ campaign management firms. For whatever reason, judicial campaigns have begun to resemble campaigns for other offices—more politicized, negative, and costly (see California Voices). This can be problematic because California's code of judicial ethics proscribes candidates from discussing cases or issues that could come before the courts or from mischaracterizing their election opponents.

Appellate and Supreme Courts   The process of becoming an appellate or Supreme Court justice is a combination of initial appointment and later election, but there are additional layers of evaluation. Although the governor makes the initial appointment, two other groups have substantial input. First, the state legislature requires that the California State Bar Association's Commission on Judicial Nominees Evaluation investigate nominee credentials and rate their fitness for office. Five grades are possible: exceptionally well qualified, well qualified, qualified, unqualified, or "not qualified at this time." These ratings make little news because so many lawyers are deemed well qualified by their peers. In a notable exception, African American appointee Janice Rogers Brown received an "unqualified" rating by the bar committee, due primarily to her lack of adequate judicial experience. Wilson appoint her anyway and eventually won praise by judicial conservatives. In 2005, U.S. President George W. Bush elevated her to the U.S. Court of Appeals. Second, a nominee needs approval by a three-member Commission on Judicial Appointments, consisting of the chief justice of the Supreme Court, the attorney general, and the senior presiding justice of the court of appeals. Although this group normally approves a

---

B o x 9.1   California Voices: The Angst of a Judicial Candidate

I bought space on slate mailers, as suggested by my campaign consultant. Being a political naïf, I did not realize that my name might appear on highly partisan and/or issue-oriented slates—like on the candidate slate of the "Republicans Against Abortion" and on the slate for "Pro-Choice Democrats." Did I fail to sufficiently inform myself? (Who has time for that?) Given the mandatory disclaimers on slate mailers, does it matter? I was asked to respond to questionnaires. While some were legitimate—requesting my background information and soliciting my views on how the administration of justice might be improved—others were blatantly political. They demanded to

know whether I believed *Roe v. Wade* was incorrectly decided and whether prayer in the schools should be permitted. They said a refusal to answer would be construed as a negative response. I ignored them. Was there a better way?

Question: Should judges wage campaigns much like other office holders? Why? Why not?

NOTE: Judicial candidate Rivera won her Contra Costa judgeship and is now associate justice for the First District Court of Appeal.

SOURCE: Excerpted from Maria P. Rivera, "The Complexities—and Importance—of Running a Fair Campaign," *California Courts Review* (Fall 2007–Winter 2008), 16.

---

governor's choice, a split vote can embarrass the governor and spell future trouble for the nominee. Both Rose Bird and Cruz Reynoso were approved by 2 to 1 votes, raising public doubts about their fitness. Once confirmed by this group, the appellate or Supreme Court justice takes the oath of office and begins work.

The voters have input at the next gubernatorial election. In these "retention" elections, the justices have no specific opponents and run solely on their records. For example, one ballot item would read: "FOR ASSOCIATE JUSTICE OF THE SUPREME COURT Shall ASSOCIATE JUSTICE CARLOS MORENO be elected to the office for the term provided by law?" State Supreme Court justices face all California voters. Appellate justices face only the voters in their respective appellate districts. Once they win, they serve 12-year terms after which they face another retention election. If they are filling an unexpired term, they serve only the remainder of the term and then face election. Usually voters pay little attention to what judges do, but 1986 was different. In a historic election, California voters rejected Chief Justice Bird, and Associate Justices Joseph Grodin and Reynoso, allowing then-governor George Deukmejian to appoint their successors. The

justices' support for defendant rights and consistent opposition to the death penalty, despite public support for it, fueled a well-organized "anti-Bird Court" coalition. A 1998 effort by anti-abortion activists to unseat Chief Justice Ronald George and Justice Ming Chin was unsuccessful but forced them to raise $700,000 for their retention elections. The fall 2010 ballot was more typical. According to the National Institute on Money in State Politics, not one California appellate justice or Supreme Court justice raised or spent anything to be retained.[11]

Judicial Discipline

As we have seen, voters can, but rarely do, oust sitting judges. Does that mean lawyers and judges can do most anything they want? Not quite. The California Constitution provides for the impeachment of state judges "for misconduct in office."[12] This involves impeachment (an indictment of sorts) in the Assembly and a trial in the Senate. Aside from this rarely used method of judicial discipline, there is a complex system of judicial accountability involving not only the public but also the legal profession. Judges are held to professional norms and subject to peer review.

Professional Norms   Lawyers learn to think and behave like judges during law school, a process called **judicial socialization**. First, they learn about judicial ethics. For example, judges are not supposed to decide cases in which they have a personal stake. Yet some do. One trial court judge issued an order releasing from custody his own son who had been arrested for drunk driving, an action roundly criticized in the legal community. Second, they learn to appreciate the rule of precedent—*stare decisis*. Judges are expected to make new decisions by relying heavily on previous ones, especially those of higher courts. Third, judges render decisions within certain limits such as sentencing standards, jury instruction rules, and uniform legal procedures. Whereas the general public cares primarily about verdicts, judges are equally concerned with procedures used to achieve verdicts. In a state and nation governed by the "rule of law," procedure is the all-important vehicle through which courts ascertain truth.

Peer Review   Socrates once said, "Four things belong to a judge: to hear courteously, to answer wisely, to consider soberly, and to decide impartially." What happens when a judge does otherwise—yelling at attorneys and their clients or calling two juvenile assailants "bitches" or giving preferential treatment to friends and family? These are the kinds of complaints handled by California's Commission on Judicial Performance. This independent state agency consists of 11 members, including judges, attorneys, and lay citizens.

Its primary duty is to investigate charges of willful misconduct by judges. According to a recent annual report, the commission examines a surprising variety of complaints involving judges' on-and off-the-bench behavior. They may include offensive courtroom demeanor, disparaging the attorneys present, moral turpitude, sexual harassment, and using court resources for personal business.[13] Various versions of a code of conduct have guided judges since 1949. Today's **Code of Judicial Ethics** was adopted by the state Supreme Court in 1996 and revised in 1999. These canons represent a judicial consensus, and it behooves all judges to heed them.

Of the hundreds of complaints filed against California judges each year, most come from litigants and their families and most of them are upset with court personnel other than judges or with a disagreeable legal result. Very few of these complaints result in public discipline such as removal from office. The Commission usually issues "advisory letters" or "private admonishments" known as "stingers" to correct problem behavior.

The Ballot Box   Although few voters pay attention to disciplinary matters, they do react to well-publicized or controversial decisions they do not like. When judges consistently make decisions outside the broad political beliefs of Californians, sooner or later they may suffer the consequences at the polls. In the 1986 election, three Supreme Court justices were defeated largely due to their adamant opposition to the death penalty; they had reversed 52 of 55 death penalties by early 1986. In some cases, they seemed to stretch reason, at least in the opinion of some Californians. For example, the court majority overturned one death sentence, finding the defendant lacked intent to kill, even though the victim had been decapitated and was missing both hands.

At the local level, unpopular decisions can lead to recall efforts, even though these tend to be unsuccessful. For example, one Los Angeles judge who sentenced a shopkeeper to mere community service for killing a suspected teenage shoplifter spent $300,000 to fend off a recall attempt. She eventually resigned. A Sacramento judge faced a recall attempt by ruling that Proposition 22, the gay marriage initiative, did not outlaw same-sex civil unions. As a general rule, judges chafe at the notion of strict electoral accountability. Sacramento Superior Court Judge Roger Warren once echoed the paradox of judicial accountability: "We don't want judges who are totally immune and divorced from real life, and on the other hand we want them to be sufficiently independent so that they can make decisions based on principle."[14]

HOW COURTS MAKE DECISIONS

In previous chapters, we examined how legislators and executives make policy and share power. Judges do both as well. But court decisions are different from policy decisions made in other branches. They result from pretrial and trial activity. As elsewhere in the nation, trials in California are based on the concept of **adversarial justice**. Determining truth and justice involves a contest between two conflicting sides. Each presents only information favorable to its side. Judges and juries find the "truth" in and around conflicting claims.

In any California courtroom, the process one sees is rather generic. The steps may vary somewhat depending on whether the case is criminal or civil. Criminal cases involve alleged wrongs against society (murder, armed robbery, and so on). That is why such cases are entitled "People" v. whomever the defendant might be. Civil cases involve disputes between individuals in society (usually involving financial transactions, real estate, personal property, business relationships, family relationships, and personal injuries).

The Criminal Process

According to the *California Penal Code,* criminal offenses can be infractions, misdemeanors, or felonies. **Infractions** (traffic tickets) involve no jail time. **Misdemeanors** are lesser crimes for which a person may be sentenced to time in county jail. **Felonies** are more serious crimes for which a person may be sentenced to state prison or to death. Many crimes may be misdemeanors on the first offense but become felonies if repeated. "Wobblers" are crimes that can be treated as misdemeanors or felonies if the judge has necessary sentencing discretion.

Criminal cases feature numerous steps and decision points. We will examine what happens before, during, and after trials. Throughout the process, an enormous amount of discretion is available to virtually everyone but the defendant.

Pretrial Activity The first decision is obviously the decision to arrest someone. Police exercise discretion at this point based on their own attitudes, the nature of the crime, the relationship between the suspect and the victim, and department policy. The second decision is the decision to prosecute. Prosecutors, called "district attorneys" in California, make that decision based on the quality of evidence and witnesses, office policy, and the availability of alternatives such as alcohol education programs. Which charges to file can vary depending on local prosecutorial policy. For example, "junk" crimes such as minor shoplifting and unreturned rental videos are rarely prosecuted in megacounties such as Los Angeles. San Diego prosecutors often return illegal immigrants to Mexico rather than press charges. At one time, poorer counties could ill afford lengthy murder trials, but state responsibility for trial court funding should rectify this situation, at least to some extent. Overall, district attorneys play a dominant role compared to judges or defense attorneys.

Two conflicting values play out at this stage. On the one hand, courtroom work groups (prosecutors, defense attorneys, judges, and other court officers) often operate on an **assumption of guilt**. "If you are there, you are there for a reason," so the reasoning goes. According to judicial scholars and practitioners, this logic is based less on prejudice than on daily experience. Plea bargaining is the logical result of this value among court professionals. On the other hand, the legal value of **innocent until proven guilty** is an essential ingredient of the American legal system. Judges constantly remind prospective jurors and juries that this value must undergird all they do.

After charging, several other steps occur. During an **arraignment**, a judge informs the accused of the charges and the legal options available. In a felony case, a **preliminary hearing** determines if there is probable cause to hold a trial. That decision is called an **indictment**. In addition to district attorneys, grand juries sometimes issue indictments. These bodies are citizen boards, selected from auto and voter registration lists. They tend to be used in complex or sensitive cases and when witnesses need protection. Most criminal arraignments are accomplished with dizzying speed given the volume of cases judges must face. When people talk of "assembly line justice," they are usually referring to the arraignment calendar.

As we noted, defendants and prosecutors often bypass trials using **plea bargaining**. Both sides benefit. By pleading no contest or guilty, often to a lesser charge, defendants can avoid unpredictable juries and know for certain what a sentence will be. Overworked prosecutors may be under pressure to avoid lengthy and costly trials; they may also regard the evidence in particular cases too weak to entrust to a jury. Whatever the motivation, judges usually rubberstamp plea agreements negotiated by prosecutors and defense lawyers. How often does this occur? Well over 90 percent of criminal cases are disposed of before an actual trial. Without plea bargaining (euphemistically called "case management"), judges and lawyers alike believe the criminal justice process would grind to a halt. California's *Three-Strikes Law* has reduced the number of defendants willing to accept a plea agreement if it constitutes a "strike."[15]

The Trial   At the trial stage, the first step is selecting a jury. Criminal trials can be heard before a judge only (bench trials) or a jury made up of one's peers. Sometimes a defendant can choose which type. Bench trials are common for less serious offenses. They constitute more than 20 percent of all criminal trials in California. Prosecutors and defense attorneys traditionally have played key roles in the selection of juries. Juries of less than 12 are possible in misdemeanor cases. Because felony cases require 12-member juries and convictions require unanimous verdicts, picking the "right" jury is essential to both the prosecution and the defense. The process is both art and science, as jurors are asked about anything in their backgrounds that would tempt them to prejudge a case. While judges are in charge of this *voir dire* process, attorneys may ask some questions and may remove some potential jurors without stating a reason (peremptory challenge). On occasion, picking the right jury means moving a trial site due to unfavorable pretrial

publicity (a "change of venue"). In the famous 1992 trial of Los Angeles policemen accused of beating African American Rodney King, many legal experts believed the outcome was predetermined when the trial was moved to suburban Ventura County.[16] A jury dominated by whites acquitted the officers. In 2004, the media-saturated Scott Peterson murder case was moved from Modesto to Redwood City; he was found guilty anyway.

Misdemeanor trials must begin within 45 days of arraignment, 30 days if the defendant is in custody. Felony trials must begin 60 days after arraignment unless the defense requests a delay. Judges usually grant such requests. Based on the notion that "justice delayed is justice denied," criminal cases take priority, forcing lengthy delays for civil cases that have no such time constraints.

The steps of a trial are rather predictable. After opening statements by both sides, the prosecution presents evidence consisting of witnesses and various exhibits (direct examination). The defense cross-examines the witnesses. The defense makes its case in much the same fashion. As the trial ends, both sides give closing arguments, lawyerly interpretations of the case. The judge instructs the jury, if there is one; the jury deliberates and decides guilt or innocence.

The Verdict and Sentence   After the trial, the judge determines a sentence if the accused is found guilty using state-imposed guidelines. Generally speaking, judges are guided by a determinate sentencing law that sets finite prison terms and gives judges less discretion than they once had. Within these bounds, judges do have discretion based on restitution to victims, the need to protect society, or other special conditions. For example, they may require juvenile offenders to clean up graffiti, not just pass the time in a Youth Authority facility.

The Civil Process

Most courtroom time is devoted to civil cases—disputes involving individuals, businesses, and government agencies. As mentioned earlier, civil cases are constrained by mandated deadlines. When can a civil litigant expect justice? On the whole, 90-some percent of limited and unlimited civil cases reach disposition within two years; the process may take longer in some metropolitan counties. Justice delayed may well be justice denied when evidence becomes stale or when potential witnesses become unreachable. There are distinctive stages to the civil processes including pretrial activity, the trial itself, and a judgment.

Pretrial Activity   First, an aggrieved party, the plaintiff, files a **complaint** against a particular party. It consists of a specific claim (say someone breaks an ankle in a sidewalk hole) against a defendant and a proposed remedy (usually a dollar amount to cover medical expenses and possibly pain and suffering). The defendant is informed of the claim and files an answer. The next step is called **discovery**, the gathering of information to prepare for a possible trial. This process can involve **depositions** (oral testimony under oath) conducted by the lawyers involved, **interrogatories** (written questions and answers), and research into various documents and materials.

Every effort is made to settle the case before a trial actually begins. Sometimes the process is formal, involving ADR—**alternative dispute resolution**. It takes two forms. Generally speaking, **mediation** is voluntary and **arbitration** is governed by law or by prior agreement. An arbitrator's decision is legally binding. California requires a "mandatory settlement conference" as the trial date approaches. As one court administrator puts it, "Show them an open courtroom and they settle." Out-of-court settlements can range from mutual apologies to millions of dollars. To avoid lengthy, costly, public, and unpredictable trials, some corporate and celebrity litigants use retired judges who charge up to $10,000 per day for their legal know-how and settlement experience. For example, actors Brad Pitt and Jennifer Aniston finalized their divorce in this manner to avoid unwelcome prying by the public. Some legal experts are concerned about the fairness of this "rent a judge"

trend at least in some cases. Because decisions are achieved in private, important settlements escape any public scrutiny. Furthermore, not all litigants can afford this form of speedy, boutique justice. With or without private judging, the vast majority of California's civil cases are settled without a public trial.

The Trial   Trials are available for those who cannot or will not settle. The process in court is similar to the process in criminal trials. In a jury trial, three-fourths of the jury must agree for a verdict to result.

The Judgment   At the conclusion of a trial, the judge or jury decides whether a wrong was committed, who was responsible, and what damages, if any, should be awarded. Lawyers for the losing side may file posttrial motions asking to set aside or reduce any damages awarded. Judges (trial and appellate) may reduce damages they think are excessive; this occurs most commonly with punitive damages intended to punish or make an example out of a defendant.

Juries and Popular Justice

Well over 11,000 jury trials take place each year in California and, for many Californians, serving on a jury is their primary exposure to the legal system. In both criminal and civil cases, juries are charged with deciding questions of fact and reaching appropriate verdicts. One superior court judge calls his jurors "visiting judges" who determine the truthfulness of witnesses. Yet, jurors may not necessarily research decisions as judges would. Microcosms of the local community, juries have been known to weigh facts selectively or interpret them in light of their own experiences. This has been called **popular justice**. The extreme of this is the centuries-old doctrine of **jury nullification**—when individual jurors or entire juries follow their consciences rather than the law. For example, to many Californians, the jury in the O. J. Simpson murder trial chose to ignore certain incriminating evidence. In recent years, California juries have been known to resist "Third Strike" guilty verdicts because the sentencing requirements are too harsh. Defenders of the practice believe juries have the right, even duty, to ignore what they regard as unjust laws. Because nullification on the part of even one criminal jury member can result in a hung jury and a mistrial, the California Supreme Court unanimously ruled that trial judges may remove jurors suspected of this behavior. Said Chief Justice Ronald M. George, "A nullifying jury is essentially a lawless jury."[17] In civil cases, popular justice is still alive and well in the form of huge—sometimes exorbitant—cash settlements to wronged parties (automobile crash victims). Accordingly, some civil defendants (insurance companies) are willing to settle out of court for what they trust will be a lesser amount.

HOW COURTS MAKE POLICY

Courts not only make decisions, they make policy. Public policy is what governments choose to do or not do. Individual policy decisions can be made by a host of public officials, including those in the judiciary. Individual court decisions might not seem like broad policy statements; it depends on which level—trial or appellate.

Trial Court Policymaking

Trial court judges in California, as anywhere else, are primarily finders of fact. They make public policy in less obvious ways. First, they reflect policy preferences over time in many cases. This is called **cumulative policymaking**. Years of decisions in comparable cases reveal certain patterns, which vary from judge to judge. As a trial court judge, former California Chief Justice Malcolm Lucas was labeled "Maximum Malcolm" due to his typically harsh sentences in criminal cases. Second, judges generally reflect community norms. These norms are part of a community's local legal culture. Because these cultures vary from place to place, a form of judicial diversity results. For instance, California's big city judges may decide certain cases differently than

would their counterparts in rural communities. Charges of disturbing the peace, loitering, or obvious marijuana use may be treated differently in university towns than in wealthy residential enclaves. Third, trial judges' decisions reflect their own ideological perspectives. For instance, legal norms aside, conservative judges tend to side with insurance companies in claims cases or with management in labor disputes; liberals with claimants and organized labor. This fact is not lost on governors who fill trial court vacancies. For example, Governor Gray Davis preferred jurists who favor the death penalty and a woman's right to choose an abortion. According to law professor Gerald Uelman, "A wrong answer … [on these issues] is likely to end the inquiry and the candidate's judicial aspirations."[18]

Appellate Court Policymaking

Unlike trial courts, California appellate courts decide matters of law, not fact. They can confirm, reject, or modify public policy with a single decision. Although guided by *stare decisis* (the rule of precedent), they are not wedded to it. They can enter the "political thicket" of partisan conflict or avoid it. The choice is theirs. When Californians think of judicial policymaking, they usually think of the California Supreme Court, and rightfully so. We will consider briefly this court as policymaker under three past chief justices: Bird (1977–1986), Lucas (1986–1996), and Ronald George (1996–2010).

The Bird Court Rose Bird, a former public defender, presided over a court that viewed itself as change agent and problem solver. Remember, California courts have long assumed their independence from the federal judiciary. The California Supreme Court was a national trendsetter in this regard. In 1955, it ruled that illegally seized evidence could not be used in court. The U.S. Supreme Court agreed six years later. The California court stipulated various rights of accused persons one year before the famous *Miranda* decision did the same nationally. The Bird court was both independent and active. It overturned numerous death sentences, widened opportunities for liability suits, nullified several initiatives, and generally favored environmental protection and the rights of workers, renters, women, and homosexuals. By the early 1980s, the Bird court was so active, one superior court judge exclaimed: "Nothing is sacred any more. It's difficult for trial judges to know what the law is. They change it every 10 minutes."[19]

The Lucas Court The historic defeat of Bird, Reynoso, and Grodin in 1986 allowed Governor Deukmejian not only to name their replacements but also to shape the court's future policy role. A succession of appointments by Deukmejian and his successor, Wilson, left the court with only one liberal, Stanley Mosk, a 1964 appointee of Pat Brown. Under Lucas, the court became less activist, less assertive, and less willing to use the state constitution to establish new legal doctrines. That is, the Lucas Court tended to follow the lead of the U.S. Supreme Court rather than forge its own policy and law. In criminal cases, it was reluctant to overturn guilty verdicts. Whereas the Bird Court often found "reversible" errors, the Lucas Court found most errors to be harmless, minor defects that do not endanger the right to a fair trial. Most important, the Lucas Court upheld more than 80 percent of death penalty convictions, in remarkable contrast to the 94 percent reversal rate of the Bird Court. Lucas made numerous legislative enemies when he upheld the most important elements of Proposition 140, the term limits law.

The George Court Associate Justice George became Chief Justice in 1996. Under his leadership, the Supreme Court continued many of the trends and policies set by the Lucas Court. Possibly due to greater diversity on the Court (three women, one Asian American, and one Latino), it could not be neatly divided into ideological voting blocks. Different majorities emerged on a case-by-case basis. The court still retains its independent-mindedness relative to federal law and even state election trends. During his years as chief justice, the Court negotiated one legal minefield after

another from abortion to civil rights to gay marriage. In general, the George Court took longer to decide cases—well over a year in many instances—and wrote longer opinions that other courts, including the U.S. Supreme Court.[20]

Replacing George in 2011 was Tani Cantril-Sakauye, a 20-year veteran of both trial and appellate courts. The Judicial Nominees Evaluation Committee rated her "exceptionally well qualified," the Commission on Judicial Appointments confirmed her unanimously, and the voters elected her in the November 2010 general election. Based on her judicial experience and work with the Judicial Council, her operational priorities included adding more judgeships, retaining current judges and justices, improving the case management system, and building more court facilities. In an era of spending cuts, she defended the increased spending these priorities would entail: "Courts are places of last resort, so to cut them is to do great harm to the public where it has no access to justice and no ability to enforce the laws that are passed by the executive and legislative branches."[21]

CRIMINAL JUSTICE AND PUNISHMENT

The policy role of California's courts is most visible in the area of criminal justice. Coping with endless waves of defendants is a challenge shared by other policymakers, the federal courts, and society in general. California's criminal justice system demonstrates both the diversity of the state and the hyperpluralistic nature of its political system. The state's judiciary has been affected by sweeping social trends, changing sentencing laws, the perennial issue of capital punishment, and the state's investment in new prisons.

Social Trends

In many ways, court cases simply mirror broad social trends. They include changing demographics plus the widespread use of guns and drugs. First, population experts have noticed a rise of young, minority males who statistically contribute more than their fair share of street crime (see Figure 9.2). Experts attribute this to reduced employment opportunities, residential segregation, the presence of gangs, and the absence of positive role models in minority communities. Despite tough law-and-order, "build more prisons" rhetoric by elected officials, crime rates are largely dependent on these economic and demographic trends.

Second, the widespread availability of handguns and assault weapons also colors the crime picture in California. The statistics are sobering. In recent years, dealers have sold nearly 500,000 handguns and long guns annually; black market sales would account for more. More than 70 percent of all homicides in the state involve firearms, most of those handguns.[22] More Californians die of gunshots than die in motor vehicle accidents. Gun-related homicides are extraordinarily high among young, urban youth. Although handguns outnumber assault weapons, the latter are increasingly used against the police, in

Male	94	percent
Race		
White	25	percent
Black	29	percent
Hispanic	40	percent
Other	6	percent
Crimes against persons	58	percent
Average age	38	
Average reading level	7th grade	
Foreign-born	16	percent
2nd/3rd strikers	26	percent

F I G U R E 9.2 California's Prison Population, 2011

Question: What larger issues regarding incarceration in California does this prisoner profile raise?

SOURCE: Joseph M. Hayes, *Just the Facts: California's Changing Prison Population* (San Francisco: Public Policy Institute of California, July 2011).

drive-by shootings, and by California's gang culture. In short, the state is awash in weapons. In recent years, the state legislature has responded by toughening its ban on certain assault weapons, limiting handgun purchases, discouraging the manufacture of cheaply made handguns, and requiring safety devices for all weapons sold, transferred, or manufactured in California.

Third, drugs and alcohol figure in many of California's criminal cases. Because criminal cases take priority over civil cases, they have in effect swamped the courts. As we noted, the courts have responded by creating so-called drug courts to better manage this aspect of the overall workload of the judiciary.

Sentencing Mandates

California courts are not only affected by social trends, they must abide by the state's sentencing policies. Traditionally, the state legislature sets sentencing policy. For example, before 1977, California judges worked with an "indeterminate sentence" policy adopted by the legislature. The idea was that convicts would stay in prison until "rehabilitated" or until the completion of a broadly defined term (say, 1 to 5, or 1 to 10 years). The policy reflected an optimistic view that most convicts could be rehabilitated. The only problem was that "rehabilitated" convicts returned to prisons at alarming rates (a phenomenon called *recidivism*). In 1976, the legislature passed the *Uniform Sentencing Act,* specifying narrower sentencing ranges within which judges can work. In 1994, California voters further amended sentencing policy by passing the state's *Three Strikes* law. Some scholars have called this reform "the largest penal experiment in American history."[23] *Three Strikes* made sentencing even more uniform by providing 25-years-to-life sentences for anyone convicted of a third felony, whether violent or not. In recent years, some prosecutors have used the discretion granted them by the law to scale back the number of life sentences they seek in third-strike cases. Even though the U.S. Supreme Court eventually upheld the law, critics contend that people are being sentenced too severely for petty crimes such as stealing cigarettes or, in one famous case, a slice of pizza. Defenders say Three Strikes fulfills its intent—incarcerating habitual, repeat felons.[24] Voters must agree—they rejected Proposition 66 in 2004, a measure that would have narrowed third strike-eligible offenses to violent or serious felonies.

California's diverse population seems to have an impact on sentencing decisions. One study concluded that, at almost every stage of California's criminal justice process, whites fare better than African Americans and Latinos. They are more likely to have charges reduced or receive rehabilitative placements versus prison time. Why the disparity? Researchers believe judges tend to follow probation reports, which weigh individual backgrounds in recommending sentences. Because many minorities come from lower socioeconomic backgrounds (a phenomenon associated with higher crime rates to begin with), many have prior records—a major factor in sentencing decisions. Also, whites plea bargain more often than minorities. If they are materially better off, they can more easily afford restitution to a victim, a sentencing alternative that can avoid jail or prison time.[25]

Capital Punishment The ultimate sentence is death. Age-old arguments over both its morality and its effectiveness have characterized its history in California. The penalty has been a political football in recent decades. In 1972, both the U.S. and California Supreme Courts ruled the death penalty unconstitutional relative to their respective constitutions due to its capricious and arbitrary use. In the federal case, *Furman v. Georgia* (1972), Justice Potter Stewart regarded the death penalty as cruel and unusual "in the same way that being struck by lightning is cruel and unusual." One year later, the state legislature reinstituted capital punishment by adding "special circumstances" under which it would be employed (such as killing during a robbery, multiple homicides, and murder of police officers). Like other states, it also established bifurcated trials; the first stage would determine guilt or innocence, the second stage would determine the appropriate sentence. In 1976, the U.S. Supreme Court ruled in *Gregg v.*

Georgia that such efforts to reduce the penalty's arbitrariness were permissible and that capital punishment was allowable where such measures were employed. In 1977, the legislature further amended the law by permitting mitigating evidence to be allowed at the sentencing stage. In 1978, California voters passed an initiative extending the special circumstances noted above, but the Bird Court usually found ways to overturn particular death sentences. Since that time, the California Supreme Court has hesitated to overrule death penalty verdicts. By 2011, there were 710 inmates on death row—more by far than in any other state. In 1992, California resumed actual executions and by 2011, executions had numbered 14. Due to lengthy appeals, far more have died due to suicide or natural causes, such as old age or illness.[26]

Just as the idea of capital punishment has evolved in California, so has its implementation. The general goal has been this: State-imposed death should at least be as humane as possible. Accordingly, the gas chamber replaced hanging in 1938. A 1993 law allowed the condemned to request lethal injection and in 1994, a federal judge essentially mandated its use by ruling the gas chamber to be cruel and unusual punishment. With this presumably more humane method, those slated for execution are strapped to a gurney and injected with a cocktail of three chemicals. Lethal injection itself has faced a series of hurdles. In 2006, a federal judge halted executions in California until the state could demonstrate that the poisons used did not inflect excruciating pain as critics claimed. Over the next several years, the California Department of Corrections and Rehabilitation developed a plan to improve its lethal injection procedures. In the meantime, the U.S. Supreme Court ruled in 2008 that lethal injections did not violate the U.S. Constitution's ban on cruel and unusual punishment if they were humanely administered. Finally, the state was ready to execute another prisoner, but in 2010, delayed again the execution of child killer Albert Greenwood Brown. Court reviews of the state's new lethal injection protocol took so long that by the scheduled execution date, a key drug needed was unavailable.

Aside from the methodology of capital punishment, why are there so many Death Row inmates and so few executions? California houses 20 percent of the nation's death row inmates but accounts for only 1 percent of the nation's executions. While there are limits to endless appeals, allowable appeals may take decades to complete. Many appeals cannot even begin because qualified lawyers are unwilling to take them on. As a result, some death row inmates have been there for more than 20 years. Furthermore, there is not one capital punishment policy for the state. The imposition of the death penalty continues to be, as it always has been, dependent on local prosecutorial practice. Because district attorneys in each county decide who is charged with special circumstances offenses, California has in effect 58 death penalty policies.

One of the constants surrounding this topic has been historically broad public support for the death penalty. What they prefer in the abstract and how they would decide in a case and two different matters. In a 2010 poll, fully 70 percent of California voters supported its use for serious crimes. But, when given a choice between imposing a life sentence and the death penalty for first-degree murder, 42 percent opted to impose a life sentence.[27]

Prison Politics   Correctional policy in California is at once exorbitantly expensive and arguably ineffective. If "You get what you pay for" is at all true, how can this be? To be sure, California's correctional system is the largest in the world. California has 33 prisons, 40 work camps, 12 community correctional facilities, and 5 prisoner-mother facilities. In 2011, those facilities housed over 160,000 prisoners; another 104,000 were on parole. In addition, each of the 58 counties operates a jail system that houses those convicted of lesser crimes or who are awaiting trial. Most of these facilities are overcrowded but voters hesitate to approve the tax increases necessary to expand the jails or add new ones. State funding to do so is also limited. In recent decades, several bond measures funded the construction of new state prisons but, even then, California has shipped some prisoners to out of state facilities to relieve pressure at in-state prisons.

The pressures that have resulted in both costly and ineffective incarceration are several. *First*, the legislature devised longer, determinate sentences where offenders are given mandatory terms which must be served prior to any parole. These were applied to many categories of crime including lesser offences. Remember, third strikes that trigger very long sentences can be for relatively minor felonies. *Second*, correctional facilities have experienced high levels of **recidivism**—criminal relapses, often habitual, that result in additional prison time. Although about 10,000 prisoners are released on parole each month, many return to prison. While some return because they committed additional serious crimes, many do so because of technical parole violations (such as missed meetings with parole officers or failed drug tests). Violations aside, few parolees are trained or equipped for life outside prison. Estimates are that two-thirds of all California parolees return to state prison within three years, the highest recidivism rate in the nation.[28]

Third, the longer convicts remain in prison, the more expensive their care becomes. Housing a healthy prisoner can run nearly $40,000 per year. Housing elderly, sick, or gravely ill prisoners can cost many times that amount. Some are so ill that they must be treated in traditional hospitals surrounded by around the clock prison guards to prevent their (unlikely) escape, all at prison expense. Although a "medical parole" law was enacted in 2010 to relieve the state of these costs, its implementation has been slow. In light of the budget crisis in recent years, one exasperated legislator exclaimed, "It's maddening. We don't have millions of dollars to squander on this nonsense."[29]

Fourth, the federal courts have regarded prison overcrowding and inadequate medical care as cruel and unusual punishment in violation of the Eighth Amendment to the U.S. Constitution. In California, a federal court removed control of the prison health care system from the state and appointed a federal receiver to oversee necessary reforms, until improvements no longer violate the Eighth Amendment. In 2011, the U.S. Supreme Court rendered a judgment on the state's slow progress toward that end. In the *Brown v. Plata*

California Department of Corrections and Rehabilitation

Prison Overcrowding California's MuleCreek

case mentioned earlier, the Court ruled that, due to severe overcrowding, the state had to reduce its prison population by 33,000 inmates. At the time of the ruling, the capacity of California's prison system was 80,000 prisoners and it housed over 143,000. Writing for a 5-4 majority, Justice Anthony M. Kennedy referred to suicidal prisoners being held in "telephone booth-sized cages without toilets" and the terminally ill suffering and dying before seeing a doctor. He noted that upwards of 200 prisoners may live in a gymnasium and that over 50 inmates may share a single toilet.

In response, Governor Brown offered to accelerate his plan to transfer thousands of prisoners to less costly county jails and to divert nonviolent offenders to drug treatment programs and other supervised alternatives to prison. Republican legislative leaders proposed "fast-tracking" the construction of new prisons and pressuring the federal government to house in its prisons undocumented inmates now housed in California prisons.[30]

Pressures to fix California's corrections system come at a time when budget cutting is the norm, including programs much closer to the public's heart than humane treatment of criminals. In fact, surveys suggest that likely voters not only oppose tax increases that would help fund prison reform, 70 percent of them support spending *cuts* for prisons and corrections. According to pollster Mark Baldassare, "Public opinion is an obstacle to finding solutions to prison overcrowding."[31] This makes prison spending on vocational training and other programs to prevent recidivism vulnerable to the budget process. But it may encourage the consideration of alternative sentencing approaches advocated by criminal justice experts.

CONCLUSION

California's judiciary manifests several trends in California politics. First, the legal profession in California certainly does not mirror the state's growing ethnic and cultural diversity. It remains largely white, middle class, and male in membership. To be sure, more women are seeking legal careers and gaining professional strength. Second, in terms of workload, the judiciary is clearly affected by the state's diversity. Criminal caseloads denote population changes plus widespread use of alcohol, drugs, and guns. Civil caseloads reflect a large, increasingly complex and regulated economy, plus an increasingly litigious society. Third, access to the judiciary is problematic, especially for the poor. Although public defenders, court appointed attorneys, and legal aid clinics provide low-or no-cost legal help, the poor in California do not enjoy the quality and quantity of legal assistance available to the middle and upper classes.

Fourth, in terms of governance, the judiciary carries out some vital functions (such as dispensing case-by-case justice and reviewing legislative and executive actions) but it also contributes to the "divided government" problem that is now the norm in California. The judiciary's role is a two-edged sword. On some occasions, it contributes to policy paralysis by allowing political struggles to continue for years or even decades in the courts. The history of capital punishment illustrates this point. On other occasions, the judiciary can break the gridlock between the other two branches, as it has in areas such as reapportionment. Jurists do not make these decisions in a vacuum. Interest groups strategically use the courts to achieve policy preferences they could not obtain elsewhere in government.

California's judiciary also reflects political fragmentation and hyperpluralism. Judges themselves are relatively insulated from the electorate, rightly so in their view. Yet they can occasionally feel the pressure and even the wrath of volatile voters. But holding judges accountable is no easy task for voters. Trial court judges share power with policing agencies, courtroom work groups, and juries. On occasion, juries define facts, the law, and justice on their own terms. In making decisions, all judges respond to professional norms, statutory laws, conflicting interest group demands, and their own sociological and political backgrounds. In an age when voters seem to think that political parties make no difference, recent appointments to the California Supreme Court suggest the opposite.

The policymaking role of California's judiciary will continue to be important and on some issues paramount. The courts will always been needed to validate, implement, or repair initiatives proposed by interest groups and passed by the voters. As the federal government continues to shift policy responsibility and accountability to the states, state courts will have no choice but to respond with policies that reflect each state's political culture and environment. California is no different.

KEY TERMS

judicial federalism (p. 174)

superior courts, district courts of appeal, the California Supreme Court (pp. 175, 176)

Three-Strikes Law (p. 175)

Missouri Plan (p. 178)

judicial socialization (p. 180)

Code of Judicial Ethics (p. 180)

adversarial justice (p. 181)

infractions, misdemeanors, felonies (p. 181)

assumption of guilt, innocent until proven guilty (p. 181)

arraignment, preliminary hearing, indictment (p. 181)

plea bargaining (p. 182)

complaint, discovery, depositions, interrogatories (p. 183)

alternative dispute resolution,

mediation, arbitration (p. 183)

popular justice, jury nullification (p. 183)

cumulative policymaking (p. 184)

recidivism (p. 188)

REVIEW QUESTIONS

1. How does the dual judicial system help explain judicial independence in California?

2. If you were a California appellate court judge, how would your work day differ from that of a trial court judge?

3. If you were a lawyer aspiring to become a judge, what would you do or not do to reach that goal? How would you be held accountable once you reached your goal?

4. Describe the various steps of the civil and criminal process.

5. How do both trial and appellate courts make policy? How has state Supreme Court policy shifted in recent decades?

6. What factors explain who is charged and sentenced in California?

7. Describe the pressures faced by California's correctional institutions.

WEB ACTIVITIES

The State Bar of California
(www.calbar.ca.gov)
This site includes law profession news, trends in legal education, bar exam information, efforts to diversify the profession, and expanding access to attorneys by low and moderate income Californians.

Judicial Branch of California
(www.courts.ca.gov/)
This site contains a wealth of data on California courts including opinions, procedures, administrative issues, latest developments, and links to other law-and court-related Web sites.

California Department of Corrections and Rehabilitation
(www.cdcr.ca.gov/)
To learn more about capital punishment in California, prison populations, or specific prison facilities, this site is helpful.

NOTES

1. See http://www.calbar.ca.gov/. The total number of attorneys including inactives, judges, and those not eligible to practice law in California swells to over 200,000, by far the nation's largest bar.

2. Philip Hager, "Poll Finds Wide Legal Ignorance," *Los Angeles Times*, May 2, 1991.

3. For an account of both Mosk's career and this doctrine, see Bob Egelko, "Justice Stanley Mosk," *California Journal* 32 (August 2001), pp. 26–31.

4. The relevant cases were *People v. Anderson*, 1972; *Serrano v. Priest*, 1971; and *Mukley v. Reitman*, 1966.

5. *Brown v. Plata*, 563 U.S. ___(2011).

6. Ronald M. George, 1997 *State of the Judiciary Address*.

7. John T. Wold, "Going through the Motions: The Monotony of Appellate Court Decisionmaking," *Judicature*, 62 (August 1978), pp. 61–62.

8. An appellate opinion is published if it establishes a new rule of law, involves a publicly visible issue, or contributes significantly to legal literature.

9. Judicial Council of California, *2011 Demographic Data Reports* (Accessed at www.courtinfo.ca.gov) and Justice at Stake Campaign (accessed at http://justiceatstake.org/state/California).

10. David Balabanian, "Justice Was More Than His Title," *California Law Review*, 70 (July 1982), p. 880.

11. For details, go to www.followthemoney.org/.

12. Article IV, Section 18b.

13. Data on specific cases, especially removal of judges can be found at the Commission on Judicial Performance Web site. (www.cjp.ca.gov/).

14. Sheryl Stolberg, "Politics and the Judiciary Coexist, But Often Uneasily," *Los Angeles Times*, March 21, 1992.

15. Legislative Analyst's Office, *A Primer: Three Strikes— The Impact After More Than a Decade* (Sacramento: Legislative Analyst's Office. October, 2005).

16. Henry Weinstein and Paul Leiberman, "Location of Trial Played Major Role, Legal Experts Say," *Los Angeles Times*, April 30, 1992.

17. Quoted in Maura Dolan, "Justices Say Jurors May Not Vote Conscience," *Los Angeles Times*, May 8, 2001.

18. Gerald F. Uelman, "A 'Death-Qualified' Judiciary," *California Lawyer*, 19 (September 1999), p. 27.

19. Quoted in K. Connie Kang, "Brown's Court Legacy: Crusaders against Social Injustice," *California Journal*, 13 (September 1982), p. 311. Another article evaluating the Bird Court is Bob Egelko, "The Court's National Stature Has Waned Under Bird," *California Journal*, 17 (September 1986), pp. 428–433.

20. Steven R. Barnett, "Longer and Later," *California Lawyer*, 25 (April 2005), pp. 221–22, 66.

21. Nancy McCarthy, "Still Awed by the Judicial Branch's Top Job, The New Chief Justice Digs In," *California Bar Journal* (December, 2010). (Accessed at www.calbarjournal.com/).

22. Bureau of Firearms, California Department of Justice (http://ag.ca.gov/firearms/).

23. Franklin E. Zimring, Gordon Hawkins, and Sam Kamin, *Punishment and Democracy: Three Strikes and You're Out in California* (New York: Oxford University Press, 2001).

24. Janet Weeks, "Arguing the Third Strike," *California Lawyer*, 19 (December 1999), pp. 39–42, 78–79.

25. Greg Krikorian, "Study Questions Justice System's Fairness," *Los Angeles Times*, February 2, 1996; and Ted Rohrlich, "Blacks, Latinos Get Longer Sentences, Study Concludes," *Los Angeles Times*, June 30, 1983.

26. California Department of Corrections and Rehabilitation (www.cdcr.ca.gov/) and Rone Tempest, "Death Row Often Means a Long Life," *Los Angeles Times*, March 6, 2005.

27. Mark DiCamillo and Mervin Field, "Seven in Ten Californians Continue to Support Capital Punishment," *The Field Poll Release #2351* (July 22, 2010).

28. Thomas Hoffman, "The Debate Around Parole Reform in California," *Federal Sentencing Reporter*, 22:3 (February, 2010).

29. Jack Dolan, "Despite Medical Parole Law, Hospitalized Prisoners Are Costing California Taxpayers Millions," *Los Angeles Time*, March 2, 2011.

30. David G. Savage and Patrick McGreevy, "U.S. Supreme Court Orders Massive Inmate Release to Relieve California's Crowded Prisons," *Los Angeles Times*, May 24, 2011.

31. Mark Baldassare, et al., *PPIC Statewide Survey May 2011* (San Francisco: Public Policy Institute of California, May 2011).

10

Community Politics

Introduction

The Role of Community

The Limits of Community Government

Counties

The Shape of California Counties

The Shape of County Government

California's Troubled Counties

Cities

How Communities Become Municipalities

"Cities" Without "Government"

How California Cities Are Run

Cities and Counties: An Uneasy Relationship

Special Districts

What Makes Them Special?

The Stealth Governments of California

Special District Politics and Problems

School Districts

Regional Governments

Regional Coordination

Regional Regulation

Conclusion: Diverse Communities, Diverse Governments

Key Terms

Review Questions

Web Activities

Notes

IN BRIEF

Chapter 10 surveys the most diverse set of institutions in California politics: local government. The thousands of local governments in California can be grouped into five types: counties, cities, special districts, school districts, and regional governments, plus privatized versions of local government such as urban villages and homeowner associations. This chapter considers the idea of community and the functions of local governments in those communities. Such governments are limited in their capacity and even in their willingness to govern effectively.

All six types represent diversity and fragmentation in California politics. With each type, we examine how local governments are established and how local officials exercise power.

Also surveyed are the inherent limits of local government, the role of the state in local affairs, and the fiscal and policy problems that each type of government faces. In recent years, all local governments have faced revenue volatility due to voter-enacted tax cuts, reduced aid from the state, and the ups and downs of California's economy. In general, cities are more fiscally healthy than counties.

California's numerous local governments represent a rich diversity of governing styles and institutions, allow ample opportunities for citizen participation in politics, and provide a wide assortment of options for living in community. There is a downside to this diversity, however. According to political scientists, the sheer numbers of local governments in California reduce political accountability and undermine the ability of local governments to manage problems, especially those that spill beyond their boundaries.

INTRODUCTION

"Divorce L.A. Style" was the title of a *Newsweek* article on the desire of many San Fernando Valley residents to secede from the City of Los Angeles.[1] By the time of the November 2002 election, two divorce proposals were on the ballot: the San Fernando Valley and Hollywood. "Breaking Los Angeles apart is not the answer," pleaded the mayor.[2] Although both proposals went down to defeat, Rancho Cordova in Northern California chose to incorporate that same election day. Four more Riverside County communities incorporated in recent years—Wildomar, Menifee, Eastvale, and Jurupa Valley—bringing the total number of cities statewide to 482. While technically possible, county splits have been unsuccessful since 1907. For example, citing a multitude of differences with their coastal neighbors, disgruntled residents of Northern Santa Barbara County tried but failed to form a new Mission County. Viewed historically, California has been breaking apart into cities and other local governments since becoming a state (see Figure 10.1).

Chapter 10 explains these community-level governments.

There are myriad local governments, laid side-by-side and on top of each other across the state. Picture several jigsaw puzzles stacked one on top of each other. That is what local government looks like in the Golden State. Cities, counties, special districts, and various regional governments are the official local governments of California. There are also various "urban forms"—places that look and behave like cities but most definitely are not governed like them.

The two broad themes of this book, diversity and hyperpluralism, are vividly represented in California's local politics. The state's profound diversity plays itself out at the community level. Communities are where people work, pursue various lifestyles, raise families, educate their children, and go about civic life. It is where neighbors do or do not get along, where California's polyglot of racial and ethnic groups live—in harmony or otherwise. From school board meetings to city hall hearings, it is in community that values collide

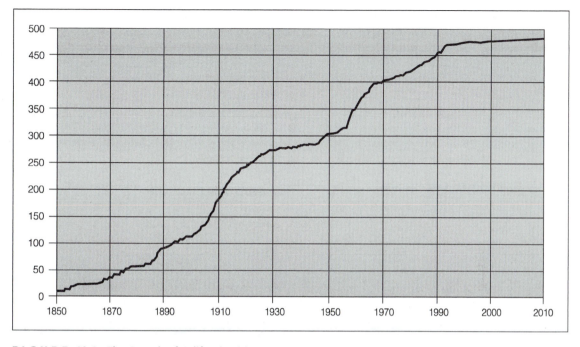

FIGURE 10.1 The Growth of California Cities

Question: What do you think is the local impetus to incorporate, to form cities?

SOURCE: Paul G. Lewis, *Deep Roots: Local Government Structure in California* (San Francisco: Public Policy Institute of California, 1998), p. 23; updated by author.

and cultures clash. Communities are where the American notion of individual sovereignty (power in the hands of the individual) rubs up against the need for group norms, responsibility, and expectations. In short, California communities are vivid expressions of a culturally pluralistic, differentiated society. At this level, the struggle for power and control between individuals and groups is constant.

California communities also represent government at its most fragmented level, and are one manifestation of what we call hyperpluralism. Fifty-eight counties, 482 cities, over 1,000 school districts, and about 3,800 other special districts all present diverse approaches to community governance. During most any weekend drive, a California motorist will encounter (unknowingly in most cases) dozens of governmental jurisdictions;

and these do not include a growing number of quasi-governments such as neighborhood homeowner associations. Californians may complain that their local governments are ineffective; they can hardly object that there are too few of them. Los Angeles County alone has nearly 500 subdivisions of government. Across the state, there are so many local governments, citizens are often unsure which government provides which service and whom to call when a problem arises. As Kim Alexander put it, "I currently have twenty-two people I elect to represent me at all levels of government, and I can't name them—and I'm President of the California Voter Foundation."[3]

Hyperpluralism also suggests a host of public policy problems beyond the reach of governing institutions. Increasingly, problems facing local officials spill beyond their reach. And funding shortages, an absence of public support, and lack of political will leave those public problems within their reach unaddressed—for years, decades, or longer. Local interest groups and regional forces, economic and demographic, usually dictate where growth occurs more than does local government. Furthermore, the growing dominance of the state in local matters has fostered both local dependence on the state and resistance to it.

The Role of Community

The late U.S. House Speaker Thomas P. "Tip" O'Neill once said, "All politics is local." A corollary could well be: "All politics begins at the community level." Local governments in California's communities perform three generic yet important functions: providing services, socializing community members, and managing conflict.

Providing Services   Local governments deliver various goods and services to their residents. These include education, garbage disposal, water, sanitation, building inspection, law enforcement, and fire protection. To some extent each community can determine the mix and quality of services to provide. But most services are either fully expected by local residents (law enforcement) or flatly required by the state (welfare). The question, "Which level of government, state or local, should pay for what services?" has been at the heart of recent budget battles in Sacramento. Those who believe the primary purpose of local government is to provide tangible services tend to think local government can and should operate as an efficient business.

Socializing Community Members   In addition to services, local governments provide varying degrees of personal attention to community residents. Most newcomers are assimilated into local society; they learn what behavior is acceptable and unacceptable. These norms can vary from community to community or even from neighborhood to neighborhood. For example, numerous conflicts (parking, noise, and partying) occur in college towns

between students and permanent residents. Gang graffiti (called "tagging") may be quietly tolerated in some neighborhoods but vigorously opposed in others. The presence of immigrant workers waiting curbside for day labor jobs may be ignored in some communities but actively opposed in others. Regulation of behavior by local government is called the "police power." This fundamental power makes it possible for governments to regulate public health, safety, and morals.

Managing Conflict   One of the most important functions of local government is managing conflict among people and groups. Some conflicts are essentially arguments over policy such as service complaints, land use controversies, and budget allocations. Others reflect deep-seated social and cultural divisions in a community—divisions among racial and ethnic groups, rich and poor, homeowners and renters, or newcomers and old-timers. The more heterogeneous a community population or the more a community values extensive political participation, the more visible conflict will be. Such conflicts become political because government is expected to intervene. Political conflict is common in cities of all sizes. The larger cities of California contain numerous and diverse ethnic and income groups. A growing number of California communities no longer contain a single ethnic or racial majority—they are "majority-minority" cities. As many of these groups have become more politically conscious, they have become more politically assertive. Small, relatively homogeneous and presumably peaceful communities often experience high levels of political involvement, no matter how small the issue. Both settings require the management of conflict, at times intense conflict.

The Limits of Community Government

Despite expectations that local governments provide all three functions, California communities are limited in doing so. Three limits discussed here are the privatization of development, state power, and the myth of apolitical politics.

Privatization of Development Historically, California's communities were regarded as economic entities. The growth of these places was dictated by a tradition of **privatism**—an ongoing succession of private economic transactions. The Big Four, land speculators, and private utility companies were the essence of early privatism in the Golden State. To be sure, local government had a role to play, usually accommodating, assisting, and at times subsidizing those private interests. Because many local governments have continued this traditional role, they have remained largely ineffective in controlling private interests when public and private interests clash. How this applies to land use politics is addressed in Chapter 12.

State Power In 1868, shortly after California's admission to the Union, an Iowa judge promulgated a judicial doctrine that to this day governs a great many state/local relationships. Judge John F. Dillon wrote, "Municipal corporations owe their origin to, and derive their powers and rights wholly from, the legislature. It breathes into them the breath of life, without which they cannot exist. As it creates, so it may also destroy. What it may destroy, it may … control."[4] The idea that states dominate local governments was adopted by the U.S. Supreme Court, other state courts, and, naturally, state legislatures. In California, "Dillon's Rule" underlies all state-local relationships. True, the state allows significant **home rule** (a measure of local self government). But Article XI of the California Constitution stipulates local powers and even the very existence of local government. While this legal doctrine is obscure to average Californians, local officials know it all too well. For example, California expressly preempts local governments from regulating certain aspects of

© AP/World Wide Photos

Gang Graffiti/Graffiti Cleanup
In the Panorama City section of Los Angeles, evidence of gang activity covers a neighborhood phone booth. To control gang behavior, the city imposed a controversial injunction on 100 members of the gang, prohibiting them from carrying pagers, blocking sidewalks, and congregating in public.

Question: To what extent can a city's police power truly curtail some forms of urban behavior?

gun ownership. California local officials also find they must defend their sources of revenue from being diverted by the state.[5]

Apolitical Politics   A final limit on local self-government in California is the enduring assumption that party politics corrupts governing. As noted in Chapter 4, the Progressives wanted to take "politics" out of government, meaning the corrupting influences of political parties and bosses. Their solutions included nonpartisan, at-large local elections, and professional city management. California political scientist Eugene Lee once described the nonpartisanship ideal: "City government is largely a matter of 'good business practice' or 'municipal housekeeping'.... There is little room for 'politics.' Therefore, it is not necessary to establish organized political competition as suggested by the partisan ballot."[6] The Progressives believed good government meant the efficient provision of various municipal services. They underestimated government's role in reflecting and managing political conflict. Even today, some local officials sincerely believe that an entire constellation of social and political issues are beyond the scope of local government. Like it or not, local governments find that they are caldrons of California's diversity—expected to articulate, address, and even solve the pressing problems faced by various individuals and myriad groups.

California's local governments are both numerous and richly diverse. We now survey the most common local governments in California: counties, cities, special districts, school districts, and regional governments.

COUNTIES

One of the most diverse units of California local government is the *county*. California, as did other states, borrowed the county idea from British local government tradition. Originally, a county was a territory administered by a count. It was both a local government and a subdivision of a central government; counties retain this dual role today.

In fact, unless prohibited by the state constitution, the legislature may delegate to counties any task belonging to the state itself. In addition to providing state-mandated services, counties provide to unincorporated areas an assortment of services typically provided by cities (law enforcement, transportation, etc.).

The Shape of California Counties

In many ways, California's 58 counties reflect a bygone era. Consider the map in Figure 10.2. At the time of statehood, California had relatively few large counties. Southern California was one vast desert; much of it still is, as San Bernardino County's boundaries attest. The Sierra foothill counties are elongated and relatively small for a reason. During the Gold Rush, it was thought that miners should be no farther than a day's horseback ride from a county seat where mining claims were filed. Those boundaries remain today.

At the time of statehood in 1850, California had 27 counties. In the late 1800s and early 1900s, new counties were formed, reflecting population growth, power shifts, and emerging local rivalries. Giant Mariposa County (encompassing much of Southern California) was subdivided into twelve counties. San Mateo broke away from San Francisco. Farmers and ranchers, fearing the early growth of Los Angeles, helped form Orange County in 1889. The last breakaway, Imperial County, formed east of San Diego in 1907. Despite vast demographic and economic change, the shape of California's counties has remained fixed since 1907. The reasons are several. First, local political cultures developed and calcified in that span of time, giving each county its own identity. Second, because county split elections are countywide in scope, selling a split to an often skeptical voting majority is problematic as those Santa Barbara County residents can attest. Third, the start-up costs for a new county (infrastructure, personnel, and tax base) are so high, county splits seem financially unfeasible.

This static situation has resulted in tremendous differences between modern California counties. Geographically, San Bernardino is the nation's largest (20,000 square miles). It is 200 times larger than San Francisco County, and embraces about 20 percent of the entire state. Los Angeles County is home to over 10 million residents (more than that of 42 other states); within its borders are 89 cities.

At the other end of the spectrum is tiny Alpine County, home to less than 1,200 people not one of whom lives in a city. Some counties have experienced persistent growth while others have languished in California's economic backwaters.

FIGURE 10.2 California's Counties

California's 58 counties come in all shapes and sizes; their boundaries have not changed in over a century despite massive population growth and change.

Question: How would you redraw these boundaries if given the chance? How so?

The state expects all 58 to perform similarly as units of government but the resources for doing so vary widely.

The Shape of County Government

Legally speaking, there are only two types of counties: **general law** and **charter**. California's 44 general law counties follow state law relative to the number and duties of county elected officials. Fourteen charter counties are governed by a constitution-like document called a "charter" that replaces some general laws regarding elections, compensation, powers, and duties. Charters also provide a limited degree of home rule or authority over certain offices and governing structures and require voter approval initially and for subsequent amendments. California's urban counties have charters, and two-thirds of all Californians live in those counties. Both general law and charter counties are the primary units of local government in rural and some suburban areas.

Answering the classic question, Who governs? at the county level is no easy task. Authority and responsibility—in short, power—is widely-dispersed and shared among the following decision makers.

Boards of Supervisors In California, each county's legislative body is a five-member board of supervisors (San Francisco is both a county and a city with an 11-member board and one mayor). Board members serve for four-year staggered terms and are elected during June primary elections in even-numbered years. If they do not garner a majority of votes (50 percent plus one), a November general election runoff is necessary. Although the elections are technically nonpartisan, informed voters likely know the partisan leanings of better-known candidates, especially incumbents. Their names sometimes appear on those partisan slate mailers discussed in Chapter 6. In the past, county supervisors were "good old boys"—older white men with business backgrounds. In recent years, more women have become supervisors and in a few counties, they have constituted board majorities. Over the years, service on a board of supervisors has been a stepping stone to the state legislature or other elective posts. Occasionally, the reverse occurs. Given the considerable powers of county boards, attractive salaries (supervisors in ten counties earn over $100,000 annually plus benefits), and a fundamental desire to remain in public life, some termed-out state legislators welcome a run for county supervisor.

Boards adopt county budgets, determine some service levels, and make numerous decisions affecting unincorporated areas. The most contentious policy issues often surround land use. Although county planning commissions make many land use decisions, supervisors hear various appeals and make final decisions. Where to locate shopping centers, housing projects, or unpopular industries (sometimes called LULUs—locally undesirable land uses) pit counties against cities, neighborhood against neighborhood, and occasionally neighbor against neighbor. Ironies abound. On the one hand, a small but controversial land use project might fill a room with surly citizens on both sides of the issue. On the other hand, discussion of a multimillion-dollar expenditure deep inside a county budget may attract little or no public interest whatsoever. Boards of supervisors hire *chief administrative officers* or CAOs (called county managers in some places) to carry out board policy and administer county routines. Preparing and monitoring annual budgets plus preparing board meeting agendas consumes a lion's share of a CAO's time.

Counties also provide for a variety of other elective officials. Together, they are California's local version of the plural executive we described in Chapter 8. The exact arrangement of these positions varies from county to county. The most common elected officers are district attorneys, sheriffs, various fiscal officers, clerks, and school superintendents. Typically, they serve four-year terms and are elected during statewide elections.

District Attorney The "people's lawyer" in each county is an elected district attorney. While the DA's duties are not limited to criminal prosecutions, that is their most essential function. As noted in Chapter 9, district attorneys can exercise a great deal of discretion in setting prosecution policy in a county. Below the elected DA is a staff of deputy DAs and investigators. Some California DAs have become well-known because of the occasional celebrities they have prosecuted (Los Angeles's Gil Garcetti and O. J. Simpson, and Santa Barbara's Tom Sneddon and Michael Jackson). Public defenders (who provide criminal defense counsel for the poor) are not elected—making them potentially more dependent on a board of supervisors. Given their crime fighting and "law and order" reputations, district attorneys usually have a competitive advantage over defenders and private lawyers when judgeships become available. The post of DA can be a stepping-stone to much higher office. Kamala Harris was San Francisco's DA before becoming state attorney general and Earl Warren, both governor and U.S. Supreme Court Chief Justice, was once DA for Alameda County.

Sheriff The chief law enforcement and public safety officer for a county is an elected sheriff. This office is one of the oldest law enforcement positions in the common law tradition. While anyone can run for this position, successful candidates are usually law enforcement professionals. Sheriffs administer an office, numerous deputy sheriffs, the county jail, and in some cases the coroner's office. The coroner conducts inquests of all questionable deaths. Through contractual arrangements, county sheriff departments often provide law enforcement to cities that cannot or will not provide their own.

Fiscal Officers Several county officials focus on finances. Assessors determine the value of taxable real estate and personal property. Tax collectors/treasurers distribute tax bills and collect and deposit revenues. Auditors/controllers allocate revenues to all eligible local governments (county, cities, schools, and special districts). Because their tasks are largely ministerial (administrative in nature with little room for personal discretion), they generate little controversy and few political enemies or opponents—usually. In 1994, Orange County declared bankruptcy because its treasurer, Bob

Citron, invested $1.7 billion of county funds in risky Wall Street securities.[7] The county recovered from that debacle within a few years.

County Clerk/Recorder These individuals wear several hats. First, they maintain county documents and records, such as real estate transactions and marriage licenses (they also can perform civil marriage ceremonies). Second, as a registrar, this office registers voters, maintains voter lists, verifies initiative signatures, and conducts all federal, state, and local elections in the county. Voters rarely hear from clerks and usually reelect incumbents.

County Superintendent of Schools In some ways, this position is an oddity in county government. California's county school superintendents often respond to separately elected county boards of education, not boards of supervisors. They do not administer local schools because district-appointed superintendents do that. The offices headed by superintendents provide staff, payroll, training, and other support services to local school districts. Due to economies of scale, they can provide those services more cheaply than many local school districts acting separately. Although the California Constitution Revision Commission recommended that this office be abolished, there is little public concern one way or the other.

Other departments vary in size depending on the size of the county. Commonly offered services include local transportation, land use planning, public health, welfare, personnel, and probation. In fact, California's counties play a critical role in administering CalWORKs—the state's version of the federal Temporary Assistance to Needy Families program (TANF), which is discussed in Chapter 13.

California's Troubled Counties

Governing California's counties is particularly challenging today, but some of these challenges are inherent to county government in America. In the 1800s, British observer James Bryce observed that American citizens are less attached to county government than other levels: "[The county] is too large for the personal interest of the citizens: that goes to the township. It is too small to have traditions which command the respect or touch the affections of its inhabitants: these belong to the state."[8] Lord Bryce considered counties artificial entities. He could well have been writing about California today. Several developments in recent decades have created substantial pressures for California counties, affecting their identity and their ability to govern at the local level.

Funding Pressures   Unlike cities, counties do not possess broad revenue generating authority. Proposition 13, which cut property taxes by half in 1978, also cut the counties' share of that tax. Some counties responded by closing libraries or delaying road improvements. Counties cannot cut just any program, though, because the state requires them to deliver a variety of services (welfare, environmental regulation, and public health). Some of these policy directives or **mandates** are fully funded; others are not.

In the wake of recession-driven revenue shortfalls, Governor Jerry Brown in 2011 recommended shifts in state and local program responsibilities and the requisite funding required—a process called realignment. If his proposals became reality, counties would incur both greater program responsibilities and the resources to pay for them. This could include corrections, health and human services, and juvenile justice.[9]

Issue Spillover   Modern policy problems in California ignore political boundaries. Smog readily moves across county lines, frustrating the ability of any single county to deal with the problem. Regionwide population growth has swamped some urban and "urbanizing" counties with traffic jams on obsolete road systems. Some welfare recipients, crushed by housing costs along coastal California, have moved to the state's more affordable interior. Ironically then, the poorest California counties—those with the fewest governmental resources—also

attract the neediest Californians including parolees, welfare recipients, at-risk children, and patients requiring publicly funded health care. The fact that one in five residents is poor in several Central Valley counties underscores the severity of this problem.[10]

Political Responsiveness   In a representative democracy, people expect elected bodies to be responsive to their wishes. This is problematic for county boards. In smaller counties, boards of supervisors are often ideologically conservative and pro-growth regarding development. Even in the face of desperate need, some boards champion a low-tax, low-spending ideology. Furthermore, with the possible exception of San Francisco, how can a five-member board possibly represent the diverse interests found in larger counties even if they are elected by district? The Los Angeles board has been called the "five little kings" by critics who believe it cannot possibly meet the needs of the county's ten million plus residents. Some reformers argue that larger boards in larger counties would allow greater opportunity for minority representation and political responsiveness.

For a variety of reasons, some communities seek to separate from counties, incorporate, and become municipalities. Often, they are dissatisfied with county services and/or want greater control over land use development. In sprawling counties, government offices may be too distant to be of practical use. Many recent incorporations stem from a local desire for control, image, and identity—those same qualities Bryce considered missing from county government in the 1830s. The communities that manage to incorporate drain county budgets further by reducing the county's share of property and sales taxes.

CITIES

Although California has its share of open space, most of its residents are fundamentally urban. Today, more than 80 percent of the state's

TABLE 10.1 **California Cities and Towns: Contrasts in Median Household Income**

California's Richest Communities and Towns		California's Poorest Communities and Towns	
Hidden Hills	$250,001	Clearlake	$28,239
Los Altos Hills	$218,922	Westmorland	$28,397
Woodside	$214,310	Firebaugh	$28,555
Rolling Hills	$205,147	Woodlake	$29,241
Hillsborough	$202,292	Arcata	$29,506
Atherton	$185,000	Lindsay	$29,556
Palos Verdes Estates	$170,068	Point Arena	$29,583
Portola Valley	$168,750	McFarland	$29,690
Monte Sereno	$167,417	Arvin	$29,915
Piedmont	$167,013	Tulelake	$29,926

The richest communities tend to be on California's coast and the poorest in rural and agricultural regions of the state.

Question: How might a community's wealth affect its politics?

NOTE: Income is expressed in 2009 inflation-adjusted dollars.

SOURCE: U.S. Bureau of the Census, 2005-2009 American Community Survey.

residents live in cities and 68 of those cities have more than 100,000 residents. California's earliest cities (San Diego, Los Angeles, Monterey, and San Francisco) were located along the coast, when passage by ship was one of the few travel choices available. Subsequent cities developed along major land transportation routes: roads, railroad routes, and later, freeways. Growing cities needed adequate water to develop and urban giants such as Los Angeles and the Bay area channeled it from great distances. Smaller urban areas developed local reservoirs to capture runoff water, tapped into agricultural water projects (like the Central Valley Project), or even built desalinization plants (converting coastal salt water into potable fresh water).

California's 482 cities have developed their own identities through economic specialization. Central Valley cities serve surrounding farm areas. Large central cities are home to banking, legal, corporate, and information services. Other cities are manufacturing centers that attract many commuters. Still others in scenic locations (including coastal cities, mountain communities, and California's wine growing regions) attract tourists. Many suburbs are bedroom communities, offering housing, some shopping, and little else. Others have attracted "clean" industry, shopping malls, and opportunities for recreation.

California's cities, including suburbs, defy overgeneralization. Together, they now represent the state's economic and ethnic diversity. For example, Table 10.1 depicts a considerable range in median household incomes among 20 of California's cities and towns. Demographers have observed that where metropolitan regions are becoming more polarized, where the middle class leaves, and the remaining poor and rich live separate lives in separate communities. One Wayne State University study found Greater Los Angeles to be the nation's most economically segregated region.[11] Ethnic diversity also characterizes California cities. In a growing number of them, no single racial or ethnic group constitutes a majority of a city's residents. These are California's majority-minority cities.

How Communities Become Municipalities

If voters in a locale wish to incorporate, they usually initiate such a proposal via a petition. A countywide **local agency formation commission** (LAFCO) studies the possible impacts of the new city. LAFCOs were established in 1963 to foster the orderly development of local government and to prevent urban sprawl. Usually consisting of two city council members, two county supervisors, and one public member, LAFCOs in recent years have been particularly sensitive to the revenue losses counties experience when new cities are formed. After a favorable LAFCO vote, the voters decide whether or not to incorporate. New cities with fewer than 3,500 people must be **general law cities**, operating under the general laws of the state. For example, a state general law requires every city to maintain a current general plan, a document that guides the city's future physical development including design, land uses, expansion plans, and infrastructure goals. Larger ones can choose to be general law or to adopt their own voter-approved charters. Only 120 California cities have their own charters. Some are quite detailed—Los Angeles's newest charter contains ten articles and more than 1,000 sections. Charter proponents believe these governing documents allow more flexibility for cities.

"Cities" Without "Government"

In the early 1960s, Samuel Wood and Alfred Heller wrote about the **phantom cities** of California. According to the authors, such places are "thickly settled, urban in nature. But they are not cities in the traditional sense of being more or less self-contained settlements controlling their own destinies. They are phantom cities."[12] Included were unincorporated cities (generalized urban growth outside city boundaries), special interest cities ("cities" dedicated to one industry or land use type, such as housing), contract cities (jurisdictions that buy some or all of their services often from counties), seasonal cities (recreation oriented communities which become bustling "cities" only during the tourist season), legitimate cities (but with problems that extend well beyond their borders), and regional cities (entire metropolitan areas without effective governments to match). All these phantoms exist today.

In recent years, a newsworthy example has been the City of Vernon in Los Angeles County. The city is home to only 112 residents but also 1,800 businesses and 55,000 weekday commuters. Dominated by heavy industry, it contains no schools, libraries, privately owned housing, or grocery stores. In fact, one city manager called Vernon's status as a municipality a sham. In the wake of chronic political corruption (bloated salaries, rigged elections, and misappropriation of funds), the state legislature attempted to dissolve this arguably phantom city.

A variation on phantom cities has been so-called **urban villages** or **edge cities**—conglomerations of shopping malls, industrial parks, office "campuses," institutions, and residential housing. Orange County's urban village—the Costa Mesa-Newport Beach-Irvine complex—is considered California's third largest "downtown." In these "post-suburban" communities, a consumer culture predominates.[13] The development of such places may overlap several jurisdictions that would otherwise manage their growth. They also blur traditional relationships between central city downtowns and surrounding suburbs.

Even at the neighborhood level, a growing number of middle-class Californians live in housing developments governed not by city hall but by **homeowner associations** (HOAs). Today, an estimated 7 million Californians live in over 40,000 common interest developments (CIDs). Developers initially establish them and all homeowners are automatic members. Elected boards of directors operate under assorted bylaws and documents called "C, C&Rs" (covenants, conditions and restrictions). In some respects, these documents are analogous to city charters. No wonder they have been called "shadow governments." Like cities, state law governs many aspects of HOA operations. The powers of HOA boards are both substantial and picayune—from maintaining private streets to mandating exterior paint colors. These powers are largely unregulated by the state; significant disputes are often taken to court. Many associations augment local law enforcement with security gates and alarm systems. Do such neighborhoods foster "cocoon citizens" who flee community life around them, as some critics suggest? Although research suggests that CIDs are less diverse than the larger communities that surround them, there is little evidence that these residents have seceded from public life generally. Nonetheless, these "privatopias" could be considered the newest phantom cities in contemporary California.[14]

How California Cities Are Run

As with counties, California cities are general law or charter; they are governed under the general laws of the state or operate under their own voter-approved charters. With the exception of the City and County of San Francisco, city governments in California follow one of two forms—mayor-council or council-manager.

Mayor-Council   Nationally, the **mayor-council form** predates the Progressive movement and tends to have strong mayors with substantial legislative, budget, appointive, and administrative powers; full-time city councils with members elected by district; and substantial partisan influence on elections and personnel. California has its version of mayor-council cities, including San Francisco, Los Angeles, and San Diego (See Figure 10.3). There are exceptions to the national norm, though. As you recall, California cities must be officially non-partisan. Also, California mayors in mayor-council systems are less powerful than their national counterparts. For example, the mayor of Los Angeles shares administrative powers with numerous managers, boards, and commissions, although his appointive powers increased under a revised charter. He remains able to veto ordinances passed by the city council. California's big city mayors maximize what powers they do have by becoming visionaries and seeking bold policy initiatives. For example, in 2006 when popular dissatisfaction with public schools was high, Los Angeles Mayor Antonio Villaraigosa sought partial control of the sprawling Los Angeles Unified School District. While that effort failed a legal challenge, he does operate a small educational partnership that controls ten schools.

What do city councils do in strong-mayor systems? As with all councils, they pass ordinances (local legislation), approve budgets, confirm appointments, and decide land use projects. They also have the power to reject decisions by other city bodies, such as rejecting a proposed utility rate increase. Compared to their counterparts in other states some, city councils in California's larger cities are small. San Francisco has 11 members on its board of supervisors and Los Angeles has 15 council members. In contrast, New York has 51 and Chicago 50.

Council-Manager   A much more prevalent city government pattern in California is the **council-manager form** (see Figure 10.4). In this form, typically part-time, modestly paid city councils hire professionally trained city managers or administrators who appoint most department heads and run the day-to-day affairs of their cities. Like their counterparts in larger cities, city councils adopt ordinances (local statutes), allocate revenue, determine the extent of public services offered, and make land use decisions. In smaller cities, council members are usually elected on an at-large (city-wide) basis and often possess a volunteer ethic, a take-it-or-leave-it attitude toward their jobs. Many do little more than respond to city manager proposals. Some are elected on single issues such as a controversial land use project and remain singularly focused. All in all, the primary power of most city councils in this system is to veto or second-guess the recommendations of city managers. As with county supervisors, council members used to be white, male, and middle class; but political times have changed. City councils today are more diverse—representing a wider range of economic interests, more ethnic minorities, and many more women.

Most mayors in California council-manager cities are council members chosen by their

A California gated community
In California, gated communities come in all varieties—from exclusive adult communities (as pictured above) to middle-class condominiums to mobile home parks.

Question: Should local governments approve more privatized neighborhoods in California? Why or why not?

colleagues to be mayor, although a growing number how have direct election of mayors. Although they preside over council meetings and grant more media interviews, they are in many ways equal to other council members. They rarely possess a mandate to lead in any meaningful sense. Their mayoral duties are largely ceremonial: cutting ribbons, presenting congratulatory resolutions, and speaking at various social functions. When their cities are successful, they rarely get the credit, but when community problems arise, they can easily become scapegoats.

In council-manager systems, city managers play powerful roles. They represent the Progressive ideal that "politics" and "administration" can be separated. City managers are directly responsible to the council. Although a growing number have long-term contracts, their tenure still depends on a council majority. "Three votes on any Monday night and I am out of a job," said one. A primary responsibility of the manager is to build agendas for council meetings. Between meetings, managers hire and supervise department heads, provide budget leadership, study the city's long-range needs, and otherwise do the council's bidding. In recent years, they have had to devote growing chunks of time to finance. Some develop statewide reputations as fiscal wizards, able to generate revenue

CITY OF SAN DIEGO ORGANIZATION
(All City Functions)

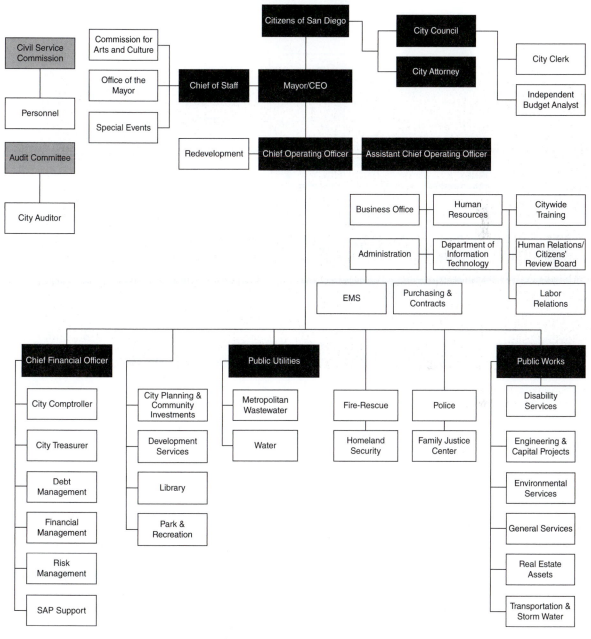

F I G U R E 10.3   San Diego's Strong Mayor Organization Chart

SOURCE: San Diego City Organization Chart from www.sandiego.gov/orgchart/pdf/allcity.pdf

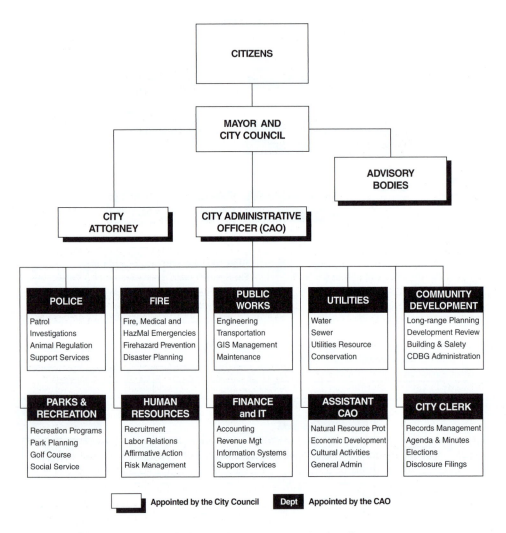

F I G U R E 10.4 San Luis Obispo's Council-Manager Organization Chart

SOURCE: Council-Manager Organization Chart from www.ci.san-luis-obispo.ca.us/orgchart.asp

from unlikely sources. Contrary to Progressive thinking, good city managers *are* good politicians. As a general rule, they know how to credit their elected bosses and steer clear of scandal (see Case in Point).

A city manager's ability to get along with a city council is paramount. Council factions often determine a city manager's success. A manager can be too entrepreneurial and dynamic (thereby competing with the mayor and council) or insufficiently dynamic (and therefore ineffective as city hall and

community leader). In recent years, the biggest problem managers have faced is how to meet unrealistically high expectations such as proposing cuts in government services without inflicting the inevitable pain that ensues. As group diversity and conflict become commonplace in California cities, so does criticism of these career professionals. No wonder city manager turnover tends to be high.

Regardless of city size or system type, city governments depend on various commissions and boards to govern. Large cities have many of them

---

B o x   10.1   Case in Point: Bell, California

How on earth did a relatively poor, blue collar city near Los Angeles with a population of 38,000 largely Latino and Hispanic residents become a national symbol of local government run amok? A 2010 investigation by the *Los Angeles Times* revealed that Bell City Manager Robert Rizzo earned nearly $800,000 per year (the highest city manager salary in the nation) and stood to retire with an annual pension nearing $1 million. Numerous other city officials also earned substantially more than their counterparts elsewhere. All but one of the part time city council members earned nearly $100,000, well beyond the average $4,800 earned by members in similarly sized cities. The sheer weight of Bell's city hall payroll required continual tax increases and dubious fee hikes. All this occurred in a city where the annual per capita income was only $24,000.

The roots of the scandal date to a 2005 state law that limited city council pay in general law cities like Bell. Ironically, the law was a reaction to high council salaries in neighboring South Gate. In response to this new law, the Bell City Council authorized a special election seeking to make Bell a charter city, thereby exempting it from those salary caps. The little-noticed election attracted a scant 390 voters, most of whom voted absentee.

Measure A's backers never revealed its true intent, cost, or consequences. After the vote and in quid pro quo fashion, the council raised Rizzo's own pay.

Now that Bell was a charter city and the council could set its own pay, how could it do so under the public's radar? The council's base pay would be only $1,800 but the members proceeded to assign themselves about $19,000 annually for serving on each of several boards and commissions—bodies that met concurrently with regular city council meetings if they met at all.

After the scandal came to light, the voters recalled the entire city council and most administrative officials resigned or were fired. Many were indicted on charges involving misappropriating public funds, conflict of interest, and falsifying public documents.

While the Bell case is sensational and extraordinary, it demonstrated how vigilant residents and the media need to be in monitoring the work of their local officials. It also showed how practices in one city can accelerate larger efforts to downsize public sector salaries and pensions.

SOURCE: Adapted from various Los Angeles Times news accounts including Jeff Gottlieb, "Bell Council Found Loophole in Law to Allow Big Salaries", *Los Angeles Times* (July 22, 2010).

---

whereas small cities might have only a few. Some commissions may actually operate harbors, airports, or public works enterprises. Others merely advise or make recommendations to elected policymakers. The most common are planning commissions that advise city councils on land use matters. They can exercise considerable power, as any developer can attest. Other boards provide advice on social services funding, libraries, the arts, and other matters. Service on these boards provides lessons in governing, and occasionally that first step toward elective office.

Cities and Counties: An Uneasy Relationship

California cities and counties invariably joust for influence and, more importantly, revenue. In general, California cities are in better fiscal shape than California counties. The reasons are clear. First, California cities have fewer policy responsibilities

mandated by the state such as welfare, jails, and public health. As a result, they are unburdened by rising caseloads in those areas. Second, cities have more flexibility than counties. County boundaries are fixed, while cities can annex unincorporated land for future development. Furthermore, new cities can form, capturing revenue generated from suburban population growth. For instance, by the time Wildomor and Menifee incorporated, Wildomar's population was more than 20,000 and Menifee's more than 72,000—providing a built-in revenue base from the first day of cityhood. Also, cities can pick and choose what services to provide and at what levels. If they want to provide police protection or garbage collection without maintaining expensive bureaucracies, they can "contract out" for those services. Third, cities have more opportunities to raise revenue than counties. When Proposition 13 cut California property taxes, cities sought other revenue sources. Because one cent of the state sales tax is returned to where it was collected, cities tend to favor revenue-rich commercial projects such as shopping malls, auto dealerships, and "big box" retailers like Costco and Wal-Mart—the **fiscalization of land use**. Although counties can also approve such developments, shopper-friendly building sites tend to be within city boundaries.

Cities (and a few counties) have also generated revenue by creating about 400 **redevelopment agencies** intended to improve and revitalize depressed or blighted areas. These agencies invest in new, largely private-sector development and then capture the "tax increment," the amount of increased property taxes attributable to new development in order to plan future projects. Results can include office complexes, in-town malls, entertainment facilities, convention centers, and other mixed-use projects. Counties may create such agencies but usually have fewer areas to declare as blighted. Under redevelopment law, these tax increments need not be shared with other local governments that would otherwise be entitled to them.

Therefore, it is not surprising that redevelopment agencies have become targets of criticism in recent years. They have always been accused of seizing private property through their eminent domain powers in order to foster economic development—which can enrich city coffers but also developer profits. Some critics suggest that the presumed benefits to a community of redevelopment are often illusory. Calling them essentially "piggybanks," Governor Brown in 2011 proposed eliminating these agencies and redirecting their considerable revenues to cash-strapped school districts, counties, and the state itself. Even the defenders of these embattled agencies have recommended changes in how they operate.[15]

SPECIAL DISTRICTS

They have been called America's "forgotten fiefdoms." There are nearly 30,000 of them across the country; they outnumber cities. California claims about 3,400, not including more than 1,000 school districts. Four counties have more than 200 of them; most counties have 50 to 200. They are special districts. Many of them were formed years ago to extend urban services to rural areas.

What Makes Them Special?

While California's special districts together provide 50 different services, nearly 85 percent of them provide only one service such as water or fire protection. Other services include community services, reclamation, sanitation, recreation, and even cemeteries (we consider school districts separately). Special districts do what general purpose local governments (cities and counties) cannot or will not do. They can assess property taxes, issue bonds, and charge user fees that are tied directly to the service provided. Not only do they spend vast sums on these services, they manage billions of dollars in budget reserves.

A San Joaquin irrigation district was California's first special district. Created in 1887, its purpose was to provide steady water supplies at predictable prices to area farmers. Since that time, special districts have multiplied in the Golden State. They became attractive to communities that desired a particular service and local control over its provision. Cities and counties rarely resisted, because these districts did not threaten existing political structures or boundaries; they simply added new, noncompeting layers of local government.

California special districts are either **dependent** or **independent**. Dependent ones are actually subdivisions of cities and counties. They commonly fund parking lots or street lighting through separate assessments, which, in effect, insulate a particular service from the larger annual budget battles faced by general purpose governments. City councils and county boards of supervisors provide policy direction. Counties also maintain county service areas (CSAs) to provide one or more services in unincorporated communities. These districts sometimes give way to municipal incorporation efforts by residents who want more home rule than these districts can provide. California's 2,300 independent districts are separate legal entities with their own elected boards that provide and finance the particular services noted earlier.

Special districts epitomize the diversity of local government in California. Some are tiny slivers of government that quietly provide a specialized service at modest cost to relatively few people. Others are gargantuan. The Southern California Rapid Transit District and the Metropolitan Water District of Southern California are two of the nation's largest. The latter's jurisdictional tentacles reach to the Eastern Slope of the Sierra Nevada—channeling precious runoff water to nearly 19 million Californians in six counties. Acting as a giant water wholesaler, this district maintains water supplies, determines water rates, establishes mandatory conservation programs, and levies fines against non-complying client agencies.

The Stealth Governments of California

The largest special districts are powerful indeed. But most are virtually invisible and in many ways unaccountable to average Californians. They are the stealth governments of California in that relatively anonymous elected boards govern them. Although their meetings must be open to the public, the public rarely shows up and the media rarely report their actions. One cemetery district manager could not recall someone from the general public *ever* attending a meeting. Special district elections are often the misnomers of democracy. Challengers are rare and elections are sometimes canceled when no one steps forth. Voter turnout is typically low unless these elections are folded into California's primary or general elections. On occasion, lavish business-trip spending, exorbitant managerial salaries, or bloated cash reserves make news and inspire calls for reform. But special districts usually operate outside the limelight, much like private businesses. No wonder many citizens express a combination of ignorance and apathy regarding these stealth governments.[16]

Special District Politics and Problems

Political scientists are often critical of special districts. First, they represent the height of governmental fragmentation. Why should the Bay Area have two dozen separate transportation agencies? Why should a patchwork of neighboring water agencies trip over each other to provide a commonly scarce resource? Why shouldn't single purpose agencies have to weigh competing priorities like general purpose cities and counties do? Defenders of special districts disagree. To them, special districts foster home rule by providing particular services tailored to particular locales—customized or "boutique" government, if you will. According to the California Special Districts Association, "There is a clear identification between agency name and service provided, which has resulted in a high degree of accountability and responsibility to the public, and a high degree of customer satisfaction"[17] (see Figure 10.5).

Second, contrary to their association's claims, critics of special districts believe that many of them lack true accountability and transparency, two key ideals of representative democracy. Any government agency that is empowered to raise its own revenue but is largely ignored by voters and the media is apt to spend those revenues in potentially controversial ways. For example, one small water agency with 17 employees and serving under five square miles paid its general manager $258,000 in 2011. Another water district paid fully half of its employees over $100,000 per year in salary and benefits. While some of them were scientists and engineers, news of this sort has fostered a general dissatisfaction with public sector pay and benefits among private sector workers.

In spite of these concerns, most of California's special districts have successfully resisted elimination, consolidation, or other reforms. But, as journalist Peter Schrag observed, "As California's ever-more desperate leaders cast around for both savings and efficiency—and maybe for a little better government generally—special districts should make for fat, tempting targets."[18]

> **Pros**
>
> They can tailor services to citizen demand.
> "Special districts only provide the services that the community desires."
>
> They can link costs to benefits.
> "Only those who benefit from district services pay for them. Those who do not benefit do not pay."
>
> They are responsive to their constituents.
> "Small groups of citizens can be quite effective in influencing special districts' decisions."
>
> **Cons**
>
> Special districts can lead to inefficiency.
> "Many special districts provide the same services that cities and counties provide. Overlapping jurisdictions can create competition and conflict...."
>
> Special districts can hinder regional planning.
> "It can be difficult to organize the various water, sewer, and fire services in one region to provide equitable services for all residents."
>
> Special districts can decrease accountability.
> "The multiplicity of limited purpose special districts can make it harder for citizens to gather information. [They] have a hard time finding out who's in charge."

F I G U R E 10.5 Special Districts Pros and Cons

SOURCE: Kimia Mizany Lewis and April Manatt, *What's So Special About Special Districts? 3rd ed.* (Sacramento: State Senate Local Government Committee, 2002).

SCHOOL DISTRICTS

California's 1,000 plus school districts are different enough from other special districts to warrant separate consideration. As a group they, too, exemplify both diversity and hyperpluralism—our continuing themes. They range in size from the mammoth Los Angeles Unified School District, with nearly 700,000 students and a $5 billion budget, to several hundred districts composed of single schools. As a group, these districts educate the state's children and youth, a growing segment of the state's population. Increasingly, they serve an ethnic rainbow in California—people groups from the four corners of the Earth.

Organizationally, school districts reflect the assumption that politics and education can and should be separate. With the exception of Los Angeles (which has a seven-member board),

California's local school boards consist of five members. All run on nonpartisan ballots; some are elected at large and others are elected by district. Like other units of government, district-based boards must reapportion every ten years and have been under pressure to better reflect California's minority groups. Boards typically meet several times a month. Most boards receive nominal pay or only minimal fringe benefits and have been common stepping stones to higher office, especially for women. Nowadays, women reach higher office through a variety of local offices (city councils, county boards of supervisors) in addition to school board service.

Professionally trained superintendents head educational staffs—teachers, support personnel, and other administrators. Usually possessing doctorates in education, superintendents prepare board agendas, systemwide budgets, and various policy proposals. Whereas small districts may be "lean and mean," large districts employ huge numbers of administrators, often a bone of contention among lesser-paid teachers. Board members and administrators are destined to conflict. Elected board members represent accountability in a representative democracy. They bring to meetings the "commonsense" views of parents, taxpayers, and neighbors. By contrast, education professionals bring expertise including educational practices, trends, and jargon that might be foreign to their boards.

Unlike most other special districts, school districts operate under close scrutiny—by parents, various interest groups, and the state government on which they depend heavily. The state's influence is pervasive. First, about 60 percent of school funding comes from state aid (based on ADA—average daily attendance figures). Second, California's massive Education Code dictates in surprising detail what districts can and cannot do. Third, the state Department of Education also affects local districts by administering statewide testing of various grade levels in various subjects, influencing curricula, approving textbook lists, and inspecting district performance. The federal government once played a relatively modest role by funding or subsidizing certain programs (such as school lunches) and enforcing various civil rights laws. Now the U.S. Department of Education oversees the No Child Left Behind Act of 2001, a law that holds the states and local school districts accountable to achieve certain educational standards and Race to the Top, an incentive-based program launched by U.S. President Barack Obama. Although it requires heightened performance and accountability, the federal portion of the state's education budget hovers around ten percent.

Pressures on California school districts will mount in the future as enrollments grow and financial challenges mount. Education policy will continue to be a battleground involving ethnic, religious, and ideological groups—each demanding that their priorities be reflected in the curriculum and in education policy generally. At one level, they must cope with a host of social phenomena such as divorce, juvenile delinquency, drug abuse, and many inattentive parents. At another level, they are supposed to respond to a growing school-age population, parent demands for greater choice, state expectations for reform, ethnic diversity, and the usual assortment of local conflict and controversy.

REGIONAL GOVERNMENTS

A few years ago, a three-mile bike path from Burbank to Los Angeles became both a source of community pride and of intergovernmental frustration. Through the Burbank stretch, cyclists passed well-tended neighborhood gardens and white picket fences. By the time they reached the North Hollywood part of Los Angeles, riders faced waist-high weeds, discarded mattresses, and graffiti-marred industrial warehouse walls. As one reporter put it, "It's a tale of one bike path, two cities, and too many bureaucrats." It turns out that the Burbank portion was monitored and maintained by one city department. Accountability for the Los Angeles portion was spread over three departments, one of which flatly refused to begin maintenance of the path until the project was fully complete.[19] This seemingly minor example demonstrates the potential challenges local governments encounter when working together toward a common goal. If a several mile bike path can become an interjurisdictional muddle, consider the mega-regional dilemmas of traffic gridlock, affordable housing, periodic water shortages, and climate change issues such as air pollution. Here we consider the role and importance of regional governance in California.

Because these policy challenges spill beyond jurisdictional boundaries, local governments acting alone will invariably be unprepared to deal with them. Thinking in regional terms would be a start, and regional governments already exist in California for that purpose. Californians rarely thirst for regional government. The proliferation of local governments in a region has allowed greater local identity, access to policymakers, opportunity for influence, and insulation from problems faced by nearby jurisdictions. Supporters of regional government point to two models in California: coordination and regulation.

Regional Coordination

The coordination model is best exemplified by the state's 35 regional planning agencies. Twenty-two of them are **councils of governments** (COGs). COGs are confederal—much like small United Nations—groups of autonomous counties and cities in a region coming together to deal with issues of common significance. The federal government designates them as *metropolitan planning organizations (MPOs)* and requires them to draw up long-range plans for transportation, growth management, hazardous waste management, and air quality. But they usually lack the legal authority to implement their plans. At minimum, COGs provide a forum for the member jurisdictions to communicate with each other. While COGs continue to receive federal funding due to federally mandated tasks, the also rely on member dues, transportation planning funds, consulting fees usually paid by member agencies, and sales tax "add-ons" that county voters have approved for transportation improvements. In addition to the state's required regional councils are 13 regional commissions that focus exclusively on transportation planning and policy.

Of the nation's nearly 700 regional councils, SCAG (the Southern California Association of Governments) is the largest—its members include six counties and 190 cities, representing more than 19 million persons. ABAG (the Association of Bay Area Governments) does planning for a nine-county, 100-city region. In these large metropolitan areas, subregional councils enable more local governments to participate and allow more detailed planning than otherwise possible. Numerous other COGs cover only one county

(such as Kern, Humboldt, Fresno, Merced, San Diego, Sacramento, and Santa Barbara). The members of these councils are city council members and county supervisors chosen by their peers and serve on a volunteer basis. Not only do COGs lack significant legislative authority, their voting members typically and understandably put local interests first. They resist giving a regional agency the power to dictate policy to member local governments. Yet, to the extent that knowledge is power, the COGs' ability to issue reports and studies often frames local policy debates.

Regional Regulation

Regional agencies that employ a regulation model have the power to both write and to enforce various rules and regulations, usually in the field of environmental pollution. For example, the San Francisco Bay Conservation and Development Commission can veto any waterfront construction that threatens the bay itself. The Tahoe Regional Planning Agency has similar powers relative to Lake Tahoe. Of the state's 35 air quality districts, the South Coast Air Quality Management District (SCAQMD) is one of the more active and controversial. As other districts do, the SCAQMD studies problems, writes plans, and then issues rules. Its rules either discourage, control, or ban polluting emissions from primarily stationary sources (power plants, factories, and corner gas stations) and consumer products (paints, solvent-based products, etc.). Some programs are incentive-based such as exchanging older leaf blowers, lawn mowers, and school buses for newer ones, resulting in reduced noise and lower emissions. These region-wide regulatory efforts usually involve complex trade-offs among various agendas, mandates, and organized interests.[20]

Regional government in California seems to be at a crossroad. Two contrary political forces explain the dilemma. On the one hand, some government officials and business leaders would like to strengthen or require regional approaches to admittedly regional problems. There are even state regulatory agencies that impact regions and communities in areas such as toxic pollution, water resources, environment, and waste management. On the other hand, pressure has been growing to empower grassroots groups and strengthen home rule *below* the local government level. NIMBY (not in my back yard) and environmental groups have flourished by opposing land use projects of both local and regional significance. These contrary goals lock horns profoundly in an increasingly diverse and hyperpluralist state.

CONCLUSION: DIVERSE COMMUNITIES, DIVERSE GOVERNMENTS

California's local governments mirror the profound diversity of the state. Cities and counties come in all shapes and sizes. Special districts, the stealth governments of California, provide single services controlled by unpublicized boards. School districts educate children and youth through high school while the state's 109 community college districts provide similar services to some high school students, college students, and adults. Regional governments face the permanent challenge of coordinating other local governments and educating them to think regionally. Private groups, such as homeowner associations, duplicate public governments but avoid (or think they do) the worst social, political, and economic problems at the local level.

Local government fragmentation mirrors a diverse state, but how problematic is fragmentation itself? Experts are not sure. Some governing problems are a function of size; some jurisdictions are simply too large or too small. The Los Angeles Unified School District might be too large to serve well its diverse school-aged population. In recent years, reformers have discussed breaking up this behemoth into smaller, more manageable districts and downsizing its largest

schools—an idea that has some popular appeal. Other districts, especially some rural counties, are so small they cannot adequately control overhead costs or provide statistically accurate evidence of student outcomes. One study suggests consolidating the tiniest districts and making them more accountable.[21] Is California overly fragmented? The layering of local governments across California's political landscape does seem to create voter confusion and the need for constant coordination. The state's regional governments help, but only help, in addressing local fragmentation. Nonetheless, local government fragmentation seems to be less of a problem in California than elsewhere. According to one study, California has fewer cities, counties, and special districts per capita than the national average. School districts have decreased in number as have the number of cities per 100,000 population (see Figure 10.6). The result has been jurisdictional stability in a sea of fiscal, political, and demographic change.[22]

That said, stable local governments do not necessarily mean governments that are accountable to California's diverse populations, or responsive to its modern policy challenges. While the ideal of homerule is sacrosanct to local officials, it has caused woes of its own. With authority come responsibility, and some local governments have lacked the latter. For example, in recent years, many cities and counties devised both generous salary packages and retirement pension formulas especially for top-level employees. In retrospect, these decisions were unsustainable in the long term and unaffordable even in the short term, especially as the Great Recession reduced once-reliable local revenues like the property tax and assets like pension portfolios. Jurisdiction after jurisdiction devoted larger shares of their budgets to retirees and pension obligations rather than substantive current programs, forcing layoffs of current workers. Several cities teetered on bankruptcy. We may be entering a new era where local government reform becomes as salient in California as budget reform, our next topic.

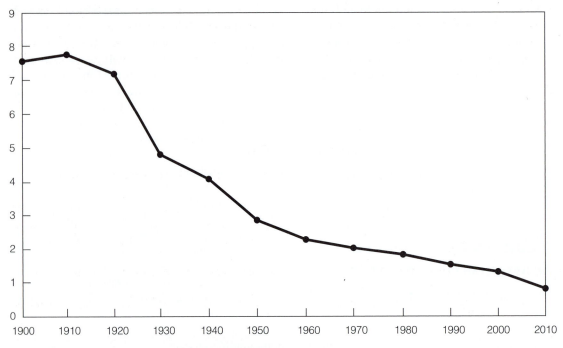

FIGURE 10.6 Number of Cities per 100,000 Population.

The graph suggests that California has accommodated population growth by expanding existing cities rather than by creating new ones.

Question: Why do many Californians seemingly prefer to live in larger cities?

SOURCE: Paul G. Lewis, *Deep Roots: Local Government. Structure in California* (San Francisco: Public Policy Institute of California, 1998). p. 23; updated by author.

KEY TERMS

privatism (p. 197)

home rule (p. 197)

general law and charter counties and cities (pp. 200, 204)

mandates (p. 202)

local agency formation commission (p. 204)

phantom cities (p. 204)

urban villages/edge cities (p. 204)

homeowner associations (p. 204)

mayor-council and council-manager forms (p. 205)

fiscalization of land use (p. 210)

redevelopment agencies (p. 210)

independent and dependent special districts (p. 210)

councils of governments (p. 214)

REVIEW QUESTIONS

1. What are the purposes of and limits to government at the community level?

2. Survey the historical forces that shaped California counties.

3. Why are California counties in trouble?

4. If you wanted your community to become a city, what would you need to do?

5. Describe and illustrate "phantom cities" from the text and your own observations.

6. What do special districts do, and why are they the stealth governments of California? Which ones exist in your home county and could any of them be combined?

7. Describe the two major approaches to regional governance in California.

8. How is local governance in California affected by home rule, diversity, and hyperpluralism?

WEB ACTIVITIES

California State Association of Counties
(www.csac.counties.org/)
Information here includes the counties' lobbying activity, issues of interest to counties, county profiles, and links to 45 specific county Web sites.

California Special Districts Association
(www.csda.net)
In addition to members-only content, this Web site provides background information on special districts and links to related local government resources.

League of California Cities
(www.cacities.org/)
The LCC site features legislative bulletins, association news, and links to hundreds of city home pages. Look up yours.

California School Boards Association
(www.csba.org/)
The CSBA is one of several education groups representing education policymakers and professionals. Its Web site contains helpful information on education governance in California.

NOTES

1. Andrew Murr, "'Divorce, L.A. Style': The San Fernando Valley Wants to Secede from Los Angeles. Can This Marriage Be Saved?" *Newsweek* (May 13, 2002), p. 38.

2. Quoted in Jim Newton, "Mayor Attacks Secession, Urges School Reform," *Los Angeles Times,* April 8, 1999.

3. Quoted in Joe Mathews and Mark Paul, *California Crackup: How Reform Broke the Golden State and How We Can Fix It* (Berkeley: University of California Press, 2010), p. 161.

4. Quoted in *City of Clinton v. Cedar Rapids and Missouri River Railroad Co.,* 24 Iowa 455, 475 (1868).

5. Gregory D. Saxton and Steven P. Erie, "Fiscal Constraints and the Loss of Home Rule: The Long Term Impacts of California's Post-Proposition 13 Fiscal Regime," *The American Journal of Public Administration* 32:4 (2002), pp. 423–454.

6. Eugene C. Lee, *The Politics of Nonpartisanship: A Study of California City Elections* (Berkeley: University of California Press, 1960), p. 173.

7. See Mark Baldassare, *When Government Fails: The Orange County Bankruptcy* (Berkeley: University of California Press and Public Policy Institute of California, 1998).

8. James Bryce, *The American Commonwealth* (London: Macmillan and Co., 1891), p. 586.

9. Dean Miscqynski, *Rethinking the State-Local Relationship: An Overview* (San Francisco: Public Policy Institute of California, 2011). (Accessed at www.ppic.org).

10. *Just the Facts: Poverty in California* (San Francisco: Public Policy Institute of California, March 2009).

11. Nancy Cleeland, "Rich, Poor Live Poles Apart in LA as Middle Class Keeps Shrinking," *Los Angeles Times,* July 23, 2006.

12. Samuel E. Wood and Alfred E. Heller, *The Phantom Cities of California* (Sacramento: California Tomorrow, 1963), p. 43.

13. For a thorough analysis of this phenomenon, see Rob Kling, Spencer Olin, and Mark Poster, eds.,

Postsuburban California: The Transformation of Orange County Since World War II (Berkeley: University of California Press, 1991).

14. Tracy M. Gordon, *Planned Developments in California: Private Communities and Public Life* (San Francisco: Public Policy Institute of California, 2004).

15. Michael J. Mishak, "California Governor Jerry Brown Defends Cutting Redevelopment Agencies," *Los Angeles Times* (January 27, 2011). For criticism of these agencies, see Steven Greenhut, "California's Secret Government: Redevelopment Agencies Blight the Golden State," *City Journal* 21 (Spring, 2011). For a more positive assessment, see *Strategic Plan for Redevelopment: New Redevelopment Realities* (March 10, 2010) (Accessed at www.calredevelop.org).

16. Little Hoover Commission, *Special Districts: Relics of the Past or Resources for the Future?* (Sacramento: Little Hoover Commission, 2000). (www. lhc.ca.gov/).

17. California Special Districts Association (Accessed at www.csda.net).

18. Peter Shrag, "Can't We Dump Some of Our 3,300 Special Districts?" *California Progress Report* (May 9, 2011). (Accessed at www.californiaprogress report. com).

19. Connie Llanoz, "Bike Paths Tell Tale of Two Cities," *Los Angeles Daily News,* September 13, 2007.

20. Wyn Grant, *Autos, Smog, and Pollution Control: The Politics of Air Quality Management in California* (Aldershot, UK, and Brookfield, VT: Edward Elgar, 1995); for more on the SCAQMD, go to www.aqmd.gov/. For links to others, go to the California Air Resources Board Web site (www. arb.ca.gov/capcoa/roster.htm/).

21. Legislative Analyst's Office, *How Small is Too Small? An Analysis of School District Consolidation* (Sacramento: Legislative Analyst's Office, May 2, 2011). (Accessed at www.lao.ca.gov).

22. Paul G. Lewis, *Deep Roots: Local Government Structure in California* (San Francisco: Public Policy Institute of California, 1998).

11

Budget Policy: The Cost of Diversity

Introduction: Budgeting as Public Policy

Where Budgeting Begins: The Economy

Economic Diversity

How California's Economy Affects Budgeting

California's Local Economies

The Budget Process

How California Budgeting Works

Constraints on the Process

Local Budget Processes

Types of Revenue

Major State Revenues

Local Revenue

Where the Money Goes

State Expenditures

Local Expenditures

The Need for Budget Reform

Conclusion: The Cost of Diversity

Key Terms

Review Questions

Web Activities

Notes

IN BRIEF

One of government's most important and contentious activities is to raise and spend money. The state of California and its local governments, like governments elsewhere, develop budgets to do so. These are government's premier policy statements, highly political documents that essentially represent contracts between policymakers and various sectors of society. As with the nation, the basis and context of California budgeting is the state's economy. The Golden State's economy historically has been diverse and continues to be. But economic upturns and downturns can significantly affect the dynamics of the budget process.

The state budget process in California is characterized by historic spending habits, significant input by various executive branch bureaucracies, and control by the governor and legislative leaders. At the local level, executive leadership and outside forces well beyond local control significantly affect budgeting.

Major California state revenues include the personal income tax, the sales tax, corporate taxes, excise taxes, the state lottery, and borrowing. Local revenues include the property tax, aid from other levels of government, miscellaneous taxes and fees, plus borrowing. Where does all this money go? The state spends most of it on the Big Three: education, health and welfare, and corrections. California's counties spend most of their revenue on public assistance and public safety activities. Cities spend most of theirs on public safety (police and fire), utilities, community development, and transportation activities.

In recent years, budgets have been whipsawed both by volatile revenues and demands for spending increases. Stormy budget debates in recent years seem to illustrate an increasingly diverse state whose policymakers can no longer achieve consensus on its arguably most important public policy.

INTRODUCTION: BUDGETING AS PUBLIC POLICY

"Funds for Disabled Restored." (2006)

"Proposed Cuts Show Depth of State Crisis" (2009)

"California's Next Budget Casualty—70 State Parks on Governor's Closure List" (2011)

"Revised California Budget Includes $6.6 Billion Windfall" (2011)

These actual newspaper headlines epitomize budgeting in California. Because of its dependence on the condition of the economy, the budget process has a yo-yo quality to it. In economic bad times, there is pessimistic debate over service cuts, denied pay increases, postponed projects, and possible tax increases. In economic good times, there is rosy talk of service expansion, restored funding, pay increases, new programs, and possible tax cuts. But even in the good years, budgeting itself is not easy. The process is cumbersome, party politics infuses deliberations, interest groups clash, and numerous external constraints limit budget options. In

Chapter 11 we discuss how and why budgeting in California works the way it does. In the end, we find that *budgeting in California increasingly reflects the state's hyperpluralistic character as increasingly diverse groups make claims on the public purse.* How policymakers respond to those demands is characterized by conflicting interest group goals and a budget process often colored or even paralyzed by the competing demands placed on it.

Before proceeding to budgeting in the Golden State, we need to explain four basic characteristics of public budgets in American politics.

1. Any *budget is simply a plan that specifies what monies will be spent (expenditures) and how those monies will be obtained (revenues).* According to political scientist Aaron Wildavsky, "Budgeting is concerned with translating financial resources into human resources. A budget, therefore, may also be characterized as a series of goals with price tags attached. Because funds are limited and have to be divided into one way or another, the budget becomes a mechanism for making choices among alternative expenditures."[1]

2. A California legislator once told some college students, "The top three issues up here are budget, budget, and budget." Indeed, *a government's budget is its premier public policy statement. Public policy* is whatever government chooses to do or not do. Particular policies are laws, programs, pronouncements, and other forms of public decisions. In a sense, "nondecisions" (what governments choose not to do) are also forms of public policy. What governments spend on these activities reflects societal priorities, what is important and unimportant. Where government obtains its money also represents the allocation of political power—who pays, who benefits, who wins, and who loses where money is concerned.

3. *Budgeting is profoundly political.* The budget process is where the sentences and paragraphs of this premier policy statement are torn apart, analyzed, and reassembled. In this regard, the budget shapes government around various spending and taxing decisions, consuming policymakers' attention spans and often dictating what can and cannot be done. Politically speaking, it reflects the state itself. California's state budget, for instance, exemplifies an assortment of phenomena: past budget decisions by both policymakers and voters, legislative/gubernatorial relationships, population growth, interest group conflict, and the health of the state's economy.

4. *Budgeting is, in essence, a contract.* Contracts represent agreements and commitments between two or more parties. Budgets serve as short-term political contracts between various participants in the political process, and between the voters and their government. At a deeper level, a budget represents a covenant or contract between a society's present and its future. For example, arguments over education spending, low-cost higher education, and new highways essentially are arguments over how best to invest in the state's future.

WHERE BUDGETING BEGINS: THE ECONOMY

To best understand the politics of budgeting in California, we need first to ask: Where does the revenue come from? In short, the basic source of public revenue is the economy. When Americans think of "the economy," they tend to think in national terms; yet there are 50 interdependent state economies that make up the whole. The health or vitality of California's economy is directly related to the revenues available both to the state government and to the state's local governments.

Economic Diversity

Historically, California's diverse and resilient economy has been one of its strengths, heralding the state as a place of opportunity for all comers. As we noted in Chapter 1, modern California possesses a balanced economy that consists of numerous sectors: service occupations, retail, agriculture, tourism, manufacturing, and a plethora of "high-tech" activities such as computers, communications, and financial services. California's modern, $1.8 trillion economy is both industrial and postindustrial—noted for innovation, sophistication, new ideas, new products, and the new jobs that follow. Over the years, California's economy has been stimulated by discoveries of gold and oil, agricultural mass production, automobile manufacturing, defense spending, the aerospace industry, and in recent decades, the revolution in technology. Also, international investment and foreign trade have contributed to making California's the eighth-largest economy in the world.[2]

How California's Economy Affects Budgeting

Two aspects of California's economy ultimately affect the budget process. *First, California's bad times and good times seem to be either very bad or very good.* During California's early 1990s recession, California's unemployment rate was twice the national rate. Several hundred thousand jobs disappeared or left the state. Given the number of military installations and defense contractors in California, cuts in federal defense and aerospace funding further eroded California's economic base. By the late 1990s, California's economy was booming—as was state budget revenue—but that was followed by another economic downturn in the early 2000s and the "Great Recession" of 2008–2010. More than earlier ones, the most recent recession resulted in increased unemployment, housing foreclosures, depressed state and local revenues, and heightened demands on state and local services. Economic volatility leads to budget volatility as policymakers agonize over ways to cut spending or raise revenue. Budget volatility also stems from the fact that, compared to other states, California has increasingly depended on the unstable income tax and less so on the more stable property tax.

Second, the state's economic trends (up or down) affect different Californians in different ways. We see it in a long-term trend toward economic inequality, especially between California's high paid sectors (like technology and professional services) and lower paid sectors (like agriculture and tourism). This is why California has higher household incomes *and* higher poverty rates than the national average. The gap is particularly acute between the wealthiest one percent of Californians and the state's middle and lower income groups.[3] Also, some differences are geographic in nature. As a rule, California's coastal economy is more varied, produces higher incomes, and is quicker to rebound from recessions than is California's inland economy where many jobs are agricultural in nature.[4]

Demographics help explain some of this. Compared to whites, California's Hispanic and African American workers earn lower wages due to lower levels of education and the poorer paying jobs that result. Immigration impacts the economy as well. Historically, immigrants relied on decent-paying manufacturing jobs to better their lives. Nowadays, they face the prospect of low-paying jobs in low-paying economic sectors with little opportunity for advancement. These economic variations have profound implications for budget making. Those who fall behind increasingly rely on tax-funded income support, medical care, and housing—the very programs that are jeopardized when the state's economy turns downward.

California's Local Economies

In Chapter 10, we noted the rich diversity of communities and local governments in California. There is also a rich diversity of local economies, which constitute the generalized "California economy." Whereas some economic trends affect all communities in the state, these local economies vary enough to create their own opportunities and challenges for state and local policymakers. Some communities depend largely on only a few sources of income—tourism, agriculture, a dominant regional shopping mall, or even the spending generated by the presence of a single state prison. Others remain militarily dependent; for better or worse, their destiny is tied to federal defense spending. Logging communities in Northern California depend on the vagaries of the construction industry. Silicon Valley communities are home to both successful technology firms and boom-or-bust Internet firms. During the most recent recession, public sector layoffs deeply affected communities where those workers lived (e.g. the Sacramento region). Large cities are so diverse that troubles in one economic sector may be compensated for by growth in other sectors. Consider Los Angeles. Today, the city's economic growth is fueled by small, minority-owned manufacturing concerns. Collectively, these companies have made the Los Angeles region the nation's second-largest manufacturing center.

THE BUDGET PROCESS

Whatever the state of the economy, California policymakers must agree to budgets every year. *The budget process is the institutional framework within which budget decisions are made.* We will discuss some basic features of the process in California, the various constraints on it, and on budgeting at the local level.

How California Budgeting Works

Although California's budget process is quite complicated, three features of it deserve special attention. It is incremental throughout, highly bureaucratic in the planning stages, and leadership-dominated in the later stages.

The Role of Incrementalism   California's budget process is **incremental**. In other words, specific agencies typically request increased funding for one **fiscal year** (July 1 to June 30) based on whatever was allocated for the previous fiscal year. To look ahead, agencies look back. In the "fat" years, when revenues continually grow, incrementalism makes budgeting easy. There is little incentive to ask whether an agency, service, or program is still needed. From the early 1950s to the present, the state budget grew steadily from $1 billion to nearly $100 billion—a reflection of California's economic and population growth. In the "lean" years, when revenue growth declines, incrementalism no longer works, and the potential for political conflict and gridlock increases dramatically. When revenues do not match desired expenditures, agencies accustomed to incremental growth can face less money than in the past. At minimum, they must settle for status-quo budgets.

The Role of the Executive   The governor and the bureaucracy dominate the planning stage, which takes about 18 months to complete. For example, the formal process to build the 2011–2012 budget (July 1, 2011, to June 30, 2012) began early in 2010, as agency budget planners developed spending estimates. Negotiations between the governor's office, agency staff, department heads, the Department of Finance (DOF), and its director take nearly a year. According to political scientist Richard Krolack, this is when DOF "earns its reputation as the most powerful department in state service."[5] The end product is a budget the governor unveils at a press conference

and submits to the legislature by January 10, 2011. The state constitution requires that the budget be balanced; if expenditures exceed anticipated revenues, the governor must propose additional sources of revenue. Governors often balance their budgets by proposing severe cuts, confident that the legislature will never approve them.

Incrementalism dominates the bureaucratic process. Projecting revenue is largely a guessing game as DOF officials must estimate future growth based on current trends, such as job growth and economic productivity. They might be on target; maybe not. At this stage of the process, career administrators provide continuity, given the comings and goings of their appointed bosses and elected officials, and form alliances among California's many interest groups. Masters of incrementalism, they can provide the most plausible reasons for retaining or increasing any agency's funding base.

The Role of Leadership   A third feature of California budgeting is that the external part of the process is leadership-dominated. When the governor submits the "budget" to the legislature, lawmakers actually receive several documents: the *Governor's Budget Summary* (a document highlighting the governor's priorities); the actual *Governor's Budget* (a large phone book-sized document); a *Salaries and Wages Supplement;* and the budget bill itself (listing each expenditure line by line). The process is leadership-dominated in that these bills are submitted only to the two fiscal committees— the Assembly Budget Committee and the Senate Budget and Fiscal Review Committee. Standing policy committees (e.g., Education) are not directly involved. The two fiscal committees divide into subcommittees (such as Education and Health and Welfare) to study in depth portions of the overall budget. The Legislative Analyst's Office issues several reports throughout the process, beginning with the Analysis of the Budget Bill and concluding with an assessment of the enacted budget. These reports sometimes challenge the governor's budget assumptions (e.g., what to expect in state revenues or federal aid). During legislative consideration, the governor proposes revisions, the most notable

---

Did You Know...?

From 1980 through 2010, the California legislature met its constitutional deadline of June 15 for sending an approved budget to the governor only five times. During those 30 years, a final budget was in place by July 1 only ten times. There were only three on-time budgets in the 2000s. Upset at these delays, voters approved Proposition 25, that not only lowered the threshold to pass budgets to a simple majority, but also prohibited legislators from collecting their pay or living expenses until a balanced budget has been passed by June 15.

NOTE: The 2011–2012 budget was on time.

SOURCE: Secretary of State, *General Election Official Voter Information Guide* (November 2, 2010).

---

being the **May Revision**. Included may be new spending priorities and, more important, updated revenue estimates. Depending on the economy, these revenue updates can represent bad news (shortfalls where revenues drop more than anticipated) or good news (windfalls where revenues exceed previous estimates). In 2011, the "Revise" revealed a windfall of $6.6 billion more than expected only four months earlier—suggesting the economy was on the mend. Good news or bad, the May Revision affects budget deliberations greatly.

Although budget disagreements occur annually, some budget years move along more smoothly than others. In some years, the full fiscal committees vote on their respective budget bills and send them on to the floors of each house well before state-imposed deadlines. A conference committee is supposed to hammer out differences, allowing time for floor votes before the constitutional deadline of June 15. The governor is supposed to sign the budget before July 1, the first day of the new fiscal year. Once the *Budget Act* is passed, **trailer bills** follow. These 16 bills implement the budget by specifying exact taxes, fee increases, and spending formulas in broad policy areas such as education or transportation. In recent years, on-time budgets have been rare and delays can take months (see Did You Know...?). When this happens, some payments to those doing business with the state are delayed as well.

In the event this process breaks down, the **Big Five** (the governor, Assembly speaker, Senate president pro tem, and minority leaders in both houses) meet behind closed doors to hammer out compromises necessary to achieve the votes needed in the Assembly and Senate—a simple majority to pass the budget and a two-thirds majority to raise taxes. This group is designed to force budget decisions when protracted stalemates seem likely. The presumption is that caucus members will follow the instructions of these leaders and dutifully ratify their compromises.

Although the state's budget process is dominated by a relatively small number of legislators, recent budget deadlocks can be traced to larger forces. As we noted in Chapter 7, newer legislators (Republicans and Democrats) have been more partisan and often more determined to have a budget voice on the floor. With majorities numbering less than two-thirds, achieving that percentage of votes is increasingly difficult. Even the Big Five have been ineffective at producing annual budgets on time because that is not their only goal. Fearing they would be boxed into approving tax increases or extensions, most Republicans in 2011 refused to even negotiate the budget with Governor Jerry Brown. As members of an unofficial "Taxpayers Caucus," most flatly rejected any tax increases whatsoever, whereas legislative Democrats favored a combination of tax increases and spending cuts. This forced the Democrats to pass a budget that relied on the usual mix of unrealistic revenue assumptions and dubious accounting maneuvers—prompting Brown's historic veto of the entire budget and a docking of legislative pay by the state Controller.

Once approved, the legislature sends the final budget along with the trailer bills to the governor to be signed. The overall budget consists of three types of funds. The *general fund* is the largest. It finances the bulk of ongoing state programs. *Special funds* encompass revenues for which spending is restricted by law, such as transportation and the state's Tobacco Settlement Fund (California's share of payments resulting from tobacco-related litigation). *Bond funds* consist of bond revenues used for capital outlays and other projects. Together, these funds support nearly 170 different departments and agencies, local governments, and individual Californians.

Constraints on the Process

In 1987, the *Economist,* a British periodical, carried an article entitled "The State That Tied Its Own Hands,"[6] referring to the budget constraints faced by California policymakers. Little has changed over the years. Here, we describe six of those constraints.

The Need for Supermajorities In November 2010, voters approved Proposition 25 that lowered the legislative votes required to pass the annual budget from two-thirds to a simple majority (21 in the Senate, 41 in the Assembly). The old supermajority requirement was passed by voters back in 1933 with little regard for its long term consequences.[7] Proposition 25 did not alter the **two-thirds requirement** to raise taxes and this remains a major impediment to on-time budgeting. If recession-era budgets cannot be balanced through spending cuts alone, some taxes must be raised or previous tax increases extended. But that requires a two-thirds vote. So, the very reasons it was difficult to pass a budget in the first place remain in place when it comes to raising revenue. In effect, two constitutional requirements clash: 1) the mandate to balance the annual budget and 2) the need for a two-thirds vote to raise the revenue that a balanced budget may require.

The Annual Budget Myth The California Constitution also requires the governor to submit a budget each year, but there is nothing sacred about annual budgets. Long-term economic, social, and political trends (all of which affect budgeting) ignore arbitrary calendars. Economic and business cycles can last for many years. An approved budget

on any July 1 is merely a primitive and temporary snapshot of the state's economy, its tax policy, and its expenditure choices. One-year budgets encourage California policymakers to "cook the books" through arcane budget maneuvers, lending the appearance of a balanced budget. The California Constitution Revision Commission recommended that a two-year budget be adopted (four years in the case of capital outlays).[8] Some California cities and several other states already do so.

Cruise Control Spending One constraint, which we call **cruise control spending**, has to do with the relatively automatic nature of many spending decisions. For example, large portions of the budget are spent on **entitlements**—those payments to individuals who meet eligibility requirements established by law. CalWORKs (California's major welfare program) and Medi-Cal (California's version of federal Medicaid for the poor) are entitlement programs. As caseloads grow, so does spending. Other increases are based on the growth of certain populations (school-aged children and prisoners). Cruise control spending is also evident in cost of living adjustments—COLAs. This spending technique gives eligible groups *automatic upward adjustments* in the funding they already receive, such as welfare payments or state employee pension increases. Yearly cost-of-living increases by policymakers easily become yearly expectations by recipients. During the fat years, the legislature routinely grants these increases. During the lean years, cutting these commitments is possible but nevertheless painful for the recipients and their allies in the legislature.

Narrow Spending Another constraint is the tendency to restrict spending by creating narrow categories of funded activity, called *categorical spending.* In education alone, there are well over 100 separate funding pots: from special education, to addressing the needs of poor students, to training algebra teachers. Each category alone has merit and a constituency willing to defend it from cuts or elimination. As one legislator put it, "Over time, I think we went crazy. Every special interest that had a little idea decided to categorize."[9] These programs tend to persist even though they may perpetuate obsolete approaches, foster spending disparities, and resist fiscal accountability.

Third Rail Issues "Touch it, you die!" **Third rail issues** refer to politically volatile issues that policymakers avoid, fearing voter wrath. Until recently, the federal Social Security and Medicare programs have illustrated this phenomenon. In California, Proposition 13 has been a third rail issue. Because it has become such an antitax icon, California lawmakers usually hesitate to make even needed reforms. In one exception, Proposition 38 in 2000 lowered the threshold for local school bond approvals from two-thirds to 55 percent, making it easier to expand local campuses or meet other needs. In recent years, the mere prospect of raising or extending taxes appears to have itself become a third rail issue, at least among legislative Republicans. Nearly all of them signed a pledge sponsored by the national group Americans for Tax Reform, vowing to "oppose and vote against any and all efforts to increase taxes."[10]

Ballot-Box Budgeting The initiative process is also an important sacred cow in California. It has given voters greater control over controversial issues and, to the consternation of many Sacramento policymakers, control over budgeting as well. One estimate suggests that more than 30 percent of California's appropriations are governed or locked in by voter initiatives.[11] This phenomenon, called **ballot-box budgeting**, has affected the budget process in three ways. First, some initiatives have fundamentally restructured state and local relationships. For example, Proposition 13 cut property taxes so severely that the state government "bailed out" cities, counties, special districts, and schools with surplus revenues. Greater aid meant greater control, which local governments feel even today. As we noted in Chapter 10, school districts are now heavily dependent on state support.

Second, some initiatives and propositions have furthered the practice of **earmarking** (allocating or restricting certain revenues to certain purposes). For example, in 2002, voters approved Proposition 42,

a constitutional amendment that required all gasoline sales tax revenues be spent on mass transit, roads, and highways. On occasion, voters will even approve tax increases if they are connected to (or earmarked for) perceived needs or desired benefits. For instance, Proposition 10 (1998) increased cigarette taxes to fund early childhood development programs. When earmarked revenues (fees to hunt and fish) are embedded in the State Constitution, changing them is unlikely. While some policymakers may bemoan earmarking, it does encourage otherwise tax-averse voters to fund programs they regard as beneficial.

Third, some initiatives effectively restructure the budget process by skewing spending priorities or otherwise restricting fiscal actions. In effect, voters set parameters within which policymakers must work. For instance, Proposition 98 (1988) has had the most profound impact on overall state spending priorities. This constitutional amendment established a complex formula for setting minimum annual funding levels for K—12 schools and community colleges. While its intent was to stabilize education funding and better tie it to enrollment and income growth, it unrealistically assumed revenue would grow indefinitely.[12]

Fourth, voters affect budgeting by readily approving bond measures that fund singularly worthy projects but encumber the state with cumulative long-term debt obligations. Elected officials themselves recommend borrowing as Arnold Schwarzenegger and the legislature did with Propositions 1A through 1E in November 2006. The revenues from those voter-approved bonds were to help fill short-term revenue shortfalls while policymakers pursued more permanent budget solutions. Most bonds are single purpose in nature and, when viewed separately, seem like worthwhile endeavors. For example, three separate bond measures on the Fall 2008 ballot authorized the issuance of nearly $27 billion in general obligation bonds to fund alternative energy programs, housing for veterans, children's hospitals, and early planning toward inter-city high speed rail service.

The result of all these constraints has been what one editorialist called a "fiscal pretzel." Policymakers find themselves negotiating merely at the margins of $100 billion budgets. Although antitax crusaders Howard Jarvis and Paul Gann are gone, the initiative process gives voters awesome powers to make complex taxation and spending decisions. They also tend to paint policymakers into a corner in terms of budget flexibility.

Local Budget Processes

Given the diversity of local governments in California, we can make only broad generalizations about how they raise and spend money. First, as we noted, local revenues depend on a host of factors including the nature of the local economy. The more diverse the economy, the more stable will be a community's revenue base. Second, local budgeting parallels state budgeting in many respects. Departments and finance offices build their budget requests; the mayor, city manager, school district superintendent, or special district manager submits a formal budget to the elected governing body; that group take input from the public during public hearings; and, after revisions are made, adopts a final budget. California local governments normally use the same July 1 to June 30 fiscal year timetable. With some exceptions they, too, use annual budgets.

Third, the public is largely apathetic. Duly advertised budget hearings are often sparsely attended. Proposition 13 effectively eliminated the

Cartoon 11.1 California in a corner

Question: To update this cartoon, what other paint cans would you add? If you were the governor, what would you recommend to offset the limitations imposed by ballot box budgeting?

SOURCE: 1993 Paul Duginski.

need for local governments to set property tax rates; as a result, most voters lost interest in the subject. Exceptions include local interest groups such as chambers of commerce, taxpayer groups, or recipients of local grants. Fourth, the local budget process is at the end of a "fiscal food chain." The federal and state governments respectively monopolize the income tax and the sales tax. What is left for California's local governments? The answer is the property tax, assorted "nickel-and-dime" taxes, fees, and aid from governments higher up the chain.

Gridlock at the state level jeopardizes budget making at all levels. Because the state and its local governments use the same fiscal year and because state budgets are often late, local governments build budgets with only guesses as to what the state will do. The "locals" that depend heavily on state aid are often "held hostage" until the state budget is adopted. School districts are in a real bind. They must make midsummer budget decisions (and hiring decisions well before that) using the previous year's attendance figures and estimates regarding next fall's enrollment, all the while closely watching the state budget process.

TYPES OF REVENUE

California's state budget consists of a general fund (for ongoing operations), special funds (revenues and expenditures segregated for specific purposes), and bond funds (revenues and expenditures involving borrowed monies). The entire 2011–2012 budget neared $100 billion, including all these funds. Here, where we examine particular revenues and expenditures, we focus on the general fund.

If a budget is the premier public policy statement, what can be said of the money raised to fund it? *Revenues are by-products of other policies and ultimately mirror society's values.* In this section, we describe major revenue sources used by California state and local governments. Each has its defenders and critics based on the following criteria.

Equity   Fairness or equity generally refers to citizen ability to pay a particular tax. Not all taxes are alike in this regard. A **regressive tax** is one where the effective tax rate falls as taxable income rises; it imposes a greater burden on lower than upper income groups. A flat sales tax disproportionately burdens the poor, who must spend a greater percentage of their incomes to pay it. That is why most groceries are exempt from the sales tax. A **progressive tax** rate increases according to one's ability to pay. The income tax is progressive in that rates climb (up to a point) as incomes climb. The property tax is regressive (based on real estate value not household income) but the wealthy tend to pay plenty of it because they own higher valued properties. California's overall tax system is both progressive and regressive in that income, sales, and property taxes are all part of the revenue mix. In the end, tax equity depends on one's income level. While affluent Californians indeed pay taxes in large dollar amounts, the poorest families pay out a greater share of their income in taxes than do the wealthy. According to one study, the lowest 20 percent of California households pay 11.1 percent of their income in state and local taxes. The top 1 percent pay 7.8 percent.[13] In recent years, the meaning of equity has come to include the "benefit principle" (those who receive benefits from government should pay for those benefits). State park campsite fees use the benefit principle.

Yield   Another criterion is yield, the amount of revenue collected given the effort required to collect it. From the government's perspective, the sales tax is the easiest to collect—retailers do it. The property tax is more cumbersome to collect, especially if people appeal their assessments or request lower valuations due to drops in home prices. The state income tax is much more cumbersome to collect for both government and taxpayers. Parking ticket fines have been so hard to collect that California occasionally sponsors amnesty programs, allowing people to pay accumulated fines without late penalties. In the absence of an enforceable sales tax on Internet purchases, California taxpayers are

---

Did You Know...?

Of the 611,318 California taxpayers with incomes over $200,000 in 2008, 2,431 paid no California personal income tax whatsoever. How so? They claimed enterprise zone tax credits, miscellaneous deductions, the research and development tax credit, and stock market losses.

SOURCE: California Budget Project, *Who Pays Taxes in California* (Sacramento: California Budget Project, April, 2011). (www.cbp.org/).

---

supposed to keep meticulous records, voluntarily declare such purchases on their annual state tax returns (line 49), and pay a so-called use tax. Obviously, the yield is slim to none.

Certainty   Will revenues be steady, regardless of economic or other conditions? Or are they uncertain and unpredictable? Consumption taxes, such as the sales tax, are considered elastic, and therefore unstable. During a recession, people tend to spend less and therefore pay less sales tax. In recent years, California's income tax revenues have become quite volatile, reflecting the gyrations of the stock market. On the other hand, the property tax is usually stable and dependable because it grows slowly and does not depend on the incomes of those who own taxable property. We say usually. In the wake of the housing crisis of the late 2000s (risky real estate loans, subsequent bank foreclosures, and resultant drops in home sales and prices), local assessors were forced to reduce property values and consequently the taxes based on those values. Local budgets were hit hard in the process.

Accountability   In a representative democracy, this criterion suggests that taxes should be explicit or transparent, not hidden. California indexes the personal income tax to make it less hidden. That is, the tax is adjusted each year by the rate of inflation to prevent taxpayers from being pushed into higher tax brackets without a real increase in income. Prior to indexing, taxes "increased" without taxpayers realizing it. At the local level, many taxes such as special assessments appear only in the fine print on their property tax bills.

Acceptability   A final criterion asks whether a particular tax is generally acceptable to the citizenry. True, everyone complains about taxes but some sources of revenue are more politically acceptable or tolerable than others. For example, many nonsmoking Californians readily support higher taxes on tobacco products. Obviously, smokers find those taxes less acceptable. Although many Californians perceive their overall taxes are too high, information in "Box 11.1—Are Californians' Taxes Too High" suggests that California is only a moderate tax state.

Major State Revenues

California's revenue system is a patchwork of taxes that were put into place during the 1930s. Experts regard the structure as complex and incomprehensible to average Californians. Indeed, most Californians themselves do not know how the state budget works and misperceive basic budget facts. Specific revenues described below are found in the pie chart found in Figure 11.1.

Personal Income Tax   The largest source of state revenue is the personal income tax. Adopted in 1935, it largely parallels the federal income tax: Taxpayers pay at different rates based on wages, salaries, stock options, and other forms of income. For most Californians, the state's standard rates range from 1 to 9.3 percent. In 2004, voters approved Proposition 63, which established a one percent surcharge on taxable incomes over $1 million to be spent on mental health services. It takes only $47,000 in annual income for an individual to reach the 9.3 rate; double that for couples.

Box 11.1   ARE CALIFORNIANS' TAXES TOO HIGH?

Although many Californians think their taxes are much too high, compared with other states California ranks in the middle on many taxes and near the bottom on still others. When state taxes are measured relative to personal income, this is how California ranked in 2009–2010:

Sales taxes	20
Alcohol	41
Tobacco	45
Motor Fuels	44
Individual income	6
Corporate income	4
All state and local taxes collected	15

NOTES: Rankings represent taxes collected as a percentage of personal income in the 50 states not including the District of Columbia.

SOURCE: California Budget Project, *Who Pays Taxes in California?* (Sacramento: California Budget Project, April, 2011) (www.cbp. org/).

All in all, the income tax constituted over 55 percent of the state's 2011–2012 general fund. Yet, in one major survey, only 29 percent of California adults knew the income tax is the state's top revenue source.[14]

Sales Tax   The second largest source of state revenue is the sales tax. Constituting about 27 percent of the 2011–2012 state general fund, it began in 1933 at a modest 2.5 percent tax on retail sales subject to the tax. The current statewide rate is 8.25 percent, including 2 percent for local government activities. Because it is inherently regressive,

necessities of life, such as food, prescription drugs, and utilities, are not taxed. In addition, voters in numerous counties and cities have approved sales tax "add-ons" to fund local transportation or other projects. The actual effective sales tax can be as high as 9.75 (Alameda and Los Angeles Counties), making those rates among the nation's highest.

While the California sales tax seems high, it is limited to tangible goods, not services such as legal advice or medical examinations, the kinds of economic activity that comprise a substantial portion of the California economy. What about tangible

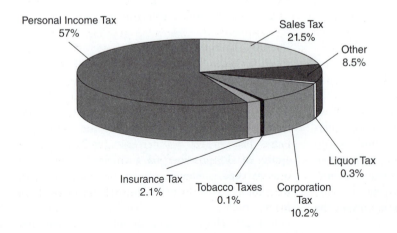

Personal Income Tax 57%
Sales Tax 21.5%
Other 8.5%
Insurance Tax 2.1%
Tobacco Taxes 0.1%
Corporation Tax 10.2%
Liquor Tax 0.3%

FIGURE 11.1 General Fund Revenues and Transfers

Question: If your intent as a legislator was to cut taxes in general or for specific groups, how might this chart inform you

NOTE: Of a general fund over $88 billion for Fiscal Year 2011–2012, the bulk of revenues came from the personal income tax and the sales tax. Some revenues like bonds and motor fuel taxes are restricted to certain types of spending and are not included in the general fund.

SOURCE: *California State Budget*, 2011–2012 California Department of Finance (www.dof. ca.gov).

goods ordered online? Here confusion reigns depending on whether the retailer has a physical presence in the state. If you buy this textbook at a campus bookstore, you pay the California sales tax; if you buy it at Amazon.com, you do not. Presumably, Amazon owes the tax but is not required by law to collect it. This tax loophole costs the state an estimated $1 billion annually and disadvantages physical retail stores. The 2011–2012 budget closed this loophole but Amazon both filed a lawsuit and pursued a voter referendum to halt the change.

The state's sales tax is fraught with other loopholes and dichotomies—a testimony to benevolence, good intentions, and interest group clout. Numerous exemptions provide "targeted tax relief" to a variety of sales ranging from animal feed and farm harvesting equipment to horse-racing breeding stock to meals for students and the elderly.

Corporate Taxes California businesses pay a variety of taxes. The corporation tax is levied on all corporations doing business in the state. Nonprofit corporations are exempt. The flat rate is 8.84 percent of profits earned in California. There are two kinds. A franchise tax is imposed on corporations for the privilege of doing business in California. The corporate income tax is levied on those businesses outside California that derive income from California sources. A controversial unitary tax is levied on corporations based on income earned outside of California. Financial institutions, including banks, pay an additional 2 percent of income in lieu of personal property and local business taxes. The politically powerful insurance companies pay only a 2.35 percent tax rate on insurance premiums sold. Insurance taxes constitute only 2.2 percent of the 2011–2012 general fund, bank and corporation taxes over 12 percent. Businesses and corporations claim this is too high but many of them can take advantage of deductions and credits not available to individuals. In some cases, these breaks are so generous that some businesses and corporations declare enough losses (on paper at least) to avoid paying any state taxes. This is often the case with small businesses.

Excise Taxes Numerous other taxes complement these larger sources of revenue. Excise taxes are assigned to particular items when they are made, sold, transported, or consumed. For example, California taxes tobacco products, alcoholic beverages, horse racing, and gasoline. They resemble sales taxes but are levied separately. Historically, California's "sin" taxes on tobacco and alcoholic beverages have been relatively low due to interest group pressure in Sacramento. Yet, voters have approved several propositions significantly increasing the tax on tobacco products. The tax on cigarettes now stands at 87 cents per pack. Taxes on alcohol depend on the beverage but are quite low. For example, although the sales tax on liquor is $3.30 per gallon, the tax on beer and wine is only 20 cents per gallon. Traditionally, "sin" taxes were considered a dependable, albeit small, source of revenue. Small indeed. They amount to only 0.4 percent of the 2011–2012 general fund. Because smoking and alcohol consumption have declined somewhat in recent years, analysts predict that this source of revenue will remain minimal.

The excise tax on motor fuels (mostly gasoline and diesel fuel) is added to the regular sales tax plus substantial federal excise taxes, all of which are included in the retail price at the pump. Gas stations collect it and motorists rarely think about it. California's gas tax was raised to 18 cents per gallon thanks to Proposition 111 in 1990. Even that amount may be inadequate. Hybrids and other fuel-efficient cars consume less gasoline than older "gas-guzzlers," sport utility vehicles (SUVs), or trucks. Consequently, their owners pay less gas tax in the process. Experts think that basing the tax on the price of a tank of gas, not the number of gallons in the tank (much like the standard sales tax), would make the tax more inflation-sensitive than it is now. The gasoline tax is regressive, as are most excise taxes. Experts believe that the poor pay a greater share of their income in gasoline taxes than do the wealthy, even though fewer of them drive.

The Lottery Joining many other states, Californians approved a statewide lottery in 1984. To sell voters on the idea, one-third of the proceeds were earmarked for education. Nowadays, 54 percent of each lottery dollar goes to winners, 35 cents to education, 7 percent to ticket sellers, and 6 cents to administrative costs. Although participation in the lottery is purely voluntary, it is more regressive for the poor who participate than for the more affluent. As a source of public education revenue, lottery proceeds are small, unpredictable, and inefficient. It amounts to less than two percent of all K-12 spending in the state.[15] Accordingly, critics complain that the lottery has not lived up to its potential. In fact, California is dead last among lottery states in percapita sales, amounts of lottery advertising, retailer participation, and prize payouts.[16] Of course, in some parts of the state, the California Lottery faces intense competition from Indian casinos. Furthermore, those who oppose gambling in general on ethical grounds believe that the lottery encourages chronic and addictive gambling by highly vulnerable Californians.

Debt Some government policies require more money than current revenues can provide. Adding a new state park, prison, office building, or state university campus takes huge sums for land acquisition and construction costs. These capital improvements are normally funded through external borrowing. Although the State Constitution limits the debt the legislature can incur, it places no such limits on the voters. Therefore, when policymakers need to borrow for capital improvements, they seek voter approval to issue bonds. Why borrow? The rationale is that long-term financing pays for projects used and enjoyed by future generations. When the state borrows money, it issues bonds that are purchased by investors. The wording of the bond tells the investor its worth, the interest rate to be earned, and when the bond can be redeemed.

Two types of bonds are used in California: **general obligation** and **revenue bonds**. General obligation bonds are backed or secured by the "full faith and credit" of the state, meaning general revenues paid by taxpayers. They finance projects that do not in and of themselves produce revenue, such as schools, prisons, and freeways. Revenue bonds are backed by the future revenue generated by the facility being financed. "Lease purchase" bonds can be paid from any source—the general fund or project-generated revenue—and do not require voter approval. In recent years, several toll road projects in California have been financed through these bonds assuming that future tolls would pay back the bonds. Because revenue projections are only projections, interest rates on revenue bonds are typically higher than on general obligation bonds. In recent years, California voters have approved numerous general obligation bonds to fund rail transportation projects, school construction, prisons, and park acquisition. Backed by Governor Schwarzenegger and the legislature, they also borrowed $15 billion to close budget shortfalls. Although some voters resist such deficit financing, bond approvals are understandable. Voters can anticipate tangible results without paying directly for them.

Just as families can incur too much debt, so can governments. How much is too much? Proponents of borrowing claim that it is the only effective and politically feasible way to finance needed public improvements and that the mammoth size of California's economy makes such borrowing affordable. Furthermore, bond proceeds arguably create needed jobs, especially during economic downturns. Opponents of borrowing claim that interest paid to investors inflates the real cost of capital projects and gives voters the impression that they can get something for nothing. Borrowing for infrastructure improvements may be understandable. Borrowing in lieu of taxes to meet routine annual expenses is unacceptable even during economic downturns.

Who is right? One authoritative answer comes, not from Sacramento, but from bond-rating services in New York City. When Standard and Poor's Corporation or Moody Investor Services say the State of California is borrowing too much, California's credit rating suffers. This effectively makes California bonds more risky and harder to sell. This forces the state to offer higher interest

Courtesy of David G. Lawrence

Lottery Fever
Small convenience stores in California offer myriad lottery games to shoppers. They also receive hefty bonuses if they sell a winning ticket.

Question: Should public officials encourage gambling as a way of raising funds?

rates, which of course increases borrowing costs. Depending on economic conditions, budget difficulties, and borrowing trends, these services have both upgraded and downgraded California's credit ratings. In recent years, the ratings have been very low, forcing the state to offer higher interest rates to attract investors.[17]

What happens when state revenues drop but current-year expenses and spending demands do not? In times like these, the governor and legislature may "balance" budgets by borrowing from (some say "raiding") other public assets such as teacher and state worker pension funds or other special funds. This short-term borrowing may last

only one day (to cover cash flow) or more than a fiscal year (during economic recessions). These funds are so huge that borrowing from them is tempting. For instance, the legislature and Governor Schwarzenegger once treated $1.2 billion of the gasoline tax earmarked for transportation as a loan to the general fund. Loans from pension and special funds are usually paid back with interest, so these fixes come at a price.

In terms of debt as a revenue source, many experts believe that California now faces a period of **structural deficits**, where the state's current revenue mix is insufficient to meet current spending commitments without corrective action. Many of these expenditures are driven by caseload and population growth, spending formulas, increased costs to the state (such as wage increases and debt service), and court orders. These structural gaps can only be closed by long-term policies that increase revenues, decrease spending, or provide for a combination of the two.

Local Revenue

Traditionally, the property tax has been a distinctly local revenue source to pay for property related expenditures. California's *ad valorem* (based on value) property tax is primarily governed by the provisions in Proposition 13. As we noted in Chapter 4, it froze existing residential and commercial assessments at 1978 levels. Growth in that value, hence the tax, could not exceed two percent per year, no matter how high the actual value had risen. Over time, new construction and property sales would trigger new assessments based on updated, higher values.

The property tax is generally considered regressive in that it is not dependent on ability to pay. Regressivity is most severe for renters, who pay the tax indirectly through their rents but enjoy none of the other financial benefits of home ownership. The revenue effect of Proposition 13 was a substantial cut in property tax revenue followed by increased aid from the state and higher local fees. Proposition 13 essentially restructured the fiscal relationship between local governments, notably counties and school districts, and the state.[18]

But Proposition 13 illustrates a more general axiom regarding revenue in California local government: *Revenue strategies in California communities are first and foremost dependent on factors external to local decision making.* These factors include the state of the overall economy, federal and state aid, voter initiatives, and interest rates. For instance, during period recessions, people spend fewer dollars and therefore fewer sales taxes. Federal aid to local governments has dwindled in recent decades. Proposition 13 cut property tax revenue, leaving a multitude of local governments

to divvy up what was left. When the Federal Reserve Board cuts interest rates, local revenues on deposit earn less interest.

Local governments have responded to these trends as best they can. As a group, California cities receive only 21 percent of their general revenues from local property taxes and 29 percent from sales and use taxes. Increasingly, they depend on assessments, service charges, and miscellaneous fees to balance their budgets. Many cities have attracted large shopping malls, which generate voluminous sales taxes. They have also aggressively pursued user fees associated with particular services (such as land use permitting, swimming pool use, recreation programs, and bicycle licenses). Some fees serve no purpose but to raise additional income (such as cable television franchise fees and business licenses).

California counties have also raised fees considerably for public health and environmental inspections and processing land use projects. In many counties, inspectors once seen only infrequently now show up like clockwork, in part because of their fee-generating potential. On the whole, though, counties have proved less nimble in recovering from the long-term impact of Proposition 13. Most revenue-rich shopping malls are within cities, not unincorporated areas served by counties. They are also heavily dependent on the vagaries of state budgeting to administer state programs, including occasional voter initiatives such as Propositions 218 and 26. In 1996, voters approved Proposition 218—*The Right to Vote on Taxes Act.* It required local governments that seek new or increased assessments to do three things: (1) specify how assessed properties will benefit, (2) assess rather than exempt other local government property, and (3) hold a "mail-in" election of all affected property owners. In 2001, the California Supreme Court allowed certain local fees to bypass 218 requirements. In November 2010, voters narrowly passed Proposition 26. This constitutional amendment classified some local fees as taxes, thereby subject to a two-thirds vote of local voters. The measure may not hamper local officials as much as they once feared. Preexisting fees were not subject to the initiative and potential new fees might well fall under several of the measure's exemptions.

These initiatives have caused a situation in which there are more severe limits on local revenues than state revenues. In response, the state has increased its own aid to California's local governments, enabling them to increase spending well beyond their own ability to pay for that spending with local-only revenues. According to one study, this system of state-local transfers has encouraged excess local spending, clouded budget accountability, and exacerbated the state's ongoing budget crisis.[19]

Like the state, local governments may borrow money for needed projects. Voters may approve additions to the portion of sales tax that local governments receive. They may also approve various benefit assessments or special district charges that are added to their property taxes or parcel taxes. **Parcel taxes** are usually modest charges levied per property type, not property value. For example, a single family home might pay $49 per year for a school remodel or for library support. Historically, such levies have been difficult because Proposition 13 required a two-thirds vote of the people. As we noted, Proposition 39, lowered this threshold to 55 percent but only for school district bond issues. Since then, more school bond measures have passed than otherwise would have been the case. One method of financing has sidestepped Proposition 13. The *Mello-Roos Community Facilities Act of 1982* allows local governments to establish community development districts and then tax land slated for development within those districts. Future property owners who had no say in the matter pay the taxes that fund needed infrastructure improvements and public services.

WHERE THE MONEY GOES

As the state of California and its communities divide policy responsibilities, spending policies result not only from clear policy choices but also from incremental, historical decisions that develop their own political momentum. Because we devote the last two chapters of this book to public policy specifics in the Golden State, we will only briefly survey state and local expenditures here.

State Expenditures

Occasionally, newspaper reporters uncover legislators' spending ideas: $2 million for a San Francisco aquarium, a $150,000 model curriculum on human rights and genocide, or $149,000 for a California trade office in Armenia. Although such projects might confirm voter suspicions about wasteful spending, they do not reflect where most state revenue actually goes. Note Figure 11.2. A staggering 90 percent of the 2011–2012 state general fund went to education, health and human services, and corrections—the "Big Three" of state budgeting. This spending trio in California is quite typical of spending patterns in other states. We should call this spending "state initiated" because about three-quarters of state revenues are actually spent by local governments (e.g. school districts, community colleges, police departments, sheriffs, and county health and human services departments). This may be why the perceptions of average Californians are so mistaken. The survey we cited earlier indicated that only 16 percent of adults thought that education was the top state spending item. Fully 45 percent thought it was corrections and prisons.

Education Public education from kindergarten through community colleges consumed about 40 percent of the 2011–2012 general fund, just over the amount required by Proposition 98. Spending for education remains enrollment-driven. The school-aged population in California has been growing at a much faster rate than the general population but is beginning to slow in many communities. Where enrollments grow, so will the need for more classrooms and more teachers. Higher education (including the University of California and the California State University system) consumes nearly 12 percent of the 2011–2012 general fund. Due to the Great Recession, California's public university

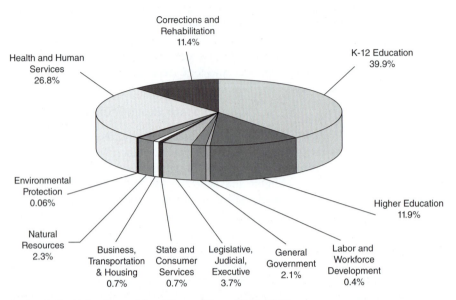

FIGURE 11.2   General Fund Expenditures (2011–2012)

The above percentages are based on general fund expenditures of nearly $89 billion. Not included are bond-based expenditures and special fund expenditures including highways.

Questions:
1. How will some slices of the budget pie expand parallel with population growth in California?
2. Does it surprise you how little money is spent on operating the major branches of government?

SOURCE: California State Budget, 2011–2012 (www.dof.ca.gov/).

systems (UC and CSU) have had to cut spending, raise fees, and seek greater productivity.

Health and Welfare   Addressing the health and welfare needs of California's poor, aged, blind, and disabled claimed nearly 27 percent of the 2011–2012 general fund. Caseloads have dropped somewhat in recent years due to job growth, welfare reform, and budget cuts. Expenditures in this area largely represent direct payments to individuals (such as CalWORKs) and to providers of particular services (medical doctors and hospitals). Within this portion of the budget, costs for Medi-Cal (California's version of federal medical care for the poor or Medicaid) have soared in recent decades due to rising medical care costs and federal requirements to serve more medically needy groups. Even so, Medi-Cal caseloads have declined somewhat in recent years. Today, nearly 20

percent of Californians—about 7.7 million people—qualify for Medi-Cal in any given month. The national average is under 16 percent.

Corrections and Rehabilitation   California's correctional system consumed over 11 percent of the 2011–2012 general fund—up from 3 percent in 1969–1970. This dramatic increase is the result of a combination of factors: rising crime rates, increases in crime-prone populations, and tougher sentencing policies (more prison time and less parole time). Increased sentences were partly mandated by Proposition 8, the 1982 "Victims' Bill of Rights." The state's *Three Strikes* law (see Chapter 9) also incarcerated more felons for longer periods of time. As a result, California's prison population jumped from 35,000 in 1983 to about 142,000 in 2011. This does not include responsibility for another 107,000 parolees.

What Is Left Other state operations (such as environmental protection, resource management, business regulation, the state courts, the legislature, and a host of executive branch agencies) consume the remaining 9–10 percent of the general fund. Most of the executive branch agencies portrayed in Chapter 8 spend little compared to the population-driven portions of the state budget. Efforts to balance state budgets by cutting these government operations will always have limited success because they constitute so little of the overall budget to begin with. Public opinion survey results do not aid the quest for balanced budgets, whether we are discussing revenues or expenditures. California voters are cool to tax increases in order to solve budget deficits. But, they have a hard time identifying which programs they would cut. In one *Field Poll*, they heavily opposed cuts in a number of the state's largest spending programs—schools, higher education, law enforcement, health care for the poor and disabled, and mental health.[20]

Local Expenditures

The two general purpose local government institutions in California are cities and counties. While California cities vary greatly in size and spending patterns vary, on average they spend their revenues accordingly (excluding the City and County of San Francisco).[21]

Individual cities can vary substantially from these averages primarily due to their size. Generally speaking, the smaller the city, the less likely it will be to manage utilities, airports, museums, hospitals, and mass transit systems. Controlling for size, cities, unlike counties, can pick and choose many of the services they wish to provide.

California counties present a much different spending picture. For the most part, this is because counties deliver services on behalf of the state. As noted below, the two largest spending commitments are on public assistance and public protection. Public assistance includes welfare, social services, general relief, care of wards of the court, and veteran services. By far the largest expenditure in this area is the CalWORKs program. Public

protection includes the local courts, sheriffs' departments, jails, and fire protection. The counties' health and sanitation responsibilities include public health, medical care, mental health, drug and alcohol abuse services, and sanitation costs. Other spending categories include general government (county boards of supervisors and administrative offices), roads, education administration, recreation programs, cultural facilities, veteran memorial buildings, and interest on county indebtedness.[22]

City Spending Category	Percentage
Public Safety (police, fire, emergency)	27
Public Utilities (water, gas, electric)	19
Transportation (streets, transit, airports)	16
Health (solid waste, sewers)	10
Community Development (planning, engineering)	8
Culture and Leisure (parks, recreation, libraries)	8
General Government (legislative, management, legal)	11

County Spending Category	Percentage
Public Assistance	30
Public Protection	33
Health and Sanitation	18
General Government	10
Public Ways and Facilities	4
Debt Service	3
Recreational and Cultural Services	1
Education	1

THE NEED FOR BUDGET REFORM

In reviewing the politics of budgeting in California, we see diverse interests confronting rather rigid political structures and economic trends. As Richard Krolack has put it, "California's budget is a complex process with many nuances and intangibles."[23] That said, three patterns of budgeting in California emerge:

1. *California budgeting is both volatile and cyclical.*
    The state's reliance on the personal income tax and sales tax heavily depends on the health of the state's economy. When the economy is growing, those revenues grow and so do public budgets. In these fat years, more revenue is available for all manner of policies and programs; those revenues can accommodate higher school and university enrollments, larger prison populations, and greater MediCal caseloads. Tax cuts are even possible. When the economy is stagnant or in recession, the opposite occurs. In these lean years, programs and expectations must be cut or scaled back. This revenue volatility is challenging in the face of long-term spending commitments.

2. *California budgeting is group-differential*—that is, it treats different groups in different ways. Consider the combination of all California taxes. The total tax burden on Californians is a function of how progressive or regressive different taxes are. Income taxes are highly progressive; sales, excise taxes, and property taxes are regressive. In general, *higher income Californians benefit from the state's tax policies.* Although they pay a large share of California's income tax, the wealthy can take advantage of numerous tax credits and deductions to offset their tax liabilities. Lower income families pay lower income taxes or possibly none at all but they are hit hard by regressive sales, excise, and property taxes. On the spending side of the equation, *lower income Californians benefit from many state expenditures,* especially in the areas of health and human services. They also have access to relatively low-cost higher education at the state's community colleges.

3. *California budgeting needs reform.* Today, California's budget process is, in the words of the California Constitution Revision Commission, "crippled" and "dysfunctional." Structural deficits seem to be a permanent feature of budgeting in the nation's largest state. There is an overreliance on the most volatile sources of revenue to fund permanent, growing, population-driven spending. During the budget process in Sacramento, policymakers lurch from one temporary, short-term budget fix to another—thereby "kicking the can down the road," as they themselves put it. A chorus of reform groups have recommended fundamental changes in the budget process. The following major reforms have been proposed:

- Use multiyear strategic planning to frame budget decisions and allow multiyear budgets

- Restructure the state revenue mix to reduce volatility

- Allow simple legislative majorities to raise or extend taxes

- Move the fiscal year start to October 1

- Require prudent reserves for "rainy day" budgets

- Limit borrowing to cover annual budget deficits

- Curtail the use of accounting gimmicks that delay and cloud budget accountability

- Ensure that local property taxes remain at the local level

- Stabilize and simplify local revenues and state/local fiscal relations

- Gradually reduce the ballooning costs of public employee pensions.[24]

Although voters eliminated the supermajority requirement for the legislature to pass annual budgets, the legislature still needs a two-thirds majority to raise taxes. Legislative Republicans and conservatives oppose reducing that threshold because they fear runaway spending and tax increases, given various demands for state services. Moving the beginning of the fiscal year to October would parallel the federal budget process and given California legislators more time after the May Revision to come to a budget consensus.[25] Even if these budget reforms were in place, policymakers would continue to face incessant spending pressures from infrastructure needs to services tied to a growing and increasingly diverse population.

CONCLUSION: THE COST OF DIVERSITY

At the outset of this chapter, we noted that a budget is a government's premier policy statement. In a representative democracy, it seems to say, "These are the things that we, the people, want to do as a society—both today and on behalf of future Californians." The consensus assumed in that statement seems missing from contemporary budget politics. State and local budget makers might epitomize fiscal gridlock to many Californians but they are not the root cause of the problem. The true cause of annual budget struggles stems from economic change, population growth, group competition, and partisan conflict.

In a sense, budgeting in California puts dollar signs on "the politics of diversity." To the extent that the tax system benefits the rich, it benefits only one segment of Californians. To the extent that state expenditures benefit the poor (public assistance, Medi-Cal), the middle class (higher education, highways), the wealthy (tax credits and low corporate taxes), or particular interests (farmers, renters), they divide 38 million Californians into groups. To the extent that the budget process itself divides power, fragments decision making, encourages group competition, and incurs gridlock, it exhibits hyperpluralism. This is all the more true when California voters wrest budget decisions from elected budgetmakers—"ballot box budgeting."

Budget experts have long regarded California's operating budget as relatively generous to those in need. But to what extent will that generosity continue, given other demands on state resources? The foremost budget question Californians and their policymakers will need to address is this: How can the state and its communities agree on budgets in an age when societal and therefore political consensus is lacking and quite possibly unachievable? The alternative is "every group for itself" in the nation's largest and most diverse state.

KEY TERMS

fiscal year (p. 223)

incrementalism (p. 223)

May Revision (p. 224)

trailer bills (p. 224)

Big Five (p. 224)

two-thirds requirement (p. 225)

cruise control spending, entitlements (p. 225)

third rail issues (p. 226)

ballot box budgeting (p. 226)

earmarking (p. 226)

regressive and progressive taxes (p. 228)

general obligation and revenue bonds (p. 232)

structural deficits (p. 233)

parcel taxes (p. 235)

REVIEW QUESTIONS

1. Describe the general characteristics of public budgets.

2. How do state and local economies affect state and local budgets?

3. How does the California budget process work? What constrains the process?

4. Using various criteria to evaluate taxes, describe the major sources of state and local revenue in California.

5. Describe the Big Three of California spending. How do cities and counties spend their revenue?

6. How does budget policy in California describe the "cost of diversity" and reinforce the theme of hyperpluralism?

7. Which budget reforms do you think are the most necessary? Which ones are most achievable?

WEB ACTIVITIES

California State Department of Finance
(www.dof.ca.gov/)
This agency advises the governor on the annual budget and makes available numerous documents on past and current state budgets and the state's economy.

Legislative Analyst's Office
(www.lao.ca.gov/)
This site provides nonpartisan, authoritative analyses of the state budget and other policy issues.

Advocacy Groups
California Budget Project
(www.cbp.org/)
This group conducts various budget studies and advocates fiscal equity and fairness in California.

California Taxpayers Association
(www.caltax.org/)
This organization's mission is to "protect taxpayers from unnecessary taxes."

NOTES

1. Aaron Wildavsky, *The New Politics of the Budgetary Process* (Glenview, IL: Scott, Foresman and Co., 1988), p. 2.

2. Legislative Analyst's Office, *CAL Facts: 2011* (Sacramento: Legislative Analyst's Office, 2011) and *CAL Facts: California's Economy and Budget in Perspective* (Sacramento: Legislative Analyst's Office, 2006).

3. Deborah Reed and Jennifer Cheng, *Racial and Ethnic Wage Gaps in the California Labor Market* (San Francisco: Public Policy Institute of California, 2003) and California Budget Project, *New Data Show That California's Income Gaps Continue to Widen* (Sacramento: California Budget Project, 2009) (Accessed at www.cbp.org/).

4. *Numbers in the News: The California Economy in 2010* (Palo Alto: Center for the Continuing Study of the California Economy, March 2011).

5. Richard Krolack, *California Budget Dance: Issues and Process,* 2nd ed. (Sacramento: California Journal Press, 1994), p. 49.

6. "The State That Tied Its Own Hands," *The Economist* 304 (July 11, 1987), p. 30.

7. Tony Quinn, "Origins of a Stalemate," *California Journal of Politics and Public Policy* 1 (2009) (www.bepresscom/cjpp/).

8. California Constitution Revision Commission, *Final Report and Recommendations to the Governor and the Legislature* (Sacramento: California Constitution Revision Commission, 1996), p. 10.

9. Quoted in Deb Kollars, "A Labyrinth of Spending: Special Programs Have Grown into Vast Bureaucratic Jungle," *Sacramento Bee,* February 2, 2003.

10. Jack Chang, "National Anti-Tax Group Warns California Republicans to Stick to Pledge," *Sacramento Bee* (January 6, 2011).

11. John G. Matsusaka, "Direct Democracy and Fiscal Gridlock: Have Voter Initiatives Paralyzed the California Budget?" *State Politics and Policy Quarterly* 5 (Fall 2005), pp. 248–264.

12. Legislative Analyst's Office, *Proposition 98 Primer* (Sacramento: Legislative Analyst's Office, February, 2005). (www.lao.ca.gov/2005_98_primer/).

13. California Budget Project, *Who Pays Taxes in California?* (Sacramento: California Budget Project, April 2011). (www.cbp.org/).

14. *PPIC Statewide Survey: Californians and Their Government* (San Francisco: Public Policy Institute of California, January 2011).

15. For more on the state lottery, go to www.calottery.com/. This official Web site includes considerable data on the lottery's operation and its funding of public education. Buried deep in the site is a piece on the problem of chronic gambling.

16. Steve Wiegand, "Slumping California Lottery Searches for a Winning Hand," *Sacramento Bee,* August 17, 2008.

17. To locate current ratings, go to www.treasurer.ca.gov/ratings/.

18. Isaac William Martin and Jack Citrin, eds. *After the Tax Revolt: California's Proposition 13 Turns 30* (Berkeley: Institute of Governmental Studies Press, 2009).

19. Bruce E. Cain and Roger Noll, "Institutional Causes of California's Budget Problem," *California Journal of Politics and Public Policy* 2:3 (2010). (www.bepress.com/cjpp/vol2/iss3/1).

20. Mark D. Camillo and Mervin Field, "Voters Express Views on Dealing with the State's Huge Budget Deficit," *Field Poll Release #2368* (San Francisco: Field Corporation, March 16, 2011). (www.field.com/fieldpollonline/).

21. State Controller, *Cities Annual Report, Fiscal Year 2008–2009* (Sacramento: California State Controller, 2011).

22. State Controller, *Counties Annual Report, Fiscal Year 2008–2009* (Sacramento: California State Controller, 2011).

23. Richard Krolack, *California's Budget Dance,* p. 111.

24. *A Budget For All Californians: Improving the Transparency and Accountability of the State Budget* (Sacramento: California Budget Project, 2006), and Public Policy Institute of California, *California Budget* (San Francisco: Public Policy Institute of California, 2011).

25. John Decker, *California in the Balance: Why Budgets Matter* (Berkeley: Institute of Governmental Studies Press, 2009).

12

✳

Policies Stemming
from Growth

Introduction: Growth in California

Why California Grew

The Drumbeat of Growth

Structuring Local Growth

Slowing Growth in California

Water: Making Growth Possible

Storing Water

Moving Water

Water Policy Alternatives

Housing: For Many, the Impossible Dream

The California Dream

Housing Policy as "Filter Down"

The Housing Crisis and Beyond

Transportation: Stuck in Traffic

The Problem

California's Transportation Policies

Energy, Environment, and Climate Change

Energy

Environment and Climate Change

Policy Options

Conclusion: A New Growth Policy for California?

Key Terms

Review Questions

Web Activities

Notes

IN BRIEF

Many state and local policies in California stem from the state's incessant population growth. Chapter 12 frames the issues of water, housing, transportation, and the environment in terms of the growth that makes them policy problems in the first place.

For decades, policymakers not only accommodated existing growth, they "built" a California that would actually encourage future growth. A political division of labor made new development relatively painless. Local governments approved individual projects, while the state provided the infrastructure required. As growth continued, so did its negative effects. The result was reduced public support for the policies and taxes that had made growth possible. Political pressures in recent years have pitted Californian against Californian: farmers and city dwellers over water, new and old residents over housing, freeway drivers and mass transit advocates over traffic gridlock, and environmentalists and business over pollution.

Many of these policy problems stem from basic assumptions deeply engrained in California and national politics: that water is "free," housing is a private sector activity, widespread car ownership is a given, and government is responsible to clean up private sector-generated pollution. Recent attempts to solve these policy problems have included market approaches to water availability and environmental pollution, plus modest public investment in rail transit. Affordable housing will likely remain an elusive goal. Policymakers have focused more on building the infrastructure needed to accommodate growth than on controlling the growth itself. In a diverse and hyperpluralistic state, this may be all policymakers can do or hope to do.

INTRODUCTION: GROWTH IN CALIFORNIA

In a public television documentary on the habitat of the bald eagle, narrator George Page declared, "California is where America meets its limit, a fitting place to realize that growth cannot extend itself forever. Growth itself has its limits." Many Californians would agree. In their view, the state's quality of life is gradually being undermined by the very growth that had sustained it for so many years. Ominous warning signs abound: air quality improvements offset by still more cars, traffic gridlock in metropolitan areas, fertile farmland giving way to housing subdivisions and shopping malls, and pockets of smog throughout the Golden State. Furthermore, there is worrisome evidence that global warming is affecting California's environment, possibly resulting in chronic water shortages. The recent Great Recession added to these challenges. It slowed economic expansion, decimated jobs, and virtually halted housing construction—the raw fuels of growth—but it also hampered state and local government efforts to address past growth and what would assuredly be future growth, especially in inland California.

This chapter discusses growth and its ramifications in the Golden State. Numerous policy issues important to Californians, such as housing, transportation, water, and environmental pollution, are rooted in population growth. We will look at the nature of California's growth, how specific growth-induced problems are addressed, and the efforts to manage growth itself. The central question is this: *How do California policymakers accommodate current and future growth without (1) degrading various qualities of life sought by diverse groups and (2) endangering the state's once-pristine environment?* This question brims with conflict ranging from the highest levels of state government down to interneighbor disputes over lifestyles, cars, noise, and fences. It also reflects the inability of a complex, fragmented, and hyperpluralistic political system to address, solve, or even keep pace with the problems that stem from growth.

An undercurrent in this chapter deals with evolving and diverse notions of what "quality of life" means. From the problematic neighbor who defines this term differently than the rest of the block to state and local debates on the subject, "quality of life" has come to represent alternative perspectives on what living in California was, is, and should be like. In the decades to come, as Californians become more numerous, culturally diverse, and politically divided, competing qualities of life will haunt, challenge, and elude policymakers.

Why California Grew

In California's history, population growth has resulted from several factors in and out of government. California boasted a favorable climate and scenic environment in which to live, work, and play. Gold Rush miners inundated parts of California, and others were lured by savvy marketing efforts of the state's railroads, citrus growers, and real estate entrepreneurs. Local governments boosted their own locales while state government accommodated the pro-growth interests of the railroads and other industries. World War II brought increased federal spending and wartime employees to California. Growth-hungry city officials encouraged and enabled military-related growth.[1] After the war, military bases remained open and military spending continued.

California developed a de facto pro-growth policy in the postwar period. A statewide water system, new highways, and a complex master plan for higher education set the stage for future growth while accommodating growth pressures at the time. These bipartisan efforts, supported by business and labor, created not only a physical infrastructure to support more households but also a social infrastructure to support people's rising expectations. A new statewide political consensus viewed growth as positive and beneficial. In addition, national policies in effect subsidized growth in California by helping to fund the Central Valley Project (a massive water project) and the state's interstate highway system. During this pro-growth era, new housing

kept pace with population growth. Much of it was suburban, low in density, and relatively cheap, considering the high demand for it. Necessary infrastructure (roads, highways, water projects, sewer systems, and schools) was funded through generous federal subsidies, state bonds, and growing general fund revenues. For decades, accommodating growth was relatively painless and uncontroversial.

The Drumbeat of Growth

Although rates of population growth in California fluctuate, this can be said: The state's long-term growth has been and will continue to climb upward. California's 2010 population of nearly 38,000,000 is only one aspect of the state's growth challenge. The state's compound annual growth rate in the last 50 years has been more than twice the national rate. In 1940, California's population was 5.2 percent of the nation's; by 2010, it was 12 percent. Although the annual growth rate dropped from 1.6 percent to under one percent in recent years, that still meant the projected growth of 340,000 per year—over 900 per day (see Figure 12.1).

Growth rates vary within California. In recent years, California's inland counties have experienced the highest population growth rates. Here growth was due to natural increases, urban and suburban "flight" (people fleeing crime and congestion), and an influx of retirees. This trend will continue in the future[2] (see Figure 12.2). But in terms of absolute population increases, the largest numbers have been in the coastal and near-coastal counties of California including Los Angeles, San Diego, Orange, San Bernardino, and Riverside counties.

The impacts of the state's historic growth have concerned many Californians. Beginning in the 1960s, some questioned how long rapid growth could continue without threatening the state's quality of life.[3] By the 1970s, the dominant growth consensus began to crumble. Why? First, California's political leaders sought to downsize government's role in fostering the state's growth. Governor Ronald Reagan (R, 1967–1974), while

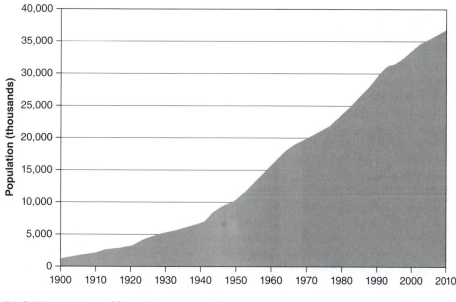

F I G U R E 12.1   California's Drumbeat of Growth

Questions: Are future growth rates destined look like past growth rates? Why? Why not?

SOURCE: California Department of Finance, U.S. Census Bureau, *Just the Facts: California's Population* (San Francisco: Public Policy Institute of California, 2011).

not objecting to growth itself, opposed the "big government" that growth made possible. His successor, Jerry Brown (D, 1975–1982), reduced infrastructure investment, especially in highway construction and large water projects.

Second, economic restructuring altered the prospect of unlimited growth without apparent cost. California's heavy manufacturing base declined, as did growth in personal income. So did taxpayer willingness to fund more public improvements. Proposition 13, which substantially cut property taxes in 1978, reinforced this unwillingness. It also cut funds local governments relied on to provide the infrastructure required by new development. Instead, developers were charged for infrastructure costs, which, of course, were passed on to new-home owners. Pressure to develop farmland near cities grew. As one Lompoc, California, farmer put it: "I could make a whole lot more money growin' condos than farming." As environmental public awareness increased, development in ecologically sensitive areas (such as waterfronts, flood plains, and

estuaries) became politically unacceptable. Voters approved the *Coastal Act of 1972* to limit coastal development where land use demand always exceeded supply. By the 2000s, Californians were of two minds on growth. Many favored more commercial development while wishing to discourage the added growth that accompanies such development.[4]

Third, settlement patterns fed a popular desire to limit growth. Although California was not as densely populated as New Jersey (239 versus 1,195 people per square mile in 2010), Californians *perceived* that they were overcrowded. This was because most of them lived in the state's coastal or near-coastal counties. Indeed, nearly three fourths of the state's population in 2010 lived in only 8 of 58 counties (San Diego, Orange, Los Angeles, Riverside, San Bernardino, Santa Clara, Alameda, and Sacramento). In recent years, the highly developed coastal strip has both lengthened and thickened. An urban corridor now extends from Santa Barbara to Ensenada,

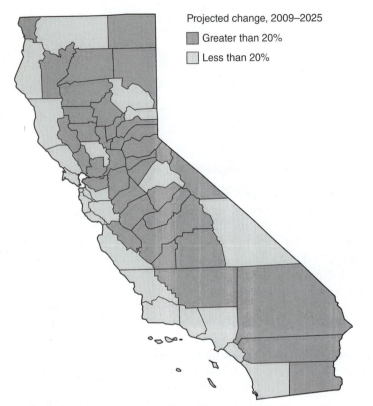

Projected change, 2009–2025

■ Greater than 20%

□ Less than 20%

FIGURE 12.2 California's Growth: Inland and Coastal Contrasts

Question: What will be the impact of greater growth in inland California?

SOURCE: California Department of Finance; Hans Johnson, *California Population: Planning for a Better Future* (San Francisco: Public Policy Institute of California, January 2011), p. 3.

Mexico—arguably the nation's first bi-national megalopolis. Furthermore, development has moved inland in the three largest metropolitan areas (San Francisco, Los Angeles, and San Diego). Today, "edge cities" mix high-density commercial, professional, and residential uses while creating environmental impacts often beyond the control of any single government. The Los Angeles Basin boasts 26 such edge cities, the largest concentration of them in the nation.[5] These growth patterns result in some of the nation's costliest housing and busiest freeways.

Structuring Local Growth

Population increases are not the whole story. Californians equate "growth" with new housing projects, industrial parks, and shopping centers—decisions that are local in nature. How are these decisions made, and who makes them?

Land Use Planning Cities and counties have planning or community development departments staffed by professional planners. They process various land use proposals, from simple room additions to massive multiuse projects. They make recommendations to a planning commission, which in turn advises a city council or county board of supervisors. They comment on the overall merits of a project, assess its environmental impact, and place conditions on approval to reduce those impacts. At both levels, public hearings allow citizens to comment on the project. After a project is approved, a developer must begin construction within a certain time period. During construction, numerous inspections make sure a project conforms to the many building standards and conditions placed on it. Developers pay **impact fees** to "mitigate" the impacts of development—new roads, water systems, sewers, even schools—costs once borne by taxpayers.

Tools Planners Use   A wide variety of policies govern project approvals. For instance, each California community has a state-required **general plan** or overall blueprint for the physical development of the area. Such plans contain general goals for future development, zoning maps, and other maps projecting future development. These documents must contain various "elements" or chapters that address land use types, traffic circulation, housing, conservation, open space, and safety. General plans do not determine or predict when growth will occur. Timing depends on economic conditions, developer initiative, and decisions by local governments.

Other planning tools abound. **Zoning ordinances** divide areas into districts to regulate the type and density of development. A typical zoning map will contain several residential zones (from low-density single family homes to high-density condominiums or apartments) in addition to commercial areas, manufacturing areas, parks, open space, and other uses. These ordinances establish minimum lot sizes, setback rules (distances between a structure and a lot line or the street), maximum densities, height and bulk requirements for structures, and parking and landscaping requirements. **Subdivision regulations** dictate how a parcel of land can be divided into smaller lots including minimum lot sizes, street standards, and other public improvements required of developers. Planners also make use of statewide **uniform building codes**, which regulate the physical components of construction (roofing, heating, electric wiring, ventilation, sanitation, and earthquake resistance). **Planned unit developments (PUDs)** integrate many of these tools for housing developments or more complex projects. They allow developers to be more innovative and grant local officials more flexibility and control.

These policies do not necessarily appease residents who adamantly oppose specific projects or the overall momentum of growth in their communities. How do local officials address their concerns? First, they can control the timing of development by imposing temporary building moratoria or annual housing quotas. Sometimes, economic conditions play a role as well as we saw with a recession-era decline in construction activity. Second, zoning ordinances can also be modified through "down zoning" (reducing legally allowed building densities on undeveloped land). Because down zoning often spreads remaining development across more land, it can result in *more* traffic congestion, not less.

Slowing Growth in California

Opposition to development in California is common, especially along California's coast. It reflects a desire to improve quality of life and a desire to slow down the pace of growth. These concerns ebb and flow with the relative health of the economy.

Quality of Life Concerns   Numerous public opinion surveys have documented this concern about development and its impacts. In a 2001 poll, 60 percent of California adults thought their communities were growing rapidly. They thought that the negative consequences of rapid growth included traffic congestion, high housing costs, urban sprawl, loss of open space, and pollution. Consequently, most respondents thought that the Golden State would be a less desirable place to live in the future.[6] In recent years, these quality of life concerns have extended to a variety of economic issues beyond the control of land use policymakers, including heavy job losses, the crisis in home mortgages, and resulting bank foreclosures.

Slow Growth Politics   Voicing these concerns, various groups and individuals across the state have advocated various growth control measures. They have included requiring developers to fund infrastructure improvements, limiting growth rates, reducing zoning densities, prohibiting development on agricultural and rural land, purchasing open space, and subjecting development decisions to city- or county-wide voter approval. City councils and county boards of supervisors enact some of these controlled growth or "smart growth" policies but upset voters initiate others, a practice dubbed "ballot box planning." Some initiatives address growth in general (e.g., creating urban growth boundaries) or seek to veto particular projects (e.g., a new Wal-Mart store). Although critics decry the shortcomings of citizen initiatives, they do give voice to local slow-growth sentiments and provide a check on local planners and developers.[7]

What explains this desire to limit growth? Several factors emerge. First, urban Californians indeed experience daily the impacts of growth; the freeways they ply daily seem more like parking lots. They view once-pristine open space now covered with housing tracts and shopping centers. Ironically, in some communities, no-growth views are shared even by newcomers. Second, many Californians seem ambivalent regarding growth. They may favor the idea of affordable housing but oppose its actual construction in their communities.

In one survey, two-thirds of respondents believed low-density family housing should be encouraged, yet also believed suburban sprawl is a very or somewhat important problem in their region.[8] Third, opposition to growth often centers around specific projects close to home. Typical controversies involve **LULUs** (locally undesirable land uses) such as landfills, toxic cleanup sites, drug abuse centers, and many traffic-generating projects. Even places of worship and schools may be opposed as LULUs. Downtown merchants may oppose the development of competing shopping malls, warehouse retailers, and factory outlet stores. Individual homeowners may fear the potential loss of property values. Common strategies used by **NIMBYs** ("not in my back yard" opponents) may include circulating antidevelopment petitions, packing public hearings with project opponents, placing initiatives on the ballot, and filing lawsuits.

WATER: MAKING GROWTH POSSIBLE

One way or another, a variety of public policy issues can be traced to long-term population growth in California. Some policies have made growth feasible, such as the provision of water throughout the state. Other policies such as housing, transportation, and environmental protection address the impacts of growth. In this chapter we explore several growth-related issues, but water comes first for a simple reason: Increasing the supply of water and moving it around has been a necessary prerequisite to California's growth. Water drew people to the state and determined where they would settle.

California is really two states divided by water: Northern California has it, and Southern California wants it. Yet, in a sense, all of California is semi-arid. In response, California policymakers have always assumed that *water not used by people is water wasted*—an assumption that defies the state's physical geography. Rain and snow are more frequent and plentiful in Northern California. As a result, the Sacramento-San Joaquin Delta region has been called "the great Central Valley mixing basin where a hundred rivers become one."[9] Once an inland sea, it now is a labyrinthine estuary of sloughs, waterways, and levees that channel drinking water to over half the state's population. In contrast, Southern California claims only two percent of the state's natural water supply. But that never stopped its impulse to grow. Southern California possessed an asset of its own: a pleasant climate. Several mountain ranges plus gentle coastal breezes protected Southern California from the heat and grit of the desert interior, creating a Mediterranean climate. The only resource missing was water. But as novelist Edward Abbey observed, "There is no lack of water [in the desert], unless you try to establish a city where no city should be."[10]

Storing Water

One marvel of California water is how it is stored for later use. California winters can be wet, but not all winters are equally wet. California endures cycles of wet years and droughts, which can be terrifying (see Box 12.1). Winter precipitation is saved in three great storage systems, two of which are nature's own. First is the Sierra Nevada snowpack. Some of the world's heaviest snowfall can occur

---

B o x 12.1   CALIFORNIA VOICES: Steinbeck on California Water

The water came in a thirty-year cycle. There would be five or six wet and wonderful years when there might be nineteen to twenty-five inches of rain, and the land would shout with grass. Then would come six or seven pretty good years of twelve or sixteen inches of rain. And then the dry years would come, and sometimes there would be only seven or eight inches of rain. The land dried up and grasses headed out miserably a few inches high and great bare scabby places appeared in the valley. The live oaks got a crusty look and the sagebrush was grey. The land cracked and the springs dried up and the cattle listlessly nibbled dry twigs. Then the farmers and the ranchers would be filled with disgust for the Salinas Valley. The cows would grow thin and sometimes starve to death. People would have to haul water in barrels to their farms just for drinking. Some families would sell out for nearly nothing and move away. And it never failed that during the dry years the people forgot about the rich years, and during the wet years they lost all memory of the dry years. It was always that way.

Question: To what extent does Steinbeck's observation explain actual water policy and politics in California?

SOURCE: John Steinbeck, *East of Eden* (New York: Viking Press, 1952), pp. 5–6.

---

in the Sierras, creating a year-round source of run-off water. Second is the state's underground water basins or aquifers (the airspace in soil and geologic formations displaced by water). Groundwater accounts for one-third of California's water supply. A third storage system is artificial, consisting of numerous reservoirs—surface lakes created by damming rivers and capturing run-off from adjacent mountain ranges. Such reservoirs dot the California landscape. These three storage systems face dangers from both periodic drought and incessant population growth. Due to less frequent precipitation and warmer winters, scientists predict that by 2050, the Sierra snowpack could shrink by 25 percent, thereby reducing flows to the reservoirs. Even with adequate inflows, reservoirs lose water to evaporation and become choked with silt. Underground aquifers pose their own challenges. When they are pumped excessively, "overdrafting" occurs. This not only lowers the water table but allows agricultural chemicals to invade rural aquifers and salt water to invade coastal valley aquifers.

Moving Water

Some say California water is never where you want it, when you want it. But Californians were never deterred by that fact. As water law developed, so did various water rights. If you lived on top of or adjacent to a source of water, it was yours (**riparian rights**). If you were the first to find or "create" a source of water, it was yours (through **prior appropriation**). If you used someone else's water with their knowledge, it was yours (**prescriptive rights**). Combined, these rights encouraged the movement of water throughout the state. California's earliest water projects were localized irrigation systems consisting of earthen dams and even hand-dug canals and ditches. In time, these efforts were dwarfed by four immense projects that would forever change the face of California: the Owens Valley and Colorado River Projects, the Central Valley Project, and the State Water Project. The politics behind these projects reminds one of Mark Twain's observation: "In the West, whiskey is for drinking, water is for fighting." As we survey these projects, as portrayed in Figure 12.3, remember that water is measured in acre feet. An acre-foot is the amount of water needed to fill one acre to a depth of one foot, enough to supply two urban households.

Water for Los Angeles The City of Angels' unquenchable thirst began in the late 1880s. Through civic boosterism, Los Angeles's population was booming, but a lengthy drought left city officials and business interests desperate. Combining controversy and intrigue, Los Angeles interests

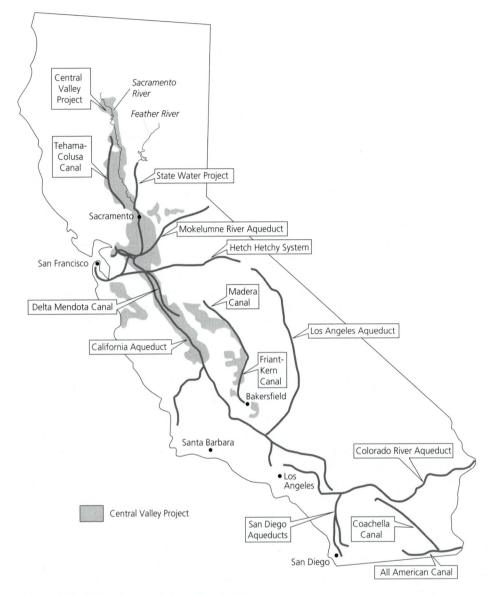

FIGURE 12.3 California's Plumbing System

quietly purchased land in the Owens Valley east of the Sierra Nevada range. The goal? To divert the Owens River through 233 miles of aqueducts, tunnels, and pumping stations. In 1905, the *Los Angeles Times* audaciously announced the news: "Titanic Project to Give the City a River."[11] Drought-

panicked Los Angelenos approved the bond measures required to build the Los Angeles Aqueduct. The project created one prerequisite to future growth—*surplus water* (more than people immediately needed). But tapping the Owens Valley was not enough, not for Los Angeles. Fueled by now-permanent growth, more bond issues, a cooperative federal government, and the belief that anything was possible, the city proceeded to harness the Colorado River. The Hoover Dam, completed in 1941, channeled the Colorado River to Los Angeles via a maze of dams, canals, tunnels, reservoirs, and pumping stations. In addition to water, this project created a second prerequisite to urban growth: *electrical power.* The Metropolitan Water District of Southern California was formed to build and operate the project. In concert with cities, counties, and other water districts, this giant water wholesaler "became and remains a Southern California growth machine." Northern Californians tend to criticize L.A.'s thirst, but they have played the same game. In 1913, San Francisco dammed up the Tuolumne River inside Yosemite Park (over naturalist John Muir's objections), establishing its own permanent water supply. Because it "created" more water than it could ever use, the city was able to sell surplus water (60 percent of total supplies) to other Bay Area communities—spurring *their* growth.

Central Valley Project   In contrast to Southern California, the state's heartland is laced by two sizable river systems, the Sacramento and the San Joaquin, plus their tributaries. As crops replaced native grasses and national markets replaced local ones, valley farmers yearned for a steady, weatherproof water supply. As in Los Angeles, a lengthy drought forced political action. In the case of the valley, underground overpumping provided the impetus for the 1931 *State Water Plan.* The 1936 Central Valley Project (CVP) was an effort to implement the plan. The U.S. Bureau of Reclamation assumed control after the state failed to finance it, and the bureau has run it ever since. The largest federal water project in the country, the CVP consists of an intricate network of rivers, dams, aqueducts, and power plants stretching nearly 500 miles from Shasta Dam in the north to Bakersfield in the south. It supplies about 20 percent of California's developed water and at heavily subsidized rates. According to one report, the average price for irrigation water from the CVP was less than two percent of what Southern Californians

pay for drinking water.[12] Cheap, plentiful, agricultural water has skewed its uses. One crop, alfalfa, consumes more water than the residents of Los Angeles and the Bay Area *combined.*

State Water Project   These projects did not end the political battles over water. California's postwar growth continued unchecked. Conflicts rose between urban and rural users, irrigation and flood control interests, and a confusing patchwork of water agencies. No single state agency had the power to referee this hyperpluralistic water anarchy. In the 1950s, a new Department of Water Resources published the *California Water Plan,* a visionary document that detailed the State Water Project (SWP). It clearly recognized Californians' penchant to live where water is scarce. A massive bond measure to fund the plan barely passed in 1960, thanks to overwhelming support in Southern California. Its first project was the Feather River Project, which "tamed" the flood-prone Feather River at Oroville and moved its water through the Delta and further south via the California Aqueduct. The project moves water a total of 700 miles through 19 reservoirs, 17 pumping stations, 8 hydroelectric power plants, and about 660 miles of open canals and pipelines. Of the contracted water supply, 70 percent goes to urban users and 30 percent to agricultural users.

In the 1980s, another north/south water battle focused on the Sacramento-San Joaquin River Delta, the largest estuary in the Western United States and an indispensible hub of California's water supply. The trick has always been to use and move Sacramento River water through the Delta without allowing seawater from San Francisco Bay to intrude and endanger farmland. To solve this problem, the California Department of Water Resources proposed a "peripheral canal" to channel fresh water east of the Delta and directly into the California Aqueduct. After years of study, the legislature approved the project in 1980. An anti-canal referendum drive was launched by two strange political bedfellows: environmentalists concerned about the Delta's fragile ecology and large-scale farmers upset at probable water price hikes. In 1982,

California voters defeated the canal project by a 2 to 1 margin; Northern Californians by a 9 to 1 margin. In the late 2000s, the idea of a peripheral canal resurfaced, now to save fish populations endangered by the enormous pumps used to move Delta water. In addition to benefiting the fish, a new canal would protect southbound water from aging earthen levees and prevent future saltwater intrusion. Supporters and opponents once again divided along north/south lines. Nonetheless, after extensive study, researchers have concluded that a peripheral canal is the most cost effective way to promote a reliable water supply and the environmental sustainability of the Delta ecosystem. In the 1990s, a federal partnership (CALFED) was formed to coordinate efforts among the Delta's constituencies. In 2009, the legislature updated these efforts with the passage of the Delta Reform Act. This law established the Delta Stewardship Council, a planning group charged with two coequal goals: 1) providing a more reliable water supply for California, and 2) protecting, restoring, and enhancing the Delta ecosystem.[13]

Water Policy Alternatives

Continuous population growth has matched every large-scale water project in California. But how many more dams, canals, and reservoirs can the state afford and the people support, given heightened competition for limited tax dollars? Adding more surface storage (dams and reservoirs) has met more opposition than in the past. Some experts believe added reservoirs will generate less "new" water than advocates claim, especially if the Sierra snowpack shrinks. The construction and environmental costs are substantial as well. Average Californians appear split on which approach is best. Fifty percent of poll respondents feel the state should emphasize water efficiencies; 43 percent prefer building new storage capacity.[14] These views have been mirrored in the state legislature where many Republican members favor new reservoirs and Democratic members prefer conservation-oriented approaches.

Many experts now believe a multifaceted "portfolio" approach is the most cost effective and politically feasible way to plan for California's water future. This policy mix should include:

1. Employing urban water efficiencies (new plumbing codes, improved technology, and tiered water rates to discourage waste);

2. Greater use of recycling (using reclaimed but nonpotable water for irrigation and landscaping);

3. Groundwater "banking" (better management of underground aquifers, especially in the Central Valley, where progress has been slow); and

4. Taking climate change into account (due to potentially higher sea levels and flooding).[15]

In some respects, water is a highly contentious issue in California not only due to its variable supply but the hyperpluralistic nature of California politics. Agricultural interests, urban users, and defenders of endangered fish populations (water's newest constituency) all have different perspectives on water and its provision. They also employ their own channels of influence at the state, regional, and local levels. Given current and growing demands on California's arguably finite and potentially reduced supply of water, this commodity that made the state what it is will continue to engender political conflict. Time will tell whether California can move beyond what one columnist called "California's perpetual water gridlock."[16]

HOUSING: FOR MANY, THE IMPOSSIBLE DREAM

If providing water to a growing and thirsty state seems challenging, consider the Golden State's version of the American Dream—owning a home. Here we consider the challenge of providing adequate, affordable housing for all Californians.

The California Dream

Although the American Dream has meant home ownership, it acquired a semirural dimension in

California. According to California historian Kevin Starr, "At the core of the [California] dream was the hope for a special relationship to nature."[17] In terms of housing, this meant a single-family, detached home with landscaped front, rear, and side yards, and plenty of privacy. The ideal was a residential suburb, far from the congestion, filth, and heterogeneity of the central city.

With the blessings of local government, single-family developments spilled across the landscape. The gridiron plan (resembling a checkerboard), considered efficient by American developers, left little room for common community uses such as neighborhood parks. This dispersed, low-density pattern occurred in California just when the automobile industry itself was expanding. Affordable cars became necessities as Californians consumed one housing tract after another, well away from where they worked. Retail businesses and even factories followed homeowners to suburbia. In the process, the idealized rural lifestyle became increasingly elusive, as if just beyond the next golden hill. For a period of time, the California middle-class "dream house" became ever larger—more and larger rooms, multiple baths, and roomy garages.

Housing Policy as "Filter Down"

Although the federal Housing Act of 1949 envisioned "a decent home and suitable living environment for every American family," governments (federal, state, and local) have not, nor ever will, built much housing. True, federally guaranteed mortgages have helped promote middle-class housing and some publicly owned rental housing exists. But for the most part, it is a private sector activity. California's "policy" has largely mirrored the nation's: *Build housing for the haves and their housing will filter down to the have-nots.* **Filter down policy** assumes that, as people on the upper rungs of the economic ladder move up to better homes, the ones they vacate will be made available to those on the lower rungs. Private builders propose and construct the housing, and private lenders finance its purchase. Local governments determine and enforce development standards. A smattering of

government aid assists a small percentage of the have-nots in their quest for housing.

Does filter-down work? Yes, if there is equilibrium between the supply of housing and the demand for it. But this equilibrium has been rare in California due to several factors. First, developers gravitate to housing that local governments will approve. Communities often resist less costly starter housing or apartment buildings and developers understandably prefer more profitable higher end housing. Also, locally imposed "pay to play" impact fees can add tens of thousands of dollars to the cost of a house. Second, California's constant population growth keeps demand for housing high, even when economic conditions retard construction or put home loans out of reach. This results in residential overcrowding, home sharing by both families and individuals, and an inability for some to move.

The Housing Crisis and Beyond

This private sector-dominated system imploded in the late 2000s, dashing the American Dream, let alone the California Dream, for many. How did it happen? As more and more people sought homeownership, home prices increased. As prices rose, others thought they also needed to buy or homeownership would forever be out of reach. Californians stretched their own finances to enter the housing market.[18] This drove prices still higher, resulting in what experts believed to be an unsustainable housing "bubble." Lending practices made matters worse. Many lenders aggressively marketed subprime loans (adjustable rate mortgages with initially low interest rates) to many first-time homebuyers who would not have qualified for traditional fixed-rate loans. As a consequence, homeowners in many places were spending upwards of 50 percent of their incomes on housing. When these mortgage rates adjusted upward or when the inevitable balloon payments came due, some borrowers had to default on their loans. Lenders were forced to foreclose those properties, take title to them, and accept huge loan losses in the process (see Photo 12.1). Thinking home values would rise indefinitely, other homeowners had borrowed from their

Courtesy of David G. Lawrence

The Housing Crisis Next Door
This Riverside, California, house was one of over a million-plus foreclosed homes in the state during the housing crisis.

home equity to finance second homes, cars, boats, college tuition—you name it. As the real estate market began to stagnate and home values dropped, some Californians found their loan balances were more than their homes were worth. Eventually, this created a backlog of unsold homes and a precipitous drop in the production of new housing. Many other Californians encountered their own housing crisis when they became unemployed.

In the aftermath of this housing crisis, many homeowners became renters. They would sit out the California Dream at least for a while. Aghast at the miseries faced by homeowners, many renters vowed to continue renting, concluding that the California Dream was more of a nightmare. The one silver lining in this crisis was that it lowered home prices and interest rates, thereby putting many homes within reach of many first time homebuyers. Tightened loan requirements limited new borrowers to those better qualified to afford home ownership in the first place.

As the housing crisis subsides over time, two interconnected housing challenges will continue to face California: affordability and supply. If we use the U.S. Department of Housing and Urban Development definition of affordability—spending no more than 30 percent of household income on housing—much of California's housing remains unaffordable. This is especially true of renters, low-income residents, and first-time homebuyers. In the first quarter of 2011, 72 percent of all first-time homebuyers could afford entry-level homes in California. This figure is somewhat higher inland and lower along the coast. But only 53 percent of households could afford a median priced home in the state. That figure drops to 39 percent for the San Francisco Bay Area.[19]

Why is California housing so expensive? First, there is a shortage of appropriately zoned land, especially along California's highly desirable coast. This has forced many who work in coastal cities to move inland, driving upward home prices in those areas. Second, many communities actually resist the construction of new housing, including "affordable" housing like rental units or "starter" housing. Opponents disfavor housing on flat land (because agricultural land needs preservation) *or* on hillsides (because of fire and flooding dangers). Third, many city officials believe housing does not generate enough property taxes to pay for the services it requires. They prefer sales tax-laden retail uses (such as auto malls and shopping centers) that require minimal public services. As noted earlier, this has been called the **fiscalization of land use**. This phenomenon spans the state and the consequences are dire. Renters are particularly vulnerable because many are lower or moderate income individuals and families. Rents often rise faster than their incomes, forcing them to spend even more of their incomes on housing. Also, because so many homeowners became renters during the recession, the rental markets tightened and became more competitive.[20]

TRANSPORTATION: STUCK IN TRAFFIC

California's legendary love affair with the automobile poses seemingly insurmountable challenges related to the state's growth. Consider this: One federal agency estimates that the average Los Angeleno wastes 38 hours per year in traffic; in San Francisco, it is 30 hours, in San Diego, 29.[21] Freeway speeds are slowing, and, on many urban freeways, the "rush hour" itself has disappeared into a cloud of heavy traffic—all day, every day. A single accident can tie up traffic for hours more. Bus and rail transit riders are not exempt from traffic delays. In fact, simple door-to-door commute times are longer for bus riders than automobile drivers. Smaller California communities also experience congestion as growing numbers of vehicles outpace narrow roads and surface streets. Throughout California, the number of vehicle miles traveled will continue to outpace both population growth and state highway capacity (see Figure 12.4).

The Problem

Although traffic congestion is easy to see and experience, it is a complex policy problem. Three factors help explain why.

Personal Choice True, Californians love their automobiles. Before widespread car ownership, streetcars and trolleys augmented walking, and living "in town" was actually desirable. The automobile essentially reversed those preferences. The automobile symbolized American individualism and personal choice. As a 1926 *Los Angeles Times* editorial put it, "How can one pursue happiness with any swifter and surer means than the automobile?" In modern times, acquiring one has become a rite of passage to adulthood. For many California college and university students, "wheels" are as fixed an expense as tuition, room, board, and books.

There is no escaping the congestion that results from these personal choices. Given the proliferation of car ownership, one household may claim at least one vehicle per driver. People can feel the effect. Once-picturesque residential streets are lined bumper to bumper with cars, more than city hall planners ever anticipated. Lengthy commutes may be the logical extension of personal choice in individualistic California. In this view, the "jobs/housing imbalance" (as urban planners call it) is really a rational choice tradeoff between relatively

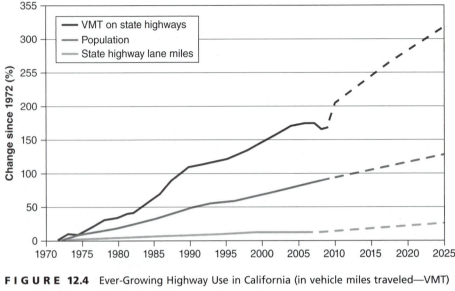

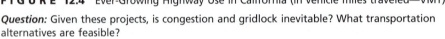

FIGURE 12.4 Ever-Growing Highway Use in California (in vehicle miles traveled—VMT)

Question: Given these projects, is congestion and gridlock inevitable? What transportation alternatives are feasible?

SOURCE: California Department of Transportation; California Department of Finance; Louise Bedsworth and Ellen Hanak, *California Transportation: Planning for a Better Future* (San Francisco: Public Policy Institute of California, June 2010).

short commutes and affordable but distant housing. So is the choice of so many to avoid mass transit (buses and rail) as inconvenient. Compared to driving personal vehicles, buses are too slow and rail stations often are too far from homes or places of employment.

Urban Development Patterns Personal choice affects traffic, but so does the legacy of urban development in California. Cities dispersed as waves of newcomers arrived. Massive highway projects connected downtowns with the suburbs. These highways once accommodated the growth of suburban commuters, but no more. Even those who found jobs closer to home discovered local surface streets as clogged as the freeways. Urban and suburban sprawl has permeated California. Dispersed development has made the construction of rail-based mass transit systems exorbitantly expensive and often unfeasible.

Environmental Effects California's motor vehicles do more than create congestion. Consider

smog. The chief component of smog is ozone (which occurs when hydrocarbons and nitrogen oxides react to sunlight). Nitrogen oxide forms during the combustion of fossil fuels. California's combination of climate and terrain creates what the Air Resources Board calls "Mother Nature's perfect smog chamber." Long before statehood, Native Americans called the Los Angeles Basin the "Land of a Thousand Smokes." California smog reaches farther than most people realize. Central Valley smog can affect sequoia seedlings in the high Sierras, and Southern California smog can reach Arizona's Grand Canyon. Vehicle smog is acute for several reasons. First, while California is only average among the states in automobile ownership, the sheer volume of vehicles—gasoline and diesel—makes California's air among the nation's dirtiest. Second, California's older vehicles can emit twice the pollution of newer ones. The worst offenders nowadays are less regulated off-road and heavy duty vehicles. They account for 80 percent of smog-forming emissions.[22]

Smog is only one vehicle-related culprit. Automobile contaminants (oil, grease, antifreeze, and small tire particles) wash into streams and waterways. Traffic noise, fumes, and toxic road dust are also major problems as ribbons of freeways snake through metropolitan areas. Asthma, heart disease, and cancer can result. According to University of Southern California researchers, the number of Californians who die each year from breathing sooty smog may be double or triple official estimates of over 9,000 per year.[23]

California's Transportation Policies

Transportation policies in California are supported by $13 billion worth of federal, state, and local funds (gas tax revenues and bond funds). It was $20 billion only a few years ago. Those dollars largely reflect a broader policy that can be summarized in one sentence. *California's transportation policy has tended to favor and accommodate the automobile.* Local governments typically approved traffic-generating developments and provided the local streets that were required. Large-scale state and national highways and the interstate system were shared responsibilities, but the primary policy-maker was the State of California. For years, even the agency titles (Highway Commission and Division of Highways) belied a policy bias. In 1923, a two-cent per gallon gasoline tax was established to finance this policy of accommodation. In the late 1940s, a new building program began, to which was added the interstate system in the 1950s. Opposition to more freeways rose on occasion. San Francisco voters rejected them in 1964. In the 1970s, Governor Brown wanted to change the state's emphasis from highways to mass transit. Yet demand for highways continued and, by the 1990s, the renamed Department of Transportation (Caltrans) was understaffed, underfunded, and backlogged with unfinished projects. While highway capacity increased by only four percent in the 1980s and 1990s, California's population grew by 50 percent. The result? Two-thirds of states spend more per capita on highways than does California.

Recent developments suggest some change in transportation policy. First, California voters have demonstrated some willingness to improve the state's transportation infrastructure. In 1990, a slim majority approved a gas tax increase (Proposition 111) and a mass transit bond measure (Proposition 108). After turning down two subsequent bond measures, voters in 2002 approved Proposition 42, which required that motor fuel taxes be used only for transportation programs. After policymakers diverted nearly all of Proposition 42 protected funds to balance state budgets, voters approved Proposition 1A in 2006. This prevented the state from borrowing (critics call it "raiding") transportation funds for other than transportation purposes. They also approved another transportation bond issue worth nearly $20 billion. At the local level, voters in more than 20 counties have approved half cent or more sales tax add-ons for city and county road improvements. Some counties have used these funds to augment state funding or finance their own local road projects.

Second, a 1989 law permitted Caltrans to build toll roads—quite a departure for a state traditionally wedded to *free*ways. Toll roads, a given in many states, are a point of contention in California. While easing some traffic congestion, these roads use so-called value pricing, which inflates tolls considerably during rush hours. Critics have called them "Lexus lanes." Despite a host of financial and jurisdictional problems, others defend toll roads as an important, if partial, answer to the backlog of state road projects. Third, efforts have begun to improve rail transit throughout California. Residents and tourists alike are familiar with BART, the Bay Area Rapid Transit system that links San Francisco with its suburbs. In more recent years, several commuter rail systems have linked outlying suburbs to Los Angeles, San Jose, and other cities. Planners have also advocated high-speed (200 mile per hour) rail service between Los Angeles and San Francisco with links to San Diego in the south and Sacramento in the north. Such a system would relieve the estimated 70 million passenger trips made each year now made by vehicles and air travel. In November 2008, voters approved another Proposition 1A, which will fund initial work on this massive effort.

All these strategies aim to alter fundamental behavior of Californians regarding transportation. The challenge in doing so is monumental. The public resists pricing tools to discourage driving (higher gas taxes and toll roads) and moving jobs, not just housing, closer to transit stations requires a daunting mix of public and private sector commitments.[24]

ENERGY, ENVIRONMENT, AND CLIMATE CHANGE

California's population growth has severely affected the state's quality of life in two broad areas: energy and environment. Energy policies address the oil, natural gas, and electricity demands of a complex, energy-hungry economy and the lifestyles of nearly 38 million residents. Environmental policies address the impacts of economic and population growth on the quality of the state's water, air, land, and natural resources. In recent years, environmental concerns have expanded to include climate change or what many now call global warming.

Energy

The electricity crisis of the early 2000s highlighted a host of energy-related concerns. Californians suffered both spiraling electricity prices and infuriating gaps in service—brownouts and blackouts. At the time, the British journal *The Economist* declared, "One of the wealthiest regions in the world is on the brink of an energy crisis of third-world proportions. How did California come to this?"[25] The answer to that question lies in a confluence of public policies and events—electricity's version of the perfect storm. The key decision was the passage of AB 1890, a 100-page law that sought to replace a patchwork of regulatory practices with an open-market approach. Electricity generation did become

more competitive, but other developments worsened the situation:

- Wholesale energy prices floated freely while policymakers froze retail prices.

- No new power plants were built to replace old plants and meet increased demand.

- Stable long-term energy contracts were disallowed.

- Energy generators and traders (like the infamous Enron Corporation) "gamed" the system by withholding capacity to spike short-term prices.

- Encouragement of energy conservation was neglected.

- The two largest public utilities became insolvent, requiring state aid to avoid bankruptcy.

In short, California's approach to deregulation failed. To many, the outcome was a bitter lesson in how *not* to deregulate. In response, Governor Gray Davis and the legislature offered still more reforms, including these: (1) using public funds to bail out financially strapped public utilities, (2) selling energy bonds to repay state costs, (3) renegotiating costly energy contracts, (4) streaming the construction of new power plants, (5) encouraging consumer conservation, and (6) researching alternative energy resources (such as solar and wind). Subsequent policies have encouraged more energy production as well as the reduction of energy waste and the development of alterative energy sources including wind, solar, biomass, and non-petroleum transportation fuels. Energy experts also advocate a pragmatic mix of strategies to craft a crisis-proof energy policy.[26]

Environment and Climate Change

Continued efforts are also under way to address environmental pollution in the Golden State. The sheer size of California magnifies the scope of the problem. California is the 12th-largest emitter of carbon in the world. But population is only one part of the equation. The development of new technologies (silicon chips, synthetic materials, and industrial processes) also adds new toxins to the environment. The long-range impact of environmental pollution has been called **climate change** or global warming. This is caused by a buildup of gases that allow the heat of the sun to penetrate the atmosphere but prevent it from escaping—the greenhouse effect. California contributes its share including 1.4 percent of the world's greenhouse gases and 6.2 percent of the U.S. total. The largest human sources come from transportation, electricity production, and industrial uses. The scientific community now agrees that this long-term warming trend would raise ocean levels (inundating California's coastline), threaten the ozone layer (worsening the state's already high skin cancer rates), alter plant growth patterns (endangering the agricultural base of the state), and diminish the Sierra winter snow-pack (reducing California's water supply).[27]

The short-term impact of environmental pollution is more immediate and visible. A derailed train spills chemicals into a scenic river, destroying all manner of life in its path. Residents near toxic waste dumps trace their illnesses to those dumps. Beaches are plagued or even closed by untreated sewage, elevated bacteria levels, storm runoff, and oil deposits. The California Air Resources Board indicates that more than 90 percent of Californians breathe unhealthy levels of at least one air pollutant during some part of the year. The most vulnerable residents—children, the elderly, and those with respiratory problems—may be advised to stay indoors on "smog alert" days.

When policymakers address issues such as global warming, they look to public support. In California, they have found it. Public opinion surveys suggest that Californians believe global warming is a threat to the state's economy and quality of life. About 54 percent believe its effects have already begun. Respondents, though, divide along party lines. When asked if global warming is a serious or somewhat serious threat, 86 percent of Democrats concur compared to 77 percent of independents and only 41 percent of Republicans.

By large margins, Californians support state efforts to reduce greenhouse gases.[28]

Policy Options

Increased media coverage and continued population growth give environmental and global warming issues a sense of urgency. In what seems like an uphill battle, California policymakers now rely on five separate but interrelated approaches based on a fundamental truth: *The private sector largely creates pollution, but it is government's responsibility to eliminate it.*

Monitor It Understanding the scope and components of any problem is necessary to finding a solution. Accordingly, California policy provides for the collection of data related to pollution and global warming. For example, AB32, the California Global Warming Solutions Act of 2006 charged the California Air Resources Board (ARB) with measuring greenhouse gas emissions from industrial sources and maintaining a statewide greenhouse gas emissions inventory. The ARB has also begun to develop specific emission reduction limits to be achieved by 2020.[29]

Regulate It A second approach has been to issue regulations, set standards, and order offenders to comply. Sometimes called **command and control**, this approach has been implemented by numerous state agencies. For example, the legislature periodically authorizes the Air Resources Board to set emission standards for various types of vehicles and to establish deadlines for compliance. Given California's share of the nation's automobile market, these regulations spur manufacturers to innovate and seek more fuel efficient hybrid and fuel cell technologies. In 2008, the Board mandated that utilities increase to one-third the amount of electricity produced from renewable sources such as wind, solar, and geothermal. The *Integrated Waste Management Act* required that 50 percent of the state's solid waste be diverted from landfills by the year 2000. In response, local governments required

AP Photo/Michael Caulfield

Farming the wind
These wind turbines near Palm Springs serve the Los Angeles Department of Water and Power. While wind is infinitely renewable, critics view wind turbines as noisy, ugly, expansive, and the source of numerous bird kills.

Question: If cleaner sources of energy cost a bit more than traditional sources, would you be willing to pay the added cost?

trash haulers to provide recycling opportunities. Also, the 2006 global warming law established a cap on allowable greenhouse emissions and required that the state reduce them by 80 percent (to 1990 levels) by 2020.

Some regional agencies have also used the regulatory approach. The South Coast Air Quality Management District has issued tough regulations requiring emission reductions from autos and stationary sources such as power plants and industrial sites. Although the command and control approach seems heavy-handed, it has fostered new recycling techniques and some new products (unleaded gasoline, low-emission equipment, alternative fuels, and recyclable plastic).

Move It Another "solution" to pollution in California has been to send the more solid forms of it somewhere else. Indeed, by the late 1980s, more than 30 other states were receiving toxic waste from California. In recent years, such exports have slowed considerably but the state still generates two million tons of hazardous waste each year. Ironically, strong environmental laws in California make intrastate waste disposal difficult and costly. Where it is feasible, large amounts of waste have been stored near poor, ethnic minority communities, a practice sometimes called "environmental racism." NIMBYism has discouraged the siting of new toxic waste facilities almost anywhere. With nowhere to go, many toxins are simply stored in garages, warehouses, and industrial facilities. It is the duty of the California Department of Toxic Substances Control to regulate this waste, seek reductions in it, and clean up old waste sites.

Price It   A recent development in environmental protection has been a market-based approach. For example, by determining a price or market value for nitrogen oxide, government can create incentives for companies to offset existing sources of smog when plants expand. Also, as we noted, cities put a "price" on automobile commutes when they charge high fees for all-day downtown parking. At some point, some drivers may consider cheaper, cleaner alternatives such as mass transit, ridesharing, biking, walking, or telecommuting from home. Pricing incentives assume a partnership between the private and public sectors, but this is just beginning in California. The state's global warming law requires the ARB to implement a **cap and trade** approach. With cap and trade, the government sets pollution caps and issues credits to polluting businesses. Credits allow businesses to pollute as long as the aggregate pollution is under the cap. Companies that successfully reduce emissions can sell their credits to less successful businesses. Overall, carbon emissions could be limited or capped but clean companies could sell whatever quotas they do not use to polluting companies to offset the excess carbon they produce. Proponents believe this approach is the most effective way to fight global warming at the least cost to taxpayers. Using the idiom of the "carrot and stick," they think rewards are more effective than punishments. Opponents, including many environmentalists, believe that the state should never subsidize chronic polluters. They prefer the stick of fees and fines to force compliance. As often happens, continued implementation of cap and trade depended on the outcome of a 2011 lawsuit against the Air Resources Board.

Replace It   One last policy option in California has been to replace fossil fuels and hydroelectric power with renewable sources of energy such as solar, wind, geothermal, biomass, and small-scale hydropower (see Farming the Wind photo). In the past, "green power" was not attractive to utility companies because it cost more to produce and was less predictable (due to cloudy days and sporadic winds). In recent decades, the state has offered tax credits and incentives to develop some renewables (solar power, e.g.). Today, the California Energy Commission offers cash rebates for the development of small wind turbines and fuel cell sources of energy. Under the California Solar Initiative, utility companies offer their customers rebates to install solar electricity systems. The latest "replace it" strategy occurred in 2011. Governor Brown signed into law a requirement that one third of the state's electricity be from renewable sources such as wind and solar by the year 2020.

CONCLUSION: A NEW GROWTH POLICY FOR CALIFORNIA?

California has experienced phenomenal growth throughout its history. A generalized pro-growth consensus among policy leaders aided post-World War II growth. Population growth continued unchecked, local governments readily approved commercial and residential development, and the state provided the necessary infrastructure. Notable were vast water projects, highways, and a comprehensive education system. By the 1960s and 1970s, concerns about too much growth were raised. Development sprawled across the landscape, an automobile-dominated transportation system seemed to choke on itself, smog was a permanent reality in much of California, and news of environmental damage was commonplace.

Growth as a potent issue has an ebb and flow quality to it. By the late 1980s, concern over growth in California entered the mainstream of

California politics. But California's economic recession in the early 1990s consumed political attention in Sacramento; in later years, education, energy, immigration, and global warming seemed to supplant growth as dominant issues. Yet the drumbeat of population growth fuels most other issues in the state.

To the extent that policymakers consider various "solutions" to the problem, they will need to include the following ideas.

A Statewide Growth Strategy   You may have been impressed with the number of agencies at all levels that address land use, water, housing, transportation, and environmental protection. This jurisdictional fragmentation can and does result in policy conflict. For example, some policies (such as building more freeways) encourage automobile use at the expense of mass transit. Building more housing might conflict with the protection of open space. One solution would be a comprehensive, future-oriented statewide growth strategy. Such a strategy would both control growth itself and accommodate growth that cannot be controlled. In recent years, the Great Recession temporarily dampened these long-term efforts.

Controlling California's population growth itself is a much more difficult challenge. It seems to be treated as a given that policymakers can do little about. After all, in a diverse, representative democracy that values freedom, how does government tell families to have fewer children? How can a state on its own barricade an international border? In light of private property rights, how do local officials tell people they cannot build houses on land zoned for that use? No wonder policymakers are at best ambivalent about population growth control.

Rethink Home Rule   Under the engrained doctrine of home rule, local governments can and should make their own decisions about growth. Yet this approach ignores the impact that decisions in one community might have on its neighbors. Interjurisdictional turf battles may result, but managing regional growth does not. Proposed solutions to the home rule "problem" include giving greater land use authority to existing councils of governments (COGs), establishing still larger superagencies to manage regional growth, and reducing the power of single-purpose, single-minded agencies that focus exclusively on water, air quality, or transportation. Progress on this front is slow.

Defiscalize Development   In the current era of economic trouble and tight budgets, local governments have depended less on the state and federal governments to subsidize local growth and its infrastructure. This trend, coupled with Proposition 13, compelled local officials to approve projects that pay more in taxes than they consume in services (e.g., shopping centers). In turn, communities compete to attract such projects while shunning less lucrative ones (e.g., low-income housing). Numerous reform groups now seek "smart growth" strategies that manage, steer, and coordinate land use decisions while decoupling them from their revenue impacts.

Reduce Population Growth   At the center of the issues discussed in Chapter 12—land use, water, housing, transportation, energy, the environment, and climate change—is, and will continue to be, population growth. One grassroots lobbying organization, Californians for Population Stabilization (CAPS), addresses that issue head-on. They point to high fertility rates within the state and "over-immigration" to the state—noting that California is growing as fast as India. CAPS urges more family planning, strict immigration controls, and other policies to protect what they consider to be a quality of life enjoyed by all Californians. Some of these ideas are controversial because they challenge behavior deeply rooted in the state's diverse ethnic and cultural groups. They also assume that government is capable of enacting a comprehensive, far reaching set of policies addressing population growth. Yet any growth management efforts that ignore population growth itself will likely miss the mark in California.

KEY TERMS

impact fees (p. 246)

general plan, zoning
  ordinances,
  subdivision
  regulations (p. 247)

uniform building codes
  (p. 247)

Planned unit
  developments
  (PUDs) (p. 247)

LULUs and NIMBYs
  (p. 248)

riparian rights, prior
  appropriation rights,

prescriptive rights
  (p. 249)

Filter down policy
  (p. 253)

fiscalization of land use
  (p. 255)

climate
  change (p. 259)

command and control
  (p. 259)

cap and
  trade (p. 261)

REVIEW QUESTIONS

1. Why did California grow and why does it continue to do so?

2. Describe land use politics at the local level.

3. Explain the rise and meaning of California's no-growth movement.

4. Delineate the major components of California's plumbing system.

5. What is the California Dream and to what extent do filter-down policies fulfill it?

How do you plan to pursue this dream in the future?

6. Explain California's ongoing relationship with the automobile.

7. Outline the major approaches to environmental pollution in the Golden State.

8. To control the impacts of growth in California, what has been recommended and what do you recommend?

WEB ACTIVITIES

Business, Transportation, and Housing Agency
(http://bth.ca.gov/)
This state mega-agency provides links to a number of data-rich agencies dealing with housing and transportation.

California Environmental Protection Agency
(www.calepa.ca.gov/)
This is a similar umbrella agency with links to boards dealing with air, water, and solid waste pollution.

Public Policy Institute of California
(www.ppic.org)

As you can see from the illustrations and endnotes in this chapter, this think tank has issued numerous growth related studies and public opinion polls.

REALTOR.com
(www.realtor.com/)
To appreciate the challenge of home ownership in California as portrayed in this chapter, go to realtor.com, locate homes for sale in various California communities, and determine how much income you would realistically need to afford typical monthly payments. What if anything should the state do to make homeownership more affordable?

NOTES

1. Roger W. Lotchin, *Fortress California, 1910–1961: From Warfare to Welfare* (New York: Oxford University Press, 1992).

2. Hans Johnson, *California's Population: Planning for a Better Future* (San Francisco: Public Policy Institute of California, January 2011).

3. Examples include Raymond Dasman, *The Destruction of California* (New York: Macmillan, 1965) and Samuel E. Wood and Alfred E. Heller, *California Going, Going ...* (Sacramento: California Tomorrow, 1962).

4. California Opinion Index, *A Compilation of California Public Opinion on Growth and Development* (San Francisco: The Field Institute, May 2002).

5. Joel Garreau, *Edge City: Life on the New Frontier* (New York: Doubleday, 1991), especially Chaps. 8 and 9 on Southern California and the Bay Area, respectively.

6. Mark Baldassare, *PPIC Statewide Survey: Special Survey on Growth* (San Francisco: Public Policy Institute of California, May, 2001).

7. To understand the scope of this practice, see Tracy M. Gordon, *The Local Initiative in California* (San Francisco: Public Policy Institute of California, 2004).

8. Mark DiCamillo and Mervin Field, *The Field Poll,* Release #2045 (May 15, 2002).

9. Erwin Cooper, *Aqueduct Empire* (Glendale, CA: The Arthur H. Clark Company, 1968), p. 202.

10. Edward Abbey, *Desert Solitaire* (New York: Simon and Schuster, 1968), p. 126.

11. Quoted in Norris Hundley Jr., *The Great Thirst: Californians and Water, 1770s–1990s* (Berkeley, CA: University of California Press, 1992), p. 148.

12. *California Water Subsidies* (Washington, D.C.: Environmental Working Group, 2004). (http://archive.ewg.org/reports/watersubsidies/).

13. Jay Lund et al., *Comparing Futures for the Sacramento-San Joaquin Delta* (San Francisco: Public Policy Institute of California, July 2008). See also the Delta Stewardship Council website for extensive background and updates. (http://deltacouncil.ca.gov/).

14. Mark Baldasarre, et al., *PPIC Statewide Survey: Californians and the Environment* (San Francisco: Public Policy Institute of California, July 2009).

15. Ellen Hanak, *California Water: Planning for a Better Future* (San Francisco: Public Policy Institute of California, 2011).

16. George Skelton, "There's Still No End in Sight to California's Water Wars," *Los Angeles Times,* April 3, 2008.

17. Kevin Starr, *Americans and the California Dream, 1850–1915* (New York: Oxford University Press, 1973), p. 417.

18. Hans Johnson and Amanda Bailey, *California's Newest Homeowners: Affording the Unaffordable* (San Francisco: Public Policy Institute of California, 2005).

19. These data are maintained by the California Association of Realtors. For updates, go to www.car.org/marketdata/.

20. For more on this rental dilemma, see *Locked Out 2008: The Housing Boom and Beyond* (Sacramento: California Budget Project, 2008). (www.cbp.org/).

21. U.S. Bureau of Transportation Statistics (Available at www.bts.gov/).

22. Louise Bedsworth and Ellen Hanak, *California Transportation: Planning for a Better Future* (San Francisco: Public Policy Institute of California, June 2010).

23. Janet Wilson, "Study Doubles Estimate of Smog Deaths," *Los Angeles Times,* March 25, 2006.

24. Louise Bedworth, Ellen Hanak, and Jed Kolko, *Driving Change: Reducing Vehicle Miles Traveled in California* (San Francisco: Public Policy Institute of California, 2011).

25. "California's Power Crisis," *The Economist* (January 20, 2001), p. 57.

26. Charles J. Cicchetti, Jeffrey A. Dubin, and Colin M. Long, *The California Energy Crisis: What, Why and What's Next* (Hingham, MA: Kluwer, 2004).

27. Louise Bedworth and Ellen Hanak, *California Climate Change: Planning for a Better Future* (San Francisco: Public Policy Institute of California, January 2011). See also the California Climate Change Portal at www.climatechange.ca.gov/.

28. *PPIC Statewide Survey: Californians and Their Environment* (San Francisco: Public Policy Institute of California, July, 2010).

29. California Air Resources Board (www.arb.ca.gov/).

13

✳

Policies Stemming
from Diversity

**Introduction: The Challenge
of Diversity**

**Social Issues: Abortion
and LGBT Rights**

Abortion

LGBT Rights

**Education: Coping with Growth
and Diversity**

Pressures on Education

Education Reform

**Higher Education: An Uncertain
Future**

The Majoritarian Ideal

Rethinking the Plan

*Higher Education for
Undocumented Students*

Social Programs

Welfare Policy

Health Policy

Conclusion

Key Terms

Review Questions

Web Activities

Notes

IN BRIEF

In Chapter 13, we consider the cultural diversity of California and its impact on five policy areas: abortion, LGBT rights, education, higher education, and social programs. Policy conflicts in these areas are struggles among competing groups—cultural hyperpluralism and ensuing political conflict seem best to describe this state of affairs.

In California, as elsewhere, the issues of abortion and gay rights mirror a diversity of values and fundamental disagreements over what constitutes personhood and marriage. Public education (K-12) must deal with population growth, ethnic diversity, social change, and variable funding. Education reforms are frequent, and they vary in effectiveness. Multicultural politics is evident even in textbook adoptions and testing. California's Master Plan for higher education promises affordable access to colleges and universities for all qualified Californians, yet observers wonder if it will be able to handle future demands.

California's array of social programs serve a growing, diverse population, many of whom do not fully participate in the political process. Programs to alleviate poverty involve all levels of government and are aimed primarily at the "deserving poor." In terms of medical care, state-regulated private insurance and Medi-Cal cover many Californians, at dramatically rising costs. Yet many working Californians are both uninsured and uncovered by government assistance. The worst-off seem to be the deinstitutionalized mentally ill, some of whom are homeless. These are the challenges facing an emerging multicultural democracy—one depicted by population growth, cultural diversity, and group conflict.

INTRODUCTION: THE CHALLENGE OF DIVERSITY

To Californians, neighborhood conflicts are commonplace. African Americans may complain about the *ranchera* music of their Hispanic neighbors. One neighbor's redwood trees may block another's rooftop solar panels. One increasingly Asian community in Southern California found that Asians were avoiding home with "4" in the house number, thereby flattening sales. The city council had to consider allowing people to change their own house numbers—for a fee. These actual incidents illustrate the most profound, long-term challenge facing the Golden State: building a diverse, multicultural society that is at peace with itself. In terms of the nation's motto, *E Pluribus Unum* (out of many, one), the likelihood of California's political system forging an *unum* out of a *pluribus* is an open question. There never has been one monolithic culture in California, but even the myth of one is diminishing. Politically speaking, the notion of an overarching public interest—what founder James Madison called "the good of the whole"—seems increasingly elusive in California.

California is at a major juncture in its political development, a time when the broad forces of growth and diversity are colliding and will likely change how politics is done. In Chapter 12, the policy issues of water, housing, transportation, and pollution were used to explain the larger question of population growth and its consequences. Chapter 13 examines the issues of abortion, gay rights, education, welfare, and health to emphasize the larger topic of cultural diversity and its consequences. Cultural diversity is nothing new in California's political development. Historically, minority cultures were either extinguished or separated from the larger society. In the 1500s, a Spanish culture largely replaced California's Native American culture through disease and conquest. Mexicans subsequently dominated the region of California until the mid-1800s. The discovery of gold brought white settlers from other U.S. states and Europe. Historians refer to this influx of non-Hispanic whites as the "Americanization" of California. These settlers intermarried widely, creating a dominant culture—a process sociologists call **cultural amalgamation**. For much of California's history as a state, Euro-Americans have been the dominant cultural group. At times, they discriminated against Chinese and Japanese immigrants, and against African Americans and Latinos, enforcing a **cultural separatism**, often through housing segregation. The dominant pattern in modern times has been **cultural assimilation**; to "succeed," minority groups need to adopt the practices and characteristics of the "host" society.[1]

As the white majority in California continues to shrink in size (see Figure 13.1), the traditional idea of assimilation into a "majority" culture begins to lose meaning. In a growing number of California cities, no ethnic group constitutes a majority. Some observers believe that California now faces **cultural hyperpluralism**: various ethnic, racial, religious, and other groups balancing the ideal of "one people" with the reality of group identity.

Cultural hyperpluralism goes beyond ethnicity. It is also evident in a variety of policy conflicts involving educational and lifestyle issues. Sociologist James Davison Hunter describes these conflicts as "political and social hostility rooted in different systems of moral understanding."[2]

According to this perspective, several policy debates in California and the nation (such as abortion, gay rights, and certain educational policies) can ultimately be traced to differing views of moral authority. The goal of opposing groups is not peaceful coexistence but winning a war of values. As you consider the policy topics in this final chapter, ask yourself this question: Are there in California "permanent and aggregate interests of the community," as Madison put it in the *Federalist*, No. 10, or simply an unending parade of policy clashes between conflicting groups or factions?

SOCIAL ISSUES: ABORTION AND LGBT RIGHTS

Some public policy issues do not involve large expenditures of public funds. They cannot be viewed as government programs, run by permanent state agencies. Unlike the annual state budget, they do not consume vast amounts of policymaker time. Yet they stir human emotions, produce conflict, and divide Californians unlike most other public policies. We call these policies **social issues**. Here

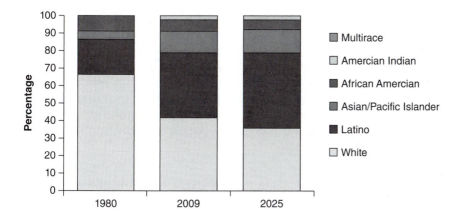

FIGURE 13.1 The Ethnic Composition of California: Past, Present, and Future

Question: What aspects of California (social, economic, and political) might be different or remain the same with an eventual Hispanic majority?

SOURCE: Hans Johnson, *Just the Facts: California Population: Planning for a Better Future* (San Francisco: Public Policy Institute of California, January 2011).

we focus on the two most familiar ones—abortion and gay rights, now known as LGBT rights.

Abortion

Abortion is one of the most controversial political issues for both the nation and California. In the Golden State, the controversy actually preceded the U.S. Supreme Court's famous decision in *Roe v. Wade* (1973), which established a woman's right of privacy relative to giving birth. Before the 1960s, abortion in California was relatively rare and largely illegal. Prosecutions were rarer still, because it was assumed physicians knew best what to do. During the 1960s, legislation was introduced to legalize what many doctors were already doing—performing abortions to protect the life and health of the mother. As medical procedures improved, the woman's health became a less important justification for abortion. In 1962, publicity surrounding a pregnant woman who had taken the drug Thalidomide, plus a rubella epidemic, heightened public awareness of the philosophical issues involved. Was a damaged life still worth living? Few Californians had bothered to ask that question before. Physicians no longer controlled the abortion issue when the general public began asking what being a "person" really means. In 1967, Governor Ronald Reagan signed the *Therapeutic Abortion Act* (the "Beilenson bill") that clarified abortion practice in the Golden State. Allowable reasons to seek an abortion were expanded to include rape and incest, the mental health of the mother, and whether or not the infant would likely be deformed. There were restrictions: Only licensed physicians could perform abortions and only in accredited hospitals. While many factors explain abortion rates, many observers conclude that Beilenson, coupled with *Roe* a few years later, increased dramatically the number of abortions in California. According to state statistics, only 518 legal abortions occurred in 1967. In 1980, the year Reagan was elected president, there were 199,089 abortions performed. The total from 1968 to 1980 was 1,444,778.[3]

The California law and the *Roe* decision also unleashed two grassroots movements, each supporting a conflicting fundamental right—the right to terminate a pregnancy versus a right to be born.[4] The political divide between these two movements is deep and wide. One group calls the unborn "fetuses;" the other, "babies." Even group labels are politicized. According to one side, those calling themselves "pro-choice" are actually pro-abortion. According to the other side, self-described "prolife" groups are not only antiabortion, they are antichoice. Granted the conflict, where do Californians stand on abortion? A majority has been consistently pro-choice over the last 20 years. See Table 13.1 for a recent snapshot of voters' opinions on abortion in the Golden State. Much is at stake for both sides. While accurate statistics are illusive, it appears that abortion rates have declined nationwide and in California for several years. Several recent U.S. Supreme Court cases, *Webster v. Reproductive Health Services* (1989) and *Planned Parenthood v. Casey* (1992), while not overturning the right to an abortion, upheld several state restrictions on its use. In effect, this moved the political war over abortion to the states. In California, the battle is waged on several fronts. The first is among policymakers and the interest groups that influence them. In Sacramento,

TABLE 13.1   Californians and Abortion

Do you favor laws that would make it more difficult for a woman to get an abortion, favor laws that would make it easier to get an abortion, or should no change be made in existing laws?

Make Abortion Easier to Obtain	Make No Changes to Existing Law	Make Abortion Harder to Obtain	No Opinion
22%	49	24	5

SOURCE: The Field Poll, *Release #2350* (July 21, 2010).

interest groups such as the California Pro-Life Council and the California Abortion Rights League have lined up predictably for or against Medi-Cal funding of abortions for the indigent. As the state's Medicaid program for poor families, Medi-Cal funds about 80,000 induced abortions per year. A second front has been in state courts. For example, in 1997, the California Supreme Court on a 4 to 3 vote struck down a never-enforced law requiring teenage girls to obtain parental or judicial approval for an abortion (*American Academy of Pediatrics v. Lungren*).

A third front has involved occasional protest activity. In the 1990s, antiabortion and pro-choice groups faced off outside clinics that performed abortions but several court cases limited the ability of pro-life groups to block clinic access. Abortion protests have become less frequent as antiabortion activists focus more on counseling and abstinence education.

A fourth front has been the court of public opinion. In recent years, a majority of California voters have reflected a pro-choice sentiment, as Table 13.1 suggests. Other polling data suggest that support for abortion rights declines the longer a woman is pregnant. A majority favors parental consent for teenage abortions but also supports late-term abortions if the mother's life is in danger.[5] A fifth front now includes the ballot box. Across the nation, several state legislatures have passed laws that restrict access to abortions, especially for minors. In the face of legislative inaction, abortion foes in California have opted for the initiative process. If nothing else, they have been persistent. Voters narrowly rejected both Proposition 73 in 2005 and Proposition 85 in 2006. Both would have required parental notification before a minor could terminate a pregnancy. Encouraged by these close votes, they submitted Proposition 4 that qualified for the November 2008 ballot. Proposition 4 was a constitutional amendment that would have prohibited abortions for dependent minors until 48 hours after a physician notified a minor's parents, legal guardian, or if necessary, another adult relative. Once again, voters rejected this measure, this time by a 52 to 48 percent margin.

To sum up, California's political climate today is largely pro-choice but with qualifications. California Democrats, who are more pro-choice than Republicans, control the legislature. Recent governors (Pete Wilson, Gray Davis, Arnold Schwarzenegger, and Jerry Brown) have been pro-choice. Even pro-life Republicans prefer discussing other issues such as taxes when running for office. This climate is supported by the state constitution's explicit right of privacy (Article I, Section 1). Although this provision was not passed with abortion in mind, it does provide a vehicle to defend abortion rights in California courts.

LGBT Rights

As with abortion rights, advancing the rights of California's lesbian/gay/bisexual/transgendered community has been waged in several political arenas and over several issues. The most visible and controversial issue has been same-sex marriage, discussed in Chapter 4. Here, we emphasize the less visible efforts to limit discrimination against LGBT people and providing domestic partner benefits for same-sex couples.

These less visible efforts have occurred primarily within the formal legislative process and have focused on civil rights short of same-sex marriage. In 1999, Governor Davis signed the landmark Domestic Partnership Act, establishing a domestic partners registry and granted a limited number of state benefits enjoyed by heterosexual married couples such as hospital visitation rights and health insurance coverage for partners of public employees. Legislation in 2001 expanded those rights. Recent state budgets have included funding to aid LGBT victims of domestic and school violence. In 2011, Governor Brown became the first state governor in the nation to sign legislation requiring school textbooks and history lessons to include the contributions of LGBT Americans.

The third arena has been local government. A growing number of counties and cities have passed ordinances barring discrimination against gays and lesbians. These rights vary from place to place, but they include public and private employment, public accommodations, education, housing, and lending practices. In order to do business with them, several cities now require private contractors to provide domestic partner benefits. On all these fronts, the overall issue continues to reflect fundamental cultural divisions in the state.

EDUCATION: COPING WITH GROWTH AND DIVERSITY

Unlike abortion and LGBT rights, education is a public service deeply-rooted in California's political history. Yet the state's educational system faces unprecedented challenges. In Chapter 10, we discussed school districts and how they are organized to implement education policies in California. Here, we analyze the challenges districts face in doing so. They include enrollment growth, ethnic diversity, and social change.

Pressures on Education

Pressures, many of which are external to the educational system itself, buffet California educators and students alike. Here we consider enrollment growth, ethnic hyperpluralism, social conflict, and funding challenges.

Enrollment Growth   In recent decades, the most significant challenge has been the sheer growth of California's school-aged population. Historically, education enrollments have reflected a boom-or-bust pattern. Enrollments surge and slow based on birth rates and immigration. For example, some classrooms that were jammed with Baby Boomers in the 1960s stood empty in the 1970s, only to be filled again in the 1990s. In recent years, birthrates have declined; future growth rates of school-aged children are expected to mirror overall population growth in California. The ebbs and flows of school enrollments vary across the state. Some school districts face school closures and teacher layoffs while other face the dire need for more classrooms, schools, and teachers. One would

think that slowing enrollments should make it possible for school districts to catch up on infrastructure and other needs but recent budget crises have prevented that. One school district in Riverside County was poised to open a new state-of-the-art high school in 2011 only to postpone the opening for lack of funding.

Ethnic Hyperpluralism   The ethnic composition in California's public schools has been shifting for some years and will continue to do so well into the 21st century. Ethnic and cultural hyperpluralism are increasingly the norm. Consider Table 13.2. Latinos constitute a slight but growing public school majority. These percentages vary dramatically throughout California. Diversity is more than ethnicity, as language differences illustrate. According to the California Department of Education, about a quarter of the state's K-12 students are English learners (EL). That is, they are not proficient enough in English to succeed academically in mainstream English programs. Of Hispanic K-12 students, nearly half are EL; that number can be much higher in some districts. Although Spanish is the most common first language for many students, it is by no means the only one. Students come from families where nearly 50 major languages are spoken. For many years, educators dealt

TABLE 13.2   Public School Diversity in California

	1987–1988	2010–2011
Latino or Hispanic	30.1%	51.4%
White	50.0	26.6
African American	9.1	6.7
Asian	7.3	8.5
Filipino	2.1	2.6
American Indian/Alaska Native	0.8	0.7
Pacific Islander/Hawaiian	0.5	0.6
Two or more races	–	1.8

Question: To what extent are these trends evident in your community?

SOURCE: California Department of Education and the Demographic Research Unit, California Department of Finance.

with this language diversity by offering bilingual education. EL students were taught in both their first languages and in English, with the goal of making them eventually proficient in English. Many non-English speakers enter California schools at all grade levels, bringing a variety of language "readiness" with them. Growing frustration with the results of bilingual education resulted in the passage of Proposition 227 in 1998. It required all instruction to be in English; for transition purposes, EL students could participate in sheltered English immersion programs for a maximum of one year. In recent years, some families, including English speaking ones, have sought out "dual language" or "dual immersion" programs to garner the benefits of being bilingual.

Social Conflict Broader social changes affecting all segments of society have introduced new levels of conflict in California schools. Two-income parents, single parents, child abuse, parental neglect, and poverty have changed the very mission of public schools. Teachers are not only educators but also disciplinarians, surrogate parents, counselors, social workers, detectives, and nurses. Problems stemming from gangs, gang attire, graffiti, guns on campus, and drug use are increasingly routine. Student behavior often reflects differences based on race, ethnicity, income, gender, sexual orientation, and religious faith. Some students even formed their own ethnic clubs. But, a few high schools have experienced a counter-trend, the creation of "gay/straight" alliances—clubs designed to discuss matters of sexual orientation with tolerance and acceptance in mind.

The Funding Challenge In absolute numbers, California spends far more on education than any other state, more than $64 billion in 2011–2012. This translates to over $11,000 per pupil from all funding sources. California's numbers are less impressive when measuring state-only, per pupil spending. According to the education think tank EdSource, California ranked only 28th in expenditures per pupil in 2007–2008 (the most recent comparative data available). While its teachers are relatively well paid, California ranks below average in numbers of administrators, counselors, and librarians.[6] Education spending in California results from numerous pressures involving court decisions, statewide propositions, enrollment growth, and substantive education policymaking.

1. In one court decision, *Serrano v. Priest* (1971), the California Supreme Court ruled that California's education finance system based on local property values created spending disparities between districts, in violation of equal protection provisions of the state constitution. Proposition 13 centralized education funding and that funding is largely equal between districts. Yet, spending differences remain. Federal aid and various specialized grants from the state vary between districts and schools. Basic aid districts (often in wealthy communities) depend solely on property taxes to fund schools. As a result, their annual per pupil expenditures can be considerably higher than if they received state funding.[7] While local superintendents, principals, and school boards may be tempted to raise fees for after-school activities and other expenses, state law prohibits them from doing so. These limits do not apply to fundraising. Accordingly, affluent districts often receive contributions from parents, booster clubs, and foundations—sources not realistically available to poorer districts.

2. California voters have made numerous decisions directly relating to statewide education funding. As Figure 13.2 suggests, these actions have ranged from tax cuts to funding guarantees and massive bond measures.

3. Enrollment change can whipsaw education spending. Because the state provides to most districts per-pupil funding based on average daily attendance (ADA), each new student triggers another $11,000 annually in education spending from all sources. But enrollment decreases have the opposite effect, resulting in personnel layoffs and program cuts.

4. About one third of K-12 spending is from about 50 state and federal categorical programs designated to address specific programs such as special education, class size reduction, child

Year	Proposition	Effect
1978	Proposition 13	Cut property tax base of education and shifted the weight of education funding to state
1984	Proposition 84	Established a state lottery with 34 percent of ticket sales dedicated to education
1988	Proposition 98	Guaranteed that K-12 education would receive no less than 40 percent of the annual general fund
1998	Proposition 1A	Provided a record $6.7 billion in general obligation bonds for K-12 school and classroom construction
2000	Proposition 39	Reduced from two-thirds to 55 percent the vote of the electorate to approve local school bonds

FIGURE 13.2   How California Voters Affect Education Spending

Question: Are voters as competent as legislators to make complex education spending decisions?

NOTE: This brief list does not include numerous other statewide bond measures to benefit schools over the last several decades. It also does not include substantive policy decisions like the initiative to curtail bilingual education that have fiscal impacts.

SOURCE: California Secretary of State.

care and development, and gifted students (GATE). Usually, school districts have little discretion over how these funds are spent. To help districts cope with budget cuts, the state has allowed more flexibility in how these funds are spent.[8]

Education Reform

The challenges of enrollment growth, diversity issues, and funding pressures have led to several education reforms in California. In recent years, reform efforts have taken on a sense of urgency. Three areas of education reform reflect both current education trends and the politics of diversity in the state.

Improving Quality   Given the diversity of California students, educational performance is a constant challenge. Recent statistics are telling. Although some test scores have improved, especially in the lower grades, only 68 percent of California's ninth-graders graduate with their classes. Graduation rates are significantly lower for African American, Latino, and Native American males. According to Harvard University researchers, "California's failure to graduate so many of its students is a tragic story of wasted human potential and tremendous economic loss."[9] Complicating matters is the high number of California students who do not meet state criteria for language proficiency. Efforts to improve educational quality in California are nothing new. The 1983 *Hart Hughes Educational Reform Act* increased high school graduation requirements and provided for longer school days and school years. The 1992 Charter Schools Act allowed the creation of parent-, teacher-, or community-established schools that would operate independent of many state and local regulations. In 1996, after experiencing some of the highest student-teacher ratios in the nation, California launched a dramatic class size reduction program. In kindergarten through third grade, class sizes would be limited to 20 students. The results were immediate and mixed. While teacher morale and classroom manageability increased, so did local costs and shortages of classroom space and credentialed teachers. In the late 1990s, new reforms included the monitoring of individual school performance, a mandatory high school exit exam, peer assistance for teachers, various awards and incentives, and new reading programs. Dissatisfied with state-level reforms, Congress passed the *No Child Left Behind Act (NCLB)* in 2001. This was U.S. President George W. Bush's signature education policy aimed at improving educational quality. The law requires schools to (1) give standardized English and math tests annually from third through eighth grades; (2) increase the number of students scoring high enough to be labeled proficient (100 percent by 2015); and 3) face sanctions for failure to do so. As with other states, California had to set annual improvement goals and publicly identify districts and individual schools in need of improvement. Because so many performance factors are outside school control (demographics, poverty, and family support), California has been unable to meet the law's expectations. Not surprisingly, the schools most likely to meet NCLB goals are in smaller, more homogeneous districts. Those least likely to meet them have large numbers of economically disadvantaged students and English learners.[10]

Improving Accountability The politics of diversity is not limited to funding and reform issues. It also includes how students, schools, and even textbook publishers are held accountable for educational success. Textbook publishers must heed California's massive *Education Code* and work within a variety of frameworks (general curricular goals) and content standards (detailed subject specifications for each grade level). These standards guide local school districts on what to teach and publishers on what to write. For each grade level and subject area, the California Department of Education approves lists of textbooks from which local school districts can choose.

Publishers must address questions like these: Should textbooks reflect America's European heritage versus the experience of "marginalized" groups—Latinos, African Americans, gays, and women? Should reading texts be literature-based, phonics-based, or both? Are mathematics texts error-free and user friendly? Do history and civics texts adequately communicate the multicultural past and present of the nation and of California?

Student and school accountability centers around testing. As educators well know, testing itself can raise as many problems as it purports to solve, leading some to conclude that "the perfect test" is an oxymoron. Accordingly, dissatisfied policymakers move from one statewide test to another or from one testing approach to another. The current testing regime is the STAR program for grades 2-11. Layered on top of that testing are the NCLB testing requirements.

The effort of schools to comply with frameworks, standards, and tests is never-ending. One problem stems from educational policy fragmentation, frequent policy changes, and lack of policy coordination. Local educators often complain that the state adopts new standards and employs new tests without aligning new textbook and curricula materials accordingly. Furthermore, they argue that a greater emphasis on testing skews academic objectives and fosters a "teach to the test" mentality in the schools. Other questions arise over the testing of English language learners. If NCLB requires high scores of all students (including subgroups like EL students or those with disabilities), does that unfairly disadvantage those schools and districts with high EL enrollments? Is it then fair to compare and rank all California schools without regard to language, income, and other social variations among them? The NCLB law simply adds another layer to this dilemma.

Improving Choice One approach to improving education policy in California is to improve educational choice. Many parents desire choice as a matter of principle; some school reformers claim it would encourage competition between schools resulting in educational improvement statewide. The most radical proposals have involved school vouchers, certificates issued by the state that parents could apply toward private school tuition. Proponents argue that, because public schools are wasteful and overly bureaucratic, parents deserve a choice of schools. Competition from voucher-funded private schools would also force public schools to improve. Opponents have feared that vouchers would drain public education budgets and allow private schools to deny access to poor families and "problem" students—the physically impaired, English learners, or low academic achievers. California voters overwhelmingly rejected two such voucher plans in 1993 and 2000.

Short of vouchers, less radical "managed choice" options are available. Charter schools—public schools that operate with fewer state regulations—have provided educational alternatives for relatively few Californians. Compared to traditional schools, charter schools in California are less likely to serve Hispanic students, low-income families, or English learners. Are they academically superior? Results are mixed. Traditional public schools outperform charter schools at the elementary level and lag behind charter schools at the middle and high school levels. Other choices are available. State law now allows intra- and inter-district transfers. Once tied to their neighborhood school, space permitting, students may attend public schools within their districts or in other districts where their commuting parents work. Magnet schools attract students from across districts by offering specialized courses, programs, or teaching approaches. The NCLB law allows parents to seek out more successful schools but this choice is problematic if other schools are also underperforming or, due to budget cuts, cannot accommodate additional students.

In one sense, these choice-oriented policies reflect the popularity of "market" approaches to public services generally. But in another sense, they reflect a disintegration of majoritarian policymaking in education—where all Californians contribute and from which all equally benefit. General taxes still fund education, but the product itself is increasingly differentiated or fragmented. Educational choice seems a ready option for California's middle class and wealthy families. That is less the case for disadvantaged families and poorer school districts. Again,

many challenges facing education in California find roots in social, economic, and demographic trends well beyond the control of educators.

HIGHER EDUCATION: AN UNCERTAIN FUTURE

Historically, Californians have taken pride in their institutions of higher education. But population growth, increased cultural diversity, and chronic underfunding have raised some profound issues for the state's colleges and universities. Students and faculty know the symptoms of the problem only too well. Fees are raised, courses are cancelled, graduation plans are delayed, and needs outpace revenues. For many public university students, a four-year baccalaureate degree is largely a myth. How have these pressures come about?

The Majoritarian Ideal

Like other western states, California lacked a significant private college sector in the decades following statehood. In its place, the state developed a comprehensive public system of higher education, featuring high quality and open access. Initially, the *Organic Act of 1868* created the University of California. Later, state teachers colleges and junior (or two-year) colleges were added. Concurrently, numerous private colleges and universities were established with little state attention or help. Anticipating an enrollment surge by Baby Boomers in the 1960s, the legislature passed the *Donahoe Higher Education Act of 1960*—commonly called the **Master Plan for Higher Education**. According to a legislative report, what began as a modest agreement between educational institutions evolved into a "world-renowned social compact" that articulated a bold vision for the future.[11]

The plan did three things. First, it prescribed enrollment parameters for each level. The University of California (UC) campuses would admit students from the top 12.5 percent of high school seniors; California State University (CSU) campuses (formerly the teachers colleges) would admit the top one-third; and the community college system (CCC) (formerly the junior colleges) would admit any student capable of benefiting from instruction. Low fees and no tuition would provide ready access to the academically qualified at UC and CSU, although admission to any particular campus was not guaranteed. Second, the Master Plan assigned different missions to each level. UC would emphasize research, graduate programs, and offer doctoral degrees. CSU would focus on liberal arts teaching and professional education through the master's degree. Community colleges would provide standard college courses for transfer to four-year institutions, plus vocational and technical training. The transfer function was to be paramount. Third, the Master Plan created governance structures to operate each sector and to resolve the inevitable turf battles that would occur.

The entire system grew beyond all projections in the decades that followed. Today, the overall system encompasses a huge complex of campuses throughout California. UC consists of ten general campuses and one health science campus enrolling about 234,000 undergraduate and graduate students. CSU consists of 23 campuses and six off-campus centers enrolling 440,000 students, making it the largest university system in the nation. The state's 112 community college campuses and other sites enroll 2.8 million students. California's 76 accredited independent colleges, universities, professional schools, and other specialized campuses enroll another 248,000 students. Although the "privates" produce only a quarter of the state's baccalaureate degrees, they produce nearly half of the master's and doctoral degrees and most of the professional degrees. Widely-perceived as less diverse than public universities, private institutions claim to enroll 10,000 more students from underrepresented groups than does the University of California.[12]

Rethinking the Plan

In recent years, revenue shortfalls and ensuing budget deficits have hit higher education's share of the state budget. University and college administrators have responded by authorizing significant budget cuts and sizable fee increases. Students have grumbled, protested, and transferred to community colleges, private colleges, or even to out-of-state public universities. Community college fees have also increased during this period. The students least able to absorb these increases have dropped out of college altogether. How much longer could these systems tolerate both enrollment and funding pressures?

Policy discussions in recent years have focused on three interlocking issues: access, growth, and pricing. First, how can California's colleges and universities provide access to growing numbers of students when resources are finite? Access is an especially sensitive matter for California's college-bound minorities and lower income families. This challenge has been particularly acute in recent years when enrollments were reduced in response to budget cuts. Responding to this issue, a Legislative Analyst's report recommended that the CSU campuses (where access is so crucial) work to better accommodate students from their immediate regions.[13] Clearly, resolving larger access issues in all the systems would require more campuses, classrooms, courses, and funding to match. Second, rethinking California's commitment to higher education faces a backdrop of historic population growth (see Chapter 12). Each system needs several new campuses to accommodate current and projected growth, but planning has been marred by competition for scarce budget dollars. Because UC, CSU, and the California Community Colleges (CCC) are running out of physical space to serve more students, suggestions for coping with anticipated growth include new campus construction, year-round instruction, greater on-campus efficiencies, increased private college aid, and more online (Internet) coursework. Some administrators characterize these efforts as providing "authentic access"—not merely admission but real access to courses that students need to graduate in a timely manner.

Third, the era of ultra-low fees appears to have ended. Fees at UC campuses now exceed $11,000 per year; at CSU, fees are about half that. (UC officials now admit that their fees are actually "tuition." CSU official maintain the "fee" terminology; only out-of-state students pay tuition). CCC fees are still a relative bargain at under $1,000. Aside from fees, taxpayers fund a significant share of overall higher education costs. But higher education's share of the state budget pie has been slipping. Opponents of increased student fees point to the continued need for access in a time of population growth, growing numbers of price-sensitive minority students, and the relatively high total costs of attending college in California, including living expenses. Defenders of higher fees argue that there are few other choices given competition for depleted tax revenues. The Master Plan's promise of broad access to quality and affordable higher education seems strained at best.

Higher Education for Undocumented Students

One intriguing issue combines access, pricing, and federal/state conflict. Should undocumented immigrant students be charged in-state or out-of-state tuition at California's public colleges and universities? Being allowed to pay in-state tuition saves California residents as much as $12,000 a year. Federal law (the Illegal Immigration Reform and Immigrant Responsibility Act of 1996) prohibits undocumented persons from receiving in-state tuition at public institutions of higher education. It also denies them various kinds of federal financial aid. In contrast, several states with high immigrant populations including California have passed laws allowing in-state tuition for the undocumented, if they have attended high school in the state for three or more years. California's law, AB540, includes that high school exemption. It also requires students to file an affidavit (a written declaration under oath) stating that they are seeking to legalize their status or will do so when eligible.

Policy action and inaction surrounding this issue involves the courts, the U.S. Congress, and the California legislature. In 2010, the California Supreme Court unanimously ruled that undocumented students are eligible for the same tuition as

legal residents of the state. The justices reasoned that because the high school attendance exemption was available to all students regardless of immigration status, it applied to qualified undocumented students as well.[14] This ruling was likely to benefit an estimated California 40,000 students, the vast majority of whom attend the state's community colleges. Opponents of the decision vowed to appeal.

In the late 2000s, legislation was introduced in Congress that would amend that earlier law to allow states to charge undocumented students in-state tuition. The Development, Relief, and Education for Alien Minors Act, known as the **DREAM Act**, would also provide a multistep path toward citizenship for those students who were brought to the United States as children. The bill faced little chance of becoming law after Republicans gained a House majority in 2010. In 2011, the California legislature enacted the state's version of the DREAM Act, Several bills that constitute the act in California would allow undocumented students to qualify for in-state tuition as well as private and state-funded financial aid. Votes were predictably party line with Democrats in favor and Republicans opposed.

SOCIAL PROGRAMS

The Golden State has a long history of social programs that cushion the impact of life's slings and arrows. For example, California's workers' compensation system (to assist injured employees) dates back to the Progressive era. Still other programs are a legacy of the New Deal in the 1930s and the War on Poverty in the 1960s. Like other states, social programs in California are a jerrybuilt arrangement of multiple agencies and financial partnerships that span every layer of the federal system. In child-care services alone, nearly 50 programs are administered by 13 California agencies. A patchwork of social programs reflects the different times in which they were enacted, mixed priorities, and approaches, plus some measure of ambivalence toward those in need. In fact, the history of social policy typifies

ambivalent benevolence—on one hand, a caring concern for California's "truly needy" and, on the other, a reluctance to support over-reliance on public assistance. Recent recession-era budgets cut funding and services to both groups.

Taken together, California's social programs consumed about 25 percent of the state's general fund for 2011–2012. These broad areas of health and welfare spending consume about a third of the state general fund. In recent decades, this share of the budget has grown due to rising unemployment, high birth rates among the poor, continued immigration, high divorce rates, and federal mandates. Yet, recent recession-era budgets have reduced some funding and services to these vulnerable populations.

Who are California's poor? Over 13 percent of all Californians fall below official poverty guidelines. For example, that threshold in 2011 was $22,350 for a family of four (and somewhat higher in Alaska and Hawaii). If California's high cost of living is taken into account, that 13 percent figure jumps another five percent. Poverty rates are especially high for children overall (17 percent), children in single-mother households (43 percent), Latinos (18 percent), blacks (20 percent), and foreign-born heads of Latino households (22 percent). Contrary to popular impressions, most poor families are employed. Where do they live? The highest rates of poverty occur in the San Joaquin Valley (around 20 percent) and the lowest rates are in the San Francisco Bay Area (less than 10 percent).[15]

Welfare Policy

Programs to help the poor are deeply rooted in perceptions about the poor. Americans perceive the poor as either deserving or undeserving. The **deserving poor** or truly needy are poor presumably through no fault of their own. Children, the blind and disabled, the laid-off unemployed, and the elderly fall into this category. The **undeserving poor** include unemployed able-bodied adults, especially men, the "lifestyle" poor or unemployed, and abusers of drugs and alcohol. Presumably these individuals have chosen their lot in life, and the personal consequences are not society's fault or responsibility. California's policies toward those in need combine these two perceptions. The largest programs target needy families, children, those who are elderly or disabled, and other adults. While the dollar amounts and numbers served seem high, costs have actually been shaved in recent budgets in response to lower tax revenues.

1. *Families*. California's major program to aid needy families is **CalWORKs** (California Work Opportunity and Responsibility to Kids). This program implements the federal Temporary Assistance to Needy Families (TANF) program that, under welfare reform, replaced the old Aid to Families with Dependant Children (AFDC). It provides time-limited assistance (food and shelter) to eligible families in times of crisis. The state's 58 counties administer the program. In 2011, the maximum a monthly cash grant for a family was $638. For families that dip in and out of poverty, the cumulative limit on aid has been reduced from five to four years. Recipients must participate in job skills training and various work activities with the goal of becoming permanently self-sufficient. In 2011–2012, an average of 580,000 Californians per month received CalWORKs support. Is the program working? Well, yes and no. According to one study, many families have moved off the welfare rolls and into jobs. But for many, their paychecks provide little more than what they received from welfare. While many have stayed off welfare, they continue to need "transitional benefits" such as food stamps and Medi-Cal.[16]

Supplementing CalWORKs is CalFresh, the former federal food stamp program that provides nutritional assistance to eligible low-income families. Recipients receive bank-like debit cards to pay for food at participating grocery stores. In recent years, about 3 million Californians received food aid worth about $259 per household per month. Less than half of eligible California families participate in the program, one of the worst participation rates in the nation. This causes the state to lose billions in federal dollars. Experts attribute under enrollment to insufficient knowledge of the benefit, laborious paperwork, and fear among Spanish-dominant Latinos that food stamps will negatively affect their employment or immigration status.[17]

2. *Children*. Obviously, children benefit if a parent qualifies under CalWORKs. Benefits include not only monthly cash assistance but publicly funded child care while parents work or receive training. But there are many other programs to help California's high-risk children. The Child Protective Services program intervenes when there is evidence or suspicion of in-home child abuse or neglect. The state's foster care program places more than 60,000 such children with relatives, foster families, or group homes. The Cal-Learn program assists pregnant and parenting teenagers to obtain high school diplomas or the equivalent. The Child Support Enforcement Program locates and requires noncustodial parents to pay court-ordered child support.

3. *Seniors and Disabled*. A variety of programs also assist the elderly and disabled. Some of them are separated from the largest federal programs, Social Security and Medicare. People 60 years or older may receive continuing care at state-approved facilities. In-Home Supportive Services provides a variety of services to help seniors, the disabled, or blind remain in their homes. The federal Supplemental Security Income (SSI) program is part of Social Security. It provides monthly cash aid to 1.3 million aged, blind, and disabled Californians who meet the program's income and resource requirements. California augments the SSI payment with a SSP (State Supplemental Payment) grant. Maximum individual grants are about $830 per month.

4. *Other Adults*. What about those adults who are not covered by the programs just described?

Several programs exist for them. The Adult Protective Services program assists elderly and dependent adults who are functionally impaired, unable to meet their own needs, or are victims of neglect or abuse. Last, the state's Refugee Settlement Program helps refugees from other countries that locate in California become self-sufficient.

Health Policy

As Americans grow in number and live longer, medical care becomes a major policy issue at both the state and federal levels. Crises such as AIDS (acquired immune deficiency syndrome) also affect an already stressed health care system. Unlike welfare policy, health policy commingles the public and private sectors, both in terms of care and funding. The "medical industrial complex," consisting of medical professionals, hospitals, and insurance companies, dominates the system. Two simple truths govern the politics of health care. First, costly medical care does not necessarily equal good health; being healthy has a great deal to do with heredity, lifestyle, social conditions, and physical environment. Second, health services (both public and private) involve a vast transfer of wealth. In the public sector, this means in effect transferring resources from higher income (less needy) to lower income (more needy) Americans. In private sector health care, it means transferring resources from the healthy to the sick and those who care for them. Although taxes and insurance premiums fund medical care in these two sectors, people rarely receive in care exactly what they have "paid" in taxes or premiums. Redistributing health dollars in both private and public sector is a fact of life. California's approach to aiding the sick is multifaceted and increasingly expensive. It includes three broad approaches: private insurance, Medi-Cal, and deinstitutionalization.

Private Insurance In the United States, our health care system depends heavily on private insurance. Traditionally, state-regulated insurance companies paid doctors on a **fee-for-service**

basis. Each medical procedure had a price, and insurance companies unquestioningly paid whatever it was at the time it was rendered. Increasingly, insurance companies and doctors have been moving to **managed care**: networks of doctors and hospitals providing comprehensive services for a predetermined price. In recent years, only 52 percent of California's nonelderly have been covered by employer-provided or privately purchased health insurance. What about the rest? Nearly seven million Californians lacked health insurance of any kind, ranking the state near the bottom in the percentage of residents without health care. Roughly a third of those uninsured Californians qualify for Medi-Cal or Healthy Families, two major state programs. The rest are workers and their dependents whose employers provide no private health insurance (a common practice in agriculture, construction, retail, and small businesses), but who earn too much money to qualify for publicly funded care. They include the "working poor" but one-third are families with incomes over $50,000. Lack of health insurance disproportionately affects Latinos and foreign-born adults. Immigrants are more likely than the native born to work in jobs that provide no health insurance[18] (See Figure 13.3).

For years, people would lose their insurance if they switched jobs, were laid off, or a new insurance carrier discovered a "preexisting condition" such as AIDS or cancer. Although Congress passed legislation in 1996 guaranteeing the portability of health insurance coverage for those who lose or leave their jobs, that law does not help those who lack insurance in the first place. After California voters rejected two propositions that would have mandated employer-provided heath insurance, the legislature enacted "Healthy Families," a program that offered low-cost insurance coverage for the children of uninsured workers who earn too much to qualify for Medi-Cal. The plan covers usual health, dental, and vision needs. About 900,000 children benefit from this program.

In 2010, Congress passed major health care reform—the *Affordable Care Act (ACA)*. Once fully implemented, it is estimated that that 94 percent of California residents will be covered by a health

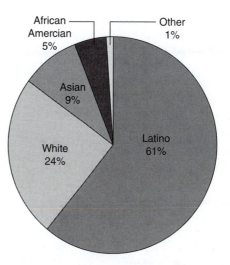

FIGURE 13.3 The Race and Ethnicity of California's Uninsured

Question: What changes to health care policy in California would alter these percentages?

NOTE: All numbers reflect the non-elderly population in 2009 (those under age 65).

SOURCE: California HealthCare Foundation, 2010. Reprinted with permission from the California HealthCare Foundation 2011.

insurance plan, a new health insurance exchange market, or revisions to Medi-Cal.[19]

Medi-Cal California's version of the federal Medicaid program for low-income individuals is called **Medi-Cal**. Medi-Cal pays for two types of care—core and optional services. Federally required core services include access to physicians and nurses, hospital care, laboratory tests, home care, and preventative services for children. Federal matching funds are available for any of 34 optional services such as hospice care, adult dentistry, and chiropractic services. CalWORKs and SSI/SSP recipients, qualified expectant mothers, and poor children automatically receive Medi-Cal benefits. Other low-income people qualify but pay for a portion of their medical care.

Medi-Cal spending generally increases or decreases in response to economic trends, various eligibility expansions, and state-imposed cost controls on health care providers. In 2011, about

Homeless in Santa Barbara

7.7 million Californians participated in Medi-Cal. In an effort to control spiraling costs, California has encouraged Medi-Cal beneficiaries to select managed care plans and providers. In recent years, almost half had done so. Furthermore, the state has reduced the number of optional Medi-Cal services it is willing to fund.

What about health care for California's large immigrant population? Are they deserving or undeserving of Medi-Cal support? This has been the subject of protracted policy debate, political hyperbole, and numerous legal challenges. The result has been public confusion over coverage and frustration over perceived costs. This we know: (1) Compared to the native-born, immigrants in California are less likely (and in some counties far less likely) to have health insurance; (2) Illegal immigrants do not qualify for publicly funded heath care (their citizen children do); (3) Immigrants are less likely to seek out regular health care, thereby incurring lower health care costs; and (4) When seeking medical care, immigrant families are more likely to pay out-of-pocket for such care.[20]

What does this discussion tell you? California's health care system faces one dilemma after another. Public spending on health care is enormous due to the growth of needy populations, the rising costs of health care for everyone, and prior spending commitments when there were revenue surpluses. Given its portion of the budget, health care is a likely target for spending freezes or budget cuts to counter revenue shortfalls. All the policy choices seem painful. Eligibility and program cuts threaten the "social safety net" for millions of the state's most vulnerable residents. Cuts in provider reimbursements threaten the already fragile finances of many hospitals and clinics, forcing some to turn away Medi-Cal patients or even close their doors. In the meantime, the public, policymakers, and health professionals wait to see how the ACA will affect this issue in California and around the nation.

Deinstitutionalization A much-less discussed health care approach in California has been the **deinstitutionalization** of the mentally ill. Historically, psychiatric patients were placed in institutions, apart from society and family. Prior to the 1960s, California had a reasonably progressive and balanced approach, including prevention and early intervention in mental cases. But in the 1960s, two trends merged. First, Governor Reagan persuaded the legislature to reduce funding for mental health programs and shift them to the counties. Second, mental health professionals embraced a new treatment philosophy that placed mental patients in communities, not institutions. Neighborhoods and families would help "mainstream" the mentally ill. In California, these forces converged in the *Lanterman-Petris-Short Act of 1968*. In effect a civil rights law, it made the confinement of unwilling mental patients exceedingly difficult.

Ironically and even tragically, many mental patients were victimized by this "reform." A decade later, Proposition 13 cut revenue for just the mental health programs these people needed. Furthermore, the ideal of community-based treatment fell far short of expectations. Anticipated community-based mental health centers never materialized. Many former mental patients did not return to families or live in group homes—they became homeless. Indeed, thousands of California's homeless population have disabilities, mental illness, or other health problems. Many call jail home because without close supervision or daily medication they lose control and commit crimes.

We should be clear that the homeless population in California is not limited to the mentally ill and the chronically homeless. Even if they are employed, many Californians live from paycheck to paycheck. A layoff, catastrophic illness, or bank foreclosure could quickly result in life on the streets. Also, job seekers who move to California are often disappointed by actual job prospects, especially during economic downturns. Advocacy groups and those who serve the homeless report an increase in the homeless population due to the state's housing foreclosure crisis in the late 2000s.

How do local governments respond to this issue? Shelters (some are open only in winter months), low-cost hotels, parking lots set aside for those who live out of their vehicles, and other "transitional housing" provide at least temporary accommodation but cannot meet the need entirely. Some California communities try to criminalize homelessness, prosecuting them for loitering, squatting, unauthorized camping, and panhandling. San Francisco has been notable for the jailing aggressive panhandlers. In contrast, nonprofit groups with local government approval offer shelters for families and single individuals while providing child care and the life skills that eventually result in permanent, independent housing.[21] At a deeper level, in California this represents a clash of civic values—authentic compassion for those in need versus the impulse to protect property values, tourism, and business interests.

CONCLUSION

California's size, diverse population, and cultural hyperpluralism affect its politics and policies in some profound ways. Many policies mirror the pushing and pulling of various interest groups based on ethnic, gender, class, lifestyle, or religious differences.

Examples abound in California. Abortion policy is essentially a continuing struggle among diverse values and contrary views over the right of privacy, moral authority, and the meaning of personhood. Education policy struggles to address enrollment growth, ethnic diversity, social change, a parade of education reforms, and funding shortfalls. Higher education faces a crossroad as the grand social compact called the Master Plan seems less venerable and more vulnerable. Even immigration impacts higher education as undocumented students seek the same benefits as residents of the state. The sheer magnitude of California's social programs reflects a subtle rivalry between California's taxpayers and tax spenders, a contest exacerbated in recent years by economic distress. Today, the broad forces of economic volatility, growth, and diversity promise to challenge California's political system as never before. Forging a new multicultural democracy will be painful and controversial, straining both govern-ment institutions and policymakers at the state, regional, and local levels. Given demographic and economic trends, multicultural democracy in California will also strain public budgets to their limits as demands for more spending by some groups confront demands for less spending by others. The old Chinese curse, "May you live in interesting times," seems particularly suited to mod-ern California politics.

KEY TERMS

cultural amalgamation, separatism, and assimilation (p. 267)

cultural hyperpluralism (p. 267)

social issues (p. 267)

Master Plan for Higher Education (p. 274)

DREAM Act (p. 276)

ambivalent benevolence (p. 277)

deserving and undeserving poor (p. 277)

CalWORKs (p. 277)

fee-for-service and managed care (pp. 278, 279)

Medi-Cal (p. 279)

deinstitutionalization (p. 280)

REVIEW QUESTIONS

1. Why is there so little common ground among foes on abortion and LGBT rights? What might common ground look like?

2. Describe the pressures facing K-12 education in California.

3. To what extent and why is the Master Plan in trouble? How might that be evident in your own experience?

4. What are the pros and cons of undocumented students receiving in-state tuition?

5. Survey California's array of social welfare pro-grams and analyze the pressures on each of them. Which Californians are easiest and hardest to help and why? In your view, does ambivalent benev-olence describe California social policy?

6. Which social programs are the most and least vulnerable in an age of tight budgets? Which should be?

7. If you were to give "deinstitutionalization" a letter grade, what would it be and why?

WEB ACTIVITIES

California Department of Education
(www.cde.ca.gov/)
This site contains a wealth of data on virtually every aspect of K-12 education policy in California.

California Post Secondary Education Commission
(www.cpec.ca.gov/)
A good source of higher education enrollment data, diversity issues, and links to all public and private campuses in California.

California Department of Social Services
(www.dss.cahwnet.gov/)
Provides complete descriptions of most major social service programs offered or funded by the state.

Legislative Analyst's Office
(www.lao.ca.gov)
The LAO provides nonpartisan fiscal and policy advice on, among other topics, K-12 educa-tion, higher education, health care, and social services.

NOTES

1. These terms were used by Milton M. Gordon in his seminal work *Assimilation in American Life: The Role of Race, Religion and National Origins* (New York: Oxford University Press, 1964).

2. James Davison Hunter, *Culture Wars: The Struggle to Define America* (New York: Basic Books, 1991), p. 42.

3. These data are cited in Lou Cannon, *Governor Reagan: His Rise to Power* (New York: Public Affairs, 2003), p. 213. California no longer formally collects such statistics outside the Medi-Cal program.

4. More detail on the early years of California abortion reform can be found in Kristin Luker, *Abortion and the Politics of Motherhood* (Berkeley: University of California Press, 1984), Chap. 4.

5. *The Field Poll, Release* #2187 (March 14, 2006).

6. *How California Ranks* (Mountain View, CA: EdSource, September 2010). (www.edsource.org).

7. Louis Freedberg and Stephen K. Doig, "Spending Far From Equal Among State's School Districts, Analysis Finds," *California Watch* (June 2, 2011). (www.californiawatch.org/).

8. For a brief overview, see *A Guide to California's School Finance System* (Education Data Partnership, April 2011). (www.ed-data.K12.ca.us/).

9. The Civil Rights Project, *Confronting the Graduation Crisis in California* (Cambridge: Harvard University, 2005).

10. S. Eric Larsen, Stephen Lipscomb, and Karina Jaquet, *Improving School Accountability in California* (San Francisco: Public Policy Institute of California, April 2011).

11. *Master Plan for Higher Education in Focus: Draft Report* (Sacramento: Assembly Committee on Higher Education, April, 1993), p. 2.

12. Data provided at the Web site of the Association of Independent California Colleges and Universities. (Accessed at www.aiccu.edu/).

13. Legislative Analyst's Office, *The Master Plan at 50: Guaranteed Regional Access Needed for State Universities* (Sacramento: Legislative Analyst's Office, 2011). (www.lao.ca.gov/).

14. *Martinez v Regents of the University of California,* Ct. App. 3 C054124 (2010).

15. *Just the Facts: Poverty in California* (San Francisco: Public Policy Institute of California, March 2009).

16. Thomas MaCurdy, Grecia Marrufo, and Margaret O'Brian-Strain, *What Happens to Families When They Leave Welfare* (San Francisco: Public Policy Institute of California, 2003).

17. *California's Food Stamp Program Participation Rate: Trends, Implications and Suggested Actions* (Sacramento: California Department of Health Services, February 2006). (www.dhs.ca.gov/).

18. Paul Fronstin, "California's Uninsured," *California Health Care Almanac* (Sacramento: California Health Care Foundation, December 2010). (www.chcf.org/).

19. *The Affordable Health Care Act: What Californians Should Know* (Sacramento: California HealthCare Foundation, May 2011). (Accessed at www.chcf.org/). See also *Expanding Opportunities: What the Federal Health Care Law Means for California* (Sacramento: California Budget Project, March 2011).

20. *Just the Facts: Immigrants and Health* (San Francisco: Public Policy Institute of California, June, 2008).

21. For an individual level case study, see Vivian Po, "California Childcare Cuts Extend Family Homelessness," *California Progress Report* (June 2, 2011). (www.californiaprogressreport.com/).

Index

Note: "f" represents figures, "b" represents boxes, "t" represents tables.

AB540 law, 276
ABC syndrome, 50
Abortion: Californians perspective, 268f
  social issue, 267–269
Abundance and Beyond, politics, 34–36
Acceptability, 229
Accountability, 229, 273
Adult Protective Services, 278, 41–42
Adversarial justice, 181
Affirmative action, 64, 65
  gerrymander, 135
Affordable Care Act (ACA), 27
Affordability, U.S. Department of Housing and Urban Development
definition, 254–255
African Americans
  diversity, 9
Age, gap, 96
Aid to Families with Dependent Children (AFDC), 277
Air Resources Board, 167
Alta California, Spain (rule), 23
Alternative dispute resolution (ADR), 183

Ambivalent benevolence, 277
America, constitutional history, 41–42
American Academy of Pediatrics v. Lungren, 269
American hybrid, 14
Americanization of California, 266
Amicus curiae briefs, 118
Analysis of the Budget Bill, 139
Angst of a Judicial Candidate, 179b
Annual budget myth, 225
Anti-Bird Court Coalition, 179
Anti-canal referendum, 251–252
Anywhere But California (ABC) syndrome, 50
Apolitical politics, 198
Appellate court, 176, 178–179, 184
  judges, role, 179
  policymaking, 184
Appointments
  making, 156
Appropriation process, 130
Arbitration, 183
Arraignment, 82
Asian Americans,
  diversity, 9

Assembly,
  committees, 131
  districts, 128f
  posts, 137–138
  speaker, 137
Assembly Budget Committee, 139
Assembly line justice, 182
Assembly Speaker, 137
Associations, 115–116
Assumption of guilt, 181
At-large elections, impact, 60
Attorney general, 163–164
  criminal investigations, 164
Authorization, 130
Automatic upward adjustments, 225

Balance of payments problem, 149
Ballot box, 180
Ballot-box budgeting, 226–227
Ballot measures, representation, 73–74
Bay Area Rapid Transit (BART) system, connections, 257
Bear Flag Revolt, 24
Beilenson bill (1967), 268
Bell, California, 77, 209b
Bench trials, 175
Bicameral legislature, requirement, 136

Big Five, budget stalemates, 224
Big Four, 27–28
  modernization factor, 27–28
Big Three, state expenditures, 235
Bill of rights, strength, 26
Bills, 126
  committee consideration,
    140–141
How many too many? 129b
  introduction, 140
Bird, Rose (Bird Court), 84–185
Blue ribbon constitutional revision
    commission, 43
Board of Equalization, 165–166
Board of Supervisors, 200
Bond funds, 225
Brown, Edmund G. (Pat), 31,
    33–34, 150
Brown, Jerry, 2, 202
  and budget, 150
  2010 election, 50
  executive orders, 158
  general veto, 60, 161f
  item veto, 158, 159f
  tax relief, 62
Brown, Willie, 137
  tenure, 138
Brown Bag advocates, 116
Brown v. Plata, 189
Budget
  annual myth, 225
  external process, 158
  General fund Expenditures,
    (2011–2012), 236f
  internal budget, reform, 158
  leadership, 58–159
  local process, 227–228
  money disbursement, 235–237
  need for reform, 237–239
  policy, 219–241
  process, 222–228
  two thirds requirement, 225
Budget Act, passage, 224
Budgeting, Big Three, 235
  constraints in process, 225–227
  economy and, 221–221
  executive, role, 223
  hyperpluralism, impact, 220
  incrementalism, role, 223
  introduction, 220–221

leadership, 223–225
  political importance, 221–225
  process, 223–225
  process constraints, 225–227
  public policy, 220–221
  reform need, 237–239
  voters, 226
Bureaucracy, 166–169
  functions, 167
  purpose, 167

Calbuzz, 102
CALFED, 252
CalFresh, 277
Californio population,, 24
California
  assembly districts, 128f
  bureaucracy, 166–169
  campaigns, contributors (ranking),
    117f
  constitution, 41–45
  conquest, 256b
  counties,(map), 199
  cultural direction, 267f
  differences, 21–22
  elections, 90–95
  federal influence, absence,
    49–51
  federal policymaking, 49–51
  foreign policy, 52
  groups, identification, 114–115
  immigrants, country origin,
    52–54
  immigration, 52–54
  international pressures, 52–54
  judiciary, 172–192
  local economies, 222
North American Free Trade Act,
    (NAFTA), 54
  policy, group struggle, 266–267
  politics of diversity, 168
Senate districts, 127f
Steinbeck opinion, 9, 249b
Supreme Court, 176, 178–179
  taxation question, 230b
  troubled counties, 201–205
California Abortion Rights
    League, 269
California Air Resources Board
  air pollutant statistics, 259

California Constitution
  Revision Commission
  recommendations, 74
California Correctional Peace
  Officers Association (CCPOA),
  clout, 168
California Energy Commission,
    261
California fiscal officers, 165–166
California Global Warming
  Solutions Act, (2006),
  (AB32), 259
California groups, 114–115
California in Washington, 49–52
California Penal Code, 181
California Political Almanac, 139
California politics, democratic
    theory, 12–13
  diversity explanation, 4–11, 17
  economy, 10–12, 11f
  elite theory, 12–14
  explanation, 4
  hyperpluralism, usage, 2, 14–16
  interest groups, 116–118
  political theory explanation,
    12–14
  pluralist theory, 13–14
California Progressivism, 60–61
California Progress Report, 102
California Pro-Life Council, 269
California Report (KQED), 105
California Republican Assembly,
  formation, 110
"California Republic"
  (inscription), 24
California State Employees'
  Association, clout, 168
California Supreme Court, 176
*California v. Cabazon Band of Mission
  Indians*, 48
California Water Plan, 251
California Watch, 102
California Work Opportunity and
  Responsibility to Kids
  (CalWORKs), 201, 225, 236,
  237, 277–278
California World Trade
  Commission, establishment, 54
Californians for Population
  Stabilization,(CAPS), 262

Californians, abortion perspective, 268–269
  characteristics, 8t
  mass media, 104–105
  political participation, 80–99
  views of California, 3f
  voting participation, 85–89
Cal-Learn program, 278
CalNews, 102
Caltrans, toll road construction 257
Campaign contributions, making, 148
Campaign professionals/pollsters, 91–92
Candidates, campaigns, contributions (monitoring), 114
  interest group support, 115–118
  money, spending, 114
Cap and trade, 261
Capital improvements, 235
Capital punishment, 187–188
Capitol Weekly, 102
Careerism, 134
Case management, absence, 182
Casework, 129
Categorical spending, 225
Centralized federalism, 46
Central Valley Project (CVP), 251
Certainty and revenue, 229
Change of Constitution, 43–44
Charter counties, 200
Charter Schools Act (1992), 272
Chief administrative officers (CAOs), 200
Chiefs of state, 162
Child Protective Services, 278
Child Support Enforcement Program, 278
Cities, 202–210
  contrasts in median household income, cities/towns, 203f
  counties, relationship, 209–210
  general law and charter, 204
  managers, 205–209
  median household income, 203f
  phantom cities, 204
  running process, 205–209
  spending category, 237f
Citizens/government linkage, political parties, 107–108

Citizens Redistricting Commission, 136
Civic education, 130
Civic engagement, 81–82
Civil process, 182–184
Civil service, 166
Class politics, 13
Clemency, 162
Climate change, 258–259
  policy options, 259–261
Clout, 167–168
Clutter, trivia and Constitution, 42
Coalition building, 144
Coastal Act of 1972, 245
Coastal communities, 4
Coastal growth, 246f
Cocoon citizens, 205
Code of Judicial Ethics, 180
Combination pattern, legislative recruitment, 132–133
Command and control, 254
Commander of chief, governor role, 162
Committee consideration, 140
Committee system, 139
Common Cause, Progressive tradition, 61
Community politics, 193–218
  cities, 202
  counties, 198–200
  diverse communities, 215
  diverse governments, 215
  introduction to, 194–196
  special districts, 210–212
  shape of counties, 198–200
  shape of county government, 200–202
Commutation of sentences, 162
Comparison ads, 112, 113f
Competing for influence, 118–119
Competing for power, 162–166
Complaint, civil process, 183
Concurrent jurisdiction, 175
Conference committees, 139, 141–142
Constancy of individualism, 14–15
Constituency differences, 160
Constitution, 41–45
  clutter/trivia, 42–43
  components, 42–44

distinctiveness, 44–45
Constitution (1849), 25–26, 41
Constitution (1879), 42–45
  contents of, 42
Constitution, right of privacy, 269
Constitutional amendments, 126
Constitutional convention, 43, 44
Constitutionalism, 40
Contract lobbyists, 116
Controlled growth policies, 247–248
Controller, 165
Conventional participation 81–82
Convicts, rehabilitation, 186
Cooperative federalism, 46
Corporative taxes, 231
Correctional system, 236
Correctional system, 236
Cost of diversity, 239
Cost of living adjustments, (COLAs), 225
Council manager, 205
  organization chart, 207t, 208t
Councils of governments (COGs), 214
Counties
  counties/cities, relationship, 210–211
  funding pressures, 202
  problems, 204–205
  spending, 235–239
Countries of origins of California Immigrants, 54f
County central committee, 110
County Clerk/ Recorder, 201
County Superintendent of Schools, 201
Courts,
  policy making role, 184-185
  organization, 174–176
Court of Appeals, 175–176
  criminal process, 181
  decision-making process, 181–184
  policy-making process, 184–185
  system, illustration, 175b
  trial stage, 182
Criminal cases, steps/decision, 181–183

Criminal justice/punishment,
    185–189
    capital punishment, 187–188
    sentencing mandates, 186–187
    social trends, 185
Criminal process, 181–183
Crises, television coverage, 103–105
Charles Crocker, (Gold Rush
    response), 27
Cross-cutting groups, 114
Cross-filling, 109
Crowd lobbying, 144
Cruise control spending, 225
Cultural amalgamation, 267
    assimilation, 267
    diversity, 267
    hperpluralism, 267
    representation, 126–129
Cultures, diversity, 17
Cumulative policymaking (courts),
    184
"Curse of California," 28, 29b

Davis, Gray (recall), 75-76
Dealignment, 125
Death penalty verdicts, overruling
    (hesitancy), 187
Debt, impact, 232–234
Declaration of Rights, 41
privacy, 44
Defense of Marriage Act, 66, 66b
Development, defiscalization of, 262
Deinstitutionalization, 123, 280–281
Democratic theory, 12–13. *See also*
    California politics
"Democratic Voters Choice,"
    (slate mailer), 112, 113f
Demographic diversity, 8
Department of Alcoholic Beverage
    Control, 167
Department of Fair Employment
    and Housing, 167
Department of Finance, 223
Department of Health Services, 167
Department of Transportation, 167
Dependent special districts, 210–211
Depositions, 183
Deserving poor, 277
Deukmejian, George, 34
Dillon's Rule, 197

Directory of Lobbyists, Lobbying
    Firms, and Lobbyist
    Employees, 115–116, 117–118
Direct primaries, 59–60, 109
Dirty Dozen states, California
    membership, 136
Disabled assistance, 278
Discovery (civil step), 183
District attorneys (DAs),
    (prosecutors) election, 200–201
    role, 181
District Court of Appeals, 175–176
Diversity, California politics,
    4–12, 97
Diversity challenge, 266–267
    divided government problems,
        190
    division, 95–97
    economic, 221
    interests and cultures, 15
    ironies, 17–18
    politics, 4–12, 97, 166–169
Donahoe Higher Education Act,
    (1960), 274
Domestic Partnership Act, 269
Do-pass recommendation, 140–141
Downzoning, 247
DREAM Act, (Development,
    Relief, and Education for Alien
    Minor Act), 276
Dual federalism, 46
Dueling views on earmarks, 51b
Duties of government, 42
Dysfunctionality, and legislative
    politics, 123–125

Early years of legislative history, 124
Earmarking, 226
Economic diversity, 11
Economic groups, 114
Economy, budgeting, 221–228
    diversity, 11, 221
    local, 222
    postindustrial characteristics, 10
    representation, 11f
    resources, 10–12
    size, 10
Edge cities, 204
Education. (*See also* higher education)
    accountability, improvement, 273

code, 278
choice-oriented policies, 274
enrollment growth, 270
ethnic hyperpluralism, 270–271
funding, challenge, 271–272
fragmentation, 164
growth/diversity, 270–274
managed choice, 274
policy battle, 164
pressures, 270–272
quality, improvement, 272–273
quality reform, 272–274
social conflict programs, 276–281
spending, voters, 272f
state expenditures, 235–236
state level reforms, dissatisfaction,
    272–274
superintendent of public
    instruction, 164
Electroneering, 116–117
Elections and Campaigns, 90–95
    national politics, 93–95
    professionals, 91–92
    role of money, 92
Electoral gaps, 95–97
Electrical power, 251
Elite media, 102
Elite politics, 13
Elite theory, 13 (*See also* California
    politics)
El Norte, 52
EMILY's List, campaign source, 94
Employment opportunities, 12
Endorsement politics, 110–112
End Poverty in California
    (EPIC), 31
Energy, 258–261
    crises, 258–259
    policy opinions, 259–261
English only requirement, 44–45
Entitlements, 225
Environment, crises, 258–259
    policy options, 259–261
Environmental protection cost,
    259–261
Environmental racism, 260
Equity (fairness), 228
Era of limits, 34, 35b
Ethnic composition of California,
    267f

Ethnic data, 7–10
Ethnic hyperpluralism, 270–271
Ethnicity, Race gap, 96
    uninsured health insurance,
        279f
Euro-Americans, arrival, 26
Excise taxes, 231
Executive
    appointments, 156
    branch management, 156
    chart oversight, 130
    orders, 158
    organization chart, 157t
    oversight, 130
    politics, conclusion, 169
    powers, 156–158
    reform, 168–169
Exit option, 82
Explaining California politics,
    1–19
Extradition, 162

Facebook/Social Networking
    Privacy Act, 143b
Fading majoritarianism, 15–16
Fairness (equity), 228
Fair Political Practices Commission
    (FPPC) establishment, 93
Farming the wind, 260b
Federal gold, desire, 31
Federal Interstate Highway Act of
    1956, 33
Federalism boundaries, 45–47
    native Americans, relationship,
        48–49
Federal Plan, 124
Fee-for-service basis, 279
Felonies, 181
Fences, politics, 52–54
Field Poll, 3, 84, 85, 237
Filipino Californians, 10
Filter down policy, 253
Fiscal communities, 139
Fiscalization of land use,
    210, 255
Fiscal officers, 165, 201
Fiscal food chain, 228
Fiscal pretzel, 226
Fiscal year, 223
Five little kings, 202

Floor action and conference
    committee, 141–142
Flower petal policy, 52
Forgotten fiefdoms, 210
Fourteenth Amendment, equal
    protection clause, 65
Fremont, John C., 24
Functional representation, 129
Functions of bureaucracy, 167
Funding challenges in education,
    270–271
Funding pressures, 202
Funds,
    bond, 225
    general, 224
    special, 225
Furman v. Georgia, (1972), 187

Gambling to fund raise, 233f
GANDA (gut and amend), 142
Gang graffiti
    tagging, 197
GATE, 272
Gay rights activists, 66–67
Gender, gap, 96–97
General elections, 90
General fund expenditures, 236f
General law, 200
General law cites, 204
General obligation bonds, 232
General plan, (physical
    development), 247
General veto, 160
    message, example, 161b
Geographic representation, 126
George, Ronald M. (George
    Court), 185
Gerrymandering, 135
Get-out-the-vote efforts,
    unreported contributions, 117
Golden Gate Bridge, WPA
    project, 31
Golden Years,
    legislative history, 125
Gold Rush (1849), 10–11, 26–27
Governance, theories, 4t
Government debt,
    incurring, 235–237
    diversity, 215
Governors

budget summary, 223
budget leadership, 158
duties/powers, 155–162
executive powers, 156–158
judicial powers, 161–162
leadership process, 151–155
legislative powers, 159–161
list of, 152t–153t
pardons, issuance, 162
personality, 154
political context, 155
political resources, 154
political skill, 154,
role of, 142
strategic considerations, 155
Governor's Budget Summary, 223
Grapes of Wrath, (Steinbeck), 9
Grassroots lobbying, 144
Grassroots pressure, 144
Gray Davis recall, 75–76
Great Depression politics, 31
Great Drought, 28
Green power, 261
Gregg v. Georgia, (1976), 187
Gridiron plan, 253
Gross state (domestic) product, 10
Group benefits and Constitution, 42
Growth, 243–248
    cities, 195b
    diversity, 270–274
    limitation desire, 247–248
    new policy, 261–262
    planner tools, 247
    settlement patterns, 248
    structuring local growth, 246–247
    water, impact, 248–252
    zoning ordinances, 247
Gut and amend, (GANDA), 42

Hart Hughes Educational Reform,
    (1983), 272
Health policies, 236, 278–281
Healthy families, low cost
    insurance, 279
Higher education, 274–276
    DREAM Act, 276
    majoritarian ideal, 274–275
    master plan, 274
    plan rethinking, 275–276
    policy discussions, 277

Highway Patrol, role, 167
Hired guns, 116
Homeowner associations,
    (HOAs) 204
Home rule, 197
Hopkins, Mark (Gold Rush
    response), 27
Housing
    crises, 253–255
    dream, 252–253
    filter down policy, 253
Housing Act of 1949, 253
Huntington, Collis (Gold Rush
    response), 27
Hybrid democracy, 77
Hydraulic Society, 5, 30
Hyperpartisanship, 96
Hyperpluralism, 2, 14–16

Ideological bias, 104
Illegal immigrants,
    reporting, 64
Illegal immigration,
    reduction, 53
Illegal Immigration Reform and
    Immigrant Responsibility Act,
    53, 276
Immigrants
    country origin, 54f
Immigration Reform and Control
    Act of 1986 (IRCA), 52
Impact fees, 246
Incrementalism, 223
Incumbent gerrymandering, 135
Independent expenditure
    committees, 92
Independent special districts,
    210–211
Indeterminate sentence policy, 186
Indian Gaming Regulatory Act,
    48, 50b
Indictment, 182
Individualism, constancy of, 14–15
Individualistic political subculture,
    22, 60
Individuals with Disabilities Act, 278
Industrialization
    rapidity, 27
Influence
    appointments, 118

competition, 118–119
    propositions, 117
Infractions, 181
In-house lobbyists, 115
Initiatives
    battles, 61–69
    campaigns, reliance on
        television, 104
    consequences of, 71–73
    Constitutional change, 44
    earmarking, 226
    legal process, 63
    mess, 69–73
    reform, prospects, 73–74
    role of entrepreneurs, 71
    usage, 44
Inland growth, 246f
In-migration,
    continuation, 8–9
Innocent until proven guilty, 181
Insurance Commissioner, 165
Integrated Waste Management
    Act, 259
Integrated Waste Management
    Board, recycling/composting
    promotion, 167
Interest differences, 160
Interest groups, 112–118. *See also*
    California politics
    actions, 116–118
    associations, 115–116
    electioneering, 116–117
    identification, 114–115
    influence propositions, 117
    influence appointments, 118
    litigation, 118
    lobbying, 115, 116
    organization patterns, 115–116,
        117
    politics, 116–117
    public relations, 116
Intergovernmental lobbying, 49
Internal budget, 158
International trade, impact, 54
Internet, social media, 105–106
Interrogatories, 183
Introduction to budgeting,
    220–221
Iron law of oligarchy, 13
Issue spillover, 202

Issuing orders, 158
Item veto message, 158, 159b

Japanese Californians, oppression,
    9–10
Johnson, Hiram, 61, 62
    leadership, 44
    political influence elimination, 31
Joint committees, 139
Judges, 176–181
    ballot box, 180
    candidates, 176
    experience, 177–178
    peer review, 180
    professional norms, 180
    selection mechanics, 178
Judgments, civil process, 182–183
Judicial discipline, 179–180
    professional norms, 180
Judicial federalism, 174
Judicial powers, 161–162
Judicial socialization, 180
Judiciary, Act of 1789, 174
    Appellate, 176, 178–179
    conclusion, 190
    court system, 175b
    discipline, 179–180
    introduction, 173
    judgeship, 176–181
    judicial discipline, 179–180
    organization, 174–176
    state courts, 174
    Supreme Court, 178–179
    trial courts, 175
Juice Committees, 125
Juries, 183–184
    nullification, 184
    popular justice, 184

KQED, impact, 105

Land
    diversity, 4
    fiscalization use, 210
    planning use, 246
Lanterman-Petris-Short Act,
    (1968), 281
La Opinion, 103
Latinos and diversity, 8
Leadership role, 137–138, 223–225

League of Women Voters
Progressive tradition, 61
Legacy of Progressive era, 76
Legal immigration, challenges, 52–54
Legal system and state courts, 174
Legislative advocates, 115
Legislative district populations, 133f
Legislative history, 124–125
reform, 124–125
Legislative politics, 122–148
Legislative powers, 159–161
Legislative process, 140–143
flowchart, 141f
Legislative program, 160
Legislative proposal, 43
Legislature and Third House
at a glance, 129f
committees, 131t, 139
executive oversight, 130
civic education, 130
functions, 126–132
leadership, 137-138
policymaking, 126
reapportionment, 134-136
recruitment, 132–133
representation, 126–132
rewards of office, 133–134
staff, 139
statistics, 133f
Lesbian/gay/bisexual/transgender
(LGBT) rights, 269–270
Lieutenant governor, 163
Life, quality (concerns), 247
Limiting community government,
196–198
Linking people and policymakers,
100–121
Local agency formation commission,
(LAFCO), 204
Lobbyists, in-house, 115
Local budget process, 227–228
Local economies, 222
Local expenditures, 237
Local interest groups, 115
Locally undesirable land uses
(LULUs), 200, 248
Local revenue, 234–235
Locke, John, 40
Los Angeles,
board of supervisors, 202

mayoral power, 202
water usage, 249-251
Los Angeles board
five little kings, 202
water, usage, 249–251
Los Angeles Times, 102–103
Lottery, usage, 232
Lucas Court, 185

Major state revenues, 229–234
corporate taxes, 231
debt, 232
excise taxes, 231
general fund revenues and
transfers, 230f
personal income tax,
229–230
sales tax, 230–231
Majoritarianism,
fading, 15–16
Majoritarian,
ideal, 274–276
policies, 34
rethinking the plan, 275–276
Managed care, 279
Managing Executive Branch,
156–158
Mandates, 46, 202
Maquiladoras, 11
Mass media
impact, 102
information/opinion/analysis,
usage, 101–102
Master Plan for Higher Education,
274–275
Material benefits, 133–134
Mayor-council form, 205
Mayor-council organization chart,
207f
May Revision, 224
Measuring public opinion, 84–85
Media bias, 104
impact, 101
Mediation, 183
Medical parole law, 188
Medi-Cal, 225, 236, 239
abortion, 269
usage, 279
Mello-Roos Community Facility
Act, (1982), 235

Mentally ill
deinstitutionalization, 123,
280–281
Merit systems, 60
Metropolitan Planning
Organization, (MPOs), 214
Mexican "control," 23–24
Mexico
independence, 23
legacy, 24
Middle class progressivism,
60–61
Minor parties, impact, 110
Miranda decision, 185
Miscellaneous groups, 114–115
Misdemeanors, 181
Mistrust of politicians, 42
Missouri Plan, 178
Modernization
factors, 30–31
politics, 26–31
Money
Constitution, 42
role in elections, 92–93
Moralistic political subculture,
21–22, 60
Motor fuels
excise tax (addition), 231
Multicultural pluralism
creation, 14
Multilevel workforce,
economy, 12
Municipalities, incorporation,
204

Narrow spending, 225
Native Americans, 7
diversiy, 7–8
federalism,
relationship, 48–49
Indian Gaming Regulatory
Act, 48–49
Spanish/Mexican mission padres,
patron-client relationship, 23
NCLB, 273
New Federalism, 47
New Growth Policy, 261–262
Newspapers
impact, 102–103
readership declining, 102

NIMBYs (not in my backyard), 248, 260

No Child Left Behind Act, 48b, 273

Non-Hispanic whites
diversity and, 8–9

Nonpartisan elections, 60, 109

Nonvoters, 87–90
voter/nonvoter gap, 95–97

North American Free Trade Act, (NAFTA), 54

Not in my backyard (NIMBY) strategies, 214

Number of cities per population, 216f

Obama, Barack,
2008 election, 108–109
Race to the Top reform, 48b

Oil (black gold),
discovery, 30

Olson, Culbert L., 31

O'Neill, Thomas P., 196

Open Primary Law (Proposition 198) (1996), 109

Organic Act of 1868, 274

Organizing to legislate, 136–140

Owens River, aqueduct, 30

Parcel taxes, 235

Partial preemptions, 46

Participatory democracy, 12

Partisan gap, 96

Partisan factors, 89

Partisan geography, 108–109, 108f

Partisan gerrymandering, 135

Party, 107–112
California style, 107–108
caucus, 137
differences, 159–160
electorate, 107
identification, 107
in government, 107
organization, 107, 110–111

Peer review, 180

Pendleton Act of 1883, 166

People and diversity, 7–10

Perceptual representation, 130

Perimeter of politics, 40

Peripheral canal, 251–252

Personal income tax, 229

Personal relations, 161

Personal staff and organization, 156

Petition referenda, 74

Phantom cities, 204

Picket fence federalism, 168

Planned Parenthood v. Casey, 268

Planned unit developments, (PUDs), 247

Plea bargaining, 182
Three-Strikes Law, 182

Plural executive, power competition, 162–166

Pluralist theory, 13–14

Police power, 196

Policies stemming from diversity, abortion, 267–270
challenge of, 266–267
coping with growth and diversity, 270–274
higher education, 274–276
LGBT rights, 267–270
social issues, 267–270
social programs, 276–281

Policy
achievement, 133
challenge of, 266–267
coping with, 279–274
higher education and, 274–276
options stemming from growth, 242–264
social issues, abortion, LGBT rights, 267–270

Policies stemming from growth, 242–264
California growth, 243–248
drumbeat of growth, 244–246, 245f
energy environment and climate change, 258–259
housing, 252–255
new growth policy, 261–262
policy options, 259–261
public agency groups, 114
reason for growth, 244
slowing growth in California, 248–252
transportation, 255–258
water availability and growth, 248–252

Policymaking
courts, 184
legislature, 126

Political action committees (PACs), 93

Political behavior types, 85–86

Political context, 155

Political culture, 21–23
definition, 21
moralistic, 21
traditionalistic, 21

Political development, 20–38
abundance and beyond stage, 34–36
idea of, 22
modernization stage, 26–31
unification stage, 22–26
welfare stage, 31–34

Political environment attributes, 4

Political information sources,

Political participation,
civic engagement, 81–82
conventional engagement, 81–82
exit option, 82
protest option, 82–83
public opinion, 83–85

Political culture, 21–22
definition, 21
moralistic, 21
traditionalistic, 21

Political environment attributes, 4

Political information sources, 102f

Political parties, 107–112
California style, 109–110
organization of, 110-111
party identification, 107
surrogate "parties," 111

Political party registration percentages, 110f

Political Reform Act of 1974 (Proposition 9), 93

Political resources, 154

Political responsiveness, 202

Political skill, 154

Political system, 4

Politicos, 130

Politics
definition, 4

Politics of Abundance and Beyond, 34–36
Politics of Modernization, 26–31
  Big Four, 27–28
  Gold Rush, 26–27
  oil, 30
  World War 11, 30–31
  water, 28–30
Politics of Welfare, 31–34
Polk, James (gold report), 25
Pollsters, major, 84
Popular justice, 184
Population growth, 243–248
  slowing of, 247–248
  Transcontinental Railroad, 8
Popular justice, 184
Post-industrialism, 10
Powell, Colin (Proposition 209), 65,
Power
  competition, 162–166
  of incumbency, 133
  sharing, clout, 167–168
  to the people, 44
Pragmatic federalism, 47
Preemptions, 46
Preferential nonvoters, 87
Preferential nonvoting, 87
Preliminary hearing, 182
Prescriptive rights, 249
Presence of Third House, 143
Presidio, Spanish system, 25
Pressure on education, 270
Pretrial activity, 181–182, 183
Primary elections, 90
Prior appropriation, 249
Prisons
  Brown v. Plata, 189
  overcrowding and reform, 188–189
  politics, 188–189
  population, 1868f
  recidivism, 188
Private insurance, 278–281
Privatization of development, 197
Privatism, 197
Privatopias, consideration, 205
Professional interest groups, 114
Professionalism
  legislative politics, 123–125
Professional management, 60

Professional norms, 180
Progressive Era, 12
  legacy and paradox, 76–77
Progressive movement politics, 31
Progressive reformers, 59
Progressive tax, 228
Progressivism
  California style, 60–61
  impact, 59–60
Proposition 1A (1966), 124
Proposition 1A (2006), 226, 257, 272
Proposition 1E (2006), 226
Proposition 4 (2008), 269
Proposition 8 (1982), 67, 83, 174 (same sex)
Proposition 8, 66–67
Proposition 9 (1974), 125
Proposition 10 (1998), 226
Proposition 11 (2008), 136
Proposition 13, cut mental health aid, 281
Proposition 13 (tax reduction), 45, 62–63, 202, 226, 227, 234 (education spending), 272
Proposition 14(2010), 109
Proposition 19 (2010), 67, 68–69, 70
Proposition 20 (1972), 70
Proposition 21 (2010), 70
Proposition 22 (2000) (same sex marriage limits), 66–67, 66b, 70
  judicial impact, 175, 180–181
Proposition 23, (2010), 70
Proposition 24, (2010), 70
Proposition 25, (2010), 70, 225
Proposition 26, (2010), 70, 234
Proposition 27, (2010), 70
Proposition 34, (2000), 93
Proposition 38, (2000), 226
Proposition 39, (2000), 235, 272
Proposition 42, (2002), 226, 257
Proposition 52, (2002), rejection, 87
Proposition 63, (2004), 45, 229
Proposition 66, (2004), 187
Proposition 73 (2005), 269
Proposition 84 (2006), 272
Proposition 85 (2006), 269

Proposition 98, (1988), governance, 226, 272
Proposition 103 (1988), 165
Proposition 108 (1990), gas tax increase, 257
Proposition 111, (1990), gas tax increase), 231, 257
Proposition 140, (1990), 16, 125, 136, 140
Proposition 187, (1994), (immigration), 107
Proposition 187, (rights limits), 64–65
Proposition 198, (open primary law), 109
Proposition 209, (1996),(rights limits), 64, 65–66
Proposition 209, (1996), (affirmative action), 166, 174
Proposition 215, (2001), 67–68
Proposition 218, (1996), 234
Proposition 227, (anti-bilingual education measure), 45, 94
Propositions in 2000s, 73t
Propositions on 2010 ballot, 70t
Prosecutors, role, 184
Prospects for initiative reform, 73–74
Protest, option, 82–83
Providing information by interest groups, 144
Providing services in communities, 196
Psychic satisfaction, 134
Public Interest Research Group (CALPIRG), 61
Public office, motivation, 133–134
Public opinion, 83–85
Public policy, 221
Public Policy Institute of California, 84
Public relations, actions, 116
Public school diversity, 270t

Quality of life, concerns, 247
Quality improvement in education reform, 272–273

Race,
  ethnicity, gap, 96
  political participation, 86f
  uninsured, 279f

Racial gerrymandering, 135
Radio, 105
Ranchos, disappearance, 24, 25
Reagan, Ronald, 34
Realignment, 202
Reapportionment politics, 134–136
Recalls
    Davis recall, 75-76
    local level recalls, 76
    state level recalls, 44, 74–76
    usage, 44
Recidivism, 186, 188
Redevelopment agencies, 210
Redistricting reform, 135
Reduce population growth, 262
Referendum, 74
Referenda
    compulsory 74
    impact, 44
    petition, 74
    usage, 44
Reform in education, 272–274
    legislative history, 124
Refugee Resettlement
        Program, 278
Regional coordination, 214
Regional governments, 213–214
Regional regulation, 214
Regions,
    diversity, 4–5
    division, 6
Regressive tax, 228
Rehabilitation, 236
Representation, 126
Representative democracy, 12
Reprieve, 162
Resolutions, 126
Resources, 5–7
Responsibility differences, 160
Responsible liberalism, 33
Rethinking home rule, 262
Revenue, *See* Major State and Local
        revenues
    acceptability, 229
    accountability, 229
    bonds, 232
    certainty, 229
    definition, 228
    equity, 228
    types, 228–234
    yield, 228

Reverse parole decisions, 162
Rewards of office, 133–134
Right of Privacy, 44
Right to Vote on Taxes Act
        (Proposition 218)
        (1996), 234
Riparian rights, 249
Roe v. Wade (1973), 268
Role of Community, 196
Role of incrementalism, 223
Role of leadership, 137
Role of National Politics, 93–95
Rules Committee, 138

Sacramento Bee, 103
Salaries and Wages Supplement,
        223
Sales tax, 230–231
    add-ons, approval, 230
Same-sex marriage licenses, 269
Same-sex unions, California
        Supreme Court, 66
San Diego, mayor-council
        organization chart, 207f
San Luis Obispo, council-manager
        organization chart, 208f
School districts, 212–213
    pros and cons, 212b
Schwarzenegger, Arnold
    governorship, 154–155
    campaign, 92
    election, 3, 75
    executive branch reform,
        168–170
    impact, 134
    initiatives, 71b
    political skill, 154
Scientific polls, 84
Secretary of State
    discretionary power, 164
Select committees, 139
Self-inflicted dictatorship, 137
Self starters
    combination and recruitment,
        132
Senate
    Budget and Fiscal Review
        Committee, 223
    committees, 131t
    districts, 127f
    President pro tempore, 138

Senate president pro
        tempore, 138
Sentencing , 182–183
Serrano v. Priest, 271
Settlement patterns
    growth impact, 244–246
Shadow governments, HOAs, 204
Shasta Dam, WPA project, 31
Sheriffs, election, 201
Short ballots, 60
Simpson, O. J., (murder trial), 184
Sinclair, Upton, 31
Single-issue politics, 15
Slate mailers
    example, 113f
    usage, 112
Slow-growth movement,
        247–248
Slow-growth politics, 247–248
Social conflict, 271
Social issues, 267–270
Social programs, 276–281
Social representation, 126–129
Socializing community
        members, 196
Soft money, 93
Solar power, 261
South Coast Air Quality
        Management District
        (SCAQMD), 214
Southern California, differences, 97
Southern California Association of
        Governments (SCAG),
        regional council, 214
Southern Pacific Railroad, 27
Spanish "rule," 23
Sparse media coverage, 104–105
Speaker pro tempore, 137
Special districts, 210–212
    advantages/disadvantages, 212b
    dependent/independent,
        210–211
    politics/problems, 211, 212
Special elections, 90–91
Special funds, 225
Specific representation, 129
Sponsorship and recruitment
    self starters, combination, 132
Spot bills, 140
Staff, impact, 139
Stagnation amid change, 124

Standardized Testing and Reporting (STAR), 273
Standing committees, 139
Standing legislative committees, 131t
Stanford, Leland (Gold Rush response), 27
Stare decisis, 184
State Banking Department, 167
State budgeting,
  Big Three, 235
State central committee, 110
State courts, 174–176
State expenditures, 235–237
  corrections, costs, 235
  education, 235
  health/human services, 235
Statehood, attainment, 24–25
State hyperpluralism, 14
State of the State speech, 160
State organizational structure, 157t
State primary turnout, 89f
State power, 197–198
State revenues, 229–234
State Senator's lament, 142b
States rights philosophy, 174
State Water Plan, 251
State Water Project (SWP), 251
State wide growth strategy, 262
Stealth governments, 211
Steinbeck, John, 109
  on California water, 249b
Storing water, 248–249
Strategic considerations, 155
Straw polls, 84
Structural bias, 104
Structural conflict, 16
Structural deficits, 233
Structural nonvoting, 87
Structuring local growth, 246
Subdivision regulations, 247
Suburban flight, 244
Superagencies, 156
Superior courts, 175
Superintendent of Public Instruction, 164
Supermajorities, requirement, 225
Supplemental Security Income (SSI) program, 278
Supreme Court, 176
  selection of justices, 178–179

and death penalty, 187
and policy making, 184–185
Surrogate parties, 111

Tagging, 196
Targeted tax reform, 238–239
Taxes,
  acceptability, 229
  accountability, 229
  certainty, 229
  corporate, 231
  equity, 228
  excise, 231
  level, consideration, 230f
  sales, 230
  yield, 228
Tax payers' caucus, 224
Tea Party movement, 111
Television,
  importance in initiative process, 72
  impact, 103–105
  media bias, 104
  sparse coverage, 104–105
  visual medium, 103–104
Temporary Assistance to Needy Families, (TANF), 201
Tenure limitation, frustration, 134
Therapeutic Abortion Act, (1967), 268
Third house, 143–144
  events, 93
Third parties, 110
Third Rail Issues, 226
Three Strikes Law, 130, 175, 186, 187, 236
Tools planners use, 247
Top-10 contributors to California campaign, 117f
Top-Two primary, 109
Traditionalistic political subculture, 21
Trailer bills, 224
Transcontinental Railroad completion, 8–9
Transportation
  environmental effects, 256–257
  highway use, 256f
  infrastructure improvement, 257–258
  personal choices, 255

policies, 257–258
problems, 255–258
urban development problems, 256
Treasurer, 165
Treaty of Guadalupe Hidalgo, (1848), 24
Trial Court Funding Act (1997), 175
Trial courts, 178, 183
  judges, role, 182
  policymaking, 184
Trial stages, 182–183
Trustees, 130
Two-thirds requirement, 225
Types of revenue, 228–235

Undeserving poor, 277
Unemployment Insurance Appellate Board, 168
Unification politics, 22–26
  1894 Constitution, 25–26
  Mexican control, 23–24
  Spanish Rule, 23
  Statehood, 24–25
Unification stage, 22
Uniform building codes, 247
Uniform Sentencing Act, 186
Unruh, Jesse, 137
Urban villages, 204
U.S. Citizenship and Immigration Services, 52, 53
U.S. Department of Housing & Urban Development, 254–255

Verdicts, 182
Vernon, City of, 204
Veto referendum, 74
Visiting judges, 183
Visual medium, 103–104
Voir dire process, 182
Voter turnout, 85
Voters
  and non-voters, 85–87, 95–96
  dealignment, 125
  disinterest, 15–87
  identification, 85–89
  ineligibility, 86–87
  personal factors, 87–88
  PPIC Survey, 86f
  preferential non-voters, 87

Voters (*continued*)
  registration rates and increase, 87
  turnout, 85–86
  decrease, 87
Voting,
  barriers, 87
  educational spending, 272b
  likely voters, 86t
  partisan factors, 89
  personal factors, 87–88
  regional factors, 89
  structural actors, 87, 88–89
Voting age population (VAP), 85
Voting Rights Act of
    1965, 135

Warren, Earl, 31, 32–33, 201
Water
  Article X, 44
  growth impact, 248–252
  Los Angeles need, 249–251
  modernization factor, 28–30
  movement, 249–252
  policy alternatives, 252
  plumbing system (map), 250f
  projects, federal government
    role, 30
  Steinbeck opinion, 249b
  storage, 248–249
*Webster v. Reproductive Health
    Services*, 268

Welfare
  policy, 236, 277–278
  politics, 31–34
Whitman, Meg, 92, 93, 150
Wobblers, 181
Women and the Constitution of
    1849, 41b
Workingman's Party, 41
World War 11,
  modernizing factor, 30

Yield, 228

Zoning ordinances, 247
Zoot suit riots, 82–83